Forgotten children

Parent–child relations from 1500 to 1900

LINDA A. POLLOCK

Published by the Press Syndicate of the University of Cambridge
The Pitt Building, Trumpington Street, Cambridge CB2 1RP
40 West 20th Street, New York, NY 10011-4211 USA
10 Stamford Road, Oakleigh, Melbourne 3166, Australia

© Cambridge University Press 1983

First published 1983
Reprinted 1985, 1987, 1988, 1993, 1996

Printed in Great Britain by
Athenæum Press Ltd, Gateshead, Tyne & Wear

Library of Congress catalogue card number: 83–5315

British Library Cataloguing in Publication Data
Pollock, Linda A.
Forgotten children: parent–child relations
from 1500 to 1900.
1. Children – History
I. Title
305.2'3'09   HQ767.87

ISBN 0 521 25009 9 hardback
ISBN 0 521 27133 9 paperback

WT

Contents

Contents

Contents

Preface

The presentation of the material may seem odd to historians, but the policy was deliberate. The history of childhood is an area so full of errors, distortion and misinterpretation that I thought it vital, if progress were to be made, to supply a clear review of the information on childhood contained in such sources as diaries and autobiographies. To that end I have relied on copious quotation as well as keeping the evidence and interpretation sections separate. That way I hoped to avoid confounding the issue even further.

I should like to make it clear that I am concerned with parental care, differentiating this from other types of care and trends in society. I believe there is no reason to assume that parental care must vary according to developments and changes in society as a whole. The history of childhood is an area dominated by myths. In this work I hope to demonstrate that the worst of the myths have no substance and also provide a surer foundation on which to base more research on this topic. It may be that I am placing too much emphasis on continuity in child-rearing practices, but I am of the opinion that changes should be investigated against this background of continuity. There may indeed be subtle changes in child care through the centuries – changes that so far lie hidden because of the prevailing interest to discover and argue for dramatic transformations.

This monograph is based on my doctoral dissertation, financed by a Social Science Research Council grant and presented to the University of St Andrews in July 1981. Several people have provided assistance during the research and writing up. John McShane (London School of Economics) supervised the doctoral thesis. He did so with aplomb and, even if I wilted at times under his comments and criticism, I cannot fault his supervision. He scrutinised reams of manuscript tirelessly and painstakingly, weeding out errors and offering many suggestions for improvement. I remain in his debt. Keith Wrightson (University of St Andrews) patiently endured a virtual avalanche of early material, studied it all and provided invaluable aid and above all encouragement. He shared his knowledge of the area with me and, through his own work on 17th-century society, has challenged the 'Black Legend' of childhood. I hope this book furnishes him with more evidence to support his views. Andy Whiten (University of St Andrews) supervised a much earlier version of this research while I was still an undergraduate and has remained interested in the progress and outcome of my studies. Both Alan Macfarlane (University of Cambridge) and Peter Laslett (SSRC Cambridge Group) read the final version of my thesis and suggested ways to turn it from a dissertation into a book. Peter Laslett, in particular, has given generously of his time to comment on the manuscript and the quality of my prose. Peter Smith (University of Sheffield) kindly let me see his paper on child care prior to publication. Mrs Pat Carroll of Cambridge University Press was a meticulous subeditor and picked up many slips and inconsistencies which I had failed to notice.

I am also indebted to my mother who typed the thesis and has also prepared the typescript for publication; she adds many finishing touches to the end product. Finally, I wish to thank my husband, Iain, who not only has endured four years of the history of childhood without flinching, but also has tolerated many lonely evenings and week-ends while I prepared the revision for publication.

To all of the above I am exceedingly grateful.

Acknowledgements

The author wishes to thank the following for permission to reproduce material from their publications or collections:

George Allen & Unwin for extracts from *The Years with Mother* by Augustus Hare (1952) and *The Amberley Papers* by Kate and John Russell (1966).

The British Library for extracts from the diary of Maurice Hewlett (Add. MSS 41075) and the diary of Peter Oliver (Egerton Collection 2674).

The Caxton Printers for extracts from *Elkanah and Mary Walker* by Clifford Drury (1940).

Essex Institute Historical Collections for extracts from the diary of Mary Orne Tucker (1941).

Evans Brothers for extracts from *Queen Victoria: Dearest Child*, ed. Roger Fulford (1964).

The Guildhall Library for extracts from MS 204 (Nehemiah Wallington).

Harper & Row Publishers for extracts from *Nancy Shippen: her Journal Book*, ed. Ethel Armes (1935).

Hutchinson Publishing Group for extracts from *Four and a Half Years* by C. Addison (1934) and *A Quaker Journal* by W. Lucas (1934).

Little, Brown & Company for extracts from *The Journals of Bronson Alcott*, ed. Odell Shepard (1938).

Liveright Publishing Corporation for extracts from *Two Quaker Sisters from the Original Diaries of Elizabeth Buffum Chace and Lucy Buffum Lovell*, ed. Malcolm Lovell (1937). Copyright renewed 1964 by Malcolm R. Lovell.

John Murray (Publishers) Ltd for extracts from *Lady Charlotte Guest: Extracts from her Journal* (1950), *Lady Charlotte Schreiber (formerly Guest): Extracts from her Journal* (1952) and *The Private Diaries of Daisy Princess of Pless* by Mary Hochberg (1950).

The Trustees of the National Library of Scotland for extracts from Adv. MS 34.7.12 (diary of Andrew Rule) and MS 983 (diary of Amelia Steuart).

Oxford University Press for extracts from *The Cowells in America*, ed. M. Willson Disher (1934), *The Journal of Gideon Mantell 1819–52*, ed. E. Cecil

Curwen (1940), *Thraliana: the Diary of Mrs. Hester Lynch Thrale*, ed. Katharine C. Balderston (1951), *Miss Weeton: Journal of a Governess 1807–1811*, ed. Edward Hall (1936) and *The Wynne Diaries*, ed. Anne Fremantle (1935).

A. D. Peters & Co. Ltd and Weidenfeld & Nicolson Ltd for extracts from *The Diaries of Evelyn Waugh*, ed. Michael Davie (1976).

Sidgwick & Jackson Ltd for extracts from *The Complete Marjorie Fleming*, ed. Frank Sidgwick (1934).

A. P. Watt Ltd for extracts from *Excitement. An Impudent Autobiography* by Sydney Horler (1933).

Dr Williams' Library for extracts from the MS diary of Elias Pledger (no. 28.4).

L. B. Wright and M. Tinling for extracts from *The Secret Diary of William Byrd of Westover*, ed. L. B. Wright and M. Tinling (1941).

Yale University and the McGraw-Hill Book Company for extracts from *The Private Papers of James Boswell from Malahide Castle, in the Collection of Lt.-Colonel Ralph Heyward Isham*, ed. Geoffrey Scott and Frederick A. Pottle. 18 vols. (1928–34).

The human environment is inescapably social. From the moment of birth, human infants are dependent on others for biological survival. Psychologically, their cognitive, social, and emotional development is also predicated on human interaction. Adult independence and self-sufficiency are achieved gradually through years of contact and interaction with others.

(Leiderman, Tulkin & Rosenfeld, 1977, p. 1)

1. Past children. A review of the literature on the history of childhood

Childhood today is a subject of intense interest to anthropologists, sociologists and psychologists among others. Children play a central role in most households and have rights protected by the state. Parents give up a great deal of their time and energy to rearing their children and would appear to enjoy doing so. But was this always the case? Many historians looking at attitudes to and treatment of children in the past would insist it was not. It is only relatively recently that the history of childhood has been considered an area worthy of research. The picture painted so far by the vast majority of writers on the subject is surprisingly similar. With an almost monotonous regularity the same idea appears again and again in the discussion of the history of childhood: that there was no concept of childhood in the past (first explicitly stated by Ariès, 1960). Many authors argue that there was no appreciation of the needs of children and thus they were neglected – some authors would say systematically ill-treated – by both parents and the state. It is claimed that there has been only a gradual realisation that children are different from adults and not merely smaller versions. Accompaniments of this realisation were a growing concern for children, at times a very strict discipline, and an increasingly closer parent–child relationship. Most researchers in this area would appear to be more concerned with finding additional evidence to support the argument than with critically appraising it.

There are a few authors, however, who think differently. They believe that both childhood and adolescence were recognised in previous centuries, although children may not necessarily have been viewed in the same way as children today.

The Ariès thesis

Philippe Ariès' book *L'Enfant et la Vie Familiale sous l'Ancien Régime*[1] is the most influential work in this field.[2] Though his sources are taken mainly

1

from French culture and society, it is clear that he believes his conclusions to be true as well for the rest of Western society. Of particular importance is his finding that there was no *concept* of childhood during the middle ages. He also suggests that, although there was no awareness of the nature of childhood in previous centuries, this does not mean that children were ill-treated. In fact, he argues that, once it was appreciated that children were different from adults, they were subjected to a stricter method of rearing and severer punishments. These two facets of his argument: that childhood as a state did not exist and that children have been harshly disciplined will be reviewed here. In addition, a theme which Ariès does not discuss, but which appears frequently in later literature – that of the formality of the parent–child relationship in past societies – will be considered.

The concept of childhood

Ariès argues that *medieval* society did not recognise childhood – ancient society 'supposaient une différence et un passage entre le monde des enfants et celui des adultes' whereas 'La civilisation médiévale ne percevait pas cette différence' (463) (ancient society 'presupposed a difference and a transition between the world of children and that of adults' whereas 'Medieval civilisation failed to perceive this difference' (411–12)) but does not explain why adults stopped regarding children as children. He deduces from paintings – a vital source of evidence in his work – that childhood did not exist in the middle ages and claims that there are so few pictures of children because a child was not deemed of sufficient importance to merit a painting. As soon as a child could do without the care of his mother or nurse, 'peu d'années après un tardif sevrage, à partir de sept ans environ' (462) ('not long after a tardy weaning (in other words at about the age of seven)' (411)), he entered the adult world.

Ariès states that in the 16th century adults were beginning to notice children as 'une source d'amusement et de détente' (135) ('a source of amusement and relaxation' (129)), but they were regarded only as the playthings of adults, there was still no awareness of childhood as a separate state from adulthood. During the 17th century, Ariès claims that, although people enjoyed 'coddling' their children ('le "mignot-age"'), they were gradually realising that children were *different* from adults and not merely smaller versions. Children were now seen as being innocent but weak, particularly by the moralists of the period. Thus

2

children had to be trained and their behaviour corrected – they were 'de fragiles créatures de Dieu qu'il fallait à la fais préserver et assagir' (141) ('fragile creatures of God who needed to be both safeguarded and reformed' (133)). These two elements of a concept of childhood were also in evidence during the 18th century and in addition the physical health of children became a matter of concern. By the mid-18th century the modern view of childhood had emerged: 'L'enfant a pris une place centrale dans la famille, et pas seulement l'avenir de l'enfant, son futur établissement, mais sa présence et son existence nue' (142) ('Not only the child's future but his presence and his very existence are of concern: the child has taken a central place in the family' (133)). Although Ariès does not provide any evidence on the actualities[3] of childhood in support of his thesis, such evidence has been presented by Demos in *Family Life in a Plymouth Colony* (1970).

Demos researched into the Puritan colony set up at Plymouth, Massachusetts, in the 1630s. He was interested in reconstructing the actual experiences of a child, criticising Ariès for not doing so, and based his judgements on such physical artifacts as house size, furniture, type of clothing, and from documents – wills, inventories and the official records of the colony. Despite the large difference in approach and theoretical orientation, Demos agrees with Ariès that there was no concept of childhood. He, in fact, believes that there was no such awareness even in the 17th century, when Ariès asserts it emerged, since children were still clad in the same fashion as adults. Zuckerman (1970) agrees with Demos on this point. Demos does suggest that there may have been some recognition of infancy as children under the age of 7 were dressed differently from adults. Nevertheless, he declares: 'Childhood as such was barely recognised in the period spanned by the Plymouth Colony. There was little sense that children might somehow be a special group, with their own needs and interests and capacities. Instead they were viewed largely as miniature adults: the boy was a little model of his father, likewise the girl of her mother' (57–8).

In *The Making of the Modern Family* (1976), Shorter emphasises how our attitude to children has changed. They no longer belong to the lowest level of the social strata but are rather the subjects of our primary concern. Almost implicit in this viewpoint is that today our treatment of children is perfect and bad parents are never found. Shorter even goes so far as to state: 'Good mothering is an invention of modernization' (168). He claims that children were held in such low esteem that they were not even regarded as human. 'Nor did these mothers often (some say "never") see their infants as human beings with the same capacities for joy and pain as they themselves' (169). Shorter does believe that there has always been a 'residual affection' between parent and child – the product of a 'biological link' – but he stresses the change in the priority which the infant occupied in the mother's 'rational hierarchy of values', this change appearing first in the upper classes of the 16th century.

Researchers such as Firestone (1971), Hoyles (1979) and Illich (1973) similarly maintain that there was no concept of childhood in past societies. For example, Hoyles argues in 'Childhood in historical perspective' that 'childhood is a social convention and not just a natural state' and believes that 'Both childhood and our present-day nuclear family are comparatively recent social inventions' (2, 16).

Other scholars have been concerned not so much with the existence or non-existence of a concept of childhood as with attitudes to children through time.[4] Most of these authors take it as given that previously children were regarded as being at the very bottom of the social scale whereas now children are an essential component of society and family life. They thus describe changing attitudes to children (for the better) through the centuries and do so regardless of their research interest and theoretical orientation: to describe social history; to apply psychological theory (Demos, 1970, 1973; Hunt, 1972; de Mause and case studies, 1976; Trumbach, 1978); to document the various child-rearing theories (Cleverley & Philips, 1976; Newson & Newson, 1974; Sears, 1975; Wishy, 1968); or to trace the development of public policy towards children (Bremner, 1970–3; Pinchbeck & Hewitt, 1969).

As has been stated, Ariès claims that there was no appreciation of the state of childhood in the middle ages; children 'did not count'. Lyman ('Barbarism and religion', 1976), studying the period A D 200–800, believes that up till the 8th century parents were ambivalent towards their offspring, viewing them both as a pleasure and an integral part of family life, as well as a 'bother'. He argues that the former was the ideal but that in actual fact the latter was more often the actuality. Though parental love was often described as natural in the 7th century, 'The continued need for legislation, as well as other scattered evidence, suggests, however, that the distance between ideals and actuality had closed rather little in half a millennium' (95). McLaughlin ('Survivors and surrogates', 1976) also found that there was 'conflict between destructive or rejecting and fostering attitudes' on the part of parents to children, this time, though, for the period spanning the 9th to the 13th century. However, through the four centuries studied 'there are also clear signs, especially from the twelfth century onwards, of tenderness towards infants and small children, interest in the stages of their development, awareness of their need for love' (117–18). In direct contrast to Ariès, McLaughlin claims that by the end of the 12th century, the notion of the child as only the property of his parents 'had also been joined by more favorable conceptions, by a sense of the child as a being in its own right, as a nature of "potential greatness", and by a sense of childhood as a distinctive and formative stage of life' (140). Both of the above studies contradict Ariès' argument that the middle ages were unaware of the nature of childhood.

De Mause is by far the most extreme of the writers in this field. In 'The evolution of childhood' (1976), his avowed intention is to propose a 'psychogenic theory of history'; that is the central force for change is the 'psychogenic' changes in personality occurring because of successive generations of parent–child interactions. In carrying out this intention, he reconstructs a horrifying dark world of childhood in the past. He agrees with Ariès that past parents were attached to their children but he argues that they were unable to regard their offspring as separate beings. 'It is, of course, not love which the parent of the past lacked, but rather the emotional maturity needed to see the child as a person separate from himself' (17). De Mause suggests that there have been six successive historical modes of parent–child relations, with children regarded as being 'full of evil' up to the 13th century. Parents of the earliest mode, the infanticidal, 'routinely resolved their anxieties about taking care of children by killing them'. From the 4th century 'parents began to accept the child as having a soul' and therefore were unable to kill them and resorted to abandonment instead (51). During the 14th to the 17th centuries the child 'was still a container for dangerous projections' but it 'was allowed to enter into the parent's emotional life'. De Mause claims that 'enormous ambivalence marks this mode' (51–2).

There was little improvement in the child's status during the early modern period. Tucker concludes from her research into 15th- and 16th-century England ('The child as beginning and end', 1976) that children were seen as untrustworthy and as being at the 'bottom of the social scale'. In fact, 'childhood was a state to be endured rather than enjoyed' (229–30). Tucker states that parents were ambivalent towards their offspring: they were unsure whether to regard them as good or evil, and also when to include them in adult society or to exclude them from it. But, she argues, attitudes were changing during this period so that a 'greater value' came to be put on the child, and a 'greater attempt is made to please him through attention to his physical welfare and happiness'

(252). Tucker decides that, by the end of the 16th century 'More and more children were being recognised as human beings with different developmental problems than adults' (252).

Shorter and Stone concur with the main thrust of Tucker's views. Shorter too found that more interest was taken in children from the 16th century on. In *The Family, Sex and Marriage in England* (1977), Stone insists that for the period 1450 to 1630 the interests of the group took priority over the individual and therefore children were ignored. Most upper-class parents as well as many of those lower down the social scale, for instance, fostered out their infants and parents in general were unmoved at the death of infants. Between 1540 and 1660, however, increasing interest was shown in childhood as a state, resulting in 'a greater concern for the moral and academic training of children' (193).

In *Children in English Society* (1969), Pinchbeck & Hewitt chart the development of public policy towards English children from Tudor times. They do not distinguish between social and parental treatment of children, but instead they look upon parental care as being influenced by social attitudes and developing along much the same lines as public policy. They deal with changing social attitudes, documenting the rise of statutory protection for children. They too maintain that children were regarded as unimportant in Tudor society: 'Infancy was but a biologically necessary prelude to the sociologically all important business of the adult world' (8). Although children were loved, they were considered to be merely the 'property of their parents' and to be miniature adults: 'They were, indeed, looked upon as little adults and therein lies the essence of the explanation of much otherwise inexplicable to us today' (348).

Hunt in *Parents and Children in History* (1972) attempts to fuse history and psychology so as to provide keys to our understanding of French notions of childhood in the 17th century from psychoanalysis. Unlike Demos (1970), Hunt is more interested in concepts than in actualities: 'I am interested in the way people felt about the family . . . the attitudes they seemed to hold with regard to the duties of parenthood' (5). His main source of evidence is Dr Héroard's diary on the upbringing of the dauphin of France 1601–10, the future Louis XIII, and Hunt uses statements from this text to generalise to the rest of French society, despite the uniqueness of the boy's position. He argues that children were regarded as being inferior to adults. For example, despite 'the efforts of doctors and moralists', 'the process of child rearing was not valued very highly and did not bring the mother much in the way of prestige or honor' (102). He states that the construction of the royal household told Louis 'as a child he was something inferior, a chattel to be used in the elaborate dealings which adults had with one another' (99). For young children, those under the age of 7, 'being the father's servant was the only role which society allowed them to assume' (152). From 7 years onwards, children were expected to behave as adults, ceasing to be only a 'consumer' and becoming a 'contributor'.

Badinter depicts a similar type of French society in her book *L'Amour en Plus* (1980). She writes that before 1760 the educators, philosophers and theologians considered the child to be 'le mal ou le péché' (52) ('an evil or sinful creature' (39)) whereas to the ordinary people a child was 'davantage, ressenti comme une gêne, voire comme un malheur' (52) ('more often considered a nuisance, or even a misfortune' (39)). Moreover, she argues, even after the publication of Rousseau's book on education in 1762 which emphasised the importance of childhood, 'il fallut près de cent ans pour effacer la majeure part de l'égoïsme et de l'indifférence maternelle' (194) ('it took almost one hundred years to subdue most mothers' selfishness and indifference' (168)).

Not all writers would agree with the above views on French attitudes to children. Hunt's interpretation of Héroard's journal is markedly at variance with that of an earlier writer, Crump (1929). The latter found that Louis' needs as a child were recognised and catered for. Furthermore the findings of Marvick in 'Nature versus nurture' (1976) are opposed to those of Badinter and Hunt. Marvick suggests that parents were concerned about the survival of their babies. Though 'Birth alone did not qualify the infant for protection that would maximize its chances for survival', once 'a bond between child and outside world had been forged the adults brought their powerful forces to bear on its behalf' (293). She adds that, although children were regarded as 'vexing and peevish' at times, they were not thought to be beyond redemption – training and 'manipulation' would ensure conformity.

Illick (1976) arrives at an almost identical conclusion to that of Marvick, but in relation to 17th-century England and America:

There is no denying that parents in seventeenth-century England were interested in their children, but that interest took the form of controlling youngsters – just as adults restrained themselves – rather than allowing autonomous development. (323)

American parents of the same time revealed great anxiety over the illness of and sorrow at the death of their children, but they were also concerned with breaking the will of their sons and daughters. An alternative view is given by Macfarlane in *The Family Life of Ralph Josselin* (1970). He based his research on the diary of a 17th-century British clergyman and describes a much more caring parent–child relationship. Macfarlane states that it appears that children were eagerly welcomed by their parents and valued highly – both for the pleasure they afforded and the comfort they would later provide. In Josselin's diary there are numerous allusions to his love for his offspring and he took a great deal of interest in their development. Wrightson's (1982) research on 17th-century diaries supports Macfarlane's findings.

Josselin's ideas would seem to be in advance of their time as, according to most scholars, there was no marked alteration in attitudes to children until the 18th century. It is held that in the later modern period, children became increasingly important and the focus of parental concern and attention. Plumb argues in 'The new world of children' (1975) that, up until the end of the 17th century, there was an 'autocratic, indeed ferocious' attitude to children. They were viewed as being full of 'Original Sin', whereas in the late 17th century 'a new social attitude towards children began to strengthen' (65). Parents adopted a 'gentle and more sensitive approach' to their offspring; they were no longer to be looked on as 'sprigs of old Adam whose wills had to be broken' (70). None the less, despite this new view of children, Plumb does not claim that there was therefore a concept of childhood in the 18th century. Children were regarded more as things than as people: 'Children, in a sense, had become luxury objects upon which their mothers and fathers were willing to spend larger and larger sums of money, not only for their education, but also for their entertainment and amusement. In a sense they had become superior pets' (90). Really? In what sense?

In *Your Ancients Revisited* (1975), Sears holds a similar point of view, though he dates the new position of children as occurring towards the *end* of the 18th century. By that date there was 'a clear increment in the empathic ethos of Western society' (3). This newly aroused empathic spirit 'dictated a change from punitiveness and brutality to kindness and compassion' in methods of child-rearing. Like Sears, Trumbach in *The Rise of the Egalitarian Family* (1978) considers the 18th century to be characterised by a rise in the 'importance of domesticity'. Accordingly parents, and particularly mothers, are more attached to their offspring – 'Eighteenth-century parents were just discovering childhood and learning to enjoy its innocence' (262). De Mause, too, asserts that there was a 'great transition' in parent–child relations in the 18th century – the intrusive mode of child care appeared. The child was no longer 'full of dangerous projections' and, since he was so much less threatening, 'true empathy was possible and pediatrics was born' (52). Other authors such as Stone and Shorter make the same point. Stone states that during the period 1660 to 1800 there was 'a remarkable change' in attitudes to children. The family became child-oriented, affectionate, with a permissive mode of child care and a recognition of the uniqueness of each child. This type appeared first in the landed and professional classes who were 'able to afford the luxury of sentimental concern' for children (405). Shorter adds that the poor remained indifferent to their offspring at least until the end of the 18th century, and in some regions considerably longer.

Smith ('Autonomy and affection', 1977) and Walzer ('A period of ambivalence', 1976) studied 18th-century America. Smith would agree with the belief that there was a more humane view taken of children in the 18th century, but only in the Chesapeake region. He begins by stating: 'Most parents in eighteenth-century Virginia and Maryland were deeply attached to their children and they structured family life around them' (32). Smith then goes on to say: 'Such an assertion could not be confidently made about parental conduct in much of the pre-industrial West' (32). He does not appear to wonder why there is such a discrepancy in parental care between America and the rest of Western society but seems to prefer to look on the Chesapeake colony as being the forerunner in novel methods of child care which the West was yet to adopt. Yet the discrepancy is easily explained once it is realised that Smith uses primary sources – mainly diaries and letters – for his own research, but relies on the arguments and conclusions of other historians, usually de Mause, to depict the rest of Western society. He is quite happy to do this, even though de Mause uses mainly secondary sources of information, comes to quite the opposite conclusion regarding parental care and is also regarded by Smith as being 'obsessed with discovering child abuse or neglect in times past' (32).

Smith argues that in Europe children were not breast-fed by the mother because they were viewed as parasites who would drain the mother, a stance which he takes from the work of Hunt. In Chesapeake, however, suckling by the mother was probably the normal feeding method. Parents were anxious about their children, revealing concern during such stages as weaning and teething. Their letters and diaries contain 'a welter of evidence of parental tenderness and affection towards young children' (39). Smith believes that childhood had become a distinctive phase for 18th-century Chesapeake. This, as he points out, is in opposition to the findings of Walzer.

Past children

Walzer considers that American attitudes to children of this period can be characterised by the parental wish to retain and at the same time reject offspring. He gives the example that, although American fathers and mothers were genuinely interested in their children, they still sent them away to school or to live with relatives. Nevertheless, he still believes that there had been a shift in parental attitudes so that children were regarded more as individuals and treated with indulgence.

Progress continued to be made during the 19th century, at least for middle- and upper-class children. Ariès, Badinter, Pinchbeck & Hewitt, Shorter and Stone all insist that the poor child was still ignored and exploited by his parents. In the matter of child labour, for example, Pinchbeck & Hewitt argue that the indifference of both parents and the community to the suffering and exploitation of children in this way 'was one of the greatest obstacles to be overcome by those seeking to establish their legal rights to protection' (355). In 'Home as a nest' (1976), Robertson argues that, by the 19th century, and in contradiction to previous centuries, European parents were being urged to find joy in child-rearing. This development was, according to Robertson, due to Rousseau. He, for the first time in history, 'made a large group of people believe that childhood was worth the attention of intelligent adults, encouraging an interest in the process of growing up rather than just the product' (407). How could *one* writer have such an influence? Robertson also believes that public responsibility for children was growing:

At the very least, however, the nineteenth century was the time when public bodies began to think of children as children, with special needs because of their helplessness and vulnerability, rather than as small adults with the right to hire themselves out for sixteen hours a day, or as the chattels of their parents. (428)

Stone maintains that, following the benevolence of the 18th century and because of the rise of the Evangelical movement, early 19th-century families imposed a strict disciplinary regime on children. Humane attitudes reappeared during the mid-19th century. He therefore concludes that the evolution of the family has been one of fluctuating change and not one of linear development. But 'The only steady linear change over the last four hundred years seems to have been a growing concern for children, although their actual treatment has oscillated cyclically between the permissive and the repressive' (683).

Bremner comes to a similar conclusion to Stone. In his book *Children and Youth in America* (1970–3), Bremner's specific intention is to review the history of public policy towards children as opposed to parental policy.

This is a valid distinction to make – and he is one of the very few authors to make it – since there is no reason why public and private policy should chart the same course, although he does not always manage to keep to his intention. His work, in three massive volumes, covers the period 1600 to 1937 and traces the path of state policy towards children in such areas as child labour, health, delinquency, children in care or in need of protection as well as the duties of parents. He believes that there has been a growing awareness of children since the 19th century, that children have risen in esteem and that sensitivity to the needs of young people and the importance of youth has been increasing. Though he recognises changes in the way children were viewed through the centuries, he does not claim that previously children were regarded as unimportant, pointing out as an example that the Puritans emigrated to New England for the benefit of their children's souls. Volume 1 of his work spans 1600 to 1864, volume 2 1865 to 1932 and volume 3 1933 to 1937. He considers that the shorter time periods of the later volumes reflect 'the great expansion of interest in, and concern for, the rights and problems of children and youth during the past century' (vii). By the end of the 19th century, Bremner argues, it was 'held that prolongation and protection of childhood was essential to human progress' (602).

Cleverley & Philips (1976), Newson & Newson (1974) and Wishy (1968) have reviewed the various theories on children and child-rearing. In *Cultural Aspects of Child Rearing*, Newson & Newson document the main theories on child care from the 18th to the 20th century and argue that there has been a great change in our attitudes towards children and hence our treatment of them. We have moved from being concerned solely with their survival and with their moral growth to taking responsibility too for their mental health and social and economic adjustment. These two writers claim that, during the 18th and 19th centuries, a 'religious morality' was prevalent and proponents of this system insisted that a child's will should be broken. During the 1920s, a 'medical morality' made its appearance: its exponents emphasised the importance of forming regular habits in infancy so that a child learnt self-control. Attitudes continued to alter and, as the 20th century progressed, an interest in the child's natural intellectual and social development led to more permissiveness in the rearing of children. Today a 'fun morality' is predominant; advice is no longer authoritarian but paternalistic, children are to be cuddled and enjoyed.

Cleverley & Philips in *From Locke to Spock* also review various theories on child care, dating from the 17th century. They take up the rather obvious position 'that the patterns of child rearing and the educational practices within a society are influenced by the theories about children which happen to be current' (vii). They believe that the writings of such theorists as Locke, Rousseau and Freud 'focused attention on facets of children that previously have been relatively neglected, children were seen in new ways, and as a result, new modes of treatment evolved' (5). Locke, for example, according to Cleverley & Philips, believed a child's mind was a blank slate to be filled by experience; Rousseau depicted the child as 'an amoral being coming to know good and evil with the later development of reason' (27); and Freud attacked the concept of the innocence of childhood. Wishy, *The Child and the Republic*, studied how the views of 'experts' on child care changed from 1830 to 1900. He too argues that there has been a progression in their beliefs: 'notions of children's depravity gave way to assumptions of their essential innocence' (i). He is convinced that the emergence of modern images of childhood date from 1750 – that is, during the Enlightenment – and that by 1850 'there existed a less hostile and less repressive attitude towards the child's will' (23).

Some general disagreement certainly exists over exactly when a more humane attitude to children emerged – McLaughlin (1976), for instance, suggests the end of the 12th century whereas Lynd (1942) points to the mid-19th; most authors opt for a date in the 18th century. But there is a consensus that such an event did occur. Moreover there is a common element in all the varying views: it would seem that a change in attitude (for the better) to children is always discovered towards the end of whatever time period is being studied, be it from 1399 to 1603 as with Tucker (1976) or from 1500 to 1800 as with Stone (1977). Furthermore, those writers who find that children are valued in the early modern period are those who researched into short time periods. This peculiarity of the literature surveyed brings into the realms of possibility that so called 'enlightened' notions of childhood have always been possessed by at least part of the community.

Because these attitudes to children are considered to be related to their treatment, the type of care given to children, as described in the literature, will be examined.

The treatment of children

Regardless of whether an author believes that the increased attention which it is suggested had been paid to children from about the 17th century on led to severe discipline being imposed on young people, or led to a reduction in the brutality to which they had been subjected, most insist that the majority of children were cruelly treated in the past. Ariès, Hoyles and Stone are proponents of the former point of view.

Ariès does not maintain that children were ill-treated in the middle ages because there was no concept of childhood. In fact, he distinguishes between the two themes: 'Le sentiment de l'enfance ne se confond pas avec l'affection des enfants: il correspond à une conscience de la particularité enfantine, cette particularité, qui distingue essentiellement l'enfant de l'adulte même jeune' (134) ('The idea of childhood is not to be confused with affection for children: it corresponds to an awareness of the particular nature of childhood, that particular nature which distinguishes the child from the adult, even the young adult' (128)). He suggests that the growing concern for children was accompanied by an increasing strictness of discipline and also constant supervision. This new severity was especially in evidence in the schools because, as Ariès makes clear, *parents* believed it was necessary for a good education. As education was not then compulsory and free, but chosen voluntarily and paid for by parents, they had more influence over the type of school which they regarded as appropriate. Pupils were encouraged to spy for the master, 'le fouet prend un caractère avilissant, brutal, et devient de plus en plus fréquent' (286–7) ('the whip takes on a degrading, brutal character, and becomes increasingly common' (258)). By the 18th century this system was declining due to 'une nouvelle orientation du sentiment de l'enfance' (292) ('a new orientation in the concept of childhood' (264)). Children were no longer regarded as weak and so in need of humiliation, but rather they were to be prepared for adult life by 'des soins et des étapes, une formation' (292) ('careful, gradual conditioning' (264)). That is the child was to be moulded into shape. Ariès then does not claim that the growing awareness of the special nature of childhood necessarily created a better world for children. In fact, he argues the opposite: that the development of the concept of childhood was accompanied by more severe methods of rearing. He concludes as follows:

La famille et l'école ont ensemble retiré l'enfant de la société des adultes. . . La sollicitude de la famille, de l'Eglise, des moralistes et des administrateurs a privé l'enfant de la liberté dont il jouissait parmi les adultes. Elle lui a infligé le fouet, la prison, les corrections réservées aux condamnés des plus basses conditions. (465) (Family and school together removed the child from adult society. . . . The solicitude of family, church, moralists and administrators deprived the child of the freedom he had hitherto enjoyed among adults. It inflicted on him the birch, the prison cell – in a word, the punishments usually reserved for convicts from the lowest strata of society. (413))

Hoyles (1979) similarly states that, after the appearance of the idea of the weakness of childhood together with the concept of the moral responsibility of the teachers, dating from the 17th century 'It is clear that the concept of childhood was becoming linked with the idea of subservience or dependence' (25). He believes that, even in this century, children are an 'oppressed' group in society.

Stone (1977) writes that in the 15th and 16th centuries children were subject to strict discipline, and that the obedience was often enforced with brutality. Towards the end of the 16th and during the 17th century, the punishments meted out to children became even more barbaric. He claims that this increase was due to the first results of the greater attention paid to children, 'a by-product of a greater concern for the moral and academic training of children', and also the doctrine of Original Sin (193). He insists that there is a large amount of evidence revealing the wish to break the will of the child, especially among the Puritans, and that corporal punishment was the main method used to do so both at home and at school. 'There can be no doubt whatever that severe flogging was a normal and daily occurrence in the sixteenth- and seventeenth-century grammar school' (164); 'whipping was the normal method of discipline in a sixteenth- or seventeenth-century home' (167); breaking the will of the child was 'the prime aim', and 'physical punishment the standard method' (170). Parents decided the careers of their sons and, higher up the social scale, also the marriages of their sons and daughters. Stone dogmatically concludes for this period that 'This picture of a severe repression of the will of the child, extending to his or her choice of a spouse, is supported by a sufficient range of evidence to be beyond possibility of challenge' (193).

However, Morgan's earlier work, *The Puritan Family* (1944), does not support this view. He states that 'there is no proof that seventeenth-century parents employed the rod more frequently than twentieth-century parents' (57). He adds: 'Granted its purposes and assumptions, Puritan education was intelligently planned, and the relationship between parent and child which it envisaged was not one of harshness and severity but of tenderness and sympathy' (61). Demos (1970) also puts forward the case for a repressive but not abusive Puritan system of child-rearing.

Even a cursory glance at the literature on the history of childhood gives the impression that children have been the recipients of cruelty from antiquity up to the 19th century. Lyman (1976) states that children were often beaten, sold and abandoned during the early medieval period and he claims that infanticide was also common. McLaughlin (1976) refers to 'the neglect, abuse and abandonment of children' during the 9th to 13th centuries (123). In her research McLaughlin found two types of child-rearing advice. In one proponents urged that children should not be beaten, emphasising the sensitive nature of the child. The other view stressed the importance of discipline and physical correction and McLaughlin believes this may 'provide a closer reflection of the actual practice of parents' (138). De Mause (1976) is also convinced that brutality to children was the accepted mode of rearing during this period.

Pinchbeck & Hewitt (1969), Stone and Tucker (1976) maintain that strict discipline was the norm in 15th- and 16th-century England. Little progress was made during the next century. Illick (1976) describes strict parental discipline in 17th-century England and America – American parents were particularly concerned with 'breaking the will of' the child (331). Cleverley & Philips (1976) argue that the Puritan educators of the 17th and 18th centuries, with their emphasis on 'man's inherent sinfulness' and strict discipline, created the 'unfree child' (22). Plumb (1975) states that 'Harsh discipline was the child's lot, and they were often terrorised deliberately, and, not infrequently, sexually abused' during the 17th century (66). Though Plumb does admit that there were exceptions, that some children were well-treated by their parents, he claims that these were a minority.

Demos (1970) argues that Puritan babies of the 17th century were gently treated: warm, breast-fed and not clothed in restrictive garments, so that 'for his first year or so a baby had a relatively comfortable and tranquil time' (134). However, after weaning, during the second year of life as a child was beginning to assert his own will, there was a radical turn towards severe discipline. Demos argues that aggression was an emotion which aroused concern, confusion and conflict among Puritans and thus a child asserting his own will would seem to sincere Puritans as 'a clear manifestation of original sin . . . Such being the case, the only appropriate response from parents was a repressive one' (136). This lack of toleration for any assertion of autonomy in the child, Demos believes, would lead in turn to a preoccupation with shame by the child in later life. This, he states, was an essential feature of the Puritan character. He takes this idea further in a later paper, 'Developmental perspectives on the history of childhood' (1973), in which he describes the Puritan method of child-rearing as being functionally appropriate to the wider Puritan culture. 'Shaming was employed as a disciplinary technique, to an extent that directly enhanced the early sensitivities in this area' (136). Puritan children who had endured such a system of discipline, as adults would be 'conditioned to respond to those cues which would ensure their practical welfare' in Puritan society (137).

In his earlier work, Demos had maintained that the Puritan way of bringing up their offspring was not excessively harsh, and he pointed to the laws of the colony to show that parents were prevented from abusing their children. He argues that the parent–child relationship was seen as reciprocal. The child owed his parents unceasing obedience and respect, but the parents had to accept 'responsibility for certain basic needs of [their] children – for their physical health and welfare, for their education (understood in the broadest sense), and for the property they would require in order one day to "be for themselves"', and there were legal provisions for those parents who defaulted in their obligations (104).

Hunt (1972) also considers the beating of children to have been common, especially in schools. As a child's emerging autonomy was regarded with hostility, attempts were made to break his will. Moreover, adults felt threatened by any show of independence, believing that if this was not stopped a child would then exert control over his elders. Hunt's book, like that of Badinter (1980), leaves the distinct impression that children were an unwanted, disturbing element in an adult's life.

Macfarlane's (1970) study of Josselin's diary is one of the very few works appearing since the publication of Ariès' book which does not claim that parents totally controlled their sons and daughters. A reciprocal parent–child relationship is described instead. In sermons to his sons 'Josselin's plea [for better behaviour] was based on the idea of reciprocity, rather than a natural superiority and authority of parents' (125). Although Josselin may have upheld the principle of parents arranging the marriages, in practice his children chose their own partners. Macfarlane argues that 'If Josselin is typical, Puritan fathers were less austere and less able to exert control over their children than some historians would have us believe' (125). He adds that historians have depicted 'the ideal of deference and humility on the part of the child, strictness amounting to absolute authority on the parents' side, but we know surprisingly little about how the actual situation corresponded to it' (111).

In contrast to most authors, Walzer (1976) stresses that children were still subjected to harsh punishments in 18th-century America. Children then had to be disciplined early and their wills subdued: 'Every opportunity must be taken to curb their wilfulness and teach them to respect and obey' (367). This training system was not based on physical chastisement but on the techniques of arousing a child's sense of shame together with playing on a child's fears. Despite the continuation of strictness, Walzer does deduce from the evidence that some progress had been made in the treatment of children. For example, a punishment had to be suited to the age and temperament of the child. His conclusions are directly opposed to those of Bremner (1970–3) and Smith (1977). Bremner states that, although children in the mid-18th century were to be disciplined from an early age so that when they were past the age for punishment they would still obey their parents, they were not to be chastised too severely. The will was not to be broken as it was feared that children would then lose all their vigour and industry. After the American Revolution, the treatment of children altered as men throughout the country tried to create new patterns of education suitable for the people of an independent and republican nation. Thus, Bremner asserts, in the 19th century children were even being spoilt too much. He does not explain, however, how a political change could have such an effect on family life.

Child care in 18th-century Chesapeake bore 'a closer resemblance to that in modern society' than that practised by parents in earlier centuries, opines Smith (32). Parents were very pleased at the birth of a child and surrounded their offspring with a warm affectionate environment. He further argues that the sources used by him indicate that children 'were not treated as depraved beings whose wilfulness and sense of autonomy had to be quashed by age two or three' (39). Parents and relatives were fond of children, often indulged them and granted them considerable freedom. There was a close relationship between parents and children and Smith believes that most Chesapeake parents, like Josselin, expected their children 'to give pleasure and comfort in return for parental tenderness and nurture' (42). They accepted the advice of such people as Locke to a certain extent – for example, allowing their children plenty of outside play – but they placed more emphasis on developing a child's freedom of movement and sense of personal autonomy, particularly in sons, than in instilling respect and obedience for parental authority.

The majority of authors agree that the 18th century also saw a transformation in the accepted mode of child-rearing in Britain. For example, Sears (1975) believed that up till the 18th century children were 'subjected to indignities now hard to believe'. Although Locke in 1690 had already expressed the idea that children should not be treated harshly, Sears claims that this point of view still had to be 'made popular for parents'. Plumb similarly argues that up till the end of the 17th century the 'common lot [of children] was fierce parental discipline' (65). He maintains that a new social attitude towards children was appearing from the 17th century on. A 'new world' was opening up for children during the 18th century: books, games, clothes especially designed for children and more entertainment in the form of museums, zoos and exhibitions all appeared and educational establishments were increasing. Plumb omits to mention that a 'new world' was opening up for adults too. Adults had not been sampling such delights as exhibitions, zoos and novels in previous centuries to the exclusion of children; they did not come into existence until the 18th century.

Plumb, like Ariès, does not regard this new world he depicts for children in the 18th century as being all beneficial. Children lost as well as gained. For example, sex now became a 'world of terror for children' and their private lives became even more rigorously disciplined and supervised. Plumb ends, however, more optimistically than Ariès, claiming, in contradiction to the rest of his paper, 'Fortunately the images that society creates for children rarely reflect the truth of actual life' (93). He concludes that, as children had more to stimulate the ear and eye in the 18th century, they had indeed 'entered a far richer world' (93).[5]

Shorter and Stone also claim that the 18th century marked the transition from cruel to kind methods of child-rearing. Stone claims that after the mid-18th century a 'permissive' mode of child-rearing was adopted. He argues that there was an intermediate stage between the severity of the 17th century and the permissiveness of the mid- to late 18th 'when parents became affectionate towards their children, but still retained very tight control over them, now by psychological rather than physical means' (433). Stone suggests that, for this period, parents were to set their children an example rather than crush them with beatings. By the late 18th century Stone states that there were some exceedingly indulgent parents who reared their children with an 'injudicious fondness'. This extremely permissive mode of child-rearing aroused public protests: 'There is an extraordinary contrast between these reiterated warnings in the eighteenth and early nineteenth centuries about excessive maternal influence and domestic affection, and the complaints in the late seventeenth century about excessive parental indifference and severity. It is a contrast that clearly had a firm base in reality' (439). How does he know? Stone believes there have been major changes in child-rearing practices during the period 1500–1800 and for him, the crucial change was the transition from 'distance, deference and patriarchy' to 'Affective Individualism' (4). Yet, even in the 18th century, Stone argues parents still appeared to control their son's choice of career and daughters were expected to conform to the ideal image of femininity: frail, pale, slim and straight, and thus they were subjected to purges, spare diets and backboards with iron collars.

Despite the general swing to permissiveness which occurred in the 18th century, Stone finds definite class differences in the methods of rearing children during this period. These differences are:

(a) Higher court aristocracy: these showed a negligent mode with the care of children given to nurses and teachers.
(b) Upper classes: these cared for their children but believed in physical punishment.
(c) Professional and landed classes: these demonstrated a permissiveness and very affectionate mode of rearing.
(d) Puritans, non-conformist bourgeoisie and upper artisans: these showed concern and love for their children, substituting prayers, moralising and threats of damnation for beatings.
(e) Lower artisans: these did want their children to have a sound education; but treated them brutally.
(f) Poor: these were brutal, exploitative and indifferent towards their offspring.

It is unclear how much these class trends conformed to actual practice. Stone, for example, merely assumes that the poor, because they were poor, were therefore cruel to their children. (For a criticism of Stone in regard to this point, see Gillis, 1979; Macfarlane, 1979a; and Scott, 1979.)

De Mause also supposes that there was an increase in empathy during the 18th century. He maintains that children in the past were systematically ill-treated: 'The further back in history one goes, the lower the level of child care, and the more likely children are to be killed, abandoned, beaten, terrorized and sexually abused' (1). In fact, he states that, up till the 18th century, when parents were more in favour of shutting children in dark cupboards than beating them, 'Century after century of battered children grew up and in turn battered their own children' (41). De Mause argues that parent–child interaction oscillated between 'projection' and 'reversal'. Parents project all their unacceptable feelings into the child and therefore feel that severe measures must be taken to keep the child under control. Role-reversal, in which the child was meant to 'mother' his parents, was also common: 'One receives the impression that the perfect child would be one who literally breast-feeds the parent' (19). He views 'the continuous shift between projection and reversal between the child as devil and as adult' as producing a 'double image' and believes that this is responsible for much of the 'bizarre quality of childhood in the past' (21). He argues that this shift was a precondition for ill-treating children, for parents were frightened of their own mothers and that it was also 'the projective and reversal reactions which make guilt impossible in the severe beatings which we so often encounter in the past' (8). Because parents lacked the maturity to see their children as separate beings, they ill-treated them. As has been stated, de Mause postulates six successive modes of parent–child relations. The infanticidal, abandonment, ambivalent and intrusive modes covering the period up to and including the 18th century have already been described. The socialisation mode existed from the 19th to the mid-20th century: the child was to be trained, not conquered, guided into the proper paths and taught to conform. The helping mode appeared in the mid-20th century: the child knows better than the parent what it needs at each stage of life. The child is not disciplined, struck or scolded and the parent plays with the child 'continually responding to it . . . being its servant rather than the other way around' (52). Exceedingly dubiously, de Mause believes that children reared by the last mode will be 'gentle, sincere, never depressed' (54).

On the other hand, in *The Rise of the Egalitarian Family* (1978), Trumbach argues that, while aristocratic parents were more attached to their children in the 18th century, discipline continued to be strict. Thus he describes the same type of relationship as Walzer. The child's 'will was to be broken, and he was to be made obedient to his parent's' (244). Slight improvement had been made, though, since whipping as a mode of punishment declined in popularity after 1750. Trumbach states that parents were concerned lest they spoilt their children and that the aim of parental discipline was to prepare children for the disappointments of the adult world.

It appears from the literature that the 18th century was unusually enlightened – inflexibility and brutality were again to be the preferred method of child care in the 19th century. Sears describes the Calvinist approach to child-rearing in the early 19th century in which, as earlier, the aim of rearing was to break wilfulness in a child and to create a respect for authority. This was to be done not by using physical punishment as a means of control, but by withholding love from the child. Pinchbeck & Hewitt argue that the first Prevention of Cruelty to Children Act was not passed until 1889 because 'of the continuing social acceptance of violence which, as far as children were concerned, was as much a feature of their treatment by their parents as it was of their treatment by their teachers' (303). They consider parent and state to be equally harsh and that statutory protection for children was gained only after a 'long and bitter struggle'.

Robertson (1976) argues that 'it was late in the nineteenth century before birching at home was abandoned by the most enlightened parents' (415–16). Robertson, reminiscent of McLaughlin, states that there was a controversy over whether children should be severely disciplined or not: some advice literature insisted on harsh whippings, other types that a child's will was to be curbed not broken, and yet others urged English mothers to make a child feel that home is the happiest place in the world. Robertson believes that, at least for England, the last was only ideal and the first two were more likely to be observed in practice. Stone also found that, at the end of the 18th century and during the 19th, due to the rise of the Evangelical movement, there was a renewed formality in parent–child relationships and again intense supervision of children with severe punishment. At this time he says beatings were less common; food deprivation and locking in cupboards being more popular punishments.

Even by the 20th century, the world was still not a completely happy place for children. In the 1920s the 'medical morality' was prevalent (Newson & Newson, 1974) which believed that children should learn self-control. The theorists of this period stated that children were never to be hugged or kissed and Newson & Newson believe that both mother and child suffered from such harsh systems of rearing. However, it is generally agreed that we have now reached 'maturity' in our dealings with children. De Mause suggests that we cater to our children's every need; Stone that we 'lavish profound affection' on our children and Sears that, apart from showing concern for the physical welfare of our offspring, we now also recognise two other needs:

One is the right of all children to the opportunity for optimal development not only in the physical realm but in the intellectual, emotional and social ones as well. The other is the right to be treated with the same dignity and equality of respect for feelings that adults receive. (62)

The formal parent–child relationship

Those authors who referred to the nature of the relationship between parents and children, described it as 'formal': parents were distant, unapproachable beings and children were inferior objects whose

21

demands need not be considered, let alone met. It is suggested that, through the centuries, this relationship has become progressively closer.

Pinchbeck & Hewitt state that parents kept their distance from their children. Children were regarded as the property of their parents and so their labour was exploited by the poor and their marriages contrived by the rich, both to the economic and social advantage of the parents. Thompson in *Women in Stuart England and America* (1974) emphasises the formal parent–child relationship in 17th-century England. This was particularly the case in wealthy families where, he states, children, often even when adult, knelt when addressing their parents.

Plumb writes that 'children and parents shared few pursuits together' in the 17th century (67). De Mause believes that 'the history of childhood is a series of closer approaches between adult and child' (3). Stone claims that distance was to be maintained between parents and children of the 16th and 17th centuries, giving examples of the 'extraordinary deference' shown to parents by their children. Bremner argues that the closer parent–child relationship which developed in America arose out of democracy: 'I think that in proportion as manners and laws became more democratic, the relation of father and son becomes more intimate and more affectionate' (349).

Macfarlane departs as usual from the above authors. He points out that there is no evidence for a formal parent–child relationship in Josselin's diary. Josselin was prepared to help solve his children's problems and once his offspring had left home, they kept in constant contact with their parents.

The evidence for the thesis

The sources used for the history of childhood are overwhelmingly secondary: moral and medical tracts, religious sermons and the views of contemporary 'experts', particularly that of Locke. For example, Tucker (1976) writes: 'The sources used are primarily early printed books which deal with children, education, pediatrics and parental attitudes' (230). De Mause (1976), when studying discipline, used 200 advice statements on child-rearing for the 18th century and Stone lists several hundred such sources of evidence. The picture given by the above sources is mainly supplemented by evidence from paintings (notably used by Ariès); fictional literature (e.g. Godfrey, 1907; Lyman, 1976); travellers' accounts (e.g. Marvick, 1976; Shorter; newspaper reports (e.g. Bremner, 1970–3; Stone); biographies (e.g. de Mause; McLaughlin, 1976); legislation (e.g.

Demos, 1970; Morgan, 1944); and such primary sources as diaries, memoirs and letters. When primary sources of evidence are used as the main source of information, for example as by Crump (1929), Lochead (1956), Macfarlane (1970), Smith (1977) and Trumbach (1978), a much less repressive picture of childhood is presented. Hunt's (1972) book is the one exception to this and this is probably due to the strangeness of Dr Héroard's diary.[6] Admittedly, the century studied by Smith and Trumbach – the 18th – is one which most authors regard as being more humane in attitudes to and treatment of children; however, Macfarlane's findings for the previous century are in direct opposition to the conclusions of other historians. Those authors who have used such sources as diaries and autobiographies as a supplement, have done so selectively and anecdotally. They often ignore any evidence contained in the text which contradicts their arguments and also present unrepresentative examples as being typical of the attitudes and behaviour of the diarist concerned.

The evidence presented for the thesis that there was no concept of childhood in the past and that parents were, at best, indifferent to their offspring and, at worst, cruel to them, is varied. That there was no concept of childhood is argued from the depiction of children in paintings, from children's dress, from the referring to children as 'it' and from the fact that dead children's names were given to later offspring. The indifference and cruelty of parents are derived from the practice of such behaviours as infanticide, abandonment, wet-nursing, swaddling and the sending of children away on apprenticeships. The educative system, family structure, the concept of Original Sin, state policies, child-rearing theories and the high infant mortality rate are also believed to have led to emotional detachment on the part of the parents, neglect and a repressive system of discipline.

Ariès in particular has relied on paintings in his study of childhood in the past, although other authors such as Demos, Plumb and Shorter have referred to them as well. Ariès regards paintings as revealing the different attitudes to children and also as depicting the growing awareness of childhood. He claims that up till the 12th century there was no appreciation of childhood; children were depicted as adults on a smaller scale, even possessing an adult musculature. This, he argues, was not due to an inability to paint children, but because 'il n'y avait pas de place pour l'enfance dans ce monde [médiéval]' (23) ('there was no place for childhood in the [medieval] world' (33)). In the 13th century the infant Jesus appeared in paintings and this theme of Holy Childhood was extended in the 14th and 15th centuries. By the 15th century there were further developments in the depiction of children: lay childhood began to be portrayed, and the naked child. By the 16th century dead children were also painted and finally in the 17th century children were deemed of sufficient importance to be portrayed alone.

The way in which children have been dressed – both with reference to their depiction in paintings (e.g. Ariès and Shorter) and their actual clothes (e.g. Demos and Zuckerman) – has been used as evidence that young boys and girls were viewed as little adults. Children of both sexes up to about the age of 7 wore a long, loose gown open down the front. After the age of 7 they adopted styles of dress. For Ariès, the type of dress worn by children in paintings was only one strand in his *melange* of evidence, whereas other authors have used this evidence by itself to demonstrate that children were not seen as children in the past. Demos claims that 'the fact that children were dressed like adults does seem to imply a whole attitude of mind' (139) and Zuckerman writes: 'if clothes do not make the man, they do mark social differentiations' (73).

Lyman, de Mause, McLaughlin and Tucker all state that infanticide and the abandonment of infants were frequent in the past and are evidence of the neglect shown to children in earlier societies. De Mause claims that infanticide was 'an accepted, everyday occurrence' in ancient times and that, by the 18th century, 'there was a high incidence of infanticide in every country in Europe' (25, 29). Tucker believes that in 15th- and 16th-century England 'Infanticide was woefully common' (244). De Mause further writes that 'Once parents began to accept the child as having a soul, the only way they could escape the dangers of their own projections was by abandonment' (51). Shorter also includes abandonment in his list of evidence for the indifference which parents felt towards their children during the 17th century. However, he does concede that for some parents poverty was the cause of abandonment and that the separation was painful.

Badinter (1980), Hunt, de Mause, Shorter and Stone, among others, regard wet-nursing as a way for parents to rid themselves of their infants – particularly as there was a high mortality rate for babies so nursed. Badinter claims that the first step in the rejection of children was this refusal to nurse and she insists that 'Pour nombre d'entre eux, il y eut, de la part de leurs parents, des choix à faire entre leurs intérêts et la vie de l'enfant. Ce fut bien souvent la mort qu'ils choisirent par négligence et égoïsme' (82–3) ('Many parents had to choose between their own interests and those of the child, and it was often the child's death they chose out of negligence or selfishness' (67)). Hunt argues that mothers were reluctant to breast-feed because they viewed the child as being principally greedy, sucking a vital fluid from a mother's body already weakened by childbirth. Thus, despite the high mortality rate from such a practice, upper-class French babies were sent out to nurse. According to Hunt, continuing the practice 'rested on one fundamental assumption: that the infant was dispensable' (108). As there was trouble getting the dauphin a suitable wet-nurse, he was often hungry. Hunt deduces from this that nurses shared the same hostility towards infants as the mothers: this inhibited their flow of milk, and therefore it was difficult in general for infants to get enough to eat. Hunt further argues that wet-nursing reinforced the child's idea that he was unwanted as it told him his mother's breasts were forbidden to him and that his father did not want him around.

The swaddling of infants has been put forward as another example of neglect. Hunt, for instance, believes that though swaddling kept a child warm and out of harm's way it also 'operated on an even more general plane as a way of caring for infants and at the same time of binding up the anxiety which adults experience in dealing with the animality of small children' (130). De Mause maintains that 'Its convenience to adults was enormous – they rarely had to pay any attention to infants once they were tied up' (37). Badinter states that the custom of swaddling allowed a mother to go about her business more conveniently and Shorter views swaddling as a means of preventing interaction with a child because the infant cannot wave his hands and feet or grasp an object.

One explanation for the neglect of children in the past appears more frequently in the literature than any other: the high infant mortality rate. (The authors would appear to regard children under the age of 5 or 6 as infants.) Because so many children died, parents found it too distressing to become emotionally attached to their offspring and therefore remained detached. Ariès writes that it was not worthwhile for parents to invest emotionally in a child to any great extent when it was more than probable that the child was going to die, and he feels that we should be surprised at 'the earliness of the idea of childhood' as infants up till the 19th century had a slender chance of survival (39). He does not appear to have considered that this fact may negate his argument. If the high infant mortality rate explained the indifference of parents to their offspring, why did this indifference not continue for as long as the high infant mortality rate continued?

Hunt concludes that the repudiation of children in French society was 'prompted by the nagging awareness, that they, the parents were not

25

able to fathom the secrets of this stage of life and were conspicuously unsuccessful in keeping children alive as well' (185–6). Pinchbeck & Hewitt believe that the high infant mortality rate was due to the carelessness of the nurse which 'was often matched by an indifference on the part of parents, an attitude almost inevitably induced at a time when parents had so many children that they ceased to take an interest in them individually' (301). In fact they claim that many child deaths were due to 'culpable neglect and cruelty'. Stone also regards the high infant mortality rate as a crucial factor in explaining the supposed difference in parent–child relations in the past. 'The omnipresence of death coloured affective relations at all levels of society, by reducing the amount of emotional capital available for prudent investment in any single individual, especially in such ephemeral creatures as infants' (651–2). Therefore, Stone asserts, parents neglected their children and this further lowered their chance of survival and heightened the indifference at their death. He considers that there was a great reduction in the number of infant burials, from 60 per cent (as a ratio of baptisms) of infants dying under the age of 2 during the period 1740–9 to 23 per cent for the period 1810–29 (477). These are impossible figures; no population could persist with 60 per cent of people dying before 2. Nevertheless, he goes on to argue that this reduction was unlikely to be due solely to such medical improvements as inoculation or such nutritional improvements as the availability of cow's milk, but instead reflects a 'change in attitude towards children, involving a greater concern for the preservation of infant lives' (477). He concludes that as children no longer die so frequently during the 20th century 'it is worth while to lavish profound affection upon them and to invest heavily in their education' (680–1).

Badinter, Mitterauer & Sieder (1982), Porter (1982), Shorter and Trumbach, like Stone, view the lack of maternal care and love as being the main contributory factor to the frequency with which young children died. Trumbach argues that such 'innovations' as maternal breast-feeding and inoculation occurred *after* the fall in the aristocratic infant death rate in the 18th century.

Ariès claims that it was the rise of an education system; Plumb, Sears and Stone that it was the concept of Original Sin and Pinchbeck & Hewitt that it was state policies which led to a strict discipline being imposed on children. The educators (and parents) believed children needed to be beaten in order to be trained and the concept of Original Sin ensured that a child would be treated harshly in order to 'cure' him of his inherent sinfulness. As children up to the end of the 19th century were subject to the full force of the law and were not protected from exploitation in such areas as employment, parental care was similarly harsh according to Pinchbeck & Hewitt. In addition, Ariès and Stone related strict discipline to family structure, although in different ways. Ariès argues that the extended 'sociable' family of the middle ages allowed children a great deal of freedom, but in the transition to the closed, nuclear family, a child became more constrained and disciplined. Stone would demur. He believes that the extended family, which placed loyalty to ancestors above all else, treated children harshly, whereas the modern nuclear family emphasises humane methods of child-rearing.

Finally, the system of apprenticeship has been blamed for the lack of closeness between parents and children. Thompson (1974) argues that this formality was due to the 'ancient tradition of boarding-out school children in other households' which was 'hardly calculated to encourage intimacy between parents and adolescent children' (155). De Mause claims that the system was also evidence for the neglect which children experienced. Morgan (1944) and Macfarlane (1970), on the other hand, disagree. Macfarlane found that, though Josselin's children left home between the ages of 10½ to 15 years, contact was maintained with their parents. Macfarlane suggests the children were sent away as a means of broadening their experience; and also as a means of removing friction and the possibility of incest in overcrowded homes. Morgan also points out that parents and offspring did keep in contact while the latter were away from home. He argues that they were sent away because parents feared spoiling their children.

Most of the material is used for the purpose of relating social history but, in a few cases such as Demos, Hunt, de Mause and Trumbach, it has been linked to psychological theory. The first three scholars have made use of psychoanalytic theory to explain their results: Demos and Hunt have relied on Erikson's (1963) theory and de Mause on Freudian theory. Trumbach has applied Bowlby's (1966) views on attachment between mother and child to his findings.

Demos, Hunt and de Mause wished to relate childhood experience to the formation of adult personality. Demos (1973) explicitly states that he was attempting 'to find certain underlying themes in the experience of children in a given culture or period in order to throw some light on the formation of later personality' (128). However, there are grave methodological problems with psychoanalytic theory. The conclusions of the above authors are based on the dubious assumption that there is a close correlation between childhood experience and adult character; that adult

27

personality reflects any interference by adults with the unfolding development of the child. Thus they ignore the influence of developmental periods later than early childhood, and the interaction of these with culture (Shore, 1979). In addition, Clarke & Clarke in *Early Experience. Myth and Evidence* (1976) provide details of a number of studies, on children who have endured some form of deprivation, which challenge 'the notion of irreversibility of effects induced by early experience' (11) and also the belief that 'early experiences exercise a disproportionate influence upon later development' (19). They point out that a child is not a passive recipient of stimulation but 'rather is an increasingly dynamic being, who to some extent *causes* his own learning experiences' (13). For them 'early learning is mainly important for its foundational character. By itself, and when unrepeated over time, it serves as no more than a link in the developmental chain, shaping proximate behaviour less and less powerfully as age increases' (18).

Material providing evidence on the transition in the parent–child relationship is more scanty. Ariès argues that the emergence of a conception of childhood could be seen in such things as: children being given special clothes, distinct from those worn by adults; children having their own toys and games; and a growing tendency to express in art the personality children were seen to possess. Stone lists such evidence for the increased attention paid to children as: the appearance of amusing children's books and toy shops in the mid-18th century; the appearance of portraits of children sitting in their mothers' laps, which Stone believes indicates a friendly association with their parents; and the decline of the infant death rate. Shorter and Trumbach also argue that the infant mortality rate declined because mothers were more concerned for the welfare of their offspring.

Explanations for the transition in the parent–child relationship

Where authors have attempted to explain why the modern concept of childhood emerged, why cruelty to children diminished, and why the parent–child relationship became less formal, they have done so with reference to:

(a) the emergence of an education system (Ariès, 1960; Mitterauer & Sieder, 1982; Pinchbeck & Hewitt, 1969)
(b) changes in the family structure (Ariès; Shorter, 1976; Stone, 1977)
(c) the rise of capitalism (Hoyles, 1979; Shorter; Stone)
(d) the increasing maturity of parents (de Mause, 1976)

(e) the emergence of a spirit of benevolence (Mitterauer & Sieder; Sears, 1975; Shorter; Stone; Trumbach, 1978).

(a) According to Ariès, the alteration in attitudes towards children from one in which children did not count to one in which they were a vital part of everyday life was due to a revival of interest in education and also to the development of the family. He argues that medieval society lacked the idea of education; it 'avait oublié la *paideia* des anciens et elle ignorait encore l'education des modernes' (462–3) ('had forgotten the *paideia* of the ancients and knew nothing as yet of modern education' (411)). Nevertheless a small group of people in the 17th century – churchmen, lawyers and scholars – were interested in the moral reform of society and recognised the importance of education in bringing this about. Ariès believes that it was this group of people who were responsible for the segregation of children from adults. He claims that schools too were instrumental in this transformation as they removed children from adult society and also extended the period of childhood – in effect creating a separate world of childhood. In *Vom Patriarchat zur Partnerschaft*, Mitterauer & Sieder state: 'There is a clear connection between the intensification of the schooling of the young and the increasing attention paid to the needs and problems of young people in their families of origin' (110). Pinchbeck & Hewitt agree with Ariès that the emergence of a system of education was mainly responsible for the emergence of a concept of childhood: 'the institutional development and acceptance of formal education in schools with the consequent isolation of the child from adult society, was a prerequisite of the emergence of modern sociological and psychological concepts of childhood' (306–7).

(b) Ariès' conclusions are based on a particular interpretation of medieval life – that of its sociability. He argues that the evolution of the family – from the 17th-century form of being open to the outside world, friends and business associates forever passing through, to the nuclear form of today where parents and children are indifferent to the rest of society, distancing themselves from the outside throng – had important implications for the development of a concept of childhood. The modern family 'se retranche du monde, et oppose à la société le group solitaire des parents et des enfants. Toute l'énergie du group est dépensée pour la promotion des enfants, chacun en particulier, sans aucune ambition collective: les enfants, plutot que la famille' (457) ('cuts itself off from the world and opposes to society the isolated group of parents and children. All the energy of the group is expended on helping the children to rise in the world, individually and without collective ambition: the children

29

rather than the family' (404)). Ariès insists that it is impossible to separate the concept of childhood from the concept of the family: 'L'intérêt porté a l'enfance . . . n'est qu'une forme, une expression particulière de ce sentiment plus général, le sentiment de la famille' (393) ('The interest taken in childhood . . . is only one form, one particular expression of this more general concept – that of the family' (353)).

Shorter sees the traditional family 'as a mechanism for transmitting property and position from generation to generation' and thus was not concerned with individual welfare (5). It was 'much more a productive and reproductive unit than an emotional unit' (5). However, due to a 'surge of sentiment' (undefined) in three areas, the traditional family became less concerned with financial status, its ties with the outside world were weakened and the ties binding family members together reinforced. Shorter believes that the 'surge of sentiment' in the following three areas was crucial to the making of the modern family, taking place in the 18th and 19th centuries:

1. Courtship: romantic love superseded material considerations for marriage.
2. Mother–infant relationship: infant welfare became the most important consideration.
3. The family: a bounding line developed between it and the community and affection and love took the place of '"instrumental" considerations in regulating the dealings of the family members with one another' (5).

Shorter is nevertheless unsure whether or not these changes were caused by the 'surge of sentiment' or vice versa.

Stone also relates attitudes to childhood to the development of the family. He associates different methods of child-rearing with different types of family, which he labels as:

Type a: 1450–1630: the open lineage family
Type b: 1550–1700: the restricted patriarchal nuclear family
Type c: 1640–1800: the close domesticated nuclear family

Family type 'a', Stone argues, placed loyalty to ancestors and living kin uppermost and the interests of the group take priority over those of the individual. Therefore the relations between husband and wife, parents and children, were not very close. Children tended not to live with their parents for long: they were first nursed out, then had nurses and tutors and finally at an early age left home for school or work. Family type 'b' was more closed off from external influences and the power of the husband over his wife and children was stronger. For this form of the family, Stone states that there is a great deal of evidence revealing the wish to break the will of the child. Stone regards family type 'c' as being the product of 'affective individualism' (Shorter's 'surge of sentiment'?). This family type practised a permissive style of child-rearing.

(c) Hoyles argues that 'The invention of childhood as a separate state corresponds with the transition from feudalism to capitalism' in about the 16th century (3). In addition, the wish of the rising bourgeoisie to have their sons educated in a particular way so as to prepare them for their adult work as well as to enable them to challenge the power of the aristocracy, led to the development of schooling and the modern concept of childhood. Here Hoyles is disagreeing with Ariès that it was the views of a small minority of priests, moralists and lawyers which were responsible for the change. He believes that it was the rising bourgeoisie and the new Protestant thinkers (living in a capitalist society, which needed educated workers) who were the agents of change.

Shorter concurs that capitalism, although this time for the 19th century, increased the value of children: 'What I am arguing is that the transformation of child care *within the family* came about as a direct result of the economic growth that nineteenth century capitalism produced' (265). Stone states that the rise of 'affective individualism' (which led to the formation of the closed domesticated nuclear family) was made possible due to the growth and spread of commercial capitalism and also the emergence of a large and 'self-confident middle class'.

(d) De Mause asserts that there was a continuous sequence of modes of child-rearing ranging from the infanticidal to the helping mode. In the latter mode, the parents show true empathic care – they are able to realise and meet the needs of their children. These modes evolved 'as generation after generation of parents overcame their anxieties and began to develop the capacity to identify and satisfy the needs of their children' (51).

(e) Shorter's 'surge of sentiment' and Stone's 'affective individualism' have already been referred to. They would appear to be examples of some indefinable spirit of humanity which appeared in society in the 18th century according to Shorter, but in the 17th according to Stone. Mitterauer & Sieder, like Shorter and Stone, believe there has been a steady evolution in the capacity for feeling affection. They write: 'Until the middle of the nineteenth century, there was, among large sections of the population little tenderness and loving intimacy' and state: 'family life has certainly gained in feelings of affection' (100, 61). Sears also suggests that, by the end of the 18th century, there had occurred 'a clear increment in the empathic ethos of Western society' (3). This newly aroused

31

empathic spirit 'dictated a change from punitiveness and brutality to kindness and compassion' in methods of child-rearing. Trumbach believes that the increase in domesticity occurring in the aristocracy in the 18th century was brought about by the egalitarian movement – that all men were equal. The ideal of domesticity encouraged both parents to take more interest in their children. Trumbach would disagree with Stone that affectionate relationships were only possible in nuclear families.

Apart from the 18th century, life appears to have been exceedingly painful for children in the past. The similarity in the views expressed by the majority of authors is striking. It has been repeatedly claimed, for example, that past societies regarded it as essential to break the will of a child. The general thesis is that there has been a progressive improvement in the status and treatment of children through the centuries.[7] The next chapter will evaluate the validity of that thesis.

2. The thesis re-examined: a criticism of the literature

Despite the lack of agreement over when changes in the treatment of children occurred and whether the emergence of a concept of childhood increased or reduced the severity of discipline imposed on children, the overall picture presented by researchers in the history of childhood varies little. It is suggested, with only a few exceptions, that parents regarded their children with indifference, that there was no appreciation of childhood as a separate state from adulthood and that harsh discipline was the normal lot for children – many authors claim, in fact, that children were systematically abused. From a functional point of view there are a number of problems with the historical thesis. For example, the following questions remained unanswered:

(a) Why would parental care have evolved in the way that has been suggested – to neglect and ill-treat offspring?
(b) Do parents ignore or abuse their offspring on a large scale in, for example, primate or primitive societies?
(c) Would not continuing brutality adversely affect a child's development?[1]

In an attempt to answer these questions a variety of divergent sources of information have been looked at: sociobiological theory on the evolution of parental care; studies of parental care in primates – both laboratory studies and naturalistic observations; evidence from anthropological studies and evidence on the effects of privation and abuse on young primates and children. Because of reasons of space and the wide-ranging nature of the evidence, the following account has to be very concise. (A fuller treatment of the above topics can be found in Pollock, 'The forgotten children', 1981, Appendix A.) None the less, it is hoped to show that it would have been difficult for the prevailing theories on the history of childhood to have been put into practice by the majority of the population. Firstly, the evolution of parental care will be considered and, secondly, its function with regard to primates and man.

The evolutionary and functional aspects of parental care

Evolutionary theory suggests that living things should be concerned with the production and rearing of offspring (Barash, *Sociobiology and Behavior*, 1977). Apart from a few exceptions, such as the worker bees who do not reproduce themselves but who rear their sister's (the queen's) offspring, it appears that this is indeed what animals do. Sociobiological theory predicts that animals should invest in reproduction as much as possible consistent with the maximisation of inclusive fitness.[2] The biological necessity to reproduce is universally strong because ultimately offspring represent the only means of leaving genetic representation in the next generation. Animals do have a diversity of parental investment strategies available to them; but the options are not unlimited. If, for instance, many offspring are produced, they will have to be given relatively little parental attention as there is only a certain total amount of time that parents can spend on their young. Alternatively, if parents choose to produce a smaller number of offspring, then they can make each one larger and/or spend more time in parental care and attention (Barash).

Therefore there are two basic strategies which animals can employ, depending on their situation, in order to maximise the survival of their young. Where there is a high loss of offspring to predators, with little the parents can do to stop it, it makes more sense to produce large numbers of offspring in the hope that some will survive. Barash calls a species which selects this parental strategy an R-selected species. On the other hand, if food supplies are scarce while predation is not a problem, parents would increase the survival rate of their offspring by producing smaller numbers so that each offspring would be given a better start in life – for example, it could be of a larger size. Barash refers to the species choosing this type of strategy as a K-selected species. R-selected species have high birth and death rates whereas K-selected species have low birth and death rates and this tends to keep the population size close to the number the environment can support. When species adapt to stable predictable environments, K-selection tends to prevail over R-selection, leading to a series of demographic consequences which favour the evolution of parental care (Wilson, *Sociobiology*, 1975).

Wilson uses the theories of such writers as Hamilton (1966), Lack (1954) and Trivers (1974) to suggest how and why parental care evolved. As has been said, one prerequisite is the adaptation to a stable environment. Once this has occurred, the animal will tend to live longer, grow larger and reproduce at intervals (iteroparity) instead of all at once. In addition, if the habitat is structured, the animal will tend to occupy a home range or territory or at least return to particular places for feeding and refuge (philopatry). Each of these modifications is best served by the production of a relatively small number of offspring whose chance of survival is improved by special attention during their early development. At the opposite extreme, species are sometimes able to penetrate new, physically stressful environments by developing protection devices which include care of offspring during the most vulnerable period of their development. The specialisation of food sources that are difficult to find, exploit or hold against competitors is occasionally augmented by territorial behaviour and the strengthened defence of the food sources when the offspring are present. Finally, the activity of predators can prolong parental investment to protect the lives of their offspring (Wilson). Wilson argues that all four of the following environmental prime movers can act singly or in combination to generate the evolution of parental care:

1. Stable, structured environments leading to K-selection.
2. Physical environments that are unusually difficult.
3. Opportunities for certain types of food specialisation.
4. Predator pressure (where parents can protect their offspring).

The essence of the theory is represented in Figure 1.

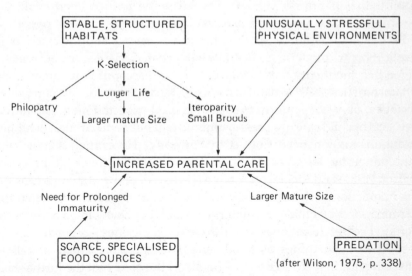

(after Wilson, 1975, p. 338)

Figure 1. The prime environmental movers and intermediate biological adaptations that lead to increased parental care

The thesis re-examined

The social systems of K-selectionists tend to be relatively well developed around complex kinship networks as compared to R-selectionists which tend towards either a social living or loosely aggregated swarms, schools or herds (Barash). Parental care is better developed within the K-selected species, consistent with the emphasis upon quality over quantity. When a heavy initial investment is made as in a long gestation period or prolonged post-natal care, extended immaturity and long life are likely to emerge as co-adaptations (Hamilton). Man is of course K-selected and has a large parental investment in offspring. Humans, if not genetically determined, are at least genetically influenced and, as good parental care is adaptive, are likely to select for it.

Sociobiological theory then, predicts that parents will sacrifice a good deal, consistent with the maximisation of their own inclusive fitness, to ensure the survival of their young. Parents should give their offspring enough care to ensure that each one has a good chance of competing successfully as an adult, even if this means producing fewer offspring. However, as Trivers has demonstrated in his paper 'Parent–offspring conflict', because parents and children only share one half of their genes by common descent, sociobiological theory also predicts a certain amount of conflict between the needs of the parent and the needs of the child. This could be over the cessation of any investment, as the weaning when it becomes more profitable for the parent to invest in another child while it is still in the offspring's interests to be fed by the mother. There could also be strife over the amount of parental investment at any one period.

Sociobiological theory certainly has its opponents and the extent of its application to modern, industrialised, urban societies is questionable given that the theory fails to take culture into account in its predictions. Characteristics of human behaviour, especially for contemporary societies, may not conform to sociobiological expectations – as Smith in 'Aspects of child care' (in press) points out, genetic and cultural evolution and transmission need not act in harmony. He examines four 'dual inheritance' models: that of Campbell (1975), Durham (1976), Lumsden & Wilson (1981) and Richerson & Boyd (1978). All of these models consider the interaction between biology and culture. Smith concludes from this examination that child care conformed largely to sociobiological expectations in preliterate societies, while in complex societies it often did not – in respect of such things as family size and the adoption of unrelated offspring, for instance. This casts doubt on the view that the further back in history one goes, the more one will find children being beaten and assaulted. What is crucial to the debate is how far can humans act in opposition to their biological inheritance? Could, for example, socio-economic and religious factors override genetic influence to the extent that parents not only stopped caring for their offspring but also actually decreased the latter's survival value by ill-treatment and abandonment?

Though parents are concerned according to sociobiological theory with the overall investment in their offspring, as Trivers has made clear, this does not prevent a clash of interests between parents and particular children. Thus, although parental behaviour functions for the good of offspring, it is not always optimal for each infant. There may be circumstances under which functional behavioural rules are not in the best interests of certain offspring and may even lead to the latter's death – as in the case of langur males who, when taking over a new harem, kill the infants in order to sire their own young (Jay, 1965). Furthermore, organisms may be living in environments to which they are not adapted and so, because their functional rules are inappropriate, destructive behaviour ensues as, for example, in many caged primates. However, in recent human populations, is it possible that either of these two types of circumstances – which could lead to the levels of child abuse suggested by many historians and psychologists – have been prevalent? Evolutionary theory undoubtedly predicts a certain amount of parent–offspring conflict, but it seems unlikely that this would go as far as the parent damaging the child as a matter of routine. It is difficult to disprove the historical thesis simply by listing the benefits of parental care – an alternative refutation would be the existence of any adverse conse-quences on the social, mental and physical development of children deriving from the lack of adequate care; this will be gone into later in the chapter. Nevertheless it does seem that parental care plays a vital role in the growth and maturation of the young: 'Attachment behaviour, contributing as it does to species survival, thus emerges as one of the most fundamental forms of social adaptation to be found in the higher vertebrates' (Goody, *The Character of Kinship*, 1973, p. 110).[3]

The young of advanced animal species are often born completely helpless. They depend on parental care for their very survival – if it is withheld the young will die. Parental behaviour is of considerable evolutionary significance. Those animals which are able to look after their offspring, at least adequately, not only increase the chance of survival for their young; but also for their race. Evolutionary theory thus predicts that living things should be concerned with reproduction and the rearing of their young. By studying the care given to offspring by animals, and also other human cultures, it is possible to discover how much of the theory is put into practice.

It appears from the studies of primates that mothers do give at least adequate protection and care to their young (Carpenter, 1965; Chance & Jolly, 1970; Hall & Devore, 1965; Hinde, 1970; Jay, 1965; van Lawick-Goodall, 1967; Rosenblum, 1968). They feed and, for the majority of the species, groom the young, protect the infants from falling from their mother and from exploring too far at an early age. Even the squirrel monkey, largely indifferent to her babies, will change her behaviour to help an incapacitated infant. The primate mother is a haven, a refuge and a fixed point of orientation for all early independent movement, except among some prosimians. The young monkey and ape escape to the safety of their mothers rather than to a nest (Chance & Jolly, 1970). A human caretaker or even a well-prepared cage can replace the mother with reference to the infant's healthy physical growth but, as monkeys are adapted to live socially, a human or cage are poor mother substitutes with reference to an infant's healthy social adjustment (Rowell, 1972).

In the ape societies, infants are born at longer intervals and the immature phase of the ape's lifespan forms an increasingly large proportion of the primate's social life. Thus the ape societies reveal more flexible, complicated parental care than the monkey societies. The gorilla and chimpanzee mothers are able to appreciate certain needs of an infant and alter their behaviour in such a way as to provide for these needs – that is they do not merely respond to a situation in a number of set ways (Chance & Jolly; van Lawick-Goodall).[4] From the various studies on the primates it seems as if enough parental care is given to ensure that at least some of the young grow to maturity and that they fit the society in which they are to live. How much is this the case in human societies?

All human infants are born helpless, dependent on adult care and adult transmission of their society's culture. To adults all over the world, children represent something helpless and weak, something to be protected, supervised and trained and also something which is a valuable asset to their society (Mead & Wolfenstein, 1955). Different cultures may possess different methods of child-rearing; but they all have the same aim; to raise their child from infancy to an independent, responsible adult capable of full participation in society. Despite the enormous differences among cultures, and although there are obviously cultural influences on child care, a great deal of similarity has been found in child-rearing practices (Ainsworth, 1967; Lewis & Ban, 1971).

LeVine ('Child rearing as a cultural adaptation', 1977) proposes the following universal goals which parents have in relation to their children:

(a) The physical survival and health of the child.

(b) The development of the child's behavioural capacity for economic self-maintenance in maturity.

(c) The development of the child's behavioural capacities for maximising other cultural values such as morality, intellectual achievement and religious piety.

LeVine believes there is a hierarchy among these goals: for example, in those societies with a high infant mortality rate, goal 'a' will have paramount place and parents will delay stimulating the child's social and cognitive development until his survival seems assured. Thus the primary function of the parental role is that of protection.

Numerous anthropological studies reveal that parents in general give at least adequate, and often more than adequate, care to their children. Such research illustrates that the protection and nurture of young children is the primary concern of almost all parents. There are variations in the way this is achieved but the main aim is the same: to ensure, as far as possible, an infant's survival (see for example Brazelton, 1972, on Mayan society; Draper's 1976 study of the !Kung tribe; Goldberg's 1972 research into Zambian infants; Kagan & Klein, 1976, on the San Marcos Indians and Marvin *et al.*'s 1977 work on the Hausa). Once it seems likely that a child will survive, parents can then turn to the task of assimilating their child into society and the actual process of socialisation will be influenced by the culture of that society (see the case studies in Whiting, 1963).[5] Thus child care appears to be a very fundamental part of human life.

Newson & Newson's (*Seven Years Old in the Home Environment*, 1976) study reveals the importance of the parental role in modern industrialised societies, particularly the function of integrating the child into the social world. They demonstrate that parents are a uniquely caring force in a child's development, having an involvement with their own child which no one else can simulate. They act as buffers for their children, preventing them from suffering the natural consequences of their actions until they reach a sufficient level of competence. The vital characteristic of the parental role is its partiality for the individual child and this explains why all the other caring agencies which have been devised can never be quite as satisfactory as an adequate parent. At the most, all community care can offer is impartiality, to be fair to every child in its care. However, that is not enough: a developing personality needs to know that to someone it matters more than other children, 'that someone will go to

39

*un*reasonable lengths, not just reasonable ones, for its sake' (Newson & Newson, p. 405). It is this aspect of parental care which may be the most important of all. In normal circumstances no child is subjected to neglect or abuse. It takes what amounts to complete social breakdown before children will be ignored or even ill-treated by their parents.

Turnbull (*The Mountain People*, 1973) studied the Ik tribe in Africa during a famine which was caused by drought. There were signs that, before the drought the Ik had been as kind, generous and light-hearted as other human beings; but with increasing starvation, they became ruthless and solely concerned with their own individual survival. Altruism was virtually non-existent; anyone who did help another was regarded as a fool. People in pain were a source of amusement to others, especially if they were old or weak. In these circumstances children were neglected by their parents – they were put out of the parental home at the age of 3 and left to fend for themselves. Turnbull notes that he 'never once saw a parent feed a child, except when Kauar did so, or when the child was still under three years old. In fact, you rarely saw a parent with a child in any context, unless it was accidental or incidental' (114). From Turnbull's evidence it is thus possible for parents to ignore and even abuse their children; but this only happens in very exceptional circumstances and in fact the Ik are dying out.[6]

The importance of parental care for normal development can be seen when infants are reared without parents or are subject to abuse. Harlow & Harlow ('A study of animal affection', 1963) removed rhesus monkeys from their mothers at birth and placed them with inanimate surrogate mothers. When these infant monkeys reached maturity, they turned out to be strikingly abnormal in their behaviour: they were socially incompetent and as mothers themselves they seriously ill-treated their offspring. Most of the infants had to be removed and reared by laboratory staff. Motherless, isolated chimpanzees show a similar type of syndrome to that of rhesus monkeys (Mason, 1968; Menzel, Davenport & Rodgers, 1963). The motherless monkeys had been deprived of the necessary interaction with their mothers and social experience and so were unable to react normally to other adult monkeys (Jolly, 1972). Attachment behaviour, seen in both man and primates, is an important, perhaps crucial, aspect of the mother–infant relationship. Mothering also requires a reciprocal interaction and this explains why inanimate surrogate mothers are useless at preventing the ill-effects of isolation.

The effects of deprivation and abuse on human development are even more striking. The large number of studies (cited in Bowlby, 1966, and see also Ferguson, 1966;[7] Flint, 1967; Franklin, 1977; and Spitz, 1945)[8] on the mental health and development of children in institutions which do not respond to them as children and individuals, make it clear that, when deprived of some kind of 'maternal' care, a child's development is usually retarded – physically, intellectually and socially. In some cases a child can be damaged for life. Thus it seems that, to ensure the normal development of a child, a basic minimum level of care from someone is required. If parents in previous centuries were as indifferent to their young children as has been suggested, then it would seem reasonable to assume, from the evidence contained in the above studies, that they produced a group of damaged children who would develop into deficient adults. Few authors are prepared to claim that past societies were largely composed of less than competent adults.

Child abuse occurs in all strata of society, although only in a minority of the population. Abusing parents tend to have been themselves abused and neglected as children – this is a factor which many researchers into the area feel is fundamental to the whole problem (Kempe & Helfer, 1972; Kempe & Kempe, 1978; Martin, H., 1976; Martin, J., 1978). Abusing parents fear spoiling the child, believe in the value of punishment and have distorted perceptions of the child (Martin, J.). There are often unrealistic demands for obedience and also role reversal where the parents expect children to fulfil their needs (Davoren, 1968; Franklin, 1977). Steel & Pollock (1968) emphasise the breakdown in 'mothering' which leads to child abuse. The parents do not see the child as a person and are unable to respond to his needs appropriately and sensitively. Daly & Wilson (1981) discuss the reasons for child abuse from an evolutionary perspective. They suggest that the likelihood of abuse and neglect occurring is increased 'under circumstances in which adults are called upon to play parent to children not their own, in which the mother–infant attachment is absent or disrupted . . . or in which parental capacities and resources are overtaxed' (406). All the above studies demonstrate that child abuse does not occur in a normal parent–child relationship; but because there is something lacking in the relationship.[9]

That child abuse is undoubtedly maladaptive is seen by the effects of abuse on children. Learning takes place in a social world; but the abused child's environment contains a number of factors which hinder the child's capacity to learn and understand (Martin, 1976). Such a child is often isolated from his peers and his mother fails either to talk or play with him. Thus speech delay is very common (Blager & Martin, 1976). In addition,

41

the child becomes inhibited and unable to play. When severe abuse has occurred, a child will display 'frozen watchfulness', refusing to participate in whatever is going on around him (Roberts, 1978). Abuse can also cause long-term damage: there is a serious risk of brain damage, eye damage and other physical defects; retarded development and emotional problems – and it greatly increases the likelihood of these children abusing their own children (Carter, 1974; Franklin; Martin, H., 1972; National Society for the Prevention of Cruelty to Children, 1976; Skinner & Castle, 1969).

The characteristics of parents in the past which have been suggested as explanations of their cruelty to children (e.g. by de Mause, 1976) are also possessed by contemporary parents who abuse their children: the fear of spoiling the child, the demands for total obedience and the wish for the child to gratify the parents' needs. Moreover, child abusers tend to have been themselves ill-treated as children, and as adults appear to have no concept of childhood: 'The severe beater of children is not capable of seeing the infant or child as an immature being without capacity for adult perception and behaviour patterns' (Davoren, 'The role of the social worker', p. 155). Therefore part, but only a tiny part, of the historians' thesis could be correct: some parents in the past possessed no concept of childhood and some parents also were cruel to their offspring. It is possible that 'centuries of battered children grew up and in turn battered their own children' (de Mause); but it would seem to be impossible, given the evolution and function of parental care to protect offspring, for all or at least the majority of children to be 'battered'. To justify such a claim, de Mause and others would have to explain how and why the abuse evolved and why, if parents now possess a concept of childhood, child abuse is still present in 20th-century society. In societies with high mortality rates, as in earlier centuries, it would be more logical to have any trait selected for which increased a child's chance of survival, rather than opting for cruelty to children which decreases it.

Parents everywhere start off with infants whom they wish to raise to independent adulthood. From the material surveyed in this section, it seems that it does not actually matter how the parents choose to go about the task, with some limitations, such as: children require a certain amount of protection, affection and training for normal development. The type of society a parent lives in will affect how that parent rears and treats a child; but it will not drastically alter the basic pattern. For example, the qualitative aspects of parental care (protection, love and socialisation) will not be altered; but the quantitative aspects (the kind of care and the type of training) may vary. Parental care has evolved as it has done in ape and human societies, because there was a need for that type of care. For parental care to have been as drastically different in past societies as has been suggested, would mean parents acting in direct opposition to their biological inheritance. LeVine claims this would be impossible:

Contemporary humans are innately programmed for attachment [between parent and child], and child-rearing practices everywhere must be accommodated to this universal tendency. In this respect, then, child-rearing practices reflect the environmental pressures that acted on our hominid ancestors, rather than those that parents experience today, and they can vary culturally only within limits established in the distant evolutionary past without inflicting developmental damage on the child. (16)

The barbaric system of child care described by many authors for previous centuries would be quite unique. The theory of prevalent systematic ill-treatment of children is highly unlikely. The next section will examine the evidence for such a theory, followed by a reappraisal of the argument.[10]

The evidence for the historical thesis

Research into the history of childhood involves relying on exceedingly problematic sources of evidence. The reconstruction of child life in the past is an area beset with difficulties, the scholar's path is strewn with obstacles. Unfortunately accounts so far of attitudes to and the treatment of children reveal little, if any, awareness of the problems involved. Several varying types of sources have been utilised in the search for material on childhood in past times (see above, p. 22). Let us examine some of these sources and the use made of them.

Child advice literature is the main source of evidence employed in works on childhood in earlier centuries. Only a few authors have relied on primary material such as autobiographies and diaries to any great extent. Quotations are taken from the contemporary books, sermons and moral tracts of the time period under study and used, not only to demonstrate what the current theories about children were, but also to infer actual parental practice. In 'Advice to historians on advice to mothers' (1975), Mechling has studied the question of whether or not parents do pay attention to child-rearing literature. She notes that the findings of several surveys in America on early 20th-century advice literature (see the Berkeley Growth Study, 'an ongoing longitudinal study of child development', and Bronfenbrenner (1958) for a review of such studies) showed that such advice is not heeded by mothers. British parents, it would seem, pay no more attention to such advice. Newson & Newson (*Patterns of Infant Care*, 1965), in a study of Nottingham parents with 1-year-old children, found that 'contemporary baby books are a rather poor indication of what actually happens in the home' (235). From their study of 4-year-olds (*Four Years Old in an Urban Community*, 1968), Newson & Newson conclude: 'We do not have the impression that mothers in Britain are strongly expert-oriented so far as child-rearing is concerned, nevertheless the majority expect to be able to find fun in parent-hood, if necessary rejecting more authoritarian advice in order to do so' (556).

Mechling considers the problem of using this type of literature in historical research and considers four methodological difficulties with its use as a source for inferring parental behaviour: the meaning of the advice, the class bias of the texts, the extent to which parents learn to be parents from reading advice books and the theoretical link between behaviour and values. She claims that there are two main sorts of advice literature: that which 'reflects' current practice and that which is the 'vanguard' of change (46). She criticises historians for not differentiating between the two types of evidence since this is important for determining what the advice means in its context. In 'The historical study of national character' (1965), Murphey makes a similar point. He is of the opinion that advice manuals are not 'descriptions of actual practice, but prescriptions of what practice ought to be' (150). Moreover, Brobeck ('Images of the family', 1976) states that such manuals are written by people who may not have been parents themselves and hence have no experience of child-rearing and who may not even have perceived behavioural and cultural patterns accurately. He also believes that, as many of the theorists are surely attempting to reform behaviour, they may recommend methods of child-rearing contrary to what actually prevailed. Both Mechling and Murphey state that the manuals are heavily biased in favour of the middle and upper classes – the literate sections of the population in past societies and also those who could afford to buy such books. Thus it is risky to generalise from them to the population as a whole.

Mechling further criticises historians for assuming that parents learn to be parents by reading advice books. She suggests instead four processes by which parents learn the art of parenting: identification, imitation, instruction and invention. She believes that people 'learn the role of parent and the entire constellation of childrearing customs associated with that role primarily through interaction with their parents' (49). She argues that, as no child-rearing manual would ever threaten the 'originally internalized parent role', advice literature plays a relatively minor role in the learning process (50).

Mechling then points out that the link between behaviour and values is more complex than historians have realised. She cites studies (Allport, 1935; Kluckhohn, 1951; Rokeach, 1968) which show that different values can produce the same behaviour and that the same values can produce different behaviour in different circumstances. Thus it is impossible to infer actual behaviour from the views expressed in advice literature. Mechling in fact contends that 'childrearing manuals are the consequents not of childrearing values but of childrearing manual-writing values' and therefore even an adequate model of inference from behaviour to values will not help those historians who use child-rearing manuals as evidence of child-rearing values (53).

The advice literature quoted from is generally of the authoritarian type; in fact most of the authors give the impression that there was no other. However, not all child-rearing theories were harsh. McLaughlin (1976) found two types of advice literature, one emphasising the importance of strict discipline and the other that children should not be beaten. She believes that the former type was the one put into practice by parents. Bremner (1970–3) gives the example of two different kinds of advice for the early 19th century – one advocating the child's will should be broken – the Calvinistic approach – and the other advocating a more gentle method of child-rearing. Murphey found the same two types of advice for the 19th century and also advice theories which were midway between the two; those influenced by Locke who believed a child was to be reared strictly so that he would not be corrupted by society. Murphey argues that the Calvinistic approach to child-rearing would only be put into practice by those parents of the Calvinistic denomination; there is no reason to suppose it was accepted by others. He further points out that there were also Calvinistic theorists who advocated an approach not unlike the gentle method of rearing. Ryerson (1961), in her study of child advice literature, and in opposition to most authors, found that advice manuals from the period 1550 to 1750 advocated a much more permissive style of child-rearing than those manuals written after 1750.[11] Thus it seems likely that harsh child-rearing theories were not as widespread as many authors have assumed. Moreover, Newson & Newson (1974) found that those mothers who did put into practice the advice of such 20th-century theorists as Watson (1928) and King (1937) that children were not to be hugged or kissed and that regular habits should be formed early on, found the method distressing. Newson & Newson argue that such theories did not pay enough attention to the parents' own needs and that both parents and children suffered from such harsh rearing modes.

Most writers on the history of childhood accepted the views expressed in child-rearing literature as being representative of that society and accepted by parents. They concentrate on those books and sermons which recommend harsh discipline and ignore any alternative advice. As it has been found that the majority of parents in the 20th century largely ignore advice literature, and that those who did follow the advice for a strict method of rearing children found it too upsetting to continue, any conclusions based on child advice literature must be suspect. Many historians seem to assume that parents are empty vessels, ready to be filled up with whatever theory on child-rearing happens to be current. However, parents bring their own views, expectations and experience to the task of rearing their children. They sometimes do, and sometimes do not, act in ways consistent with the advice literature – and because some sections of the advice may be put into practice, it is not safe to assume, as some writers have done, that the rest is. It is impossible to infer parenting behaviour from advice in manuals.

The descriptions of child-rearing provided by various travellers have been used by a number of authors (e.g. see Ariès; Hoyles; Hunt; Marvick, 1976; Pinchbeck & Hewitt; Robertson; Shorter; Stone; Thompson, 1974; Tucker, 1976). These accounts are generally used to reveal the indifference of English parents and also the indulgence of American parents during the 18th and 19th centuries. Travellers' accounts may be more descriptive than advice literature of actual practices but they are also biased by cultural differences. As Brobeck points out: 'Judgements as to whether American children act autonomously and aggressively, for example, reflect the definitions of autonomy and aggression by the culture of the visitors' (94). Murphey criticises the class bias of the reports: travellers 'chiefly saw the urban upper classes and saw them at best fleetingly' (150).

The use of paintings as an index of attitudes to children, particularly by Ariès, is just as problematical. Ariès deduces from paintings that adults became increasingly aware of children through the centuries. There are difficulties with his interpretation. For example, how far do paintings represent reality? – there is no reason why there should be any connection between the representation and that which is represented. There must have been technical improvements through the centuries so that, for instance, painters learnt how to paint in three dimensions and also how to depict such things as the proportions of a child's body. The different types of childhood portrayed in paintings through the centuries may have more to do with changes in art rather than changes in the way children were seen. In 'An appraisal of Philippe Ariès' (1980) Wilson points out that artists 'discovered' childhood through the imitation of Greek and especially Roman works of sculpture and painting during the Renaissance. Thus childhood 'was "discovered" by artists not in isolation, but as part of a widespread cultural change in which, it could be said, the representation of children was merely swept along' (145). Wilson adds that, because Ariès believes that the work of the historian consists of the extraction of history from the sources, he merely reproduces the iconographic evidence rather than analysing it (147). Ariès' conclusions from his study of paintings have also been criticised by Brobeck, Cohen (n.d.) and Fuller (1979).

Brobeck studied American portrait paintings for the period 1730–1860. He suggests that there are more adult portraits than children's, not because childhood was regarded as too unimportant a phase to be recorded, but because it is difficult to get children to stay still long enough and because adults wanted themselves and their children to be remembered by future generations as adults. Cohen ('Palatable children') looked at 158 child and 379 adult portraits for the period 1670–1860 in America. He agrees that early paintings of children do appear stiff and two-dimensional and so tend to support the idea that the Puritans regarded children as miniature adults; but argues that 'much of these paintings' significance hides under their stylized, planar surfaces' (2). He suggests that, although 17th-century Americans had little notion of age-graded groups, they did distinguish between people of different ages. Cohen's study reveals that the early painters employed certain techniques, disclosing that they did recognise childhood: 'a painter who could not deal with three dimensions and who sought to portray a "typical" yet individual human might be forced to rely on some kind of literal symbol to supply the information his visual technique failed to convey' (2). Thus, early painters noted the sitter's age, often to the month. Other devices used to indicate that the painting was of a child – and these are significant differences between child and adult paintings – are:

1. The child stands by a chair, which would give an estimate of his real height.
2. The child had bare feet.

3. The child was painted full length.

4. The child was portrayed with animals.

5. From the 19th century on the child was painted with toys or playing. Cohen deduces from this that 'Americans from the first recognised the distinctiveness of childhood' (13), although he did discover some changes in attitudes towards children. By the late 18th century children look their age, partly due to improved techniques and partly due to the need now to show the child as a child. Thus, Cohen argues, children were depicted with toys and/or playing – things which adults do not normally have or do. Cohen concludes that his examination of paintings 'has indicated that the earlier colonists thought children different from adults even as they considered childhood the beginning of a continuous progression to adulthood' (26).

Fuller ('Uncovering childhood') also investigated how childhood was depicted in art, in Europe. He argues against the idea that childhood is a product of history, that past centuries did not regard children as distinct from adults. He explains that many of the 'miniature adult' type of children's portrait were used as 'bargaining factors in the negotiation of political marriages' and so would depict the child in the jewels and dress appropriate to his state. Even when they had some other function, the portraits 'were designed to express what the parents of the child hoped he or she would become' (78). Fuller points out that today children are still depicted as miniature adults, for instance in greeting cards. He believes that 'In Renaissance art, when a child was not the principal subject of the picture, the reproduction of his or her appearance did not have to be done in a way which would immediately please specific adults. The perceptive painter often placed pictorially contingent children *within the space of childhood*' (80). Fuller gives such an example as a detail from a Crivelli painting of the 15th century in which a little girl is dressed as an adult but with the physical proportions and facial characteristics of a child.

Fuller does agree that there has been an increasing 'awareness and recognition of childhood' but finds it difficult to accept that in a civilisation in which the Christian ethic was dominant – one which 'has at its very centre the idea of the *specialness* of an ordinary child, of his separateness, and difference from the adults who surround him' (85) – there was '*no* perception of children as distinct from adults' (86). He concludes that it was 'not childhood, as such, which was transformed through history'; but instead there were profound changes in the social conditions in which childhood was lived (88–9).

It has been stressed that the adult manner in which young children were dressed illustrated the lack of any awareness of childhood (Ariès; Demos, 1970; Zuckerman). Although children after the age of 7 were clothed in adult garments this should not be taken to mean that they therefore entered the adult world. In her paper 'Childrearing among the lower classes' (1977), Hanawalt states that the accident pattern for children aged 7, taken from an analysis of coroners' rolls, indicates that the children were engaged in play rather than work. Macfarlane argues in *The Family Life of Ralph Josselin* (1970) that perhaps children were dressed differently from the age of 7 as that was the age when sexual differentiation was appropriate – boys were clad in feminine attire until that age. Stone (*The Family, Sex and Marriage in England*, 1977) too believes that dress for children depended more on 'whims and fashions than on deep-seated psychological shifts in the attitude towards children' (410). Brobeck suggests that children were depicted in adult dress in paintings as they would be more formally dressed for portraits than for school or play. Stannard (1974) agrees that children were clothed in a similar manner to adults; but he does not believe this means they were therefore viewed as adults:

> to argue in isolation of other data that the *absence* of a distinctive mode of dress for children is a mark of their being viewed as miniature adults is historical presentism at its very best – one might argue with equal force – in isolation of other facts – that the absence of beards on men in a particular culture, or the presence of short hair as a fashion shared by men and women, is a mark of that culture's failure to fully distinguish between men and women. (457)

Such treatment of infants as infanticide, abandonment, sending to a wet-nurse and swaddling has been put forward by a number of authors as evidence not only of the neglect of infants in the past but also of the general indifference to children. Hunt, McLaughlin, de Mause and Tucker state that infanticide was common in earlier centuries but the research of Hanawalt, Helmholtz (1975) and Wrightson (1975) has demonstrated that infanticide appears to have been a relatively rare occurrence. Furthermore, anthropological studies show that, even when infanticide is practised, surviving children are well cared for. For example, Konnor ('Infancy among the Kalahari Desert San', 1977) discovered that the Kalahari bush people did practise infanticide, as a means of birth control as well as for malformed infants, until recently. Despite this, with surviving babies, there were levels of smiling and responsiveness between Kalahari mothers and infants comparable to levels in modern Western society (cited in Smith, 1977). This kind of data creates difficulties for inferring from the occurrence of infanticide that surviving children were ill-treated. Infanticide and abandonment 'may have been actions taken regretfully by parents to limit family size, at a time soon after birth before attachment bonds had strongly developed' (Smith). They were last-resort methods of coping with too large a family at a time when both efficient contraception and a welfare state were lacking.[12]

Sending infants to wet-nurse is also believed to reveal the widespread neglect of children (Badinter, 1980; Flandrin, 1979; Hunt; de Mause; Shorter; Stone; among others). It is unlikely though that wet-nursing was practised on a larger scale in Britain and America. It was generally confined to the upper classes who could afford to pay for nurses and, as Wrightson (*English Society*, 1982) points out, care was generally taken in the selection of these. Wrightson suggests that interpretations of the significance of wet-nursing have been influenced by the horrific conduct of many nurses to pauper children. The callous neglect of these nurses in fact shocked many contemporaries just as it does today. The main reason for wet-nursing seems to have been pressure from husbands to resume sexual relations with their wives – it was a widely held belief that these would curdle a mother's milk and therefore should not occur while breast-feeding. In the upper classes, with their need for heirs to inherit property, coupled with the lack of alternative foods for babies, the mothers had little choice but to send their offspring to a wet-nurse. The mere existence of wet-nursing cannot be taken to mean that children in general were neglected. Schnucker (1974) in fact demonstrates that the continuance of the custom was more evidence of social inertia than indifference and cruelty.

Young infants were swaddled for the first few months of life. De Mause claims that this was enormously convenient for parents as they could then ignore the baby. Ryerson counters this argument by suggesting that a 'swaddled baby needed constant attention and care; he could not even brush a fly off his own nose' (313). Furthermore, it seems unlikely that swaddling was an example of neglect. Marvick (1976) and Trumbach (1978) argue that swaddling was a reasonable procedure given the ideas and beliefs of the time. It was intended to keep an infant's limbs straight, protect the child from harm and keep it warm. Anthropological studies, such as that of Brazelton (1972) on the Mayan Indians, reveal that swaddling is used as a protective measure. In the Mayan society there are few adults available to supervise the infants and they are therefore swaddled in order to restrict their locomotor exploration until the baby becomes more skilled and also better able to recognise physical danger. Hence swaddling is more an indicator of concern rather than neglect. It is probable that, as the physical environment of the child becomes safer, for example by guarding open fires, then the need for swaddling would decline. Thus Western societies did not stop swaddling their infants because they were more concerned about them but because there was less need to protect the infant in this way.

The majority of authors agree that the high infant mortality rate was the crucial factor in explaining parental indifference to children. Parents were unwilling to show affection towards their offspring, often neglected them thus increasing the mortality rate, and were not distressed by a child's death because so many died. The infant mortality rate has been greatly exaggerated. In England it rarely exceeded 150/1000 and in France 200/1000. With 80 to 85 per cent of all babies surviving, at least for a few years, it would have been impossible for mothers to avoid getting attached to their children. Furthermore the argument of parental indifference is not consistent with other forms of evidence. These authors are therefore claiming that there is a link between demography and emotion but, as Macfarlane (1979a) notes, there is no correlation between mortality rates and the supposed development of affection. Nor do the authors cite any studies to show that people consciously work out the expectation of their offspring and 'tailor their emotional lives accordingly' (107). In addition, evidence from anthropological research on primitive societies with a high infant mortality rate does not support the thesis that parents were indifferent to and aloof from their children in order to protect themselves from too much emotional distress (Ainsworth, 1967; Draper, 1976; Goldberg, 1972; LeVine, 1977; Marvin *et al.*, 1977). Parents living in cultures where there is every possibility that young children will die, do not 'ignore' their children but adapt their methods of child-rearing in such a way as to maximise their offspring's chance of survival. LeVine suggests that in such societies there will be an *increased* not a decreased level of responsiveness to a child's needs. Thus the infant is continually with a caretaker, crying is quickly attended to and feeding is a frequent response to crying. Marvin *et al.* found the same pattern of results in their study of the Hausa of Nigeria: Hausa care-givers maintain near constant proximity and contact with their infants and are also extremely responsive to their signals. Most authors insist that mothers and fathers in history were not distressed at the death of a child because so many died. This is quite untrue; parents were grief stricken at the loss of a child. MacDonald's (1981) study of Richard Napier's case notes, Le Roy

The thesis re-examined

Ladurie's classic work on the village of Montaillou (1978) and Wrightson's (1982) recent analysis of 17th-century texts bring to light the anguish of many parents. See also the results of this study contained in chapter 4. Macfarlane (1979a) particularly criticises Stone for his misinterpretation of the evidence on this topic. The latter, for instance, deduces from account books, which deal more with income and expenditure than the expression of emotion, that parents were totally unmoved by the death of a child.[13]

The argument of the historical thesis

The sources upon which the received view is founded are obviously suspect and are certainly not a sound enough base to warrant the grand theories which have been derived from them. Aspects of the thesis, especially the assertion that there was no concept of childhood, have been shown by later research to be completely unjustified.

Kroll in 'The concept of childhood in the middle ages' (1977) is opposed to the view that the nature of childhood was not recognised in the middle ages, writing: 'It is more likely that children then were viewed differently than children now, but still viewed as children' (384). Using evidence from documents from the areas of medicine, law and church, Kroll demonstrates that 'there was a realization and accommodation to the specialness of childhood, derived from and consistent with their [medieval people] world-views' (385). He finds that medical teachings did appreciate the specialness of newborns and young children, emphasising their vulnerability and fragility which necessitated tender care.

The law also catered for the minority status of children and laid down specific provisions to protect the lives, property and well-being of children, particularly in those areas where the crown was strong. The concepts too of adult premeditation and responsibility did not apply to children. Church writings contain evidence of an awareness of childhood – Kroll gives the example of the rules by Lanfranc in the 11th century for the regulation of monastery life. These contained special provision for children, for instance they should not be picked to administer punishment or to wash/dress the body of a dead brother. Kroll agrees that the church was ambivalent about children: regarding them both as innocent and bearing the burden of Original Sin. He concludes that, though there were no theories about the development of individuality in the child, nor elaborate developmental periods: 'at the pragmatic level,

52

there was an awareness of the smallness, vulnerability, irrationality, limited responsibility, medical fragility, and potentiality of the child that clearly designated the uniqueness and specialness of childhood' (391).

Stannard ('Death and the Puritan child', 1974) takes up the idea that the Puritans regarded their offspring as miniature adults in the 17th century and argues that there was 'no confusion or ambiguity in the mind of the adult Puritan as to the differences between his children and himself' (457). He states that there is a wealth of evidence to support this – for example, the law discriminated between acceptable behaviour and appropriate punishment for children, post-adolescent youths and adults. He believes however that, although the New Englanders of the 17th century did have a concept of childhood, it was different from that of 20th-century parents. For example, Puritan parents were intensely concerned for the salvation of their children – even though it was impossible to know who had been elected and who had not. Both adults and children were considered to be polluted and faced with the alternative of educating their children for salvation or accepting them as depraved, sinful creatures, doomed to burn in Hell, 'it is hardly surprising that Puritan parents urged on their offspring a religious precocity that some historians have interpreted as tantamount to premature adulthood' (461). These parents were not being cruel: 'When the Puritan parent urged on his children what we would consider a painfully early awareness of sin and death, it was because the well-being of the child and the community *required* such an early recognition of these matters' (475). Puritan parents were genuinely concerned for their children – they may have been polluted beings; but they were also 'Lambs in the Fold' and deeply loved. Stannard argues that the children were expected to be frightened of death and adults sympathised with rather than ridiculed their fears.

Beales in 'In search of the historical child' (1975), using sources from colonial New England, similarly attacks the claim made by Demos (1970) that Puritans did not possess a concept of childhood: 'While this essay does not suggest that colonial Americans treated their children as we treat ours, it does conclude that notions of "miniature adulthood" and the absence of adolescence in Colonial New England are, at best, exaggerations' (379). Beales states that language, law, religious thought and practice, all suggest that New Englanders recognised the immaturity of children. They possessed the concept of the 'ages of man' and these ages included old age, middle age, youth, childhood and sometimes infancy. Beales argues also that there were different ages of legal responsibility.

These concepts abounded in religious thought and practice – for instance the Puritans realised it was difficult for children to understand the intricacies of their religion. Thus for catechism in a church the children were separated according to age; for males this meant groups from 7 to 12 years and 13 to 28 years. Preachers were to take pains to convey the 'Truth' in such a manner that the children could understand it. He also found that the Puritans did not believe that children had a sufficient degree of knowledge to receive communion; there was no fixed age but the child had to be deemed to have reached a sufficient level of maturity and in practice this would be about the age of 14. Beales concludes that 'the idea of "miniature adulthood" must be seen, not as a description of social reality, but as a minor chapter in the history of social thought' (398). He believes that it was a mistaken belief which may have arisen due to the submergence of adolescent sexuality in the 19th century. This may have paved the way for a 'discovery' of adolescence in the late 19th century and also for the idea that previous generations had treated their children as small adults.

Individual authors have not been allowed to remain unscathed, but have been subject to scrutiny and criticism. Ariès' (1960) interpretation of his evidence is based on his belief in the sociability of medieval life. He is one of many authors who believe that, prior to industrialisation, the family was extended, consisting of several generations living together, and open to the outside world so that children mixed with adults from an early age. This assumption has been called into question by scholars such as Macfarlane (1979b) who emphasises the predominance of the nuclear family in early modern England. Hanawalt (1977), from her research into coroners' rolls, found that although the extended family did exist in the middle ages, the nuclear type was the most common. Her findings are corroborated by the work of Le Roy Ladurie (1978). However, it is the collection of papers in *Household and Family in Past Time*, edited by Laslett & Wall (1972) which have conclusively shown that, for as far back as we have records for, the simple family was the standard situation. Thus Ariès' belief is only partially correct at best and the discovery that the nuclear family was the most prevalent type casts doubt on his whole thesis. He also maintains that children became economically productive at the age of 7. The coroners' rolls reveal, however, that this was not the case – 'their accident pattern indicates that they were doing little work' (Hanawalt, p. 18). Ariès argues that children left home between the ages of 8 and 12 whereas the information contained in the rolls shows that such

54

children were still living at home, being trained for the work they would eventually perform as adults.

Hunt (*Parents and Children in History*, 1972) and Wilson ('The infancy of the history of childhood', 1980) point out various inconsistencies in Ariès' argument. For example, Hunt notes Ariès' statement that the young child was separated from the adult world as he 'did not count' and was thus ignored. Ariès then goes on to argue that, owing to changing attitudes towards children, the child became separated from the adult world. However, following the lines of Ariès' argument, it would seem more logical for the changing attitudes, which he claims did occur, to have increased the integration of the child into the adult world rather than to have increased his separation from it – the latter implies that the child would 'count' even less.

Ariès' main research interest lay in the field of education and therefore he virtually ignored children under the age of 7. It seems highly unlikely that a child could be regarded with total indifference by society for as long as seven years, as Ariès maintains, or that children were not weaned until the age of 7. If parents totally ignored their young children, the latter would die; human infants are all too obviously dependent on adult care and protection. Hunt criticises Ariès for failing to take into account the 'realities of biological growth': that it is impossible for the helpless dependence of an infant to last as long as seven years and that a child can communicate and sustain a complicated relationship with adults long before the age of 7. Because of Ariès' interest in education and therefore his concern with children over the age of 7, his conclusions with regard to infants are suspect. He has only assumed that young children were regarded with indifference instead of looking for evidence on how they were actually regarded.

Wilson agrees. He criticises Ariès for consciously writing from a '"present-minded" point of view', that is Ariès focused on the present and therefore searched medieval and early modern material for modern notions of a child (136). When he does not find such attitudes, he records that childhood did not exist. As Wilson notes, Ariès has merely recorded an absence of the modern awareness of childhood without investigating how children were perceived. There is evidence to suggest that childhood was recognised. For instance, Hanawalt (1977) argues that the material contained in coroners' rolls about the accidents which befell children and led to their deaths, makes it clear that those 'growing up in the medieval household went through developmental stages closely compatible with those described by Erikson' (19).

The thesis re-examined

In the first two years most accidents happened to infants in the cradle, especially being burnt from the fire. Between the ages of 2 and 3, they enter the second phase of development, 'reception to outside stimulus', and the accident pattern indicates that the children were exploring their environment – wells become more of a hazard than cradle fires (15). Between the ages of 4 and 7 the number of accidents drops sharply. This was due, Hanawalt believes, to the fact that children were now sufficiently mobile to be with adults. From the age of 8 to 12, children were independent from adults and had their own tasks to perform. Children above the age of 7 may have mixed more with adults in traditional societies, but 'this did not exclude social differentiation into groups structured by age and playing specific functions' (Wilson, p. 142). As with younger children, all that Ariès has discovered is an absence – the lack of age segregated schooling. In traditional cultures apprenticeship appears to have been an alternative to schools (Wilson, p. 143). It is probable that children have always had their distinctive role and place in society.

Hunt's study was concerned with child-rearing in 17th-century France. As I have already explained, Hunt's views on the methods of child care employed during this period have been derived from one source of evidence, the diary of Dr Héroard, doctor and mentor to the dauphin of France. This text has also been relied on by Ariès. Hunt does admit that Héroard's journal is not representative of the whole of society, but then goes on to argue that it is possible to generalise from Louis' upbringing to all parents and children in the 17th century. Thus he uses a particular example, the most 'special' that could be found, as evidence for the rest of society. For instance, there was a problem in finding a suitable wet-nurse for the dauphin and so he had trouble in getting enough nourishment. Hunt claims: 'Here, as elsewhere, the experience of the most precious child in the kingdom enables us to imagine the even more sombre circumstances of his less fortunate peers' (116), and goes on to assert that infants in general lacked sufficient nourishment. Louis was whipped as a child in the kingdom enables us to imagine the even more sombre almost universal custom', and that there was an emphatic and 'unanimous insistence on the obedience of children as indispensable to the survival of society' (134, 149). Van de Walle (1973) is of a different opinion, pointing out that there have been accounts of a more gentle and flexible mode of rearing for the same period.

In 'The character of Louis XIII' (1974), Marvick criticises both Hunt and Ariès for 'de-emphasising' the dauphin's unique situation. He was the first legitimate heir for almost 80 years and was also the first heir of a new dynasty: hence 'the embodiment of the Bourbon dynasty's future' (351). The exaggerated interest shown in Louis' sexual development, for example, was due to the fact 'that his potential performance was literally a question of state' and not, as Ariès and Hunt have suggested, the norm for society as a whole (352). Hunt states that Louis was kept in a separate household because 17th-century fathers were jealous of a potentially close mother–son relationship. Marvick, on the other hand, argues that he was nursed out because of political necessity. His mother was the king's second wife, the first having already been divorced for infertility. The queen's position was in jeopardy until she had proved her ability to have heirs and, with the prevailing belief that breast-feeding mothers should not resume sexual relations, Louis had to be sent to a wet-nurse. It should be noted, though, that because the sending of babies to a wet-nurse was very much a standard social custom for 17th-century French aristocrats, even if no more heirs were required, Louis would still have been fed by a wet-nurse rather than his mother.

Marvick also regards the diary as an exceedingly biased document. Dr Héroard was very ambitious with a political as well as medical role to play, seeking to undermine the king's influence through friendship with the dauphin and queen. He was in constant and prolonged contact with Louis and Marvick suggests he greatly influenced the dauphin, shaping his character and ensuring the dauphin's future dependence on him. Héroard's journal is therefore not an account of the normal methods of rearing children in the 17th century; it is rather the story of a child being brought up in unusual circumstances and manipulated by a politically motivated mentor.

De Mause ('The evolution of childhood') is the most extreme of all the authors. He appears to be writing a history of child abuse and not of childhood. Some of the reasons he lists for the ill-treatment of children in the past, such as role reversal and the parents' projection of their unacceptable feelings to their children, are characteristics of child abusers today (see Martin, H., 1976; Martin, J., 1978), a point which de Mause himself notes, but then ignores. De Mause is relentless in his zeal to provide evidence for his argument but he (like many other authors) provides no systematic analysis of his sources. In *Family Life and Illicit Love* (1977), Laslett especially criticises de Mause for his

evident anxiety to derive from the recalcitrant and miscellaneous mass of facts, half-facts and non-facts (misreports, misrepresentations) a connected and dramatic historical study about childhood and the way in which it has changed over time. This is done with little or no discussion on the part of the editor that literature itself is subject to fashion and change. (19)

De Mause postulates a series of modes of parent–child relations ranging from the infanticidal to the helping mode – this last, de Mause argues, appears from the mid-20th century on.

He states that parents belonging to the helping mode work to fulfil a child's expanding needs; they make no attempt to discipline and continually respond to their child, 'being its servant rather than the other way around' (52). Young people who have been reared in this way will, according to de Mause, be 'gentle, sincere, never depressed, never imitative or group-oriented, strong willed, and unintimidated by authority' (54). However, according to Shore, in 'The psychogenic theory of history' (1979), they are more likely to be 'narcissistic monsters with precariously regulated self-esteem, relationships with others based on narcissistic entitlement, and poor capacity to deal with the manifold frustrations of reality' (522). De Mause is one of the many authors who claim that parents have matured at last, and are now capable of treating their offspring with love and kindness instead of brutality. But life is not quite so perfect; not all 20th-century children receive tenderness and consideration at the hands of their parents. Any report from the National Society for the Prevention of Cruelty to Children provides more than adequate information to show that horrifying abuse is still being meted out to some children by their parents. It is as much a mistake to claim a 'happy ending' (Lynd, 1942) for the history of childhood as it is to claim that the beginning of the story was a 'nightmare' (de Mause, 1976).

Stone's (1977) book is riddled with so many problems of evidence, methodology and logic, that it prompts at least two reviewers to wonder how such an eminent historian could have written such a 'disaster' (Macfarlane, 1979a; Thompson, 1977). As Macfarlane explains, Stone's ideas are based on a general theory of the development of modern English society from a traditional, group based, kinship dominated society into the modern capitalistic system; that is there has been a gradual growth of individualism. Unfortunately Stone's description of a cold, affectionless, often brutal culture with the individual dominated by the group, bears little resemblance to the society which has been revealed to many historians of the period (Macfarlane, 1979a & b; Wrightson, 1982).

Macfarlane (1979a) censures Stone for his assumption that affection was linked to demography, his interpretation of a lack of evidence as proof of a lack of feeling and his belief that there has been a gradual evolution from backward periods in history up to the so called enlightenment of the present. Stone was unable to supplant any of his training in political and institutional history and this led him to expect a gradual progression of society along certain prescribed lines. He was convinced that it was impossible to have a loving, caring society before the 18th century and was forced to bend the evidence in order to fit his theory: he presents a distortion of the past. Macfarlane writes that Stone 'ignores or dismisses contrary evidence, misinterprets ambiguous evidence, fails to use relevant evidence, imports evidence from other countries to fill in gaps, and jumbles up the chronology' (113). Therefore Stone's dramatic and dogmatic synthesis has not one shred of sound logic and convincing evidence to support it.

Most authors have tried to relate the history of childhood to the history and development of other trends in society: Ariès links it with education, Bremner with democracy, Pinchbeck & Hewitt with public policy towards children and Stone with the growth of individualism. As Saveth in 'The problem of American family history' (1969) puts it, 'Grand theory about the American family is centered in the assumption that family structure is a variable of some larger conditioning circumstance – political, social or economic' (316). Bremner, in his account of childhood in the past (*Children and Youth in America*, 1970–3), assumes there was a match between society and the family in which the family reflects without distortion that triumph of freedom and democracy which has transformed other institutions. In other words, the story of the child is the story of liberation. However, Bremner has over-simplified, as Rothman (1973) points out – there must have been losses as well as gains.

Stone's account of the history of childhood depends on a great transition in social life which he claims occurs between the 15th and 16th centuries. Macfarlane (1979b) discloses that such a shift from a 'traditional' to a 'modern' society never in fact took place. He has found that in 15th-century England there were no wide kinship groups and the individual was not subordinated to large family structures. Thus Stone's argument rests on an error of historical fact as well as on a mistaken historical thesis.

The method of associating parental care with public care and policy is another area fraught with danger. Pinchbeck & Hewitt write in *Children in English Society*: 'The harshness of the parent was paralleled by the harshness of the State' (351). In *The Prevention of Cruelty to Children* (1955),

The thesis re-examined

Housden states: 'To parental neglect the children could add in their sum of misery, neglect by the state' and 'The general attitude of adults towards children was reflected by the treatment of child-paupers in the workhouses' (28, 30). Robertson ('Home as a nest', 1976) claims that the 19th century 'was the time when public bodies began to think of children as children, with special needs' (428). The prevailing viewpoint is that children have grown in importance from the 17th century, were treated better by parents and the state and, with the appearance of child welfare laws in the 19th century, protected by legislation from abuse. There are two assumptions in this argument. One is that parental and social treatment of young people are connected, and both have developed along similar lines. The other is that the appearance of child welfare legislation is an example of an increasing awareness of children and of their special needs. Though parental care of and public policy towards children are two different entities, they have rarely been clearly differentiated in works on the history of childhood. It is important to realise that, although the state may not have statutes and laws for the protection of children, and though it may even at times sanction such things as child employment, this does not necessarily mean that parents will also abuse and exploit their offspring. It is as absurd to claim that as it would be to claim that, once the rights of children are safeguarded by law, they will no longer be ill-treated. Before the 19th century what child protection legislation there was was concerned with the pauper, the orphaned, or the illegitimate child, and was designed to find them some means of livelihood. The absence of laws to safeguard children was due, not to a disregard for children, but to the organisation of a predominantly *rural* society. In such a society, procedures were informal and legislation was not necessary. There was certainly little possibility of enforcing such laws.

The Industrial Revolution, beginning about 1750, caused society to alter its basic forms of legal and administrative organisation in order to cope with the changes produced by industrialisation. It also brought increasing affluence, making all kinds of humanitarian legislation affordable (Birch, 1974; Briggs, 1959; Perkin, 1969; Roebuck, 1973; Ryder & Silver, 1970). Children were merely one particular case in this general upheaval.[14]

The effect of industrialisation must be appreciated if the emergence of child welfare legislation is to be understood – such humanitarian legislation was largely a response to the changing conditions wrought by the Industrial Revolution. Children should be seen in their context; it is a mistake to isolate them from the rest of society. They were and are always children of their place, class and time, subject to the same living conditions as the adults of their society. The Industrial Revolution, in the short term, brought great misery to *working-class* adults and children in certain industries. It was their exploitation that the protection legislation was designed to prevent. Children of the poor have always worked (Laslett, 1971), but industrialisation introduced very different working conditions – with the coming of machines their work was often synonymous with slavery (Helfer & Kempe, 1968).

Industrialisation also brought new roles for children in certain industries. The changed and more powerful technology which the Industrial Revolution produced, reduced and even in a few cases removed the differential in strength between the adult and the child (McKendrick, 1974). During the 18th century coal was transported underground by means of sledges which were too heavy for children to pull. The introduction of the wheeled corf and the tramway lightened the task and brought it within the powers of young children. Improvements in ventilation extended the demand for child labour as well – a child of 5 or 6 years of age could be employed to open and shut the doors used to control the air supply (Ashton & Sykes, 1964). Ashton & Sykes explicitly state in their book *The Coal Industry of the Eighteenth Century*: 'It is important to observe that it was in the coalfields where technical progress was most marked that this extension of child labour was the greatest' (73–4). Thus, not only did the Industrial Revolution transform the working environment of the child, but it also created novel types of employment for him.

Industrialisation with its factories and mills and rapid urban expansion concentrated the misery of the poor. The towns and cities concealed the evidence of poverty and injustice from the rest of society. In the small villages, the squire, though hardly on familiar terms with the villagers, would at least have some contact with them and would have some knowledge of the conditions in which they lived. But the increasing class segregation and social differentiation resulting from industrialisation, ensured that many of the middle and upper classes were wholly unfamiliar with the lives of the poor and that they were also liable to misinterpret what they saw (Middleton, 1971; Perkin, 1969; Wrightson, 1982). When the existence of such squalor became known – through the labours of determined investigators like Chadwick and Engels, and the publication of the parliamentary blue books in the 1830s which revealed the desperate plight of the working classes – the suddenness of the discovery made the shock even more acute. The transfer of workers from their homes or farms into factories also brought the terrible conditions of labour, particularly child labour, into view. It was possible to see more human misery and suffering in one visit to one factory than in a tour round the countryside (Altick, 1973; Briggs, 1972; Bruce, 1968; Perkin, 1969).

The poor child in the Industrial Revolution was the victim of the circumstances of social and economic change. The use and abuse of children in factories, mills and mines occurred before public conscience was aware of the problem, or able to take steps to see that the conditions in which they lived and worked were raised to an endurable standard (Heywood, 1978). The ignorance of, and in some cases indifference to, the situation of some of the children in society, is not confined to the 19th century, but can also be seen in the 20th. The evacuation of city children in 1940 made a large number of people aware of the poor health and bad living conditions of the lower working class (Bruce, 1968; Ryder & Silver, 1970). What is even more interesting about this example is that by 1940 the government thought that it had helped the working-class child: school meals had been introduced in 1906 and free school milk in 1921. However, the evacuation programme revealed that giving aid only to the school child was insufficient; the very young child also needed help. Thus infant welfare legislation was introduced, such as the system of Family Allowances in 1945, not because there was a sudden acquisition of the concept of 'infancy', but because the government recognised that certain sections of society had a special need of its intervention and assistance. Moreover, Spitz's paper 'Hospitalism' (1945) described the appalling manner in which orphan children were reared in 20th-century institutions and the disastrous effect this had on their development.[15]

There would not appear to have been a fundamental change in parental attitudes towards children, despite the great transformation wrought by industrialisation. Pinchbeck & Hewitt, among others, have argued that children who worked during the Industrial Revolution suffered such dreadful hardship because they were subject to economic exploitation by their parents. It is difficult to grasp how working-class parents regarded child labour in the 19th century since so many of them were illiterate. It is possible, however, to discover what some parents thought by examining the records of the Children's Employment Commissions set up in the first part of the 19th century to study the conditions in which children worked. The report of one such committee will be discussed here.

The committee of 1831–2 was formed by parliament to investigate the kind of work undertaken by children, the manner in which they were employed and the effect this had on them, with reference to a proposed 10-hour bill. This was designed to limit the working hours of children to 10 a day, and also to forbid the employment of children under the age of 10 years. By speaking out against the system of child employment in force at the time, the parents interviewed ran a real risk of losing their jobs and of being branded as trouble makers and therefore not eligible for poor relief. A variety of people were interviewed: those who worked or had worked in factories, parents with children working, mill owners and doctors.

Of the 18 parents interviewed, all claimed that they were forced to let their children work through necessity, all regarded the long hours (often as much as 16 or 17 hours a day) as unhealthy, and all wanted the proposed bill. Though the shorter hours would mean a reduction of wages, it was hoped that, by cutting children's hours, the factory owners would no longer prefer to employ them and hence adults would be employed instead. The parents were all desperately unhappy about the situation their children were in, but could do nothing about it. Although the parents disliked their children working, the social system at that time allowed them no choice. Poor relief was usually refused to a family if it contained children capable of working. When an officer for parish relief was asked by the committee:

Supposing that the parents applying for relief for their children, refused to allow them to labour in mills or factories, in consequence of their believing and knowing that such labour would be prejudicial to their health, and probably destructive of their lives, would they, in the mean time, have had any relief from the workhouse Board, or from you as an overseer, merely on the grounds that the children could not bear the labour?

the reply was: 'Certainly not' (464).

It is clear that the parents interviewed by this committee were exceedingly distressed at the effect the long hours of work had on their children. William Kershaw, whose children were working, stated: 'if it had been in my power to prevent it, they should never have gone. My wife had numbers of times upbraided me for suffering them to go, but still I thought it was better to allow them to go there than altogether starve for want of bread' (47). Joshua Drake believed: 'With regard to their long labour, I am of the opinion that it always did hurt and always will hurt the children; it keeps them unhealthy' (39). John Allen said that his children were 'very sleepy . . . I have thought I had rather almost seen them starve to death, than to be used in that manner' (108). William Bennet also considered that the hours were too long: 'Of a morning when they had to

63

get up, they have been so fast asleep that I have had to go upstairs and lift them out of bed, and have heard their crying with the feelings of a parent; I have been much affected by it' (102). They saw the factories as having a damaging effect on the morals, health and capacity for education of their children. The majority did wish their offspring to be educated so as to improve the latter's status in life. There were Sunday schools, but the parents were reluctant to force their weary children out of bed in order to attend them. Those interviewed felt that 10 hours a day was quite long enough for children of 10 years and above. This was in marked contrast to the majority of mill owners, who informed the committee that a 12-hour day would not harm a child as young as 8 years of age.

Parents of the 19th century were just as horrified by the conditions in which their children toiled as parents would be today. It is possible that mothers and fathers have always had the concept of childhood, whereas those in power had to learn not so much what a child is, but that its helplessness could be exploited by society and it therefore required state protection. Parents have always tried to do what is best for their children, within the context of their culture. It is not necessarily cruel for a child to help on the farm or with a cottage industry of his parents from an early age. In a society where there was little choice of employment as well as little help for the poor, learning the essential skills early on was probably the best thing for that child.

It seems from the literature that those authors who have tried to relate the history of childhood to other historical trends have not concerned themselves with the problem of how far *parents* are influenced by these developments.[16] They have merely assumed that, if society itself has altered over the centuries, then attitudes to and treatment of children must have changed too, in accordance with those trends. Most of the scholars have looked for *changes* in perceptions of children, but they have not kept a sense of proportion. They have not related the amount of change they have found to the amount which has remained unchanged. Ariès himself has commented in the introduction to the first edition of his book that 'within the great family types, monogamous and polygamous, historical differences are of little importance in comparison with the huge mass of what has remained unchanged' (7). The literature so far on the history of childhood leaves the distinct impression that everything has altered, the way in which young people are viewed and reared varies according to the time period in which the children live. It is at least equally likely, if not more probable, that, though parents are influenced by the differing social circumstances, and adapt to these, they do not do so to such an extent that they drastically change their methods of child-rearing.

One of the more serious criticisms of the various authors of works of this kind is that they have used attitudes towards children, mainly those expressed in religious sermons and child advice manuals, to infer the actual treatment which children received. Plumb (1975) does state that the images which society creates for children rarely reflect reality. But he is still prepared to deduce from the views of theorists like Locke how children were treated in past times. As Rothman points out in 'Documents in search of a historian' (1973), the *concepts* of childhood and adolescence may have changed, but this does not indicate that the actual experience of the young has altered. The views of theorists on children and methods of child-rearing do change over time. But we have already seen that parents do not pay a great deal of attention to the advice of 'experts', and hence there is no reason to suppose that their modes of child care have undergone as dramatic a transformation as has been suggested. Changes are obviously important, but 'Overemphasis upon the phenomenon of change neglects what remains permanent in family structure' (Saveth, 1969, p. 323). Are not the similarities, what has remained unchanged over the centuries, worth studying too?

Despite their preoccupation with changes in the status of childhood, the writers do little to explain such changes. Gnomic statements like Shorter's 'surge of sentiment' or Stone's 'rise of affective individualism' do little to elucidate those changes which the authors state have occurred. They argue that we have changed from viewing children with 'indifference' and as 'chattels' to being preoccupied with their welfare and regarding them with affection, although there is general disagreement over when these changes occurred. Such a thesis can only be valid if it can be shown *why* parents and society regarded children with indifference – could it be that infants looked different in the past? – and *why* their attitudes changed. Relating supposed changes in child-rearing to changes in society, and sprinkling the literature with various nominalistic terms is not sufficient explanation. The diverse types of parents that the authors have found for different time periods may have always been in existence. People vary in their methods of child-rearing.

Is a history of childhood possible?

Some writers feel that the sources which are available for the history of childhood are so problematic that the subject cannot be studied. Laslett

(1977), for example, decided to concentrate on the size and composition of past households rather than the actualities of child life as 'it is well known how intractable the analysis of any body of documents of this kind can be [advice literature, letters, diaries, autobiographies] so untidy is it, so variable, so contradictory in its dogmas and doctrines, so capricious in what it preserves and what it must leave out' (18). Brobeck (1976) also considers that personal documents such as letters and diaries are relatively unhelpful: 'They tend to dwell on affairs of business or the state, [neglecting] the most intimate details of family life or those which might prove to be embarrassing. In many cases, they deliberately attempt to create a favourable image of the author's own family' (94). Stone is of the same opinion. He believes that the interpretation of diaries and autobiographies is problematic, since the information they contain can rarely be checked from an independent source and they are also affected by the personality of the writer. He concludes that 'They must, therefore, be examined in bulk' (12). Unfortunately that is only half the answer. Stone has certainly made use of many primary sources of evidence, but there is no method to his examination of them.

Where an author has used personal documents in his research into the history of childhood, it is only in an anecdotal sense, to illustrate a point from the advice literature. There are only a few works, such as that by Macfarlane (1970), which concentrate on primary documents and investigate them in a systematic manner. However, unless the whole document has been analysed, it is impossible to ascertain whether or not any particular action, statement or attitude was typical of the person concerned. Parent–child interaction is a continuing process, not a series of isolated events, despite the preoccupation of the literature with punishment. We will take one example of this anecdotal and selective method. Samuel Sewall's statement that he 'whipped' his son Joseph 'pretty smartly' is often used to illustrate the strict discipline of the 17th century. That is the only occasion, in the whole of his long detailed diary, when he mentions physically punishing that son. If the circumstances leading up to the incident are examined, the whipping appears to be less the action of a severe disciplinarian and more the response of an exasperated father. Joseph had been playing during prayers and eating at 'return thanks', both activities which were bound to annoy a Puritan father. He finally threw a lump of brass at his sister, bruising and cutting her forehead. The passage in the diary recording these events gives the impression that Joseph had been irritating his father all day and the throwing of the brass was the last straw. Sewall lost his temper.

This selective use of material is not confined to personal documents but applies to all the sources of evidence. A point is made by an author and then illustrated by reference to a miscellany of sources. Such a method merely reveals that some people at some point agreed with the author's statement; it does not mean that everyone thought the same way. There is no allowance for individual differences and little systematic analysis of the various sources of evidence. If, for example, all the sources of evidence which are available were analysed separately, with full awareness of the problems pertaining to each source, and in bulk, then the prevalence of various attitudes to children and various child-rearing methods through the centuries would be revealed. Once this had been done, all the sources could be looked at together, a synthesis attempted, and in that way a more accurate history of childhood could be written than has been achieved hitherto. As it is, we still know little about how *parents actually reared* their children.

3. Issues concerning evidence

No document can tell us more than what the author of the
document thought – what he thought had happened, what he
thought ought to happen or would happen, or perhaps only
what he wanted others to think he thought, or even only what
he himself thought he thought.

(Carr, *What is History?*, 1961, p. 10)

The reconstruction of family history is difficult; there are few facts, little
that can be proven. A miscellany of various sources of evidence is
available, none of which provides a complete history of childhood and all
of which possess numerous problems. With this situation, all that is
possible is to fit all of the pieces of evidence together – almost like a jigsaw
– decide which kind of general picture they produce and then use this as a
basis for filling in the inevitable gaps. In order to able to do this with any
degree of accuracy, a systematic analysis of all available sources is
necessary. Unfortunately such an analysis has not yet been done –
although some authors have investigated child-rearing theories through
the centuries, they have still tended to concentrate on what they consider
to have been influential theories and thus there is little or no discussion of
other theories which were also in existence at the time. With reference to
child care in the past, the sources used so far have not been very helpful:
there are too many gaps left, little information on actual family life and
some of the sources used (e.g. child-rearing advice literature) do not
contribute to our knowledge of how parents reared their children in the
past. They are more like pieces from another jigsaw: how 'experts'' views
on child-rearing theory change through the centuries.

This study is concerned with providing a detailed analysis of three
types of evidence, in an attempt to throw light on child-rearing practices
in previous centuries:
(a) diaries, both parental and child diaries
(b) autobiographies
(c) newspaper reports of court cases concerning child abuse *before* The

Prevention of Cruelty to and Protection of Children Act, passed in 1889.

The primary sources

Diaries, autobiographies, letters and wills belong to the class of personal documents. The last two have been ignored in this study, unless they happen to have been included in a diary or autobiography. Letters and wills share the same disadvantages as diaries and also possess some additional ones. Letters, for example, are written with another person in mind, and this must affect what events are noted and how they are related. Wills are useful for studies of inheritance, but contain little on child care.

A total of 496 published diaries and autobiographies were read for this study, of which 80 contain no useful information on childhood. The remaining 416 are composed of 144 American diaries, 236 British diaries and 36 autobiographies only (i.e. autobiographies which were not attached to a diary or, if they were included in a diary, the diary section contained no information on child care). Of the diaries, 98 were written by children or started when the diarists were children. All American texts are signified by an asterisk. The diaries differed in length from a few pages to nine volumes and were of varying degrees of usefulness. In addition, 27 unpublished British manuscripts were looked at. Of these, 10 were discarded either because they were illegible or no use. Nearly all of the texts were found in the bibliographies by Matthews (*American Diaries*, 1945; *British Diaries*, 1950). The diary of Blundell was cited in Macfarlane (*The Family Life of Ralph Josselin*, 1970) and the diaries of *J. Bayard, *Bissell, *Bowers, *Chace, *Hadley, *Hazard, Smith and *Wister were discovered by chance when looking through the British Library catalogue. Those texts published after 1950 were found in the National Bibliography catalogue. The Appendix lists all of the texts used in the study.

The use of diaries as a main source of evidence does present a number of methodological problems:[1]

(a) that of representation: what kind of people wrote diaries and why did they do so?

(b) that of censorship: are important details omitted either by the diarist or the editor?

(c) that of generalisation: is it possible to infer the behaviour of other sections of society from the diaries?

The relationship between attitudes and behaviour is also problematical and should be considered. Let us consider these one by one.

Representation

The earliest diaries date from the 16th century; none have been found written before that date – there was little self-expressive literature of any kind. The chief impetus in the 17th century came from the Puritans with their inexorable drive to put their thoughts to paper as a means of cultivating the holy life by the techniques of self-examination and self-revelation. Obviously the diaries and autobiographies only represent the literate section of society; but within this limit the texts studied do cover a wide stratum: a Queen of England down to a poor farmer. The occupation of the writers is shown in Table 1 and their religion in Table 2.

With reference to the lower classes, much of the argument that they lived brutal, affectionless lives as in Shorter's *The Making of the Modern Family* (1976) and Stone's *The Family, Sex and Marriage in England* (1977), has been derived from a lack of evidence. It has been assumed that poor parents make bad parents, poverty has been equated with brutality. Although it is difficult to discover information relating to the lower classes, recent research suggests that the above claims are unwarranted. The book *Montaillou* (1978) by Le Roy Ladurie and articles by Gillis (1979) and Scott (1979) take issue with the belief that the poor endured a lifestyle lacking in love, joy and warmth. Hanawalt's ('Childrearing among the lower classes', 1977) examination of coroners' rolls demonstrates that the children of the working classes in earlier societies did play and also passed through similar developmental stages as modern children. MacDonald's (*Mystical Bedlam*, 1981) analysis of the notebooks of Richard Napier brings to light the depth of affection felt by many poor mothers for their offspring and their anguish when a child died. Information from parents living in poverty and whose children had to work in order to survive (see the evidence taken from the parliamentary commissions described on p. 63; Anderson's 1971 depiction of 19th-century Lancashire; and also the results of such anthropological studies as Leighton & Kluckhohn, 1948) reveals that these parents were still capable of loving their offspring and continued to regard them as children. Furthermore, Newson & Newson (1965, 1968 and 1976) have discovered from their research on 20th-century child-rearing practices that, although there are class differences and although a working-class parent is more likely to hit a child than a middle-class parent, the amount of physical punishment used by the lower classes does not even approximate to the level of cruelty that many authors have claimed existed in earlier

Table 1. *Percentage division of sources by occupation (where known)**

						Occupation					
Nationality	Church	Arts/ Science	Politics	Business/ Trade	Law	Farming	Medicine	Army/ Navy	Edu- cation	Others	Un- known†
American n = 154	21	4	8	8	3	10	3	6	10	3‡	24
British n = 279	15	11	7	6	5	5	5	4	3	10§	29
ALL n = 433	17	9	7	7	4	7	4	5	5	7	28

* The listed fields of employment cover a wide range of occupations. For example: Church covers travelling preachers up to archbishops. Business or trade covers small shop owners up to owners of or partners in large business firms. Farming covers small farmers up to wealthy land owners. Army or Navy covers soldiers/sailors up to majors/admirals. The specific occupation of the writers is given in the Appendix.

† Of the writers whose occupation was unknown, one American and 23 British (8% of the British sample) were titled aristocrats. Of the sample as a whole, 2% of the American writers were either title holders or wealthy plantation owners; 17% of the British were titled aristocrats. Of the 433 sources, 11% belong to the top ranking members of the upper classes.

‡ These were: 2 clerks; 1 anthologist; 1 fur trapper; and 1 deacon.

§ These were: 2 apprentices; 2 brewers; 2 clerks; 2 engineers; 2 ladies-in-waiting; 2 tailors; 3 yeomen; 1 alderman; 1 antiquary; 1 baker; 1 bookseller; 1 civil servant; 1 government official; 1 nanny; 1 pewterer; 1 shop-worker; 1 skinner and glover; 1 surveyor; 1 turner; and 1 watchmaker.

Table 2. *Percentage division of sources by religious belief*

			Religious belief			
Nationality	Puritan	Quaker	Orthodox*	Dis-senting sect†	Religion un-specified	Religion not mentioned/ followed
American n = 154	18	10	1	20	33	20
British n = 279	6	13	17	14	34	16
ALL n = 433	10	12	11	16	34	18

Note: It should be noted that the religious categories are based on the diarists' self-descriptions and may not be mutually exclusive.
* The orthodox section consists of:
American: 1 Church of England; 1 Protestant.
British: 21 Church of England; 11 Catholic; 8 Protestant; 3 Church of Scotland; 3 Jew.
† The dissenting sects comprised:
American: 9 Episcopal; 7 Presbyterian; 5 Methodist; 2 Baptist; 2 Mormon; 2 Unitarian; 1 Calvinist; 1 free-thinker; 1 Tractarian.
British: 12 Methodist; 7 Presbyterian; 5 Baptist; 3 Evangelical; 2 Episcopal; 1 Calvinist; 1 Christian Scientist; 1 Moravian and 7 unspecified dissenters.

working-class parents. Thus there seems to be no justified reason to assume that in past times poor parents were brutal and exploitative in regard to their children.

In order to ascertain how representative diarists were of their society, it is necessary to discover how prevalent the practice of diary keeping was. This study is concerned only with what Matthews (1950) calls the 'domestic' diary. There are numerous other types of diary: war, travel, political, purely religious and account-book. There would also appear to have been a great many diaries written. Matthews lists 363 diaries for the period 1490–1699 and there are many hundreds more for the 18th and 19th centuries. Not all diaries are included in Matthews' bibliography; for example, he omitted the detailed diary of Nicholas Blundell and, of course, could not include any diary discovered after 1950. It is also likely that there are many more diaries hidden in attics still awaiting discovery (Macfarlane, 1970). These texts are also only the surviving records, presumably from a much larger sample. In addition, there were advice books on the function of and how to write a diary published in the 1650s (cited by Macfarlane). This suggests that the writing of a diary was a common activity. Some diarists do mention reading other people's diaries or being advised by another to keep a diary. For example, William Jones (1755–1821) quoted at the start of his diary the directions of one minister on diary-keeping: 'Compile a History of your Heart & Conduct. Minute down your Sins of Omission. Register those secret faults to which none but your own conscience is privy. Often contemplate yourself in this faithful Mirror' (xiii). *Aldolphus Sterne (1801–52) noted: 'Having sometime ago read Cobbets advise eta, & having seen my descd Friends Jas Ogilvys Diary & seen, and learnt its usefullness I came to the determination to keep one, of such things as might be usefull, or interesting so here goes – ' (vol. 30, 1927, p. 63).[2] Hester Lynch Thrale (1741–1821) wrote: 'It is many Years since Doctor Samuel Johnson advised me to get a little Book, and write in it all the little Anecdotes which might come to my Knowledge, all the Observations I might make or hear; all the Verses never likely to be published, and in fine ev'ry thing which struck me at the Time' (1). Thus diary keeping appears to have been a fairly prevalent practice – the diarists themselves certainly do not consider themselves in any way odd or different from the rest of society. However, it must be conceded that diarists as a class may be exceptional rather than representative of society as a whole.

As has been said, diaries are only found from and after the 16th century. This needs some explanation. The history of diary writing is related to the development of self-awareness. The centuries of a universal church and an international culture were unsympathetic to the expression of individuality in any form. It was the Renaissance and the Reformation in the 16th century, bringing in their wake freedom of thought and con-science, that paved the way for autobiography of all kinds (Spalding, 1949).

Macfarlane (1970) lists three types of motive for keeping a diary. Some diaries are simply account books noting purchases and bills; others are intended to help the diarist recall certain events and yet others are prompted by religious considerations in an attempt to examine the soul and so correct behaviour. Spalding in *Self-Harvest* would consider the 'pure' diary as consisting of 'the outflow of the spontaneous impulse to record experience as such and so preserve it' (21). Spalding argues that the best diaries are those in which no motive is apparent to the reader and, if the diarist was asked why he kept a diary, he probably would not know. For example, Francis Kilvert (1840–79) wrote:

Why do I keep this voluminous journal? I can hardly tell. Partly because life appears to me such a curious and wonderful thing that it seems a pity that even such a humble and uneventful life as mine should pass altogether away without some record of this, and partly too because I think the record may amuse and interest some who come after me. (Spalding, 1949, p. 21)

As diaries are influenced by the personality of their writers, it is obviously important to consider why the diarists used in this study wrote diaries. Almost one quarter of the diarists (24 per cent) specifically state why they are writing a diary. Of these most write for their own amusement or improvement: 'Sitting before the fire this evening, a thought came over me to write a few lines every night, of what sort of weather we have, whether we go out or not, who comes to see us, and how we spend our time summer and winter' (*Sarah Eve, 1749–74, p. 22). '[This diary is] to be in some sort a register of my life, studies and opinions' (Benjamin Newton, 1762–1830, p. 1). 'I find it [diary] such a useful practice, and so entertaining, that I am fully resolved to continue it all my life' (Emily Shore, 1819–39, p. 138). Others used their diary as a confidant: 'To have some account of my thoughts, manners, acquaintance, and actions . . . is the reason which induces me to keep a Journal – a Journal in which, I must confess, my *every* thought – must open my whole heart . . . with the most unlimited confidence, the most unremitting sincerity, to the end of my life!' (Fanny Burney, 1752–1840, vol. 1, pp. 24–5) 'This book is quite a little friend to my heart; it is next to communicating my feelings to another person' (Elizabeth Fry, 1780–1845, p. 14). 'Treasure of my thoughts! Dear companion of solitary hours! . . . Herein I inscribe the workings of my secret soul' (*Anna May, 1840?- ?, p. 1).

Some diarists wrote for religious reasons; particularly the earlier diaries: 'I have decided to perpetuate, for the benefit of my children and grand-children, a memorial of the goodness of God' (John Townsend, 1757–1826, p. 139). 'Believing that my progress in the christian course may be assisted by the practice of noting the condition of my soul, and recording some of the events which pass around me, I feel encouraged to commence a journal' (Edwin Tregelles, 1806–84, p. 10). 'I did write down these mercies of God' (Nehemiah Wallington, 1598–1658, p. xxvii).

Other diarists wished to leave a record for their children: '[The diary is] only for the private use of such of my children as may survive me, from which by ye Grace of God they may possibly learn to escape many errors that I have committed and avoid many evils I have fallen into' (James Clegg, 1679–1755, p. 16). 'To my dear little Marianne I shall "dedicate" this book, which if I should not live to give it her myself, will I trust be reserved for her as a token of her Mother's love' (Elizabeth Gaskell, 1810–65, p. 5). 'I only intend it [diary] for the perusal of a few, and of my own child in particular . . . It is for my little Mary principally that I write this' (Ellen Weeton, 1776–1850, vol. 1, p. 3).

A few diarists wrote their diaries so that they would be able to recall events later: '[The diary] is a shorte breviat to be caried about me to helpe my memorie concerning those things & upon all occasions' (Walter Powell, 1581–1656, p. xi). 'I have all my life regretted that I did not keep a regular Journal. I have myself lost recollection of much that was interesting' (Walter Scott, 1771–1832, vol. 1, p. 1). 'These lines are penned that in after life should my life be spared I may have the opportunity of comparing myself with myself, & of calling to mind many events which might be forgotten' (*Mary Walker, 1814–97, p. 13).

Some diaries are begun as a response to a special event such as a visit to friends (e.g. *Lucinda Orr, 1764?– ?); travel abroad (e.g. Mary Damer, 1809?–40) or marriage: 'I have concluded to keep a journal of my life as I have begun with rather bad prospects – today is my wedding day. I am married privately as all parties are opposed to it' (*Caroline Phelps, 1810?– ?, p. 209). A few of the child diarists were instructed to write their diaries: a daily journal was a task imposed on Marjorie Fleming (1803–11) by her teacher who then corrected any misspelt words; Frederic Post (1819–35) wrote his diary at the suggestion of his father and John Scott (1792–1862) began 'to keep a journal, under the guidance of my dear mother' (23).

The majority of diarists give no reason for keeping a diary. Many diaries do seem to be spiritual exercises; a way of becoming closer to God and of improving the diarist's faith; but most diaries, particularly the better, more detailed ones, appear to be written in response to an inner impulse to record things, for no better reason than that they had occurred. 'I should live no more than I can record, as one should not have more corn growing than one can get in. There is a waste of good if it be not preserved' (James Boswell, 1740–95).[3] 'Sometimes after our people is gone to Bed I get my Pen for I Dont know how to content myself without writeing Something' (*Jemima Condict, 1754–79, p. 41). 'I have for some years past, kept a sort of diary, but intended to discontinue it, and make this a memorandum book – but seeing a fine snow falling this morning, and being used to make observations on the weather, began this first day of the year in my accustomed manner' (*Elizabeth Drinker, 1734–1807, p. 337).

Most diaries are very private documents, containing a wealth of trivial and personal details which were clearly not intended for the public gaze. Of the 433 texts studied, only 26 of the writers considered publication of their work (6 per cent) and, of these, only 10 began their diaries with the express purpose of publishing them later. (These tended to be the 20th-century diarists.) There may have been more diaries written with publication in mind, although the writer did not admit it. This is particularly likely to be true of those texts which were concerned with public events or the diarist's/autobiographer's work – a further 7 per cent of the total sample size. The glimpses of family life portrayed in such texts are more suspect than those contained in texts where publication was not considered – the writer, for example, may deliberately suppress anything he thinks society will condemn or which reveals himself in a less than favourable light. None the less, in the diaries studied here, there does not appear to be any significant difference between those intended for publication and those that were not. Arthur Hutchinson (1880– ?), who did intend to have his diary published, wrote that a diary has a 'singular disability – truth. In all other forms [of literature] one can either invent what is not true or suppress what is. In the diary not so. If it is not written within the confines of strictest truth it is not worth writing' (134).

Looking at one aspect of the parent–child relationship – that of discipline – those writers who at least considered publication of their work and who referred to discipline, described the same range of experiences as those to be found in the rest of the texts. For example, Anthony Cooper (1801–85) described the cruel treatment he received as a child, at home and school; whereas Sydney Owenson (1780?–1859) recalled receiving nothing but kindness as a child. John Mill (1712–1805), Jones (1755–1821) and John Skinner (1772–1839) noted the trouble they experienced with some of their children, and thus were not depicting an idealised home-life.

It is arguable that any diarist who keeps a diary long enough must consider that it will be read by others. However, most diarists appear to cherish the private nature of their diary. Privacy, in fact, seems to be the essence of a diary; a place where people can relate their regrets, hopes and dreams without fear of ridicule or disapproval. The majority of the diarists studied regarded their diaries as confidential repositories for their thoughts and viewed the thought of anyone else reading their diaries as an intrusion. Priscilla Johnston's mother wished to see her journal; but her daughter wrote in her diary: 'I do not think I shall, because showing it to anybody would, I think, take off the pleasure and value of my journal' (Johnston, 1808–52, p. 3). 'My diary is of such a nature, that I should not like to trust it to any one but my other self' (William Steadman, 1764–1837, p. 43).

I cannot but think that much curious information is detailed *not* intended for publication. Think not that *my* diary is intended for publication; but Evelyn or Burton, perhaps, thought the same . . . But if my diary might be discovered in the 20th century and printed, I would offer to the reader a few remarks:-
1. Various sentiments in this book there are, which, perhaps, I should now condemn.
2. The matters of fact in this diary, are matters of fact.
3. This diary is strictly private; it details private feelings; and feelings which, perhaps, were often to be checked.
4. Judge leniently.   (Post, 1819–35, pp. 192–3)

Censorship

Diarists (and autobiographers) do select the information which they wish to record. Thus it is possible that significant information on the history of childhood is omitted in the texts. For example, the disciplining of children would appear to be a very emotive area. Information on physical punishment may not appear if:
(i)   The diarist omitted it because:
       (a) physical punishment was so commonplace it was not thought worth mentioning;
       (b) the diarist considered physical punishment too shameful to relate;
       (c) the diarist believed society would consider it shameful.
(ii) The editor omitted any details on physical punishment contained in the original manuscript from the published text.
(iii) Severe physical punishment did not occur.
To take these in order.

The diarist. Punishment, physical or verbal, is a salient event. It generally causes distress to both the inflictor and the victim (Newson & Newson, 1976). It does not seem very likely, therefore, that punishment would not be recorded on the grounds that it was too ordinary an event – particularly as the diaries do contain a great deal of trivial information such as the food eaten or clothes worn that day and also information on the methods used to discipline children.

If the diarists did not mention physical punishment because they were ashamed of inflicting it, then at the very least, the diarists were opposed to what has been put forward as the attitudes of society to children in the past. The diarists did not simply ignore discipline – it is, in fact, one of the main recurring themes of the diaries. The parents were concerned with the way they reared their children: not spoiling; but not repressing them. They certainly did not ignore their children. The diaries frequently contain long passages on the appropriate punishment for any childish misdemeanour. These include lecturing, reproaching, sending to bed or out of the room and fining. Infliction of some kind of physical punishment from a slap to a 'whipping' is mentioned by 27 diarists (6 per cent). Whippings were noted very rarely, usually on only one or two occasions and do seem to have been a last resort. The way the event was described in the diaries does not suggest that the diarists concerned were ashamed of inflicting the punishment; but rather that they thought it justified in the circumstances. For example, Boswell (1740–95) 'beat' his son for telling a lie; *William Byrd (1674–1744) whipped his nephew 'exceedingly' for bed-wetting and *Samuel Sewall (1652–1730) whipped one son for playing truant. As any whippings are mentioned when they do occur, it appears that they were an infrequent event. Some fathers, such as Adam Martindale (1623–86) and John Bright (1811–89) complained when their child was beaten at school and *Lester Ward (1841–1931), when a school teacher, had to apologise to parents for hitting his pupils too hard on the hand. This suggests a general disapproval of physical punishment.

If the beating of children was considered by society to be perfectly acceptable, even praiseworthy, as has been suggested by some historians, then there would be no need for the diarist to conceal it.[4] Since the majority of diarists did not consider publication, then it is unlikely that the attitudes of society at large would have any influence on what the diarist wrote. If it were the case that the diarists suppressed evidence of ill-treatment because they felt society would condemn it, then this would present a serious obstacle to the thesis that the ill-treatment of past children by all was the normal method of rearing. The diaries do contain details on punishment when it occurred, hence it seems likely that the diarists simply noted the punishment as they would any other event of the day.

By attempting to assess the 'honesty' of the diarists, it may be possible to ascertain how much of what the diaries contain can be relied on. The diarists did include in their diaries actions or thoughts of which they repented. The Puritans and Methodists in particular, using their diaries as a means of spiritual improvement, were likely to note all of what they considered to be their faults and good points that day. If, for example, they considered it their duty to beat their child, then they would either record in their diary their regret at not having done so or their satisfaction in performing their duty. Other diarists also included in their diary their regrets. Gambling, failing to provide for their wife and children, ignoring their father's advice, refusing to go to Eton, losing their temper, and being impatient with their children are a few examples. The diarists did record details which they wished to keep private. Boswell (1740–95) committed adultery on numerous occasions, each noted in his diary. His wife happened to find the diary, read it and was exceedingly annoyed at the contents, so much so that Boswell decided that 'Perhaps I should not put such things as this into my Journal' (vol. 13, p. 12). However, the next time he was unfaithful, it was also recorded in the diary. It is almost as if diarists are compelled to record what actually happens as otherwise their diary would be worthless.

Elizabeth Holland (1770–1845) also wrote in her diary details of an incident which she obviously would not have wanted to be made public. She wished to divorce her husband and re-marry. The law at the time (the late 18th century) gave custody of all children to the father. Lady Holland particularly wished to keep her youngest child, Harriet, and so she wrote to her husband while he was on a business trip, telling him Harriet was dead. She then removed Harriet to a hiding place. If the plot had been discovered, both Holland and her new husband would have faced a term of imprisonment – something not undertaken lightly in the 18th century. Similarly, Thrale (1741–1821) and Charlotte Guest (1812–?) recorded in their diaries their growing love for a man they knew would be totally unacceptable to their children and their circle of peers. Claver Morris (1659–1727) admitted receiving smuggled French wine on a number of occasions. For example, he noted: 'I got up to let in Amey Rogers with 4 Gallons & 6 pints and ½ of French White-Wine' (100).

The diarists also included details of their behaviour with which they were not entirely happy, often deploring the incidents. See, for example, the diaries of Boswell (1740–95), *Byrd (1674–1744) and Dudley Ryder (1691–1756) which describe their sexual liaisons, often with prostitutes, and their ambivalent attitudes towards and later regrets for their behaviour. James Erskine (1679–1754) – a senator of the college of justice –

similarly noted: 'I drank and whor'd and followed sensual pleasures' – to such an extent that he contracted one of the venereal diseases which somewhat dampened his enthusiasm (78). John Byrom (1692–1763), Thomas Smith and Thomas Turner regretted their drinking habits. '[I was] so overcome with Liquor and in so bad a State that I knew not what I did and too bad to be mention'd; only I make my sincere Acknowledgement to my Creator and Preserver, and stedfastly promise never to commit the like beastly Wickedness' (Smith, 1673–1723, p. 187). '[I] came home drunk Oh! with what horrors does it fill my heart, to think I should be guilty of doing so, and on a Sunday too! Let me once more endeavour never, no never, to be guilty of the same again' (Turner, 1729–89 (1925), p. xiv). Unfortunately for Turner's peace of mind, he was 'guilty of the same' on many other occasions.

The diarists were concerned with recording the truth as they saw it. They were obviously selecting which events to record; but they would not appear to have been deliberately falsifying them: 'I may make bold to remark here that I know and am certain, that a strict regard has been paid to truth, throughout' (John Taylor, 1743–1819, p. 2). 'I shall say little more here than that all I write is the simple and entire truth' (Weeton, 1776–1850, vol. 1, p. 3). Some diarists were aware of how difficult it was to record only the exact truth. One, for example, was afraid that others might find him too sinful and wrote: 'Imagining that my *Journal* may fall into the hands of friends or others, I find within me, in spite of all I can do, a studious care employ'd, tho' not to misrepresent the Truth, yet to avoid setting it forth in *glaring* colours' (Jones, 1755–1821, p. 14). Others, on looking back over their diaries, believed the texts revealed more of the writer's failures than achievements: 'A diary tempts one to be cynical: a man shows himself a poor prophet or a hasty builder. Looking back on mine from now I can see the flimsiness of many hopes' (Maurice Hewlett, 1861–1923, fo. 35); 'it is only too true that an exact and honest review of life cannot be made without seeing in bold relief the weakness, vanity and imperfections of even our best efforts' (Thomas Sopwith, 1803–79, p. 16).

The diarists were honest about their feelings: four diarists, already having some children, hoped they would not become pregnant again, or admitted they were not happy when they became so; Fry (1780–1845) and *Elizabeth Prentiss (1818–78) suffered from post-natal depression after the birth of their children and Frances Boscawen (1719–1805) was terrified of childbirth. Isobel Gurney (1851–1932), on the birth of her first child, decided to answer all her children's questions; seven children later, she admitted this was one of the most 'trying' things she had ever undertaken.

The editor. There are disadvantages in using published texts. Whether or not a manuscript is published depends on someone considering it worth publishing. Most manuscripts were shortened for publication and therefore significant details may have been omitted. In some diaries many of the family details were omitted because they were considered to be too personal or, in the 19th century, not of interest to the public. Ultimately, research in this area will have to concentrate on the original manuscripts – although some of these are no longer available. For this study, the large number of sources used made it impossible to study the manuscripts – the latter are not renowned for their legibility – although an attempt was made to read a few. It is hoped that the large number of texts would help to counteract individual vagaries in editorial policy. As the vast majority of sources were used in their published form, a discussion of editorial policies is essential in order to ascertain the reliability of the results.

It appears that it is the very private nature of a diary which caused problems for the editors. Some editors were reluctant to 'bare the soul' of the diarist. 'This journal enters too minutely into the details of his daily doings, and touches too closely the secrets of his inner life, to be given to the world' (Alexander Ewing's diary, pub. 1877, p. 26). 'There are almost daily references to them [Macready's children] in the diaries, but they are mainly of too intimate a character to admit of quotation. Their faults as well as their merits are impartially recorded, but even his [Macready's] severest displeasure was seldom untempered with evidences of deep and anxious affection' (William Macready's diary, pub. 1912, vol. 1, p. 4).

There is no office involving more difficulty than that which devolves on the editor of a Diary . . . Reserve has, however, rather to do with the expediency of such a publication than with the manner in which it is conducted. A Diary is chiefly interesting as a portraiture of feelings which are discoverable through no other medium . . . In the Diary of Bishop Sandford, many passages have been repressed, which – though deeply delightful to his nearest relations – were considered of too sacred a character for the public eye.

(Daniel Sandford's diary, pub. 1830, vol. 1, p. 110)

However, it seems that in most cases, even if private details were suppressed, the editors were concerned with publishing a representative sample of the original manuscript. They often list what they have omitted: this list includes notes on books read or sermons listened to, repetitive visits, repeated observations on the weather and any item which may cause distress to persons still living at the date of publication.

It may be claimed that nothing of importance has been omitted. The diary called for compression; for Glenvervie often repeated himself, was often tedious about minor political movements which have lost all interest, given to reflections, moral or literary, which do not rise above the level of platitude, and sometimes indulged in flights of facetiousness devoid of wit.

(Sylvester Douglas' diary, pub. 1928, vol. 1, p. viii)

In making this abridgement I have endeavoured to preserve the essential interest of the Journal, while omitting such details as lists of correspondents, or of calls made and received, bald statements of commonplace happenings, and other recurrent features of little interest.

(Gideon Mantell's diary, pub. 1940, p. vi)

as a limit [on extracts] was absolutely necessary, it was resolved to be guided by the object of exhibiting individual character as much as possible, without violation of what, even at this distance of time, are felt to be the sacred privacies of the soul, or intrusion on other personalities. A great deal of what is interesting and characteristic, especially of the almost daily notes of her studies and observations on natural history, had to be omitted. But nothing which has been suppressed would tend to give a different idea of her character from what the published extracts convey.

(Shore's diary, pub. 1898, p. viii)

Some editors also included in their published version certain entries with which they did not agree. For example, Hannah Rathbone mentioned 'whipping' her infant for crying. The editor, in a footnote, remarked that, although this action did not seem very likely, it was so stated in the diary. Other editors published details which the diarist would prefer not to have been revealed. For instance, Mary Gladstone had prepared some extracts of her diary for publication but died before the diary was published. The editor of her diary considered these extracts too 'edited' and therefore ignored them and used the original manuscript. In his diary, Mill had crossed out a disparaging remark on his daughter's character;[5] but, as it was still legible, the editor included it in the published text.

In order to discover if anything significant to the history of childhood was omitted, a sample of manuscripts was compared with the published text. The American manuscripts are listed in Matthews (1974) and the British ones in Matthews (1950). The American libraries who owned the required manuscripts were asked for a microfilm or a Xerox of the text. The comparison of the British manuscripts was confined to those manuscripts which were available for study in libraries in London. The American and British diaries were considered separately and divided into

Table 3. *Manuscripts used in the comparison study*

| Nationality | Period | | | | |
	1825–50	1850–75	1875–1900	1900–25	1925–50
American	Elias Hicks	Samuel Dexter	Increase Mather	Landon Carter	William Byrd
	John Pemberton	Timothy Newell	Ann Warder	Cotton Mather	
British	Henry Hyde	Sarah Fox	Walter Calverley	Susanna Day	John Skinner
	Mary Rich	Nehemiah Wallington	Caroline Powys	Abiah Darby	Richard Rogers
				John Thomlinson	

groups according to the date of publication. The American diaries had publication dates ranging from 1760 to 1951. Manuscripts for those diaries published before 1825 (two) and for the only diary published after 1950 were not available. This left a range of publication dates ranging from 1825 to 1950, which gave five periods of 25 years. Two manuscripts were looked at from each period except that of 1925–50 where only one manuscript was obtainable. This gave a total of nine manuscripts. The publication dates of the British diaries ranged from 1750 to 1967. Manuscripts for those diaries published before 1825 (six) and those after 1950 (seven) were not available. Two manuscripts were read for each 25-year period 1825–1950, and three were used for the period 1900–25, giving 11 manuscripts. These manuscripts are listed in Table 3.

(a) Verbatim
Those manuscripts which were reproduced verbatim (or very nearly so) were: *Byrd, Henry Hyde, *Cotton Mather, *Timothy Newell, *John Pemberton, Mary Rich and John Thomlinson. In the case of *Pemberton, the editor omitted a few entries, but provided an accurate summary of them so that, in effect, nothing contained in the manuscript was excluded from the published version. The editor of Thomlinson's diary omitted a few religious entries at the beginning of the diary; but the remainder was verbatim. The editor of *Newell's diary did not omit anything in the

manuscript, although he did occasionally alter a word· or word order slightly.

(b) Less than 25 per cent omitted

The editors of the diaries of Calverley, *Hicks and Rogers omitted less than 25 per cent of the original manuscript.

Walter Calverley: The editor omitted about 10 per cent of the manuscript; details of accounts; the occasional entry on debts and the visits of friends or relatives. No family details were omitted.

*Elias Hicks: The editor omitted about 10 per cent: accounts of dreams, details of some of the religious meetings which *Hicks attended, entries regretting his poverty. The only family detail excluded was an entry describing the sending of two of *Hicks' daughters to boarding school. The editor sometimes paraphrased what *Hicks had written, but without altering the sense.

Richard Rogers: The editor omitted about 10 per cent: Rogers' frequent regrets at neglecting his studies, an entry considering whether or not to bring a teacher into the family and an entry in which Rogers recorded that too much of his time was given to delighting in his family when he should spend it appreciating God.

(c) 25–50 per cent omitted

The diaries of Day, *I. Mather, Powys, Wallington and *Warder fall into this category.

Susanna Day: The editor of Day's diary was mainly interested in Day's religious experiences and so omitted most of the family details – about 30 per cent of the diary – details on her children's illnesses, entries revealing Day's concern for the health of her children, an entry describing taking ‘dear little Agatha to school', a number of entries referring to the visiting of this daughter at school and notes on the visits Day received from her married children and grandchildren.

*Increase Mather: The editor omitted about half of *Mather's diary; these were mainly religious details: numerous entries on the meetings he attended, his struggles with his faith and details on sermons. In addition, the years 1688–97 – covering a large part of *Mather's family life – were excluded from the text. This is possibly due to the fact that the manuscript for these years belongs to a different library. The Xerox of the manuscript for this period proved to be practically impossible to decipher.

Caroline Powys: The editor omitted about half of the manuscript: parts of letters, frequent descriptions of houses and places she visited on her travels, her reason for writing the diary and entries in which she talked about other people. An occasional reference to her children was also excluded: her decision to make one of her sons a new outfit and her distress at the death of her baby daughter.

Wallington: The editor omitted about half of the manuscript: description of a period of famine, Wallington's recollection of he and his brother stealing ls from their father twice and many religious entries. In addition, the editor omitted many of the references to Wallington's children, although they are summarised to some extent in a preface to the diary. These omissions were: entries on his wife's difficulties with breast-feeding, references to the illnesses of his children, a description of the time his daughter was missing for a few hours, his wife's miscarriages, and some small details of Wallington referring to enjoying the company of his daughter and to his son as being 'merry . . . and full of play'.

*Ann Warder: The editor omitted about half the diary: the description of *Warder's voyage to Philadelphia, details on the kind of food she ate, many descriptions of the furnishings of houses she visited and people she met, entries referring to the writing of letters home and some entries on *Warder's daily activities such as sewing and mending. Some references to her children were also excluded: an entry in which *Warder hoped her 'sweet dear dearest offspring' were happy while she was away from them, her description of her delight in seeing them again and of taking them round various places in America, and an account of one son who was unwilling to go to bed, was later found asleep and taken up to bed where he gave an 'ill-natured cry'. However, *Warder wrote that, as she realised her son did not know that she had heard and as she did not wish to arouse the 'inevitable passion' if she 'corrected him', she did not. Her feelings at the death of her young daughter were also omitted – *Warder regarding this as an 'affliction' – as well as entries in which she referred to American children as spoilt in that they were rude to their parents and had too much freedom.

(d) Over 50 per cent omitted
The diaries of *Carter, Darby, *Dexter and Skinner fall into this category.

*Landon Carter: The editor left out about 75 per cent of the entries: frequent long entries on debts owed to him, bills to be paid. *Carter's state of health, observations on the weather, his religious beliefs and the running of his plantation. Very few family entries were omitted, however: some entries on family visits, an entry on *Carter's views on the contraceptive effect of breast-feeding and two incidents of discord with his sons – similar entries for other occasions were included in the published text.

Abiah Darby: The editor omitted about 75 per cent of the manuscript: Darby's reason for writing, descriptions of her parents and siblings, frequent letters to and from friends described in the manuscript, long accounts of the numerous Quaker meetings Darby attended and also many descriptions of her religious experiences. A few family details were also excluded: Darby's breast-feeding difficulties, entries on her children's illnesses and education, and notes on them going to meet their mother as she returned from her religious meetings.

*Samuel Dexter: The editor cut out about 75 per cent of the manuscript: *Dexter's reason for keeping a diary, frequent preaching details, his regret at not writing in the diary daily, many accounts of his religious struggles and of the religious lectures and conferences he attended, and a list of what *Dexter considered to be his faults. Very few family entries were excluded: the entry referring to *Dexter's distress at the death of his daughter and son – 'a bitter cup' – and his view of children as gifts from God.

Skinner: The manuscript of Skinner's diary runs to 98 long volumes, which were condensed into one volume for publication. The early years of the journal are largely omitted; they reveal Skinner's affection for his children and his enjoyment of their company. Most of the later volumes are taken up with Skinner's growing disillusionment with life and his discord with his parishioners and his children. A representative sample of this is included in the text.

For this sample almost half of the editors (eight) omitted 50 per cent or more of the manuscript from the published text. This seems a great deal; but, as has been shown in the results, this would not appear to have significantly affected the entries on family life, although there are many references to children in the manuscripts. (The published diary of Sarah Fox contained no references to children; but, after examining the manuscript, I discovered she had no children.) It would appear to be mainly incidental details which were excluded from the published texts: descriptions of places and houses visited, financial arrangements, religious meetings and repetitive entries. The editors did try to provide a representative selection and the omissions, even if on a large scale, do not detract from the overall impression provided by the published text. The omissions would not alter any conclusions; but rather provide additional evidence to reinforce them. It is of interest that Macfarlane (1970), in his study of Josselin's diary, thought he was using a complete transcript of the diary. However, he later discovered that this transcript was incomplete; but, on reading the full version, he found that the omissions did not affect his conclusions regarding Josselin's family life. Instead, these entries contained more details to support his argument.

Ill-treatment did not occur. The function of parental care and the effects of neglect or ill-treatment on children are discussed in chapter 2. From this evidence, it is unlikely that severe abuse would occur on a large scale. Thus it seems reasonable to accept that details of severe physical punishment did not appear in the diaries because it did not occur. Child abuse occurs in all socio-economic groups, although there is a tendency for it to be more common at the lower end of the scale. As all the diarists are literate, then, particularly for the earlier centuries when literacy was the mark of a higher education, perhaps it would not be expected that they would ill-treat their children to any great extent.

Generalisation

Most of the diarists belong to the middle classes; there are very few lower-class diaries or autobiographies. The diarists do leave open the possibility that certain segments of society did abuse children. This is not disputed here. Nevertheless the diarists represent a large class of people who did not ill-treat their children and who have been largely ignored in accounts of the history of childhood.

The majority of diarists were not exceptional, but ordinary people living out their lives in anonymity. Not all of them were happy – to name a few: Boswell (1740–95) and Clarissa Trant (1800–44) became exceedingly depressed; Elizabeth Freke (1641–1714) and her husband quarrelled continuously; Skinner (1772–1839) was in constant discord with his older children and his parishioners; Weeton (1776–1850) was beaten by her husband and not allowed to see her child and Thrale (1741–1821) was rejected by her daughters and society after her second marriage. Nor did they depict idealised children; some diarists admitted they found the care of their children a burden at times and the majority were aware of the faults and limitations of their children. They did not present a picture of a perfect world. A few diarists recalled ill-treatment during their own childhood; for example, Cooper (1801–85) from servants; Simon Forman (1552–1601) from his mother and siblings; Elizabeth Grant (1797–?) and Augustus Hare (1834–1903) from their parents; and John Stedman

(1744–97) from his uncle. Many more related the severe discipline they experienced at school. Freke (1641–1714) and Kate Russell (1842–74) both noted the neglect of their child by the nurse and, in both cases, the nurse was changed. Twenty-six of the diarists (6 per cent) recorded the ill-treatment of children occurring in society, such as baby-farms, infanticide and neglect. Henry Newcome (1627–95) took in his own grandchild because he could not tolerate his son's 'shameful abuse' of the child.

The diaries do reflect social changes: the 18th-century diaries recorded the introduction of inoculation for smallpox with the parents debating whether or not to take the risk and have their child inoculated. Nineteenth-century diaries are quite different from previous ones in that they do depict a much wider, more technological world. For example, the diarists noted train journeys, new forms of entertainment such as exhibitions and museums and new kinds of toys and books. If the diaries were sensitive to these changes, then it is at least possible that they would also be sensitive to drastic changes in the concept of childhood, if these did occur.

One way of assessing the possibility of generalising from the diaries would be to check how representative 20th-century diaries are of present-day practices as depicted in such studies as Newson & Newson (1965, 1968, 1976).

Diaries do not provide all the necessary evidence for a reconstruction of child life in the past. There is, for example, a lack of infant data. However, they do have a number of advantages when used as a prime source of evidence. They present a more personal, intimate picture providing glimpses into actual households. They reveal children in their context – as part of a society with adults – rather than isolated from it. They go some of the way to revealing the *actualities* of childhood rather than the attitudes to it. The child diarists present the child's point of view as a *child* rather than an adult looking back. Diaries are the closest we have available to direct observation of parent–child interaction and so are a very valuable source of evidence.

It is not possible to prove conclusively that diaries only contain the exact truth; but, on the face of all the evidence, there is more justification to accept what they say rather than reject it: The diaries do not prove that child-rearing was more kind or more cruel in the past; but what they do suggest is that there was a large section of the population whose methods of child-rearing appear to be no harsher than today. It is this section which has been omitted from most previous works on the history of childhood – because most authors have been more concerned with finding evidence to support the thesis that children were not valued in the past, rather than examining the prevalence of different attitudes at various times.

A total of 120 autobiographies were read (27 American and 93 British). Of these, only 27 were solely autobiographies; the others were written as an introduction to a diary. Autobiographies suffer from the same problems as diaries and also possess some additional ones. They are written in retrospect and generally for publication. Therefore they are likely to be more selective than the diaries in what they contain. They depend on how the writer views the actual events from hindsight, and he may attempt to show himself in a better light. They are also dependent on what the author himself remembers and thus, apart from the fact that memory is notoriously selective, are unlikely to contain information on infancy. What is of interest is to see how much similarity there is in the accounts of childhood given by autobiographies, child diaries and parental diaries.

The relationship between attitudes and behaviour

Many authors have assumed there is a predictable relationship between a given attitude and a behaviour. Stone (1977), for instance, assumes that because Puritans believed that children were innately evil, they therefore subjected their offspring to a very strict disciplinary regime. That is, the possession of the concept of Original Sin by a parent led to the infliction of physical punishment. However, psychological research on attitudes and behaviour (see Fishbein & Ajzen, *Belief, Attitude, Intention and Behaviour*, 1975, for a review of such research) reveals that there is no systematic relation between a person's attitude and a particular behaviour. Neither is there any necessary relation between attitudes and intentions, Fishbein & Ajzen defining a behavioural intention as one which 'refers to a person's subjective probability that he will perform some behaviour' (288). It has been discovered, though, that intention is a good predictor of behaviour, particularly when the action is under a person's voluntary control. An attitude can lead to different behaviours and also the same behaviour could be the result of different attitudes. Thus, in order to establish how parents did rear their children in past times, it is vital to discover their actual actions as opposed to their attitudes and concepts.

The presentation of evidence

The main study was concerned with a systematic analysis of the information on childhood contained in primary sources. Four sources of evidence have been used from the 16th to the 19th centuries inclusive: published adult diaries, child diaries and autobiographies and unpublished manuscripts. A number of texts contain more than one type of source, for example an autobiography and a diary.[6] Where this occurs, the two sources are considered separately. The child diaries include material written by older offspring still under parental authority. The autobiographies either describe the childhood of the writer (the majority) or recall his/her later life as a parent. The texts were divided into centuries according to the date of birth of the writer. It was decided to do this rather than to categorise them according to the dates or the text or the date of the specific entry because it was considered that giving the lifespan of an author would place him or her in context better.[7] The Appendix contains details of the various sources in the texts as well as information on the dates of the texts.

Both American and British sources were studied, although only those American manuscripts used in the comparison study (described in chapter 3) have been read. The data in the American and British texts are discussed separately. The majority of the British writers were English and most of the American writers came from New England (see Table 4). Table 5 shows the sample size of each source for each nationality and century.

The largest sample size is available for the 18th century and this is also the period in which the most detailed, introspective and analytical diaries are found. There are relatively few 16th-century texts, and unfortunately the diary entries in these texts are fairly brief and factual. The unpublished manuscripts, apart from that of Steuart, also contain little useful evidence. Within each topic discussed, the American data are quoted first. Where the sample size is small, for example with the 16th-century texts, all the information is discussed. With a larger sample size, a representative selection of quotations spanning the century is given whenever possible. Diarists who made the same point but are not quoted from are listed in the text, or if the list contains more than 10 writers, are referred to in the notes at the end. The evidence is therefore being surveyed and analysed, rather than being selected, or even distorted, to fit a theory. The primary objective in this study is to bring

Table 4. *Percentage d*
(where known)

Century	New England
16th	100
n = 1	
17th	93
n = 15	
18th	58
n = 87	
19th	39
n = 51	
ALL	
n = 154	

Issues concerning evidence

Table 5. *Division of sample size by natio*

Nationality	Century	16th	17th	18th	19th
American					
Total					
British					

Adult diary

* 1 writer came from Illi....
† 6 writers came from Illinois, 3 from O...
from Missouri, 1 from South Carolina, 1 from Tenn...
Toronto, 1 from Washington.

together a body of material to facilitate detailed discussion of the history of childhood (by expanding knowledge). As yet only the first steps in interpretation are possible.

Newspaper reports

until late in the nineteenth century, both Parliament and the national press were largely unconcerned with the way in which parents treated their children, regarding even the most barbarous cruelty as beyond comment and beyond public intervention since children were not then regarded as citizens in their own right.

(Pinchbeck & Hewitt, *Children in English Society*, 1969, p. 611)

In discussing this subject, Pinchbeck & Hewitt refer to the case of one woman who put out the eyes of a child in her care in order that the child might then earn money by begging. They claim that it was only because the woman was employed by the parish to look after children that her cruelty was prosecuted and that, if the woman had been the child's mother, no one would have bothered to intervene because it was accepted that parents could treat their offspring as they pleased. Thus

		Text			
		Child diary	Autobiography	Manuscript	Total
	1	0	1	–	2
		13	2	0	–	15
		60	25	13	–	98
		31	20	14	–	65
		105	47	28	–	180
16th	15	2	5	0	22
17th	39	5	14	7*	65
18th	83	14	43	7	147
19th	57	31	31	4†	123
Total	194	52	93	18	357
ALL	299	99	121	18	537

* Sample includes six diaries and one autobiography.
† Sample includes three child diaries and one adult diary.

they infer from one particular case the attitude of the whole of 18th- and 19th-century society to child abuse.

Chapter 2 has dealt with the appearance of child protection legislation, showing that it appeared as part of a general response by the state to a national crisis. The lack of such legislation until the 19th century does not necessarily mean that people condoned child abuse. In order to test Pinchbeck & Hewitt's claim that cases of child cruelty were not reported, *The Times* newspaper from 1785 to 1860 was read (excluding the years 1788 to 1790 for which there were no indices available at the time of study).

The newspaper reports of child abuse cases were found by searching the Criminal Court and Police sections of the indices to *The Times* newspaper and then looking in the appropriate newspaper. In all, 385 cases of child neglect and sexual abuse were found (19 cases were of incest) for the period 1785–1860.[8] Of these cases, 7 per cent were found not guilty and 24 per cent were to be sent to a higher court for trial. The cases which resulted in a not guilty verdict were not, as might have been expected, concentrated in the earlier part of the period covered but occurred from 1806 to 1860, typically one case every few years. The police and magistrate courts, up till 1862, could only impose a maximum penalty of £5 or two months in the House of Correction and therefore sent many cases of cruelty to the central courts where a higher penalty could be imposed. A few cases (11 per cent) involved apprentices; the earliest reported case of cruelty to a child by a parent appeared in 1787.

The manner in which the cases were reported by the newspaper provides an indication of the attitudes of the time to cruelty to children. The fact that the majority of cases were also found guilty meant that the law and society condemned child abuse long before the specific Prevention of Cruelty to Children Act appeared in 1889. Parents who abused their offspring were generally considered 'unnatural' and the cruelty as 'horrific' or 'barbaric'. The following 14 cases have been selected as representative examples of the attitudes to child abuse during the period studied.

In December 1787 *The Times* reported a case of cruelty to a child by his guardian. The report occupied a complete page of the newspaper and the judge and court regarded the case as 'very rare' with reference to the extent of the cruelty. The 3-year-old child was so ill-treated and neglected that he was physically deformed by the abuse and his appearance in court 'drew tears from almost everybody'. The case was described as one 'of the most savage transactions' heard by the court (11 Dec. 1787, p. 3).

In 1809 a 'case of the most unparalleled barbarity' was described. William Marlborough and his wife were charged with starving their 6-year-old daughter 'together with a series of other atrocious cruelties, hardly to be equalled'. The girl slept in an underground cellar on a heap of rubbish and was given very little food; 'But this however horrible to relate, was not the worst of her sufferings' as she was also beaten with a leather thong at the end of which were pieces of iron wire. Her parents said they had punished her for lying but 'The Magistrate, however . . . expressed a becoming indignation at their brutal conduct' (10 Oct. 1809, p. 3c).

The next year a mother was charged with 'barbarously beating and ill-treating her own child' – a daughter aged 4. When the mother was taken out of the office after her trial, 'it was with the greatest difficulty she could be protected from the fury of the women on the outside' (28 May 1810, p. 3e).

Elizabeth Bruce was charged with 'cruelly starving, unmercifully beating and otherwise most inhumanly treating her own son'. The trial was said to have 'exhibited a picture truly shocking to every feeling of humanity' (28 Oct. 1812, p. 3e).

A case of 'shocking inhumanity' was reported in 1817. Benjamin Turner was charged with 'inhumanly beating, depriving of food, and otherwise ill-treating three of his children'. The children were beaten till the blood flowed and salt was then rubbed into the wounds. In addition, he held his two daughters under water. The magistrate 'expatiated with indignation upon the conduct of the defendant' (17 Dec. 1817, p. 3e).

Mr and Mrs Cayzer were charged with cruelty to their children – 'by stifling the calls of humanity, they made themselves intoxicated, and then commenced a scene of barbarous cruelty, the recital of which shocked every person in the office, and in many instances was such that we cannot lay before our readers'. The magistrates 'strongly reprobated such inhuman cruelty' and, in taking the defendants to prison, the officers had great difficulty in protecting them 'from the fury of an immense crowd that had assembled' (7 Apr. 1824, p. 4c).

Patrick Sheen beat his 8-year-old son till blood flowed because the child would not stop crying and then threw him on the fire so that the child's back was burnt by the hot grate. Sheen said the child was perverse and obstinate 'adding, that he thought every father had a right to do as he pleased with his own child, and that he did not see what right other people had to interfere'. The magistrate replied that 'the law must teach the defendant that this doctrine of his was very erroneous' (17 Nov. 1824, p. 3c).

James McDougal and his wife were charged with neglecting and beating their three children. The chairman said:

that they had been convicted of a most atrocious offence, and for the sake of human nature he trusted there would never be such another instance of diabolical cruelty exercised towards an unoffending and helpless child unable to protect itself . . . How they could reconcile such inhuman conduct to their consciences, he was at a loss to conceive, without they were entirely callous to every feeling of humanity. (6 June 1829, p. 4a)

N. Weston bound his 11-year-old daughter to a bed post and struck her with a belt and buckle until her skin was cut. The magistrate thought the child's back 'was the most shocking sight he ever beheld; it was the duty of parents to correct disobedient children, but not to inflict such barbarous punishment' and regarded Weston as unfit to look after the child (26 May 1834, p. 6f).

In 1837 the 'unnatural conduct of a mother' was described – she had exposed her 2-month-old twins. The chairman told her: 'Your conduct has been the most unnatural, and of the most cruel character, I ever remember to have become acquainted with. The Court would be wanting in the common feelings of humanity did they not mark their opinion of your behaviour by a severe punishment' (6 Apr. 1837, p. 6d).

M. Noed beat his 14-year-old son with a stick which had six cords attached to the end. The magistrate stated: 'I never recollect in all my experience a case of greater cruelty' (25 May 1844, p. 8e).

A 2-year-old girl was beaten with a knotted whip by her parents so that she was severely bruised and marked. Her parents believed her to be a stubborn child who needed a great deal of punishment. On the other hand, the judge believed 'Those persons surely could not have expected to improve a poor little child's disposition by such a course of brutal treatment as they appeared to have practised on her' (30 Mar. 1848, p. 7a).

E. Butterfield inflicted four cuts on the buttocks of her 7-year-old daughter after the latter had refused to go to school. The magistrate said: 'the offence was one of such atrocious and unusual description that it was difficult to conceive how it could have entered into the heart of a mother to commit it' (23 July 1850, p. 8b).

E. and P. Hennessey neglected their child aged $2\frac{1}{2}$ to the extent that he would be crippled for life, if he survived. The judge passed the maximum sentences (two years in prison for the mother and one for the father) 'but he felt that the sentence he was about passing upon the woman might be thought inadequate to the heinousness of the offence' (21 Sept. 1853, p. 9c).

Newspaper reports would seem to be a fairly reliable source of evidence. The reports are accounts of actual behaviour and the way in which the event is reported gives an indication of how the act is regarded by society. Thus, if newspapers are not entirely 'neutral' observers, they surely reflect the attitudes of the period.

The reports given here, apart from totally refuting Pinchbeck & Hewitt's claim, reveal the sense of outrage evoked by cruelty to children. The magistrates, witnesses and general public (for the last, see especially the reports of 1810 and 1824) were all horrified that parents could inflict such cruelty on their offspring, seeming to find it completely inexplicable that the parents could do so. Such parents were regarded as 'inhuman', aberrations from the norm rather than as typical. This contradicts the arguments of many historians that adults were indifferent to children and that cruelty to children was practised on a large scale – the case in 1824 in particular reveals that parents *could not* treat their children exactly as they pleased, even when there was no specific law to protect children.

4. Attitudes to children

l'enfance n'était qu'un passage sans importance, qu'il n'y avait pas lieu de fixer dans le souvenir.

On ne pensait pas que cet enfant contenait déjà toute une personne d'homme, comme nous croyons communément aujourd'hui. Il en mourait trop . . . Cette indifférence était une conséquence directe et inévitable de la démographie de l'epoque. (29, 30)

(childhood was simply an unimportant phase of which there was no need to keep any record.

Nobody thought, as we ordinarily think today, that every child already contained a man's personality. Too many of them died . . . This indifference was a direct and inevitable consequence of the demography of the period.)
(Ariès, 1960, pp. 38, 39)

Childhood as such was barely recognised in the period spanned by the Plymouth Colony. (Demos, 1970, p. 57)
The omnipresence of death coloured affective relations at all levels of society, by reducing the amount of emotional capital available for prudent investment in any single individual, especially in such ephemeral creatures as infants.
(Stone, 1977, pp. 651–2)

The concept of childhood

Ariès argues in *L'Enfant et la Vie Familiale sous l'Ancien Régime* that there was no concept of childhood until the 17th century. He defines a concept of childhood as 'une conscience de la particularité enfantine, cette particularité, qui distingue essentiellement l'enfant de l'adulte' (134) ('an awareness of the particular nature of childhood, that particular nature which distinguishes the child from the adult' (128)). Unfortunately, the very vagueness of Ariès' definition negates his whole argument: it would be impossible not to realise that a child was different from an adult, children are all too obviously dependent on adult care and protection. If there is an appreciation of the *immaturity* of the child in either the physical (e.g. an awareness of such developmental stages as teething and the acquisition of language) or mental sphere (e.g. the need to socialise a child by discipline and education), then whoever has that appreciation possesses a concept of childhood, no matter how basic or limited this is. The point at issue is not whether there was a concept of childhood in the past, but whether this concept has become more elaborated or changed through the centuries.

Related to the above theme is the problem of socialisation – the process by which a relatively egocentric individual is moulded into a participating member of adult society. How far, if at all, were past parents concerned with this aim and what methods did they employ to achieve it are questions that have yet to be adequately answered. One way of studying the problem would be to discover not only how parents viewed their children, but also how they viewed the parental role. In addition, the parent–child interaction should be investigated: for example, by asking how far the parents accommodated the demands of their offspring and if their methods of socialisation differed with respect to the age of the child.

How parents regarded their children[1]

The 16th century. The 16th-century sources available present great difficulty to the historian in that they contain little detail and they require careful reading in order to glean useful information from them. Even so, the texts studied reveal that a concept of childhood was in existence in this century.

In the diaries children were seen as developing organisms: Anne Clifford, John Dee and Wallington referred to such things as weaning, teething and early utterances. Children also played. Dee, *William Jefferay and Wallington included entries on play in their diaries. It was realised that children needed some form of guidance. Dee, Thomas Hope, *Jefferay and Powell wrote of discipline; Richard Boyle, Dee, Hope, Humphrey Mildmay, John Oglander, Powell, Rogers and John Winthrop advised their offspring; H. Mildmay solved his son's problems at school and Boyle arranged the marriages of his sons and daughters. Children were also creatures who had to be protected and looked after. Clifford, Dee, Hope, *Jefferay, H. Mildmay, Powell and Wallington nursed their children through illness; Clifford noted leaving baby-sitters for her daughter aged 3 when she left on a visit; Wallington searched for his young daughter when she failed to return from play and Oglander sent his children to the mainland when trouble broke out on the island. Finally, children were economically dependent and had to be provided for: Boyle, Hope, *Jefferay, Powell and Winthrop recorded giving their offspring financial aid towards independence.

There was some ambivalence in 16th-century parental attitudes to children. Children brought joy and company certainly but also irritation and anxiety. The parents were pleased at the birth of their children and later delighted in their company (e.g. Clifford and Wallington enjoyed speaking with their young children, Dee was amused by his offspring's play and *Jefferay regarded his children as 'a comfort'). On the other hand, parents could be annoyed with their offspring as in the diaries of Clifford, Hope, H. Mildmay, Powell and Winthrop. Children also brought anxiety, particularly with reference to illness but also with regard to other matters, for example H. Mildmay was worried about his second son's conduct at school and Wallington was concerned when his daughter was missing for a time.

Few 16th-century autobiographies divulge how parents regarded their offspring, although Grace Mildmay (1552–1620) did appreciate the susceptibility of the young to external influences: 'It is certaine that there is foundation and ground of many great and ensueing evills when the nobilitie and great personages have no regard nor forecast what governors they sett over theyr children, nor what servants they appoynt to attend upon them' (127).

Discussion. These sources reveal that children were seen as:
1. Organisms that pass through developmental periods.
2. Organisms that indulge in play.
3. Organisms that need care and protection.
4. Organisms that need guidance, for example by education and discipline.
5. Organisms that have to be financially provided for.

These facets of a concept of childhood reappear in each century and therefore will not be considered in any great detail for the 17th to 19th centuries. Instead, the change in any type of attitude will be highlighted.

From the 16th-century texts it is quite clear that these writers possessed a concept of childhood – they were aware not only that children were different from adults, but also appreciated the ways in which children were different. These parents recognised that children were physically and mentally immature and so dependent on adult protection and guidance. It is more difficult to discover if children were seen as being at the bottom of the social scale, as has been argued by various historians (see for example Pinchbeck & Hewitt, 1969; Shorter, 1976; and Tucker, 1976). It is of significance that these parents were prepared to spend money on their offspring in order to educate them, purchase apprenticeships and set them up in independent households. The wish of G. Mildmay that parents should choose carefully any servants who were to look after their children implies that she considered children were something to be valued. Clifford (1590–1676) also noted that on her daughter's fifth birthday 'my Lord caused her health to be drank throughout the house' (105), which contradicts the idea of parental, particularly paternal, indifference. The diarists were obviously attached to their offspring, revealing a great deal of anxiety when their children were ill and also a desire to help their children when necessary.

There would not appear to have been a formal parent–child relationship: Clifford liked her young daughter to sleep with her, *Jefferay gave long detailed accounts of the natural history excursions which both he and his children enjoyed, and Winthrop's letters to his son at college were full of friendly, affectionate advice. Furthermore, the fact that some adolescent offspring continually opposed their parents' wishes suggests that these children at least were not in awe of their parents (see Pollock, 1981, ch. 8).

The 17th century. The American diarists of this period also referred to the developmental stages their children passed through as well as to their children playing (see *Byrd, *Joseph Green, *C. Mather and *Sewall). Over and above being concerned with the discipline and education of their offspring, the more articulate diarists provide information on their expectations of their children at a given age. *Byrd (1674–1744) was delighted when he took his daughter, aged about 4, to a wedding where she 'behaved herself very prettily' (1941, p. 495). *C. Mather (1663–1728) wrote that his 11-year-old son, Increase, was 'now of Age enough to know the Meaning of *Consideration*' (vol. 8, p. 49). At the age of 13, Increase was considered by *Mather old enough to 'hear from me such Documents of Piety, and of Discretion, as I shall endeavour to suit him' (vol. 8, p. 151). When another son, Samuel, reached the age of 11, *Mather was considering *'What shall I now enrich his Mind withal?'* (vol. 8, p. 435). A few months later, *Mather decided to 'Entertain *Sammy* betimes, with the first rudiments of Geography and Astronomy, as well as History; and so raise his Mind above the Sillier Diversions of Childhood' (vol. 8,

p. 473). *C. Mather also believed that his children possessed an inherently sinful nature.

Pride was another emotion roused in parents by their offspring. *Byrd wrote of his second daughter that 'her accomplishments, if a Father can be a judge [were] as great as any Damsel in this part of the World' (1942, p. 5). *Sewall (1652–1730) was similarly proud of one of his sons, 'a worthy minister' (vol. 6, p. 418). There was not a formal parent–child relationship in these American diaries: the company of their children was enjoyed by the parents; *Green (1675–1715), for example, often 'went a fishing' with his three sons (95) and *Sarah Knight (1666–1727) described her daughter waiting 'with open arms' to greet her mother after she had been away (12). Nevertheless, children were not all pleasure. The 17th-century diarists, as did the earlier writers, also described the extreme anxiety experienced by a parent when a child was ill; *Byrd and *C. Mather were in conflict with at least one of their adolescent children and *Sewall became embroiled in the problems of his eldest son.

Turning to the British diarists, Nicholas Blundell, Byrom, J. Erskine, John Evelyn, Ralph Josselin and Newcome possessed an awareness of the developing abilities of a child. For example, Evelyn (1620–1706) told a son of almost 5 years that a book would be too difficult for him to understand. This is particularly interesting as this child had reached a very high level of educational attainment by the age of 5 and has been put forward as an example of the precociousness which 17th-century parents forced on their children (see for example Illick, 1976). However, Evelyn obviously considered his son an exception to the normal child: he referred to his son's 'strange passion' for Greek, his 'strange . . . apt and ingenious application for fables', his 'astonishing knowledge of the scriptures' and concluded that his son's achievements far exceeded 'his age and experience . . . such a child I never saw' (vol. 2, p. 96). That Evelyn considered some books too difficult for his son suggests that Evelyn was not forcing the boy beyond his capabilities. Parents did not expect children to be adults: J. Erskine thought his 7-year-old son 'had a wantonness, as such of his age used to have' (72), and Newcome decided to read his children from scriptural authorities once they had reached a certain age as 'they are more capable now' (43).

As with the American diarists, no formal parent–child relationship was revealed. These parents were very much involved with their children: enjoying the latter's company, deciding on their education and solving their problems. Josselin (1616–83) described his children as 'comforts' and as 'shoots' (12, 123) growing up. Alexander Brodie (1617–80) also referred to his 'sweet' children as 'earthly comforts' (209). 'Comfort', in fact, appears to have been the standard way to describe a child by these diarists; it being the term most commonly appearing in the diaries. The diarists also tended to be proud of their children. Morris (1659–1727), for example, wished his daughter to reveal her prowess in French when he had guests and Martindale (1623–86) described his son of not quite 2, beating back a calf that used to run at children: 'I doe not think one child of 100 of his age durst doe so much' (154). Some parents at least regarded their children as hopes for the future (A. Brodie, Byrom, Josselin, Martindale, Newcome and Slingsby). Henry Slingsby (1601–58), for example, regarded his sons as 'those precious pledges wherein I had treasured all my inferior hopes, being next in care to the eternity of my Soul' (200).

Parents were ambivalent, at times, with regard to their children: child-rearing was not considered to be an easy task. Byrom (1692–1763) wrote: 'I am not without concern about the health and behaviour of the children, whose happiness so much touches me, and whose time of life is subject to such dangers as one can never guard too much against' (vol. 40, p. 240). Newcome (1627–95) was concerned that he would have rebellious offspring:

I consider the sad things that befal parents about children. May not one beg of God, that if it be his will, he will save us from such afflictions, and if he sees it good 1. That my children may be kept in health, or from sad and grievous distempers. 2. However not to die immaturely, if God see it good, esp. not untimely deaths. 3. That they may not die while they live; nor be a cross and exercise to us, by rebellious untowardliness. (105)

Newcome did not achieve his last wish – he was constantly upset at the behaviour of one of his sons (from his diary he appears to have been preoccupied with the problem of rebellious children). Another father, Richard Newdigate (1644–1710), managed to be 'pleasant with the Children', although he was 'very weary' (214) and Rule (1695– ?) referred to the disappointment he experienced with his children as 'The Greatest outward affliction this year that has befallen me' (MS, fo. 37v). Many of these diarists experienced discord from their offspring (see Pollock, 1981, ch. 8).

Two British diarists referred to the sinful nature they believed a child possessed. Oliver Heywood (1630–1702) wrote of his children: 'I am apt to over love them, but their inward deformity by the fal checks my too much dealing on their due proportions and desirable beauty' (vol. 1, p. 146). Mrs Housman (1680?–1735) tried to convince her 8-year-old daughter 'of her Sin and Misery, by Nature and Practice'; but when the child became upset, Housman softened her approach (81).

Two autobiographies supply more information on the concept of childhood. Walter Pringle (1625–67) was aware of the immaturity of a child, leaving a letter of advice to his youngest child as 'I knew not if I shall live till he comes to understanding' (24). Rich (1624–78), although she wanted some children, did not want a large family: 'when I was first married, and had my two children so fast, I feared much having so many, and was troubled when I found myself to be with child so soon'. She feared that too many children would ruin her figure and her husband thought they had insufficient income to support a large family: 'and my husband too was, in some measure, guilty of the same fault; for though he was at as great a rate fond of his children he had, as any father would be, yet when he had had two he would often say he feared he should have so many as would undo a younger brother' (32–3).

Discussion. Both the American and British texts of this century disclose parental appreciation of the capabilities of a child and the attempts to ensure that the education and advice given to a child were suited to the level of understanding the child had achieved. There is no doubt that childhood was both recognised and indulged, even if, as *C. Mather's remark reveals, the pastimes of children did not always meet with parental approval. Parents took a great deal of interest in their children and experienced much pride with regard to their behaviour and achievements – the children were indeed hopes for the future. Because these parents were involved with their offspring, the latter inevitably took up a good deal of parental time. The texts do contain evidence on parental ambivalence towards children – because the parent was so concerned for the child and/or had expectations for a child which he or she could not live up to.

Three diarists referred to the child's sinful nature (7 per cent of the 17th-century diaries). These were all Puritans and it should be remembered that Puritans did not consider that it was only children who were sinful. To a Puritan all were sinful, adult and child. They were thus not exulting in adult superiority, but simply trying to help their offspring come to terms with what Puritans regarded as an unpleasant but inescapable fact of life. These diarists were not being cruel; Original Sin was an integral part of their doctrine, and therefore they saw it as their duty to make their offspring aware of it (Powell, 1917; Schücking, 1969). Puritan parents sympathised with their children's distress and, as

Heywood's diary reveals, did not manage to consider their children as sinful as their religion demanded. Greven (*The Protestant Temperament*, 1977) discovered three child-rearing modes coexisting through the 17th to the 19th century in America – the 'evangelical', 'moderate' and 'genteel' modes. Greven characterises the evangelical parental type as being urged by his religion to view the child as depraved and thus be concerned with breaking the will of the child. He includes *C. Mather in this mode. However, Greven found that 'the truths that emerged from the feelings of many evangelical parents did not always conform to the truths that were taught by the Bible and the doctrines they also believed and acted upon' (31). This conclusion is borne out by the 17th-century texts studied here.

The images of children which these 17th-century texts provide do not correspond to those given by many historians. Hunt (*Parents and Children in History*, 1972) for example argues that children were not wanted or valued and were regarded as something to be controlled and not enjoyed. Stone (*The Family, Sex and Marriage in England*, 1977) suggests that the Puritans of the 17th century were so preoccupied with the concept of Original Sin that they were intent on breaking the will of the child. However, out of the texts studied here (at least 15 of which were written by Puritans), only 4 per cent refer to the concept of Original Sin and none wished to break the will of their child. My interpretation of such 17th-century sources as the diaries of Josselin and Martindale is markedly different from that of Stone among others. Recent research, though, does confirm my view (Greven, 1977; MacDonald, 1981; Macfarlane, 1979a; Wrightson, 1982). MacDonald argues from his study of Napier's manuscripts that children were wanted and valued – Napier's case notes provide information on the great distress experienced by women unable to bear children. In *English Society* Wrightson analyses several 17th-century diaries and comes to the conclusion that children were 'clearly desired', that parents 'found in their children a source of emotional satisfaction' (104, 114). Another author, Badinter (*L'Amour en Plus*, 1980), claims that paternal interest in children is a 20th-century phenomenon, but although 16th- and 17th-century fathers may not have taken an active part in the care of infants,[2] there is no denying the depth of their involvement with their offspring, the anxiety which the 17th-century fathers felt for their children's future and the amount of pleasure which these fathers derived from their children.

The 18th century. The American diarists saw children as bringing pleasure. *Amos Bronson Alcott (1799–1888) viewed his children as 'objects of great delight', adding: 'They are indeed the charm of my domestic life. They keep alive and vivid the sentiment of humanity, and are living manifestations of the theories of my intellect; for they are the models of our common nature from whence these theories are in no small degree framed and delineated' (55). *Benjamin Silliman (1779–1864) described his young son as giving 'only delight' to his parents (vol. 1, p. 276). There was a great deal of affectionate interaction between parents and their children. For example, *Martha Bayard (1769– ?) described returning home after seeing friends:

As they expected us the Child was kept up, and came running to the door with his Papa to meet us; never did my heart experience more lively sentiments of maternal affection and joy than in the moment I clasped him to my bosom – I could not speak; the dear fellow observing my emotions burst out a-crying, and, with his little arms round my neck, begged me not to cry, now I was with him. (59–60)

*Ezra Stiles (1727–95) enjoyed debating with his offspring, appreciating one daughter's 'ingenious and a new Thought' with regard to the scriptures (vol. 1, p. 341). *Mary Tucker (1775–1806) wrote of her adopted daughter that 'this little object grows every day nearer to my heart . . . her understanding is far beyond her years; her memory retentive, her sensibility exquisite' (315).

Apart from anxiety and discord, more evidence is given in these diaries on ambivalent attitudes experienced by parents towards their offspring. *Manasseh Cutler (1742–1823) believed that boys should board with 'sober families' when sent away to school rather than living in rooms by themselves as 'their immature age is an insuperable objection to their having so much the direction of themselves' (vol. 2, p. 255). *Carter, *Ebenezer Parkman and *William Sewall referred to the expense of children and *Huntington and *Jean Lowry mentioned the amount of time and care it took to look after children. *Susan Huntington (1791–1823), for example, wrote: 'The truth is, no one can govern a family of children well without much reflection, and what the world calls, trouble' (135). She also regretted her impatience with her offspring: '[my] unevenness of temper, which makes me impatient with the daily little faults of my children, such as carelessness, noisy and inattentive behaviour, &c.'[3] (326)

The majority of British diarists also regarded their offspring as 'delights'. For example, Jones (1755–1821) wrote of his children: 'May they ever rejoice with me when I rejoice, but never weep when I weep! May their cheerful spirits remain as long as possible unbroken! . . . May no impatience or fretfulness arising from my painful feelings ever check their sweet smiles or interfere with their innocent cheerfulness. Never let me grudge them all the happiness they can enjoy! (102) Macready (1793–1873) felt unworthy of his children: 'When I look at my children I think how little I have deserved the blessings that are heaped upon me – I *wish* to deserve them' (vol. 1, pp. 50–1). Sandford (1766–1830) derived great enjoyment from his daughters: 'S—— amuses me and pleases me very much: she has a great deal of lively humour and like her dear sister, is always cheerful' (vol. 1, p. 368).

Fry, Catherine Stanley and Arthur Young saw their children as future comforts. For example, Stanley (1792–1862) wrote: 'Are not one's children given to one that they may see for us, do for us, and that we may live over again in them when we have done living for ourselves' (324). Parents tended also to be proud of their children: W. Scott (1771–1832) believed: 'I have much to comfort me in the present aspect of my family. My eldest son, independent in fortune, united to an affectionate wife – and of good hopes in his profession; my second, with a good deal of talent . . . Anne, an honest, downright, good Scots lass, in whom I would only wish to correct a spirit of satire' (vol. 1, p. 39). Stedman (1744–97) wrote the following account of his son: 'My wonderful Johnny once drew a tooth to keep company to Mama, then physic'd and lived low for company to me, and at last innoculated for company to his brother George' (306).

Elizabeth Mascall, Rathbone, Thrale and Margaret Woods discussed how much time their offspring took up. Thrale (1741–1821), for example, remarked that her friends had reproved her for failing to note down all the sayings of Dr Johnson, and added:

little do these wise Men know or feel, that the Crying of a young Child, or the Perverseness of an elder, or the Danger however trifling of any one – will soon drive out of a female Parent's head a Conversation concerning Wit, Science or Sentiment, however She may appear to be impressed with it at the moment: besides that to a *Mere de Famille* doing Something is more necessary & Suitable than even hearing something; and if one is to listen all Eveng and write all Morning what one has heard; where will be the Time for tutoring, caressing, or what is still more useful, for having one's Children about one: I therefore charge all my Neglect to my young one's Account. (158)

A few diaries (those of Boswell, Jones and Skinner) contain evidence on the great expense of rearing children and the anxiety which an insufficient income produced. Some diarists described the impatience they experienced with regard to their children: Macready (1793–1873), for example, 'grew impatient and spoke with temper' when he tried to teach his daughter, although he continually regretted doing so (vol. 1, p. 166).

Attitudes to children

Amelia Steuart (1770?–1808) would have sympathised. She noted the exasperation her children could arouse in her, found them 'troublesome when in the house' during bad weather (102), and also wrote: 'The children sometimes put me out of humour when they are inattentive at their lessons – what a shocking example that is to them – & how ready they will be to follow it' (MS, fo. 133v). Absalom Watkin's diary contains similar evidence. Other diarists found their children too much to take at times. Fry (1780–1845) wrote: 'I feel, at times, deeply pressed down, on account of my beloved children. Their volatile minds try me' (145), and also: 'with my dear little ones I often feel myself a poor mother' (151). Woods (1748–1821) described her feelings with regard to her offspring: 'They may, indeed, in various ways, be deemed uncertain blessings; their lives are very precarious, and their future conduct proving as one could wish, not less doubtful. I already often look forward with anxiety, and the most ardent wishes for their welfare, in a state of permanent felicity' (85). Thomas Turner's (1793–1873) attitude would appear to be representative of nearly all the 18th-century diarists. He wrote to his daughter on the birth of her first child: 'You must expect, my dear child, now that you have a baby (and such an one *too*!!) to be visited with more anxiety than formerly, for bitters and sweets alternate with each other' (1875, p. 208).

Two autobiographies provide further information. *Abigail Bailey (1746–1815) described her offspring as being 'twined about my heart' (109) whereas *Hicks referred to the worry which children could cause. His sons were all invalids and died before the age of 20. None the less, *Hicks (1748–1830) recalled:

But, although thus helpless, the innocency of their lives, and the resigned cheerfulness of their dispositions to their allotments, made the labour and toil of taking care of them agreeable and pleasant . . . And when I have observed the great anxiety and affliction, which many parents have with undutiful children who are favoured with health, especially their sons, I could perceive very few whose troubles and exercises, on that account did not exceed ours. (14)

Discussion. More abstract concepts of childhood are found in the 18th-century texts, although only in a minority. The 18th has generally been regarded as the century in which more humane attitudes to children appeared and certainly the previous quotations do reveal a great deal of affection for, but also ambivalence towards, offspring. However, there is a problem with these 18th-century cases: the writers are far more articulate and far more capable of analysing their feelings. In the introspective texts, every facet of life is subjected to detailed scrutiny, not only childhood. The 18th-century writers described emotions and not just facts. Parents in the earlier centuries may not have shared the attitudes of the 18th-century writers, or they may simply not have been able to express such feelings.

If the quotations from the 17th and 18th centuries are compared, then it is revealed that the 18th-century texts do not refer to different aspects of childhood (apart from innocence) but discussed the same aspects in a far more eloquent manner. For example, both *Knight and *Bayard described their child greeting them with open arms. *Knight (1666–1727) did so in one line whereas *Bayard (1769– ?) took a whole paragraph – see also the entries of Newcome (1627–95) and Woods (1748–1821), both of whom refer to the care of offspring. Children are, though, referred to as 'innocent' for the first time (*Hicks and Jones). It is possible that this, in an age not noted for its religious fervour, was a reaction to the concept of children as depraved – only one diarist (Mascall, born 1702) in the large sample of this century referred to the doctrine of Original Sin. It is also possible that the emergence of the concept of innocence was due to the ideas of Locke (1694) and Rousseau (1763). Locke attacked the doctrine of Original Sin and Rousseau explicitly referred to children as innocent.[4]

Parents in both the 17th and 18th centuries reflected on the behaviour of their offspring, and some were unsure about their ability to regulate their children's behaviour in the long term (e.g. Newcome in the 17th century and Woods in the 18th). This suggests that, far from viewing their offspring as creatures to be repressed, parents – even though they did wish for obedient children – were aware that children possessed minds of their own and were not always willing to conform to parental expectations of conduct.

The 19th century. These diarists continued to derive pleasure from their children, as in the 18th century, particularly from their offspring's early reasoning abilities and their zest for life. *Rutherford Hayes (1822–93), for example, tried to explain death to his 4-year-old son by stating that God took good people to Heaven. He was amused when Birchie asked: 'Do He pull them up with a rope?' (vol. 1, p. 521). *Henry Longfellow (1807–82) wrote of his offspring: 'The interest with which they invest common things is quite marvellous' (176). The 'innocence' of childhood is again noted. *Miriam Colt (1817– ?) referred to 'Innocent and trusting childhood; sipping enjoyment like bees, whenever it can be found' (78), and *Ward (1841–1931) referred to his baby son as 'innocent' (186). A few diarists expressed regret at their children reaching maturity. *Amos Lawrence (1814–86) wrote: 'What strikes me most is the quickness with which our children have come and gone' (255). *Prentiss (1818–78) described her attitudes towards her children: 'I am inexpressibly happy in the mere sense of possession. I hate to have them grow up and to lose my pets, or exchange them for big boys and girls' (217).

*John Burroughs, *Lucy Lovell, *Prentiss, *John Todd and *M. Walker exhibited ambivalence towards their children. *Burroughs (1837–1921) referred to the 'joy' he experienced from having children; but also when comparing children to dogs wrote that the latter 'make no demands upon you, as does a child; no care, no interruption, no intrusion' (84). *Prentiss (1818–78), when her daughter was a few weeks old, wrote: 'I find the care of her very wearing, and have cried ever so many times from fatigue and anxiety, but now I am getting a little better and she pays me for all I do' (102). *Todd (1800–73) found the care of his young daughter very tiring. When she was aged $3\frac{1}{2}$ months he wrote: 'She cries more than any child that we ever saw. Sometimes there is not an hour in the night that we are not disturbed, and do not have to get up to still her . . . We sometimes get quite discouraged, and almost worn out with her' (209–10). *Todd later noted that Mary, at the age of 16 months 'grows well, and learns to talk fast, and to *us* is interesting; but oh, what a child! She never wants to sleep or to rest. It seems as if we should never have a night's rest or ever be free from headache and fatigue' (213).

The 19th-century British diarists also looked on their children with pleasure and affection.[5] A few described different images of childhood. Henry Alford and Cooper regarded their offspring as hopes for the future. For example, Cooper (1801–85) wrote of one son: 'How often have I meditated on his future aid and sympathy in all my thoughts and pursuits for the good of mankind' (vol. 2, p. 283). Gurney (1851–1932) wished to treat her children as adults: 'I tried to treat them [children] as if they were "grown up" people, and not as little children, and it is certain they rose to the trust placed in them, and their opinions became of value as their powers of mind and body increased' (39). Theodore Powys (1882–?), on the birth of his son, wrote: 'it is a goodly boy, and shows in its countenance, the old animal and the child man, also at times thought that beginneth to awaken, and in that thought is the life hidden' (77).

Hannah Allen, Mary Brabazon and Victoria Hanover (Queen Victoria) described their regrets as their children grew up. Brabazon (1848–1918), for example, wrote that '[This day] was a very sad one to me, as Normy [aged 13] for the first time put on manly attire, and it made me realise how time had passed, and that I must very soon bid him farewell. It is sad to feel his childhood is passing away (vol. 1, p. 56). Hanover (1819–1901) noted that her daughter of 3 was 'fast, alas! growing out of the baby – is becoming long-legged and thin' (1964, p. 273).

What is particularly striking of the 19th-century British diarists is the large increase in the references to feelings of ambivalence experienced by parents with regard to their children. Information on this topic is contained in 18 diaries[6] (32 per cent) (although it is perhaps not quite correct to regard Evelyn Waugh as ambivalent towards his offspring – he definitely disliked them). Hanover wrote: 'I have no tendre for them [infants] till they have become a little human; an ugly baby is a very nasty object – and the prettiest is frightful when undressed – till about four months; in short as long as they have their big body and little limbs and that terrible froglike action' (1964, p. 191). She also wrote of her children: 'I quite admit the comfort and blessing good and amiable children are – though they are also an awful plague and anxiety for which they show one so little gratitude very often!' (1964, p. 94). Johnston (1808–52) noted (when her children were away for a while): 'In the absence of all my precious party . . . I have had time to contemplate them; and I have perceived that I have allowed myself to be too much encumbered with cares and labours about them, so that the flowers of daily delight, love and companionship, have been in a measure choked' (169). T. Powys (1882–?), of his two young children, wrote:

The babes seem well, only there are many little disturbing influences that torment, distract and offend. I take it that Women have had almost too heavy a burden, the minding of babies being a heavier task than the bearing them. Though I believe one gains much by being thrown out of thought, set to baby games and made to brush and sweep and clean the little new life blossoms. Must they not be set in the way? (164)

Waugh (1903–66) wrote of his offspring: 'My children weary me. I can only see them as defective adults; feckless, destructive, frivolous, sensual, humourless' (1976, p. 640).[7]

One autobiography (that of William Lucas, 1804–61) contains evidence on the attitudes to children. He revealed great ambivalence with regard to his offspring and had doubts about his own competence as a parent:

I feel at times much depressed from not being able to make myself so companiable as I ought to be with my children. I never had the art of winning children or getting free with them and I do not think I now can expect to do it. It is so difficult to put up with their extreme vivacity, and so difficult to remember what we once were at their age, and to make due allowance for it. Christian humility and command of temper are great requisites and difficult attainments. When I look upon my seven boys I feel an inexpressible anxiety that they may turn out well, and feel how much depends upon my own example and character. (395)

Discussion. There are two distinctive features of the 19th-century texts: the appearance of nostalgia for childhood and also an increase in the proportion of texts (especially in the British sample) which describe ambivalence. These may be related to the massive social changes occurring in the 19th century. Perhaps the wish to retain childhood was linked to the wish to revert back to a predominantly rural society rather than live in an urban, technological one? It is possible too that the upheaval caused by the Industrial Revolution, the French Revolution and (for Britain) the wars with France – all of which deeply affected society – influenced parental attitudes to children. The writers studied were predominantly from the middle classes who were disturbed by what they believed to be the sinful state of society. In an attempt to counteract this, they perhaps may have been more concerned with the behaviour of their offspring. Three diarists, Allen, *Lovell and *M. Walker, believed their children had 'depraved hearts'. This confirms Greven's (1977) hypothesis that differing attitudes to children were in existence at any one time and opposes the arguments of other authors such as Stone (1977) that the concept of Original Sin disappeared with the 17th-century Puritans. *Lovell was a Quaker and *M. Walker a Methodist missionary.

Overall, a concept of childhood was in evidence by the 16th century, although there do seem to have been some changes in attitudes towards children. During the 18th and early 19th centuries some parents would appear to be more ostentatiously concerned with the state of childhood. Confronted with the minute dissection which many 18th-century writers applied to their lives, it is all too easy to dismiss earlier writers as 'indifferent', when clearly they were not. Though there is not the dramatic transformation in attitudes to children that has been argued (from parents regarding children as being at the bottom of the social scale to parents being preoccupied with their offspring's every need) there is more discussion of abstract notions of childhood, seen first in the 17th-century Puritans. This development is accompanied by more discussion on the undesirable aspects of childhood – the amount of time, trouble and money it took to rear children.

If the names by which children were referred to are studied, then it is discovered that they do correspond to the differences in attitudes and also reveal the growing literary powers of the writers. In the 16th century children were referred to as my son or daughter or, in the case of Clifford, 'the child'. When a more abstract term was employed, this was either 'comfort', 'benefit' or 'blessing'. In the next century children were still 'comforts' and 'blessings' and also 'plants', 'birds', 'lambs', 'flowers' and 'pledges'. In the 18th century children were 'buds', 'fruit', 'joys', 'delights', 'pleasures', 'stimulants', 'cares' and 'incumbrances' in addition to 'flowers', 'blessings', 'lambs' and 'plants'. In the 19th century children were referred to as 'lambs' and as 'balls of love', 'blossoms', 'chicks', 'gifts', 'pets', 'treasures', 'froglike', 'a plague' and 'trying'. The word 'it' used to refer to a child appeared in at least one text in each century: that of Wallington in the 16th; Josselin in the 17th; Oliver in the 18th and T. Powys, K. Russell and *Sterne in the 19th. Thus, as 'it' occurs throughout the centuries, it does not seem that the use of the word was evidence of the indifference to children before the 18th century, as has been argued by Shorter (1976). It appears that the term was used more with reference to young children – apart from Josselin's daughter who was aged 8, and not always referred to as 'it', the other children were all under the age of 5. In addition, Clifford referred to her young daughter as 'him'. It seems that young children were regarded more as sexless than worthless.

The vital question is how far, if at all, these changes in attitudes lead to or reflect changes in behaviour towards children. Did, for example, 18th-century parents treat their children any differently because they were concerned with analysing the nature of childhood? Would parents who regarded their child as depraved subject him to a system of rearing markedly different from parents who regarded their child as innocent? These questions will be considered in chapters 5 and 6.

How parents regarded the parental role

Very few parents articulated any abstract concepts of parental care (only 6 per cent of the total sample). Thus, in order to gain some idea of how they regarded parenthood, their attitudes were inferred from the behaviour they recorded, although it is realised that a specific behaviour could be the result of different attitudes. Table 6 summarises what appears to have been considered the most important aspects of the parental role, according to the evidence contained in the diaries. The manuscripts and autobiographies were too small a sample to categorise. What evidence they do contain will be discussed in relation to Table 6.

The protective function of parental care remains at a fairly constant level in the British diarists; but is much higher in the early American

Table 6. *Percentage division of parental functions as described in the diaries*

	Century							
Function*	16th		17th		18th		19th	
	A	B	A	B	A	B	A	B
n =	1	15	13	39	60	83	31	57
Educative	100	54	31	65	46	45	42	59
Protective	100	54	62	53	41	59	48	49
Disciplinary	100	31	31	23	10	23	13	22
Provider	100	39	23	28	19	21	13	13
Advisory	0	69	8	35	9	18	10	5
Trainer	0	0	15	8	18	19	16	14
Helper	0	7	14	33	17	6	7	2

* The functions were defined as follows:

Educative: The parents taught the child themselves or provided evidence to suggest they believed that education should be the subject of parental concern. For example, Heywood (1630–1702) wished to move house in order that his children would receive a better education and Smith (1673–1723) noted 'the great Circumspection' with which he chose his son's tutor.

Protective: The parents nursed their children through illness or revealed an awareness of the need to protect a child from harm. For example, Clifford (1590–1676) noted arranging baby-sitters for her daughter before going on a visit.

Disciplinary: The parents noted inflicting some type of punishment on a child.

Provider: The parents were concerned with the financial responsibility of children. For example, Jones (1755–1821) regretted signing a bond as 'I am a husband, – I am a father! I have robbed my wife and children! I *painfully* feel that I ought not to have done it.'

Advisory: The parents gave their child advice. For example, Evelyn (1620–1706) wrote: 'I gave my sonn an Office, with instructions how to govern his youth. I pray God give him the grace to make a right use of it.'

Trainer: The parents explicitly stated that they were concerned with the socialisation of a child by training or moulding the child into shape. For example, J. Taylor (1743–1819) had 'thought a deal on "Train up a child in the way he should go"'. *Huntington (1791–1823) believed that mothers 'have to mould the character of the future man, giving it a shape which will make him either an instrument of good in the world, or a pest in the lap of society'.

Helper: The parents gave the child whatever help he or she required. For example, by paying debts, furnishing a house, solving employment problems or by providing emotional support in times of crisis.

The above categories may not be mutually exclusive. Ideally a selection of diaries should have been read by another person in order to ascertain the reliability of the categories.

diarists. This is possibly due to the fact that these parents were living in a newly colonised land, fraught with health hazards and therefore tended to show more protection to their offspring. The American diarists would also appear to be less concerned with discipline from the 18th century on. This corresponds to the conventional image of the American child as being less restrained and more precocious than the British child (Bremner, 1970–3; Smith, 1977; Thompson, 1974). It is also possible that, after the American Revolution when America declared her independence from Britain in 1776, parents also severed ties with the British mode of child-rearing and set out to create a more independent child – as suggested by Bremner. On the other hand, the American sample for the 18th and 19th centuries may contain more of what Greven (1977) refers to as the 'moderate' parent. Greven argues that these parents were less concerned with the disciplining of children.

The American diarists would also appear to be less concerned with advising their offspring than the British diarists. Again this is probably related to their social situation: as emigrants to a new land they would be less able to help their children and possibly also wished their children to be independent. The large percentage of British diarists in the 16th century who advised their children results from their greater intervention in the marriage and career choice of their offspring. What is of particular interest is the rise of the training aspect of parental care – that of moulding a child into shape. It would seem to be non-existent in the 16th century, rising to a peak in the 18th. The following survey of the texts will be mainly concerned with the providing and training aspects of parental care – the other aspects will be discussed in later chapters.

The 16th century. None of the early diaries described how the diarist felt about rearing children or their attitudes to the parental role. They only noted educating and disciplining their children, nursing them when ill and endeavouring to ensure some supervision. In her autobiography, however, G. Mildmay (1552–1620) did refer to parental responsibility for the children produced: 'Parents have much to answer for before God, who neglect theyr duty in bringing up their children, or prefere any care, labour or delight in the world before that natural and most necessary imployment' (128). She believed in religious and academic education for children, that parents should endeavour 'to make theyr children good' (128), and also that care should be taken with the environment in which the child lived.

113

Attitudes to children

The 17th century. *C. Mather's (1663–1728) diary was the only one of the century to contain direct evidence on the moulding of a child. He was constantly preoccupied with the religious education of his children from their earliest years, attempting to make them come to terms with the 'sinful and woful condition' of their 'Nature'. He decided that in his duty as a parent, as well as promoting schools in the neighbourhood, he should 'grow yett more fruitful in my Conversation, with my little Birds, and feed them with more frequent and charming Lessons, of Religion' (vol. 7, p. 304). As each child reached the age of 11, or thereabouts, *Mather increased his attention to their religious state and increased his exhortations to them to strive for religious salvation. He was none the less prepared to adapt his religious training to suit the temperament of each child: 'I would carefully observe the Tempers of each of my Children. And, first, I would warn them against the peculiar Indiscretions and Temptations whereto they may be exposed in their Tempers. Then I would see, whether I can't suit their Tempers with Motives that may encourage and animate their Piety' (vol. 8, p. 91).

Another Puritan diarist, *Sewall (1652–1730) was less concerned than *C. Mather with the socialisation of his offspring. He did on one occasion attempt to make his 10-year-old son aware of the suddenness of death but then relented and comforted the child when he showed distress. His children had obviously absorbed the precepts of Puritan religion, although it is unclear from the diary whether this was due to *Sewall's training or to the sermons of other Puritan preachers.

Betty [daughter of 14] comes unto me almost as soon as I was up and tells me the disquiet she had when waked; told me was afraid should go to Hell, was like Spira, not Elected. Ask'd her what I should pray for, she said, that God would pardon her Sin and give her a new heart. I answer'd her Tears as well as I could, and pray'd with many Tears on either part; hope God heard us. (vol. 5, p. 422)

*Sewall may not have been as assiduous in the training of offspring as he should have been: 'Last night I dream'd that all my Children were dead except Sarah; which did distress me sorely with Reflexions on my Omission of Duty towards them, as well as Breaking oft the Hopes I had of them. The Lord help me to thankfully and fruitfully to enjoy them' (vol. 5, p. 399).

*Green, *C. Mather and *Sewall recorded providing financial assistance for their children. *C. Mather seemed to be obsessed with the idea of his own early death and is concerned that his children would be looked after, writing (many years before his death): 'I am now providing *Patrons* for my children, when they shall be *Orphans*' (vol. 8, p. 95).

Heywood and Housman, both British Puritans, also attempted to make their children realise the sinfulness of their nature. Housman (1680?–1735) in particular was concerned to instil religious principles into her daughter, for example the pernicious consequences of Sin; her own original depravity and the necessity to accept Christ in order to be saved. Byrom (1692–1763) was also concerned with the religious training of his children, although this was not as harsh as Heywood and Housman:

I consider them [children] as being the children of God who created them and who loves them, and that comforts me again. Let us take all occasions to incite them to love and think upon him; to look to themselves, their healths, and thoughts, and works, with a view to please him in everything they do or see or hear, &c. (vol. 40, p. 240)

Byrom was also preoccupied with the health of his offspring. For example, he wondered:

Do not children go too bare about the neck for coughs and cold weather? I am sure that herbs, roots and fruits in season, good house-bread, water porridge, milk fresh, &c, are the properest food for them, and for drink, water and milk, and wine, ale, beer, posset, or any liquor that is in its natural or artificial purity, whenever they have the least occasion for it. (vol. 34, p. 389)

Other diarists were more concerned with having enough money for their children rather than with their religious education. Mary Cowper (1685–1724) for example played for low stakes at basset: 'I played out of Duty, not Inclination, and having four Children, Nobody would think ill of me if for their Sakes I desired to save my Money' (14). Freke's (1641–1714) son was 'borne butt to two hundred pound A yeare, but By God's Blessing an my Indistry he will have after my death Above Two thousand pound A yeare' (50). At times the necessity of financial provision for offspring could cause a parent a great deal of anxiety. Newcome (1627–95) constantly hoped: 'I do not fall into reproach for not providing for my family (for this is now my constant fear lest I die and shall leave nothing for my wife and children)' (135).

Two autobiographies supply more details. Pringle (1625–67) saw himself as an adviser to his children and Rich (1627–78) wished to bring up her children 'religiously so that they might be good, and do good afterwards in their generation' (21).

Discussion. It appears from the texts that, from the 16th century, parents were prepared to accept the responsibility for the children they produced, regarding child-rearing as an essential duty. (Newson & Newson, 1976, suggest that this is fundamental to the parental role.) At least some of the Puritans wished to ensure that their children would grow up to be true to their faith. They were perhaps following the advice of such Puritan conduct books[8] as that of Gouge (*Of Domesticall Duties*, 1622), which ran to eight editions. Gouge emphasised the duty of parents to provide their children with religious instruction and advised that this religious instruction should be adapted to suit both the age and the temperament of each child. Those parents who were concerned with religious education wished to train the child in order to increase that child's chances of future salvation. Later diarists were more concerned with training the child to fit into society. Greven (1977) claims that many of the Puritans regarded the relationship between parent and child as a battle of wills. In practice, though, it seems that parents were prepared to compromise and adapt their training programme to suit the character of each child – see in particular *C. Mather's statement.

Illick in 'Child-rearing in England and America' (1976) has argued that 17th-century Americans were concerned with breaking the will of the child as advised by Locke. His sources are drawn only from New England. In the texts studied here, no parent endeavoured to break the will of the child, not even *C. Mather, despite his preoccupation with their religious education. If texts from elsewhere are used, such as the diary of *Byrd, a plantation owner from Virginia, then these reveal no evidence at all to support the idea that 17th-century parents wished to break the will of the child. *Byrd, for instance, was angry at his wife attempting to force their daughter to eat against her will. *Byrd is an example of the parental type Greven calls 'genteel' – parents who had no wish at all to break or curb their offspring's spirit.

The 18th century. The diaries of this century reveal an increase in concern with the formation of a child's character, this time not necessarily for religious reasons. The parents were concerned with 'training' the child. *John Adams (1767–1848) believed that for children there is a 'duty not less sacred than that of giving them bread . . . that of training them up in the way they should go' (16). *John Griffith (1713–76), after his wife's death, placed his children 'where they might be trained up in the way of truth' (59). *Tucker (1775–1806) wrote that the care of children 'is a burden pleasingly oppressive on my mind, to train up one little heir of immortality' (319).

*Huntington's (1791–1823) diary provides a great deal of information on how one mother regarded her function. On the birth of her first child, she was

Deeply impressed with a sense of the vast importance of a mother's duties, and the lasting effect of youthful impressions, I this day resolve to endeavour, at all times, by my precepts and my example, to inspire my children with just notions of right and wrong, of what is to be avoided and what pursued, of what is sacredly to be deserved and what unreservedly depreciated. (77)

Fifteen months later she wrote:

There is scarcely any subject concerning which I feel more anxiety, than the proper education of my children . . . The person who undertakes to *form* the infant mind, to cut off the distorted shoots, and direct and fashion those which may, in due time, become fruitful and lovely branches, ought to possess a deep and accurate knowledge of human nature. (88, present author's emphasis)

Six months after the above she noted:

Legislators and governors have to enact laws, and compel men to observe them; mothers have to implant the principles, and cultivate the dispositions, which alone can make good citizens and subjects. The former have to exert authority over characters already formed; the latter have to *mould* the character of the future man, giving it a shape which will make him either an instrument of good to the world, or a pest in the lap of society. Oh that a constant sense of the importance and responsibility of this station may rest upon me! that grace may be given faithfully to discharge its difficult duties. (100, present author's emphasis)

This is the first explicit reference in the texts studied to the socialisation of the child as opposed to a concern with his future salvation. The diaries of *Alcott, *Drinker, *James Fenimore-Cooper, *Elisha Mitchell, *Nancy Shippen and *Silliman also contain evidence on the training of a child.

The function of the parent as the provider of a child's needs continues to arouse anxiety. For example, *Alcott (1799–1888), who experienced many financial disasters, wrote that he wished, for the sake of his wife and children 'I could have a pair of profitable hands and marketable wits' (362). *Henry Hull (1765–1834) was willing to work as hard as was necessary to provide for his wife and children: 'for whose comfort I am so desirous, that I am willing to exert my strength in labouring for their subsistence both day and night, if necessary' (270). *W. Sewall (1797–1846) found that his farm did not provide a large enough income to support his family's needs. Thus he decided to start a school: '[I] rode around to most of my neighbours relative to a school which I have concluded to take charge of until harvest. I am compelled to do this for the benefit of my own children' (244).

Attitudes to children

Many of the British diarists were similarly concerned with the 'training' of their children.[9] Thomas Moore (1779–1852), referring to the 'loving and loveable nature' of his daughter felt 'how ticklish will be the steerage of such a creature, when her affections are brought more strongly out' (vol. 2, p. 245). J. Taylor (1743–1819) had 'thought a deal on "Train up a child in the way he should go"' (118). Melesina Trench (1768–1837) believed that the 'first object of education is to train up an immortal soul' (1837, p. 7). Woods (1748–1821) wrote of her children: 'I would encourage them to lay open their little hearts, and speak their thoughts freely; considering that by doing so, I have the best means of correcting their ideas, and rectifying whatever may be amiss' (427).

Mascall (1702–94) was the only diarist of the century who believed that parents should make their offspring aware of their inherent sinfulness, noting that she endeavoured 'to my utmost to convince my children of their natural sinful state, & ye necessity of a Saviour & to teach ym wt to believe & practice yt they may be saved' (13).

As in the 16th and 17th centuries, the financial aspect of parental care is again referred to in the diaries. Jones (1755–1821), for example, regretted signing a bond as 'I am a husband, – I am a father! I have robbed my wife & children! I *painfully* feel that I ought not to have done it' (197). Mantell (1790–1852), having little success in his chosen employment, wondered whether to move: 'My little ones however render it necessary that I should pause before I take a step fraught with such importance to them, and I am therefore in that anxious state of suspense, than which nothing can be more unpleasant' (47). Macready (1793–1873) wished to ensure that his children would be better provided for than he was: 'my own experience of the painfulness of struggling without assistance through life makes me nervously anxious to afford my dear children some little support in their journey through life, which I wish to be an active and industrious one' (vol. 1, p. 135).

The 18th-century British diaries contain supplementary information on parental care. Boscawen (1719–1805) wrote to her husband while he was away at sea: 'Have no anxious thoughts for the children. Assure yourself they shall be my sole care and study and that my chief purpose and the business of my life shall be to take care of them and to procure for them a sound mind in a healthful body. God give me success!' (1940, p. 54) Steuart's (1770?–1808) manuscript reveals that she also regarded child-rearing as a 'sacred charge' (MS, fo. 95). Elizabeth Wynne's (1778–1857) husband, on the other hand, was concerned that his wife would take too much care of their children. He wrote to her, also while away at sea:

if there is any subject on which I feel diffident, it is that your kindness and affection for the Children will lead you to take too much care of them, believe me nothing tends more to health than exercise and Air, and that the more they are out of the house the better . . . Consider what your boys must undergo before they arrive even at Manhood, and I am sure you will agree with me that it is not wise to bring them up too tenderly. (vol. 3, p. 96)

Maria Fox (1793–1844) thought that childhood should be a happy period; that children should be encircled in an atmosphere of kindness and love, although with some restraints:

The dear children have a constant claim, requiring the judicious restraint and direction of parental discipline. Their desire to be with us, and the enjoyment we have in their society, holds out continual inducement to indulge them, perhaps beyond the proper point, but we have ever been fearful of weakening, by undue restraints, that entire confidence they repose in us. How difficult it is, in all things, to maintain the golden mean. (309)

She was also prepared to spend a good deal of time with her offspring: 'I used to wonder, when I was a girl, that mothers were so absorbed about their children, as to have little inclination, at times, for anything else. Now, I wonder when I see a mother who is fond of going out' (250).

Hannah Backhouse and Fry were unsure how to rear their offspring. H. Backhouse (1787–1850), for example, wrote that 'Children, and the education of them, is a subject of too much anxiety. Too sensible perhaps of idleness and awkwardness; too earnest for, and valuing too highly, intellectual cultivation, easy action, and decorum of manner' (50). Finally, Townsend (1757–1826) referred to parents as 'fond and anxious parents, who have sacrificed your ease, your rest, your worldly property, your health, your all, for the comfort and prosperity of your offspring; perhaps, too, for unfortunate, for disobedient, yea, even for cruel children' (34–5).

Few of the 18th-century autobiographies provide information on parental care, although one mother, *Bailey (1746–1815), was concerned with protecting her children from the abuses of their father. (He was stern with his children and formed an incestuous relationship with at least one of his daughters. *Bailey eventually obtained a divorce.) William Carvosso (1750–1834) wished his children to be religious and, as his youngest son remained unconverted: 'I felt my mind deeply impressed with the duty of embracing the first opportunity of opening my mind to him, and talking closely to him about eternal things' (46).

Discussion. The 18th-century texts contain the first specific references to the 'training' of a child. These parents believed that a child could be moulded into shape. There was also, particularly in the British diaries, evidence on the growing unsureness of the ability of parents to rear their children properly; feelings of incompetence predominate. The 18th century is the first one in which women wrote diaries to any great extent and there would appear to be different functions assigned to the mother compared with the father. The former is concerned with the training, the latter with providing enough money for the family. Many of the 18th-century mothers were devoting every waking moment to the care of their offspring. Greven argues that 'moderate' parents were concerned with the process of the development of their children, wishing to mould their character, as in the case of *Huntington. Thus they believed that the child was not depraved but pliable and their duty as a parent was to bend the child's will in order to achieve respect and obedience without repression.

The 18th century is generally put forward as an example of humane, enlightened modes of rearing compared with previous centuries, although de Mause (*The Evolution of Childhood*, 1976) does suggest that 18th-century parents wished to conquer a child's mind 'in order to control its insides'. From a child's point of view it is debatable whether the 18th century really was more humane; a minority of children were now subjected to a rigorous training procedure in order to produce model citizens. These parents would seem to be displaying what Ariès (1960) calls an 'obsessive love' and they were clearly uneasy about their new role – as with attitudes to children, these parents were more self-consciously aware of their duties as a parent. This articulated awareness of the parental role may be due to the influence of Locke (1694) rather than Rousseau (1763). Locke emphasised how much the parent was responsible for the development of the child and the damage a parent could do by rearing a child incorrectly. Rousseau, on the other hand, suggested that a child should be allowed to develop without adult intervention. It was also Locke who argued that children should not be 'coddled'; they should be encouraged to bathe in cold water and play outside in all weathers. Wynne's husband seems to have been influenced by Locke's views, hoping that his wife would not rear their children too tenderly. The quotation from Wynne's diary is in marked contrast to that of Byrom in the 17th century who was concerned about the effects of cold weather on his offspring's health.

The 19th century. Those American diarists who recorded in their diary their efforts to mould their child appeared to be even more concerned than the 18th-century parents with having the child comply with the parents' will (*Elizabeth Duncan, *Lovell, *Prentiss, *Todd and *M. Walker). For example, when *Lovell's (1809?– ?) daughter aged 5 refused to say 'Good Morning' to a visitor, she was sent to her room, then smacked, followed by a lecture from her father and finally threatened with a stick, and Caroline at that yielded. *Lovell regarded this defiance as 'if the enemy had her completely in his power, and was trying to effect her ruin' and also as an example of 'the depraved state of the unrenewed heart' (89). *Lovell wanted her daughter to be obedient: 'We wished to train her to a habit of implicit compliance with our directions, and on this account we frequently had occasion to correct her in such a way as we thought would best promote this object' (84). *Todd (1800–73) described his view of child-rearing:

The first thing a boy needs is a good, firm, powerful constitution *worked* on him, so that in after-years he can endure great fatigue and labor. The next thing he needs is a firm, decided government over him, to which his will shall bow without any reserve, and with cheerfulness. The last thing (though the first in reality and importance) is piety – a heart submissive and obedient to God. (285)

Other parents were not so involved with the training of their offspring. *Hayes (1822–93) wrote: 'I would much prefer they would lay up a stock of health by knocking around in the country than to hear that they were the best scholars of their age in Ohio' (vol. 2, p. 437). *Emily Judson (1817–54) loved her children just as they were: 'I love them for their own sakes; for sweeter more lovely little creatures never breathed; brighter, more beautiful blossoms never expanded in the cold atmosphere of this world' (230).

The idea of parental sacrifice reappears in *Samuel Howe's (1801–76) diary (see Townsend in the 18th century): 'We must and ought to love our children with all our hearts; love them better than ourselves, but be willing to sacrifice our own feelings and inclinations for their good' (295).

On the other hand, the financial aspect of parental care seems to arouse less concern in the 19th century, although it mattered to those diarists who referred to it. *Lawrence (1814–86), for example, wrote: 'My chief care and ambition for this world now centres in the welfare of my children' (165). He gave each child a patrimony when they reached the age of 21 so that they would be financially independent.

The British diarists of this period were also concerned with the formation of a child's character (Allen, Cobden-Sanderson, E. Gaskell, Gurney, Hanover, Francis Palgrave, F. Russell and Tregelles). Thomas Cobden-Sanderson (1840–1922) trained his son of 19 months to go to sleep when put in his cot rather than to cry: 'He now goes to bed noon and night and to sleep without a cry. If this can be done, how much more may not be done? What a responsibility! What a superb instrument, gymnast of virtue and of beautiful conduct, may not a man be made early in life!' (vol. 1, p. 247). He was one of the few diarists to refer to a theorist's views on child-rearing: 'Our anxiety for his future makes us careful in ridding him of bad habits and making his will "supple" as Locke – whom we are now reading – would say' (vol. 1, p. 246). E. Gaskell (1810–65), who also read Locke, as did *Huntington (1791–1823), referred to her 'extreme anxiety in the formation of her little daughter's character' and wished to teach Marianne self-control as soon as possible. For example, Marianne at 13 months took a dislike to being bathed, however: 'this last two days she has tried hard to prevent herself from crying, giving gulps and strains to keep it down. Oh! may this indeed be the beginning of self-government' (16). At the age of 3½ Marianne was sent to infant school in the morning: 'not to advance her rapidly in any branch of learning . . . but to perfect her habits of obedience, to give her an idea of conquering difficulties by perseverance and to make her apply steadily for a short time' (34). Gaskell did hope that her daughter would not be 'adversely affected' by the school and other pupils.

Frances Russell (1815–98) had a specific aim in rearing her children. She hoped that (reminiscent of G. Mildmay in the 16th and Rich in the 17th century): 'each of my children may add some little ray of light by thought, word, and deed to help in dispelling the darkness of error, sin, and crime in this and all other lands' (227). T. Powys (1882– ?) believed that children recompense parents for their care: 'The babes reward all one's labour, every night time one feels the reward, the feeling of the Father that increaseth, that taketh away from the self and giveth to the child' (164). Hewlett (1861–1923) would appear to be satisfied with his performance as a parent, writing of his children: 'They are never out of my thoughts, and I can't reproach myself in their regard at least' (MS, fo. 79).

The parental obligation to provide for their offspring was again referred to. John Kitto (1804–54), when convalescing, was asked to walk six miles a day by his doctor and was unwilling to do so: 'However, seeing that there are so many little ones whose immediate welfare seems to have been made dependent upon my existence', he decided to walk (625). Tregelles (1806–84) was also anxious about providing for his offspring:

I have sought by insuring my life, and by a careful investment of the payments I receive for my exertions in business, to lay by a suitable provision for my family. This has cost me much toil and some anxiety at times; but I have acted from a sincere desire to do right, and not from the love of accumulation. (118)

The autobiographies contain similar information. Henry Dawson (1811–78) was upset when he could give little financial assistance to his sons to carry out their hobbies: 'It is true they tried to make a shop in part of their bedroom, but it made me melancholy to see how little they could carry out their notions in the face of such difficulties' (82). Lucas (1804–61) was very much aware of the different temperaments of each of his nine children, describing each child in his autobiography. He did not have a high regard for his competence as a father, for example he disliked inflicting corporal punishment (although he did so): 'for after all how much more important is the good example of parents when they can gain their children's affections than all systems, rules or rostrums of education' (164). Later he wrote: 'Often do I pray for more ability to guide and influence the dear dispositions of our dear children' (241).

Discussion. As in the 18th century, those parents who referred to parental care were concerned with the active formation of their child's character. There would appear to be in the American diarists a lessening of this desire, see for example *Hayes and *Judson – was this a response to Rousseau? The British diarists seem to be still following the advice of Locke – Cobden-Sanderson and Gaskell noted that they were reading his work. Locke gives a great deal of advice on how to 'weed' out a child's faults in order that a parent may 'plant what Habits you please'. However, these parents are a minority, others are not so concerned with the active formation of a child's character.

To sum up, many aspects of parental care have changed very little. Nevertheless, the amount of parental interference in a child's development would appear to increase during the 18th century. In the 17th century a small number of diarists wished to ensure that their children would be good Puritans. This training took the form, following the precepts of the non-conformist religions, of making a child aware of his inherently sinful nature and so paving the way for his salvation. In order to further the continuance of these new faiths, it would be necessary to ensure that children imbibed the religious principles so that they would conform as adults. It is not till the 18th century that some parents became concerned not with forming a child so as to ensure his salvation but with forming a child who would be accepted by society. In this development, the different attitudes of these 18th-century diarists are connected with their different rearing method – although it is unclear whether these attitudes reflected their behaviour or produced it. These parents saw their children as 'delights'; but as imperfect delights and therefore reared their children in such a way as to 'weed out' (Locke) these imperfections.

In each century some parents referred to the financial aspect of children. These parents were concerned not only with having sufficient income in order to rear their children properly; but also with leaving enough money to provide for their children if the latter became fatherless (see for example Newcome, *Hull and Tregelles). At a time when the state gave very little financial assistance to families, the expense of rearing children would be an important matter, and in the less affluent families a cause for concern.

Stone (1977) has portrayed the child-rearing practices of the English aristocracy in a very bad light. He regards them as indifferent, often cruel, parents with no interest in child care. The aristocratic texts studied here do not bear out Stone's thesis. Many such parents regarded the rearing of children as their duty, were exceedingly interested in the welfare of their young and enjoyed the company of their offspring – as shown by the texts of Clifford and G. Mildmay in the 16th century and Blundell, Rich and Slingsby in the 17th, for instance. Several aristocratic parents were just as anxious about the expense of children and as convinced of the parental necessity to ensure financial provision for them as the not so wealthy parents (e.g. Cowper, Freke and Rich).

Illness and death

It is generally agreed that past parents were at best indifferent to the wellbeing of their offspring and at worst actually harming them by neglect and abuse. Parents prior to the 18th century, it is claimed, were unconcerned when a child was ill and unmoved at a child's death. An analysis of the primary sources brings to light quite a different tale and reveals the anxiety and distress which most 16th- and 17th-century parents experienced – emotions which many authors maintain they were incapable of feeling.

The 16th century. The one American diarist for this period, *Jefferay (1591–1675), sent for the doctor 'on some small Sickness of one of my children' (71). He gives no indication of his feelings but sending for the

124

doctor implies both a concern for the child's welfare and a wish for the child to recover.

Of the British diarists, Dee, Oglander and Powell simply noted that their children were ill, although Powell did visit his married offspring when they were unwell. Dee (1527–1608) did observe when his 6-month-old son was ill: 'Arthur fell sick, stuffed with cold fleym, could not slepe, had no stomach to eat or drink as he had done before' (7). Thus he was sufficiently aware of his baby to know of the infant's normal behaviour patterns. Dee further noted that an elder son, aged 8, 'slept well' after a stick had accidentally pierced his left eyelid. This suggests that Dee was sufficiently concerned to either watch the child at night or at least inquire how he had slept the next day. Dee also hoped 'God spede the rest of the cure!' which contradicts the idea of parental indifference (125). Other diarists described their anxiety. Clifford (1590–1676) wrote when her daughter aged 2 years and 8 months was ill: 'the Child had a bitter fit of her ague again, insomuch I was fearful of her that I could hardly sleep all night, so I beseeched G O D Almighty to be merciful to me and spare her life' (54). Hope (1585?–1646) referred to the illness of one of his older children: 'The faittis of sickness increseit on my deir sone . . . The Lord pittie and spair him, if it be his holy will' (194). H. Mildmay's (1592–1667) diary contains frequent references to his son Charles (aged about 11) during the latter's illness and Mildmay was clearly worried about him: 'My poor Charles very unruly and ill; God help him and comfort with help and care.' The next day he wrote: 'This was a sad night with poor Charles and all of us God amend him' (66). Winthrop's (1587–?) son felt ill while away at university. His mother wrote to him: 'I am very sory for thy sicknes and pray to God night & day for thy good recovery which I desire with the most intire affection of my hart, and wish my self present with thee' (280).

The 17th century. Out of the 29 diarists who referred to the illness of a child, only three (*Samuel Danforth, J. Erskine and *John Pike) revealed no concern. The other diarists were all exceedingly concerned.[10] *Byrd (1674–1744) wrote when his infant son and young daughter were ill: 'I rose by 5 o'clock and sent our excuses to Colonel Hill for not going with him to Colonel Harrison's because our children were both sick. However, they came to see us in our affliction' (1941, p. 181). A few months later *Byrd's daughter was ill again and he recorded: '[I] ate no breakfast, I was so concerned for my daughter' (1941, p. 213). *I. Mather (1639–1723) noted that he 'sat up all night with Nath who continued to be ill'. The next day 'Nath continuing ill', *Mather reported he was 'much hindred in my studyes' (341). The day after that *Mather wrote: 'Much interrupted in studyes by Nats illness . . . Little doe children think, wt affection is in ye Heart of a Father' (341). *Mather believed that his son's illness was the result of *Mather's own sins. *C. Mather (1663–1728), son of the above, also believed that his sins led to the illness and death of his offspring and that he should resign himself to the will of God. However, the last point does not mean that he was unconcerned when a child was ill; on the contrary, *Mather's diary contains a great deal of information regarding his anxiety during a child's illness. For example, of one daughter, *Mather wrote:

my little and my only, *Katharin*, was taken so dangerously sick, that small Hope of her Life was left unto us. In my Distress, when I saw the Lord thus, *quenching the coal that was left* unto mee, and rending out of my Bosom one that had lived so long with mee, as to steal a *Room* there, and a *Lamb* that was indeed unto me *as a Daughter*, I cast myself at the Feet of His Holy Soveraignty. (vol. 7, p. 179)

*Mather did 'resign' his child to God, but also begged for her recovery. Of another daughter, who had recently been accidentally burnt, and was now suffering from a fever, *Mather remarked: 'My Soul was many wayes *wounded* with the deplorable State, which this *little Bird*, that had already undergone so much Calamity, was again fallen into' (vol. 7, p. 303). *Mather revealed the same anxiety when any of his offspring were unwell, yet Stone claims: 'There is little evidence in Mather's diaries that he was emotionally deeply committed to any of his children' (214).

The British diarists gave evidence of a similar concern. Freke (1641–1714) heard that her adult son was very ill 'which soe Terryfied & Frightened mee thatt I had noe Reste in mee' (46). Housman (1680?–1735), during her 4-year-old daughter's illness, wrote: 'He [God] hath been touching us in a very tender Part. Hath threatened to take from us the Delight of our Eyes, the Joy of our Hearts, with Stroke. But had Pity upon us, and in the midst of Judgement remembered Mercy' (62). Newcome (1627–95) also thought his actions could lead to the illness of one of his children. For example, when his young daughter was ill, he wrote: 'I was much afflicted herewith, lest the Lord should seem hereby to manifest his displeasure for my removing [house]' (73). Later this child was sent into the country in an attempt to cure her of rickets. When Newcome visited her: 'She met us on her feet, which was a great rejoicing to us' (93). After one of his sons recovered from a fever, Newcome noted 'that heaviness endured for a night, but joy came in the morning' (97).

Mary Woodforde's (1638–1730) son received a dangerous cut in his finger while away at school. She wrote: 'He is at a great distance from us and all his relations, but Oh, my dear Lord do thou supply all our love and care in taking him into thy special protection' (19). The manuscripts of Andrew Rule (1695– ?), Owen Stockton (1630–80) and Mrs Stockton (?) depict a similar picture of parental care. The only child diarist of this century to refer to illness, James Fretwell (1699–1772), noted that when he was unwell at the age of 18, 'my dear mother sate up with me till betwixt 3 and 4 o clock' (195).

One father did seem to be less upset by his offspring's illnesses. Elias Pledger's (1665– ?) daughter suffered from tuberculosis and her father was worried that he and his wife were more concerned with their daughter's frailty than her spiritual state: 'I fear we have loved her out of her place and have not sufficiently resigned our wils to gods, it may be we have been more concerned for y life of her body yn her soul' (MS, fo. 63). Though Pledger did pray for the recovery of his children, he seems to have been more prepared to return them to God than other diarists. When his son of 3 was ill, Pledger wrote that 'we did not desire him of god on any other acct for his service in the world & rather yn he should lived to God's dishonour we wr willing to part with him then' (MS, fo. 74). Even in this case, though, it would be unfair and unjust to accuse Pledger of being completely indifferent to his children's health.

Two autobiographers referred to the illness of their own children. Pringle (1625–67) recalled that when his eldest son was ill he (Pringle) 'submitted' to the will of God and his son recovered. Rich (1624–78) thought her own behaviour resulted in her infant son's illness, because she loved her son too much. Rich had been trying, unsuccessfully, to be more religious; but now promised God that she would improve her faith if her child's health improved – which it did. When the same son at 19 caught smallpox, Rich wrote: 'I shut up myself with him, doing all I could both for his soul and body' (29).

Discussion. It has become commonplace to argue that parents prior to the 18th century were unconcerned about the welfare of their children due to the high infant mortality rate. In order to protect themselves from too much emotional distress, parents maintained a distance between themselves and their offspring. The results from the 16th- and 17th-century texts do not support this argument; most parents were only too clearly anxious and upset by the ill-health of a child. In fact, it appears that the high rate of infant mortality operated to increase their anxiety.

Attitudes to children

Parents were very much aware of the frequency with which children died and a childish cold or cough was enough to send most of the parents into a paroxysm of panic. From his examination of the diaries of Josselin, Martindale and Newcome, Wrightson (1982) also found that the high infant mortality rate 'led not to indifference but to a persistent anxiety for their children in the face of the hazards of illness and accident' (109). More evidence on the sometimes acute unease that parents could feel can be found in MacDonald (1981). The sleepless nights endured by many 16th- and 17th-century parents and the willingness of most to nurse their offspring themselves, even to the point of sitting up all night (see the diaries of *Byrd, Clifford and *I. Mather for instance), testify to the deep emotional bonding between parent and child – and it should be noted fathers were just as anxious as mothers.

The age of the child was not related to the depth of parental concern – those parents who did not record any unease when a young child was ill, did not note any for an older child either. In the 16th century, Clifford, Dee and Powell noted the illness of a child under the age of 5. Clifford was the only one of the three to reveal any distress. However, Dee and Powell referred to the illnesses of their older offspring in the same brief manner in which they noted the illness of their younger offspring. Of the 17th-century texts, 56 per cent contain information on the illness of children under the age of 5. All the parents were upset, apart from *Danforth and *Pike who also did not record any distress at the illness of an older child. The religious diarists would appear to temper their anxiety with religious faith. Nevertheless, it seems that their actual feelings were different from those which they tried to express in terms of religious fortitude – most of the parents found it difficult to resign themselves to the will of God (Ebenezer Erskine, Housman, *C. and *I. Mather and Pledger). Thus we have parents whose strong religious convictions counselled them to feel no anxiety, but who found it impossible to maintain a state of Christian resignation when confronted with the illness of their own child.

The 18th century. Eight diaries (12 per cent) out of those which dealt with illness merely stated that a child was ill, without giving any indication of their feelings (*Carter, *Silas Constant, Goff, *Jacob Hiltzheimer, Mascall, *James Parker, *Ebenezer Parkman and *Stiles). The two British diarists would appear to be unconcerned when a child was ill. For example, Elizabeth Goff (1730?– ?) did not return home from a visit even though she knew that one daughter was very ill and her younger children had measles or whooping cough. In addition, when one of Mascall's (1702–94) sons was ill, his mother merely hoped the illness had improved his soul. The remaining diarists were evidently anxious.[11] For example, *Alcott (1799–1888) recorded sitting through the night with his daughter Elizabeth. Five years later, when Louisa caught typhoid fever while working away from home, *Alcott immediately went to collect her and both parents nursed her 24 hours a day until she recovered. *James Gordon (1713–68) wrote when his baby daughter was unwell: 'A great company here, which is rather disagreeable, as the child is so unwell' (232). When another young daughter was ill, he noted: '[I] intended to go to Richmond, but did not incline to leave my dear little child' (233).

One young mother described her state of mind during the illness of her 17-month-old daughter; *Shippen (1763–1841) recorded:

My baby thank God is much recover'd. These six days past she has been so ill her life has been despair'd off. I nurs'd her attentively – I never left her more than an hour altogether – O! what I have suffer'd! for several hours I thought she was dying – what I felt then it is impossible to describe – I have been ill too myself with fatigue & want of sleep – Mamma was much affect'd & fain wou'd have taken part of the trouble off my hands but I would not permit it. (151)

*Huntington (1791–1823) described her feelings at the illness of her infant son: 'Yesterday my little son appeared very sick. I was awake with him most of the night, and was apprehensive of two disorders, one in consequence of a bad fall, the other the effect of having been exposed to an infectious disease . . . I thought I should sink under the affliction of a separation from my child' (80). The two American child diarists who referred to illness also described parental solicitude and care – *James Gallatin (1797–1876) and *Anna Winslow (1759–1779). *Gallatin in fact believed that his mother fussed too much whenever he was sick.

The British parents revealed a similar anxiety. For example, Boscawen (1719–1805) wrote:

All three children have been ill at once. The two girls had coughs and fevers occasioned by teeth, which were lanced immediately. The boy had a violent and never-ceasing cough . . . You can imagine the state I was in. For poor Fanny I trembled, her breath and her lungs being already so oppressed that 'twas pain to hear her, and the slut [*sic*] would not drink anything, though she was dying of thirst. There was no sort of liquor I did not try her with . . . As to the dear boy, he would at all times take anything I brought him; but then I dreaded a bleeding, which would have been necessary in the measles. I did not doubt my being able to persuade him to it. I had even got his promise. But I distrusted myself. I doubted my being able to stay in the room, and the least signs of fear in me would have inspired and justified his. (1940, p. 74)

Attitudes to children

Boswell (1740–95) was 'tortured with apprehension' when he thought his 2½-year-old daughter had measles (vol. 10, p. 255). Mary Fletcher (1739–1814), when her adult daughter was ill, wrote: 'I felt it as a knife in my heart. She is my earthly all' (186). Fox (1793–1844) 'was distressed' to see her infant son's suffering when he was ill (191). Fry (1780–1845) was 'very low and anxious on account of our little baby, who appeared uneasy and in much pain. She seemed suddenly really unwell. I wish my heart not to be too much set on her, or her health' (98). Fry believed that she should resign herself to God's will: 'I desire, with regard to my dear lambs, to be ready to give them up, if called for at my hand; for we know not what is best for them; and I believe we should seek to look upon them, as charges committed to our stewardship, and not as our property' (124). None the less, in practice, she did not feel it was easy to subscribe to this belief and continued to be upset when a child was ill. W. Scott (1771–1832) of his adult daughter observed: 'Anne is ill this morning. May God help us! If it should prove serious, as I have known it in such cases, where am I to find courage or comfort?' (94) Another father, Peter Oliver (1741–1823) tried everything he could think of to help his ill daughter who appeared to be in the early stages of tuberculosis. She was taken to the seaside, taken 'frequently to the cold bath but to no purpose', and also sent into the country' (MS, fo. 18).

Grant (1797–?) was the sole autobiographer to include any details of illness. This may be because the kind, loving care Grant and her siblings received when they were ill differed markedly from the usual harsh mode they were subjected to. This example indicates the complexity of attitudes to parental care. Grant's parents were by modern standards cruel parents and yet were distressed when a child was sick, nursed the child themselves and did everything they could to make the child as comfortable as possible.

Discussion. There had been remarkably little alteration in the type of parental reaction to childish indispositions. As with earlier texts, the age of the child was immaterial with regard to parental concern during illness. Those diarists who described no distress whenever their children were ill did so for both infants and older children. If the diaries of Goff and Mascall are considered, there would appear to be definite unconcern in some 18th-century parents. Although the fact that a diarist does not specify concern cannot be taken to imply that he or she did not experience any, the fact that Goff did not return home from a visit when her children were very ill does suggest that she did not suffer from undue anxiety.

130

The religious fortitude which is revealed in the 17th-century texts reappears in some of the 18th-century texts (*Bayard, A. Darby, Fry, Faith Gray, *Huntington, Jones, Hannah Kilham, Macready, Rathbone, Elizabeth Rowntree, Sandford, Dan Taylor). These parents also found that their religious beliefs and parental emotions did come into conflict – although they firmly believed they should submit to God's will, they found it very difficult, if not impossible to do so.

There does not seem as if much could be done for sick children. Few parents called a doctor, but instead tried remedies recommended by friends and relatives – if a successful remedy was found, parents were keen to pass the idea on (MacDonald, 1981; Wrightson, 1982). The country air was believed to be beneficial by parents from the 16th to 18th centuries (e.g. *Huntington, Newcome, Oliver, Rathbone and Wallington) and was often used to strengthen ailing children.

The 19th century. Out of 48 diaries referring to illness, Thomas Acland and Waugh were the only two to remark simply that their children were ill. Waugh (1903–66) appears to have been indifferent, writing, for example, 'In the nursery whooping cough rages I believe' (1976, p. 667). The other diarists were not so unmoved.[12] *Howe (1801–76) was going to start a journey but, as his daughter of 7 was ill, he delayed his visit: 'her present illness, though other people tell me it is nothing, seems to me alarming . . . As soon as she is better, or so that I shall not worry and be pained by the thought that the poor thing is asking for Papa, I shall start' (369). *Prentiss (1818–78) recorded great anxiety when any of her offspring were ill. For example she stayed up all night with her 2-year-old daughter: 'But as we sat hour after hour watching the alternations of color in her purple face and listening to that terrible gasping, rattling sound . . . Oh, why should I try to tell myself what a night it was God knows, God only! How he has smitten me by means of this child, He well knows' (144). *Todd's (1800–73) 14-month-old daughter was very ill:

I go to her bedside and gaze, and hear her short groans, as long as I can stay and then go away to weep. Wonderful skill! in creating and planting in the human heart that wonderful passion which we call *parental*! As I go about the house (and oh, this feeling is to increase to agony!) I see her little chair, her clothes, her things; here she sat, there she sung, there she gave me her sweet looks; every spot is associated with the past, and with fear. (241)

*Todd was reluctant to lose his child: 'I know we ought not to refuse to give this dear one, this sweet child, back to her Maker and Father: she must be better off than with us; but oh, the agony of breaking the heart-strings!' (241)

The British diarists described the same concern. For example, Christopher Addison (1869– ?) was concerned about the health of his children during the first world war: 'it was painfully evident that their vigour is seriously affected by the war diet . . . I believe the limitation of sugar in one form or another, is largely responsible for their condition' (422). Later his children caught measles and his youngest son 'was seriously ill . . . so that I came away this morning feeling very anxious' (485). Addison's wife told her husband:

that if we survive this horrible time she thinks one of her most vivid recollections of it will be of an air-raid night, her trying to get Michael, age 3½, to sleep, lying on his bed beside him monotonously chanting a nursery rhyme, everything in darkness, a terrific roar of barrage and bombs, the whole house rattling and rocking whilst he is murmuring feverishly with measles bad upon him, 'scwatch me Mummy, scwatch me'. (492)

Andrew Bonar's (1810–92) diary contains information on the conflict already referred to – the conflict between religious beliefs and parental feeling. When Bonar's son, aged 2, was ill, he found that he was unable to resign himself to the will of God: 'these two days have yielded me awful proofs of the coldness of my heart. I have felt my utter inability to rouse up grateful love. I have at times felt, as it were, sickness at the discovery of my selfish heart' (207). When E. Gaskell's (1810–65) 22-month-old daughter was ill, she wrote: 'I did so try to be resigned; but I cannot tell how I sickened at my heart at the thought of seeing her no more here' (11). Mary Hochberg's (1873–1950?) young son (aged 5) had to have an operation:

He was so good and brave, but cried dreadfully when he awoke from the chloroform. I saw him when he was still under the effects of it, lying there quite quiet with a little pale face and heavy eyes and I felt miserable for him and knew more than ever how I adore him, and it was misery to have him clinging to me in pain afterwards, poor precious mite. (128)

Ten child diarists mentioned some kind of ailment and all of them referred to parental concern (Bruce Cummings, Hanover, Johnston, *May, Ann Palmer, Llewellyn Powys, *Richards, Shore, *Frank Smith and *Webb). *Caroline Richards (1842–1913), for example, wrote that, as she had a very bad cough, her grandmother became concerned and sent for the doctor; but did not approve of the doctor's mode of examination: 'He [doctor] placed me in a chair and thumped my lungs and back and listened to my breathing while Grandmother sat near and watched him in silence, but finally she said, "Caroline isn't used to being pounded"' (194). *Catherine Webb (1801–1900) was sent to boarding school but 'I was a delicate girl and as it was so very cold my Mother was afraid to have me stay' (148). Shore (1819–39) was gradually succumbing to tuberculosis. At 19 she was very ill: 'It is painful, however, to be the object of such constant care and anxiety to my parents, especially my poor father, who has harassment enough in his wearing profession without my (innocently) adding to it. It is impossible to describe how he watches me, and how, without being fidgety, he catches at any glimpse of my being better' (265).

Of the three autobiographies which provide information on illness during childhood (*Elizabeth Chace (1806– ?), Hare (1834–1903) and *Judson (1817–54)) only Hare recalled no parental solicitude. The austerity with which Hare was reared resulted in him becoming ill, but no allowance was made for him during this period and he continued with his daily lessons. Kitto (1804–54) remembered the misery he experienced when told by a doctor that the bump on the head which his baby daughter had received could prove fatal.

Discussion. The 19th-century texts contain the same evidence as the 17th- and 18th-century texts; the age of the child did not affect the concern of the parent and also the conflict between parental anxiety and religious belief was again described, although in a smaller proportion of diarists (Bonar, Gaskell and *Todd).

Overall, the results reveal that almost all parents were extremely concerned whenever any of their offspring were ill, irrespective of the century in which they lived. It seems as if the deep emotional involvement which most parents had with their offspring prevented them from feeling anything but distress and anxiety. In addition, nearly all the parents nursed their offspring themselves and were reluctant to leave children who were ill, even for short visits. Thus, they regarded the nursing of sick children as their responsibility. These results contradict the view that parents were emotionally detached from and indifferent to their children. Neither is there any significant class difference in the amount of anxiety experienced or nursing care given by a parent. The aristocrats were just as concerned and as prepared to nurse their children as the middle classes (e.g. see Clifford in the 16th century, *Byrd and Rich in the 17th and Boscawen, Grant and *Shippen in the 18th).

Parents were so anxious when any of their children were ill because any illness, no matter how slight, could all too easily lead to death. Studies on

British mortality bring to light the relatively high frequency of infant and child death in earlier centuries. Fildes (1980) states that, for the period 1680–1875, an average of 169 infants died per 1000 births. The demographers Wrigley & Schofield have established that about a quarter of children would fail to live up to the age of 10 years (cited in Wrightson, 1982, p. 105). It is likely that the American mortality rate was higher. When an illness did prove fatal, the parents' anxiety was realised and most grieved deeply. They were not 'indifferent' at the death of a child because so many died, as has been argued. The conflict between religious belief and parental love revealed in the illness section reappears in the quotations on death. The religious parents firmly believed, in theory, that a child was only lent to them and therefore they could not object when he was recalled, through death, by God. Despite this, when they actually experienced the death of a child, they found it very difficult, at times impossible, to reconcile their faith with their grief for the loss of a child. These passages are the most agonising the diaries contain; at times the parents are completely distraught. They could not come to terms with the death of a child, nor could they accept their inability to come to terms with this, believing they had lost their child and their faith.

As it has been argued that parents were particularly indifferent to the death of their young children, the information on death will mainly relate to children aged 6 and under.

The 16th century. The offspring of five diarists died as young children.[13] Two diarists revealed no emotion – Nicholas Assheton and Powell. However, although Assheton did not seem to be upset at the death of his child soon after birth, he not only attended the funeral (Shorter in *The Making of the Modern Family* (1976) argues that parental indifference to children prior to the 18th century could be seen in such things as the non-attendance of parents at the funerals of their young children); but laid the child in his grave. Perhaps some of the early diarists suffered from an inability to articulate. Although they felt grief, they were unable to express it.

Towards the end of the century three diarists, William Brownlow, Wallington and Winthrop, were able to describe their grief and revealed great distress at the death of their offspring. For example, Brownlow (1594–1675) lost numerous children shortly after birth; but this did not make him 'indifferent'. He described his feelings when two sons, who have survived for a few years also died: 'O Lord thou has dealt bitterlie with mee and broken me with breach upon breach, when wilt thou comfort mee' (121). And, on the death of the second: 'I was at ease but Thou O God has broken mee a sunder and shaken mee to peeces' (123). Wallington (1598–1658) was stricken at the death of his daughter, approximately 4 years of age: 'The grief for this child was so great that I forgot myself so much that I did offend God in it; for I broke all my purposes, promises, and covenants with my God, for I was much distracted in my mind, and could not be comforted, although my friends speak so comfortably unto me' (xix). Wallington's wife, in comparison, reproved him for mourning so deeply, saying: 'I do as freely give it again unto God, as I did receive it of him' (xix). Wallington was not convinced; he still regarded it as a 'bitter portion' when his young son died a few years later. (There was a great status differential between these two fathers: Brownlow was a baronet and Wallington a shopkeeper.)

The 17th century. Six diarists revealed no emotion at the death of an infant: *William Adams, Browell, *William Cooper, *Danforth, Heywood and Samuel Newton.[14] All of these were infants under 1 year of age; apart from the offspring of *Danforth, all of whom succumbed to a disease at the same time. As with the 16th-century diarists, perhaps some parents were unable to express their feelings. For example, Mark Browell's diary (1660?–1729) contains no emotion; but he did note that his daughter died at 'six weeks, one day and seven houres' old which implies that he paid sufficient attention to his daughter to note the precise time of her entry into and exit from the world (186).

Another father, John Hervey (1665–1751), appeared to be resigned to his fate, writing when his 6-week-old son was overlaid by the nurse: 'The Lord gave, & ye Lord hath taken away, yet blessed be ye goodness of my most merciful God, who hath left me so many alive' (44).

Other diarists revealed considerably more concern. Four American diarists expressed grief at the loss of a young child: *Byrd, *C. Mather, *Pike and *Sewall. For example, *Byrd (1674–1744) wrote of the death of his 9-month-old son: 'My wife was much afflicted but I submitted to His judgement better, notwithstanding I was very sensible of my loss; but God's will be done.' Four days later: 'My wife continued to be exceedingly afflicted for the loss of her child, notwithstanding I comforted her as well as I could' (1941, pp. 186–7). *C. Mather (1663–1728) was upset when any of his children died, finding it difficult to submit. For example, his daughter of a few months was overlaid by her nurse: 'The Spirit of the Lord Jesus Christ, helped mee, I hope, to a patient and cheerful Submission, under this Calamity: tho' I sensibly found, an Assault of

Temptation from Satan, accompanying it' (vol. 7, p. 185), and when a daughter aged 2½ was dying, he wrote: 'I begg'd, I begg'd, that such a bitter Cup, as the Death of that lovely child, might pass from me . . . Just before she died, she asked me to pray with her; which I did, with a distressed, but resigning Soul; and I gave her up unto the Lord . . . Lord, I am oppressed; undertake for me!' (vol. 8, p. 261).

Many of the British diarists who noted the death of a child mourned deeply: Byrom, E. Erskine, J. Erskine, Evelyn, Housman, Josselin, Pledger, Stockton and Mrs Stockton. E. Erskine (1680–1754) lost three children from the measles within a few weeks: 'My dear, sweet, and pleasant child, Ralph [aged 2] died on Thursday . . . His death was very grievous and affecting to my wife and me; but good is the will of the Lord' (266). After Ralph's death: 'I was called to return thanks, which I did; but towards the end, when I came to take notice of the present providence, that God had plucked one of the sweet flowers of the family, my heart burst out into tears, so that I was able to go no further' (268). A few days later Erskine wrote he had 'been sadly, *sadly*, afflicted with the loss of other two pleasant children': Henry aged 9 and Alexander aged 5. Alexander was the last to die: 'My affections were exceedingly knit to him, and I was comforting myself in having him . . . but it seems the Lord will not allow me to settle my affections on anything here below. I cannot express the grief of my heart for the loss of this child, the other two strokes being so late' (269). Housman (1680?–1735) regarded it as 'A Trial indeed . . . the greatest I may say that I ever felt' when her young son died. Rule's (1695– ?) 4-month-old daughter was probably overlaid by her mother. When she was found dead in the morning, Rule wrote: 'What a hard trial this was to us both ye lord only knows' (MS, fo. 86).

Two fathers suffered the loss of both an infant and an older child and both related more anguish at the death of the latter. Evelyn (1620–1706) was resigned when his son of a few weeks was overlaid by his nurse: 'to our extreme sorrow, being now againe reduced to one: but God's will be done' (vol. 2, p. 164) but his 5-year-old son died 'to our inexpressible grief and affliction' (vol. 2, p. 96) and his 20-year-old daughter 'to our unspeakable sorrow and affliction' (vol. 2, p. 452).

Josselin (1616–83) similarly exhibited more grief at the death of an 8-year-old than a baby. Although he did regard it as 'sad' when his infant son died: 'it was ye youngest and our affections not so wonted unto it' (47). This contrasts with the emotion he displayed at the death of his daughter Mary: 'it[15] was a pretious child, a bundle of myrrhe, a bundle of sweetnes: shee was a child of 10,000, full of wisdome, womanlike gravity, knowledge, sweet expressions of God, apt in her learning, tender-hearted & loving, an obedient child to us. . . . Lord I rejoyce I had such a present for thee . . . it lived desired and dyed lamented' (74).

Discussion. A mere glance at the previous quotations is enough to demonstrate the searing grief most parents felt at the death of a child. It seems quite inexplicable how historians could have claimed that 16th- and 17th-century parents were unmoved at the loss of a child. A study of Stone's treatment of the problem is particularly enlightening. Stone does quote Josselin's reaction to the death of his baby son and claims that Josselin was not distressed. He then omits the description of Mary's death because the grief related there contradicts his argument. (See also Macfarlane, 1979a, who makes the same point.) Though Josselin does appear to be less upset by the death of Ralph, it is quite wrong to claim he was indifferent. What is particularly interesting is that parents in later centuries were also less disturbed by the death of an infant when compared to the grief they experienced at the death of an older child. The findings of this study are supported by MacDonald (*Mystical Bedlam*, 1981) who found that 58 out of 134 cases of disturbing grief recorded by Napier, were attributable to children's deaths. As he says, 'What was familiar was not easily borne' (77). Despite urgings to the contrary, village women 'formed deep and enduring bonds with their children and were forced to suffer again and again as disease slew one child after another' (85).

The babies of four diarists were overlaid (Evelyn, Hervey, *C. Mather and Rule), the first three by their nurse and the last by her mother. Another 17th-century diarist, *Sewall, seems to have regarded overlaying as a normal occurrence, writing after a friend's son was found dead in his bed in the morning: 'It seems there is no symptom of Overlaying' (vol. 5, p. 121). It has been found from anthropological studies that one reaction to a high infant mortality rate is keeping the infant near the mother or caretaker at all times (Konnor, 1977; de Laguna, 1965; Leighton & Kluckhohn, 1948; LeVine, 1977). Other diarists such as Clifford and Wallington in the 16th century and *Bailey in the 18th century described children sleeping with an adult. Thus it seems that past parents were also organising their rearing practices to cope with the high infant mortality rate, although overlaying could be the unfortunate consequence.

The 18th century. Six diarists expressed no grief at the death of a young child: Anna Braithwaite, *Thomas Hazard (1756–1845), *Mary Holyoke, *Susanna Holyoke, *John Preston and Steadman. Other American and

137

British diarists were grief stricken,[16] for example *M. Bayard (1769?– ?) wrote, a few days after the death of her son:

Oh cruel recollection! this day my beloved Child would have been nine months old, the age that I fondly flattered myself he would have run alone – but alas! how often does a mysterious Providence cut off our hopes and blast our most favorite plans; he was a promising child as ever lived, but hard as the trial was, last Saturday he was committed to the silent grave. (122)

*Huntington (1791–1823) lost a son of almost 2 and, 11 days later, a daughter of 5 years. She noted her feelings on the death of her son:

Thus the fond and cherished babe left me at a moment's warning. It fell upon me like a thunderbolt . . . The greatest shock was the first. But my mind was unsettled all that and the next day. I hardly knew where or what I was; so little sensible had I been how this darling babe had entwined himself about every fibre of my heart. (295, 298)

When Elizabeth then died, *Huntington felt that this was too much and she 'sunk at once' (298). *Silliman's (1779–1864) eldest child died shortly before his fifth birthday: 'This bereavement took fast hold on me. The shaft of death, which never before had been discharged in this house, was levelled against my oldest son, a child of the most attractive traits' (vol. 1, p. 277).

The British texts contain similar material. Jones (1755–1821) was exceedingly distressed at the death of his 18-month-old daughter: 'what a gloom overspreads my soul! . . . My Soul seems oppressed with a load, which no length of time will ever lighten. O my dear little infant, lying dead under this roof! whose spirit I watched departing yesterday' (99–100). Jones did think his sorrow was misplaced as his daughter had gone to 'certain everlasting bliss' (99). Another father, Macready (1793–1873), mourned just as deeply at the death of his young daughter: 'I scarcely know what I did, or how I felt, except that it was unutterable and hopeless agony . . . My child is dead – my blessed, my beloved, my darling child' (vol. 2, p. 99). A few days later he wrote: 'The thought of that blessed cherub haunts me everywhere' (vol. 2, p. 101).

John Lettsom, Moore, Thrale and Trench lost a younger and an older child and all experienced more distress at the death of the latter. Moore (1779–1852), for example, revealed little emotion at the death of an infant, compared with the following outburst after the death of his 16-year-old daughter: 'I could no longer restrain myself – the feelings I had been so long suppressing found vent, and a fit of loud violent sobbing seized me, in which I felt as if my chest was coming asunder' (vol. 6, p. 21). Trench

(1768–1837) lost a daughter of only a few days old and a son of 2 within a short time of each other. After the death of her son she wrote:

The loss of my infant daughter, which seemed heavy at the time, shrinks into nothing when compared with this. She was merely a little bud; he was a lovely blossom which had safely passed all the earliest dangers, and gave clearest promise of delicious fruit . . . Oh, my child, my child! . . . when I saw you cold and motionless before me how came it my heart did not break at once. (1862, pp. 199, 201)

One child diarist, Boswell at the age of 14, wrote to his mother commiserating with her on the death of a son shortly after his birth, but adding 'besides if he had been more advanced in years it would have been much greater grief to you' (vol. 1, p. 48). This corresponds to the picture given in other texts, that infants, although mourned, are not mourned as deeply as older children.

The 19th century. These texts depict the same range and depth of grief as do the earlier writers. Two fathers (*John Lee and *James Strang) merely entered the deaths of their children. Two of Samuel Wilberforce's children died during the period of his diary (one as an adult and one as an infant) but there is no mention of these deaths in the published text. As Wilberforce did describe writing a letter of condolence to a friend whose son had died, it is likely that he was distressed by the deaths of his own offspring. *Hayes and Waugh were relatively unconcerned. *Hayes' (1822–93) son, born while his father was at war, died at 6 months of age. *Hayes wrote: 'I have seen so little of him . . . that I do not realize a loss; but his mother, and still more his grandmother, lose their little dear companion and are very much afflicted (vol. 2, p. 414). Waugh (1903–66) wrote of a daughter who died shortly after birth: 'Poor little girl, she was not wanted' (1976, p. 489). The rest described considerably more distress.[17] All three of *Lovell's (1809– ?) children died within 18 months of each other. The day after the death of her last child, aged 5: '[I] looked in vain for some token of childish play. The order and stillness of the house oppressed me. I sank under it' (109). One year later she wrote: 'Our hearts still bleed' (109). *Ward (1841–1931) wrote, after the death of his 11-month-old son: 'I need not dwell on the grief and tears which wrenched our hearts. I need not describe the void which now exists. It is the duty of this little journal to register only cold facts' (201).

The British parents suffered as much pain. Emilie Cowell (1820?– ?) recorded the anniversary of the deaths of her children in her diary. For example: 'On this day, thirteen years ago, our firstborn, our darling Joe died, three years and three months old! To this day his memory is a precious, a delicious sadness to us, but oh what wild what disobedient agony did we endure for years. God gave us many sweet children, but we pined for the one taken' (10). Mary Timms' (1808–34) daughter died at the age of 2½:

How transient are all things here below! how soon are our hopes and prospects blasted! my babe, my dear Mary Anne is taken from me, to bloom in paradise. Ah! I fondly hoped she would have been spared to us; but God has seen good to separate us, perhaps but for a little while. O how painful to nature! my heart bleeds. I am jealous of the worms; I do not like to give my Mary Anne to them; but the mandate is, 'dust thou art, and unto dust shalt thou return' . . . I know it is my duty to submit – to be resigned. (87)

Alford (1810–71) described the death of his 11-month-old son as 'our bitter loss'. However, he was quite distraught at the death of his 10-year-old son – 'the joy of our hearts and the desire of our eyes', writing: 'To think that those cherished ones, from whom we carefully fenced off every rough blast, whom we led by the hand in every thorny path, have by themselves gone through the dark valley' (191).

Discussion. When the evidence from the 16th- and 17th-century texts is compared with that from the 18th and 19th centuries, it can be seen that the thesis of a dramatic transformation in the capacity for experiencing emotion is a myth. There is no such transformation. It is the similarity in the extent and range of parental grief which is striking, not the lack of grief in earlier parents. Most parents were acutely aware of the frequency of child death, but far from inducing a state of resignation, this only served to heighten their anxiety during any illness of their offspring, and anguish at their death.

Conclusion

There seem to have been some slight changes in the concept of childhood. Children were seen by a few parents as being depraved in the 17th century, innocent in the 18th and as both depraved and innocent in the 19th. In addition, the texts, particularly in the 18th century, contain more discussion on the nature of childhood. A few of the 17th-century Puritans and a number of 18th- and 19th-century parents were also more concerned with their duties as a parent and the texts reveal the doubts of many 18th- and 19th-century writers with regard to their competence as a parent. This does not mean, however, that 16th-century parents were unaware of childhood or unwilling to accept responsibility for rearing their offspring, but rather that they do not appear to have been so consciously aware of these matters. This may simply be due to a lack of experience with the medium of writing as a form of expression, coupled with the scarcity of literary models.

Many parental attitudes to children discovered from the primary sources turn up again in 20th-century parents. Backett ('Images of the family', 1982) researched into modern middle-class parenthood. She found that these parents saw their children as passing through stages and as 'inexperienced humans'. Understanding one's own child was perceived as 'an ongoing challenge' and as a crucial requirement for good child care (361). How earlier parents such as Cobden-Sanderson, *Huntington, *C. Mather and Steuart would have agreed.

It is clear that parental ambivalence with regard to children occurs in all types of parents and in each century studied – it is also a feature of 20th-century parents (Newson & Newson, 1965, 1968 and 1976). Greven (1977) argues that, although 'evangelical' parents were in two minds about their offspring, regarding them as both depraved and innocent, this feeling was non-existent in 'moderate' and 'genteel' parents. The texts examined reveal that even parents who regarded their children as innocent could still be ambivalent towards them – many parents found the amount of time and attention which children took up both wearisome and exasperating. It seems as if it was the strength of parental affection and involvement in their own children which produced this state of mind.

As I have argued, when parental reaction to the illness or death of a child is studied through the centuries, one is struck by the lack of change. There were a few diarists who would appear to have been unmoved at the death of a child (Goff, H. Mildmay and Waugh) – these were not confined to the early centuries. A few more writers did not express any grief at the death of a child and may, therefore, have been indifferent. Again, these appeared in every century and with regard to all ages of offspring. But the vast majority of writers through the centuries were extremely distressed at the death of a child, irrespective of their class, sex or religion and no matter at what age the child died. However, it does appear that, in every century studied, young infants were not mourned as deeply as older children. It seems as if parents grieved at the death of a baby for what that infant would have become whereas, at the death of an older child, they grieved not only for what the child would have become, but also for what the child had been – as Trench in the 18th century explicitly states. There

141

is no change in the extent of parental grief over the centuries and no support at all for the argument that parents before the 18th century were indifferent to the death of their young offspring, whereas after the 18th century they grieved deeply.

Of particular interest is the number of writers who were unable to reconcile their emotion at the death of a child: Brownlow and Wallington in the 16th; E. Erskine, Evelyn, Josselin and *C. Mather in the 17th; *Bayard, Boswell, Darby, *Lorenzo and *Margaret Dow, Fry, F. Gray, Jones, Kilham, Macready, Sandford, Skinner and D. Taylor in the 18th; and Cowell, *Duncan, Timms and *Todd in the 19th. It was very difficult, if not impossible, for a parent not to react to the death of a child with all the emotional attachment of a parent no matter how strongly his religious faith urged otherwise.

5. Discipline and control

The increased solicitude of adults 'lui [l'enfant] a infligé le fouet, la prison, les corrections réservées aux condamnés des plus basses conditions'. (465)

('inflicted on him [child] the birch, the prison cell – in a word, the punishments usually reserved for convicts from the lowest strata of society'.)   (Ariès, 1960, p. 413)

Century after century of battered children grew up and in turn battered their own children.   (de Mause, 1976, p. 41)

Harsh discipline was the child's lot, and they were often terrorised deliberately and, not infrequently, sexually abused.
                                                        (Plumb, 1975, p. 66)

whipping was the normal method of discipline in a sixteenth- or seventeenth-century home . . . The breaking of the will was . . . the prime aim, . . . physical punishment the standard method.   (Stone, 1977, pp. 167, 170)

If de Mause in *The Evolution of Childhood* is 'obsessed with discovering abuse or neglect in times past' (Smith, *Autonomy and Affection*, 1977), then most other writers on the history of childhood are obsessed with the disciplinary nature of the parental role. It has been used as the litmus test of parent–child relations in the past. In fact, most works dealing with the treatment of children in earlier centuries give the impression that parents only interacted with their offspring in order to whip them. Ariès in *L'Enfant et la Vie Familiale sous l'Ancien Régime* argues that more severe forms of discipline, including a dramatic increase in adult supervision, appeared at the same time as a concept of childhood, that is during the 17th century. The majority of authors, though, believe that children have always been harshly punished at home and at school and that more humane methods of discipline did not appear till the mid-18th century (see for example Lyman, 1976; McLaughlin, 1976; de Mause, 1976; Plumb

143

1975; Sears, 1975; Shorter, 1976; Stone, 1977; and Tucker, 1976). Some authors, such as Robertson (1976) and Stone argue that children were again subjected to severe discipline and total parental control in the 19th century.

Most historians have examined the hypothesis that parents, and other adults, have evolved from treating children with cruelty to treating them with kindness. However, as has been shown in chapter 2, little systematic analysis has been applied to any source of evidence. Thus the findings of these historians merely generate another hypothesis regarding the treatment of children in the past; that a great deal of individual variation in methods of discipline has always existed and thus no century was or will be notably cruel or kind. This chapter will be concerned with the methods used to discipline children, both in the home and at school, and also with the amount of control which parents tried to exert over their children's lives.[1] The texts have been divided into 50-year time periods, from 1500 to 1900, in order to discover whether or not modes of discipline have changed dramatically over time.

Discipline in the home

Table 7 gives the extent to which the four sources of evidence used discussed parental discipline and control.

1500–49. Two adult diarists were available for this period and both referred to physical punishment. Dee (1527–1608) wrote: 'Katharin [8 years] by a blow on the eare given by her mother did bled at the nose very much, which did stay for an houre and more' (30–1),[2] and Henry Machyn (1498–1563) related that 'The iiij day of Desember was a voman [set in the] pelere [pillory] for beytyng of her chyld with rodes' (98).[3] In addition, Machyn remarked on a young apprentice beaten so severely by his master that the skin was taken off his back. For that, the master was also set in the pillory and whipped till, as Machyn noted with grim satisfaction, 'blude ran downe' (311).

1550–99. Only one American diarist was born before 1600 in the texts studied here. Although *Jefferay (1591–1675) did not mention any specific method of discipline, his diary contains some evidence on the mode of discipline he employed. He wrote of one of his daughters, who had fallen in love:

There has a gentleness come over her, also, that sets vastly well, Her brother and sister do scarce understand how she, who did at times task them so sharply on

144

Table 7. Number of sources containing information on discipline in the home

| | Source | | | | | | | | | | | | | | |
| Time Period | Diary | | | Manuscript | | | Child diary | | | Autobiography | | | All | | |
	A	B	% of sample	A	B	% of sample	A	B	% of sample	A	B	% of sample	A	B	% of sample
1500–49	0	2	100	–	–	–	0	0	0	0	0	0	0	2	100
1550–99	1	7	62	–	–	–	0	1	50	0	5	83	1	13	67
1600–49	0	9	36	–	–	–	0	2	50	0	9	82	0	20	47
1650–99	3	6	32	0	2	100	0	2	50	0	4	100	3	14	45
1700–49	5	17	32	0	2	100	1	0	11	2	11	72	8	30	39
1750–99	5	19	30	0	1	20	7	8	32	7	21	72	19	49	44
1800–49	13	21	45	0	0	0	5	12	37	10	21	97	28	54	53
1850–99	0	7	54	0	0	0	0	4	67	0	8	67	0	19	58

their duties, and did stand so for her own rights, can have become so seeming tame. Her mother and I read her more clearly; and, as she turns to us with this new gentleness in her eyes, know, as well as if she had made speech of it, that now (as life broadens and deepens) a new understanding of our love and care for her has come; and that she sees how our correctings, even (tiresome or needless seeming), were in love, to cure a fault, or a weakness that should grow to one. (133)

Of the British diarists for this period, not one noted inflicting any kind of physical punishment. There are signs that at least some of the parents wished to regulate their offspring's behaviour. For example, John Penry (1563–93), while awaiting execution for treason and with the eldest of his daughters not yet 4 years of age, wrote a long letter of advice to his children on how to conduct themselves as they grew up. He advised them on such matters as religion and marriage and obviously had intended exerting some control over his daughters' lives if he had lived. Similarly, Winthrop (1587–?) wrote letters of advice to one son at college, advising him not to become too worldly or extravagant and not to neglect his studies, and Hope (1585–1646) too wrote to one of his sons telling him to 'stay his tour, and to command him to attend his studies' (42).

Hope and Winthrop also tried remonstrating with sons who were continually in debt – though as neither father refused to bail their son out when necessary, they were implicitly encouraging their sons to continue such behaviour. Winthrop, for example, wrote to his son: 'I have disbursed a great deal of money for you, more than my estate will bear . . . I have many other children that are unprovided, and I see my life is uncertain' (285). Powell (1581–1656) told his 18-year-old son to leave home; but gave no indication as to what the problem was, only stating: 'my sone William disobedient departed my house' (23).

Other diarists, on the other hand, were not so concerned with controlling their children. H. Mildmay (1592–1667) over-indulged his second son, nicknamed 'Nompée' and his favourite child, for example, though Mildmay wished his sons to be well educated and sent his other sons to Cambridge, as Nompée disliked school, Mildmay gave in to his son's wishes and allowed him to leave. Nompée was also given money whenever he wanted it, and was generally spoilt by his father to the extent that the latter had no control over his son. Mildmay did not try to discipline Nompée himself, but rather appealed to God, writing, for example, 'Nompée a bad boy. God amend him' (63). Clifford (1590–1676) was upset by her 5-year-old daughter's behaviour. Margaret's speech had been 'very ill so as strangers cannot understand her' all winter.

Furthermore, she had been 'so out of temper' that it 'grieved' Clifford 'to think of it'. However, Clifford made no attempt to punish Margaret for 'all these inconveniences'; but instead endured them believing that her daughter was suffering from 'some distemper in her head' (110).

Ariès has claimed that past parents were indifferent to their children and thus the latter were subjected to very little parental restraint or supervision. Wallington's (1598–1658) diary reveals that parents may not always know the whereabouts of their offspring; but they would prefer to do so and are concerned if a child is missing. His daughter aged 3 years and 8 months went out: 'with a nother little childe to play as wee had thought but it semes my dafter Sarah left the other child and went herself as far as [the] fell'. Once it was realised that Sarah was missing, Wallington went out to look for her until she was brought home by a neighbour. Wallington was obviously relieved, writing that, if Sarah had not been found: 'what strange distractfull thoughts should wee have had and how could wee eate or have sleept that night with thinking what is become of our poore childe, thinking yt maybe it is drowned at the wather side or some other mischife hath befallen it' (MS, fo. 435).[4]

There are two child diaries for this period; that of Edward Tudor contains no reference to discipline whereas Clifford (1590–1676), aged 13, wrote: 'my Mother being extreme angry with me for riding before with Mr. Mene, where my Mother in her anger commanded that I should lie in a chamber alone, which I could not endure, but my cousin *Frances* got the key of my chamber and lay with me' (11). Clifford does not explain why her mother objected to her riding with Mr Mene; but as she disobeyed her mother's command it appears that 16th-century children were not as much in awe of their parents as has been suggested.

Six autobiographies are available for the latter part of the 16th century and three record physical punishment. Forman (1552–1601) wrote that, as he was the youngest, he was his father's favourite child 'but his mother nor brethren loved him not' (3). His father died when Forman was 11 and from then on life at home was none too pleasant – Forman being 'beaten' by his mother and siblings for any faults so that he left home to live with his aunt at the age of 12. G. Mildmay (1552–1620) noted that she was whipped to 'inculcate virtuous principles'. She and her two sisters were brought up to behave with decorum and propriety: their governess 'counselled us when we were alone so to behave ourselves as yf all the worlde did looke upon us, and to doe nothing in secret whereof our conscience might accuse us' (120). Mildmay's father obviously had control over how she was reared. He liked women to be reserved and serene so as to present a 'good hope of stablished mynde and a virtuous disposition to be in her. I have seen him with his owne hands (for example's sake) scourge a young man, naked from his girdle upwards, with fresh rods, for making but a showe and countenance of a saucie and unreverent behaviour towards us his children, and put him from his service' (122). Richard Norwood (1590–1675) wrote that, as a child: 'often on a Lord's day at night or Monday morning I prayed to escape beating that week, or when I was sent on an errand two or three miles into the country, that I might not lose my way' (10). *Jefferay and Wallington, however, recalled no such discipline. *Jefferay (1591–1675) wrote that his mother 'was ever a good and tender mother to me' (16) and Wallington (1598–1658) described his mother as 'very tender-hearted to her children' (x).

Discussion. The 16th-century texts provide little detailed information on discipline and control. None the less, the evidence they do contain does not support the picture given by most historians of severe whipping being the normal mode of punishment. Machyn's comment shows that abuse and punishment were differentiated and that the former was condemned long before there was any formal child protection legislation. These 16th-century parents preferred advice to commands and the remonstrations of Hope and Winthrop suggest that some parents were unable to control the behaviour of their older offspring, even when they disapproved of it. Furthermore, the very fact that Hope, H. Mildmay and Winthrop were prepared to support their rebellious sons, no matter what, implies that at least some children were allowed a great deal of autonomy. This contradicts the theory that children in the 16th century were totally subject to their parents' will.

Stone has been notably depressing in his description of upper-class child-rearing practices, regarding such parents as cruel and with no love for their offspring. Although Stone's thesis with regard to the lower classes has been severely criticised, his view of the upper classes has been accepted by recent works (MacDonald, 1981; Wrightson, 1982). However, an examination of the 16th-century texts containing evidence on discipline, of which 7 were written by a member of the upper class (Clifford, Dee, Hope, G. Mildmay, H. Mildmay, Powell and Winthrop), suggests that these parents were not so brutal. Only Dee noted the infliction and G. Mildmay the receipt of some form of physical punishment. Others such as H. Mildmay spoilt their children, Clifford tolerated what she considered deviant behaviour from her daughter and

Hope and Winthrop were reduced almost to the level of pleading for better behaviour from their older sons.

The autobiographies contain more evidence on physical punishment than the diaries. Forman would appear to be an exceptional case – not all the children in the family were treated as he was. However, both G. Mildmay and Norwood seemed to have experienced quite a number of whippings, although neither considered these unduly severe. In contrast, *Jefferay and Wallington refer to their 'tender' mother. Thus there was a wide range of parental discipline in the 16th century.

1600–49. No American diarist was available for this period. Of the British diarists, Newcome (1627–95) was the only one to state he inflicted physical punishment (4 per cent of the sample). 'I discharged my duty of correction to my poor child [aged 12], prayed with him after, entreating the Lord that it might be the last correction (if it were his will) that he should need' (302). (Newcome was continually upset by this son's behaviour later on.) A. Brodie, Freke, Josselin and Newdigate all tried remonstrating with troublesome sons. Brodie (1617–80) recorded : 'In the Evening I called for my Son, and exhorted and admonished him to self-trial, and to more exactness, sincerity and watchfulness over his heart and thoughts than ever' (96), and again later noted: 'My hart rais with indignation' against the same son (179). Freke (1641–1714) wrote a letter to her adult son: 'as I thought it my Dutty to Admonish him of his Errors. I had only as usuall a Rude Answer For Itt' (64), and Newdigate (1644–1710) also attempted to make one son improve his behaviour: 'I will this day enter my son John's Faults here, which I tell him of to make him humble' (298). This father also fined his daughters if they annoyed him.

Parents found it difficult to be as stern as they intended with their offspring. For instance, Josselin (1616–83) threatened his younger son with disinheritance and, as John did not reform, Josselin wrote: 'John declared for his disobedience no son; I should allow him nothing except he tooke himselfe to bee a servt; yet if he would depart and live in service orderly I would allow him 10/- yearly; if he so walkt as to become Gods son, I should yett own him for mine' (167). Josselin nevertheless did not carry out these threats; John remained at home and eventually inherited his father's estate. Josselin's view of the parent–child relationship was based on reciprocity rather than the natural authority and superiority of the parent. He believed that children should recompense their parents for the amount of care they had received by being obedient, although he did not attempt to force his offspring to go against their own wishes and even

149

continued to support John despite his condemnation of his son's behaviour. Similarly, Heywood (1630–1702) did try to be severe with his sons of 12 and 13 years; but relented on seeing their distress: 'on saturday morning my sons having not made their latin in expectation to goe to Halifax, were loath to goe to schoole, yet I threatened them, they went crying, my bowels workt and I sent to call them back' (vol. 1, p. 261).

Evelyn, Martindale, Pringle and Slingsby all tried to exert control over their children by giving them advice. Evelyn (1620–1706) wrote: 'I gave my Sonn an Office, with instructions how to govern his youth; I pray God give him the grace to make a right use of it' (vol. 2, p. 334). Martindale (1623–86) considered it as 'a sunshine gleam' when his son finally agreed to accept his father's advice (215). Slingsby (1601–58) was in the same position as Penry – awaiting execution – and like him wrote a letter of advice to his children:

I am to address my self out of my *Fatherly* and tender care towards You. The ground of my discourse shall be Instruction; where-to, I am confident You will be ready to give the more serious attention, in regard it proceeds from his mouth, and devotion of his heart; who with a parental and tender affection ever loved You while he was living: and now dying leaves You this *Memorial* as my *last Legacy* for your future benefit, improvement and direction. (197)

He wished his children to be true to their religion, not to be active in affairs of state, keep good company and a clear conscience and to be just. Pringle (1625–67) was the only autobiographer to note the treatment of his own offspring. Believing that he may not live till his youngest child reached the age of 'understanding', he wrote some words of advice for that child.

There was only one child diarist for this time period. Thomas Crosfield (1602–63) began his diary at the age of 16, and from the information it contains, it seems that he was on very friendly terms with his father. He recorded no attempt of his parents to force him to give in to their wishes.

Two of the 11 autobiographies for this period do not refer to discipline in any way (Newcome and Anthony Wood). Others such as Ashmole and Pringle recalled receiving physical punishment. Elias Ashmole (1617–92) related that his mother 'was continually instilling into my ears such religious and moral precepts as my younger years were capable of. Nor did she ever fail to correct my faults, always adding sharp reproofs and good lectures to boot' (26). Pringle (1625–67) wrote: 'In my childhood, tho I was much indulged by my parents . . . I was often led also to acknowledge God, in my childish concernments, such as, the getting of my lesson, on being freed from reproofs; frequently praying to escape correction, when I expected it' (3). Martindale (1623–86) worked for his father for a time and recollected that the latter gave him too much work to do and punished him if it was not done. Evelyn and Heywood recalled the general form of the discipline they received as children and both seemed to think it was fair and just. Evelyn (1620–1706), for example, referred to his father as being 'discreetly severe, yet liberal on all just occasions, to his children, strangers, and servants' (vol. 1, p. 2). Heywood (1630–1702) described his mother as 'though she was very indulgent to us, yet was she severe and sharp agt sin, especially such sins as she saw us inclined to, oh how did she disgrace sinful ways! and endeavour to prevent our falling thereunto' (vol. 1, p. 51). Freke, David Hume, Josselin and Rich recorded that they received indulgent treatment as children. Freke (1641–1714) noted that she had a very happy childhood and that she never heard an unkind word spoken to her. Josselin (1616–83) wrote that his father 'loved me exceedingly' (3) and Rich (1624–78) referred to her father as 'indulgent' and to Lady Claytone who looked after him (Rich's mother died when Rich was 3) as making 'so much of me' (2).

Discussion. The evidence from these texts is very similar to that contained in the 16th-century sources: a few parents inflicted physical punishment, others tried remonstrations and threats and yet others tried advising their offspring. Again it was the autobiographers who recalled the strictest discipline, although even here the discipline was certainly not as harsh as has been argued and it is clear that not all children were so treated. It seems that parents would like to control their offspring's behaviour, although they did not always find it possible. The evidence from Pringle and Slingsby (and Penry in the 16th century), who all wrote letters of advice for their children, suggests that the parents did think it was their responsibility to regulate their children's behaviour. However, as the diaries of A. Brodie, Freke, Josselin and Newdigate reveal, parents were not always successful in this aim. In fact they seemed to realise the limits of parental authority – Evelyn and Martindale merely hoped their offspring would heed their advice and those diarists who disapproved of their son's behaviour continued to come to the latter's aid.

1650–99. Blundell, *Byrd, Morris, John Richards and *Sewall (18 per cent of the sample of diaries) stated that they used physical punishment as a disciplinary technique. *Byrd (1674–1744) did not seem to whip his own

151

children but did record that he whipped his niece and nephew (reared by *Byrd); the former for soiling the bed and not learning to read and the latter because he also 'would not learn his books' (1941, p. 204). *Byrd did not approve of too severe a punishment as he noted: 'I quarrelled with my wife for being cruel to Suky Brayne, [niece] though she deserved it' (1941, p. 285). He was also fairly lenient with his own children, writing: 'I was out of humour with my wife for forcing Evie [daughter of almost 3 years] to eat against her will' (1941, p. 182). *Sewall (1652–1730) recorded whipping two of his sons, each on one occasion. The punishment of Joseph has already been referred to (see chapter 2). *Sewall's 10-year-old son was 'corrected . . . for breach of the 9th Commandment, saying he had been at the Writing School, when he had not' (vol. 5, p. 225). *Sewall also reared some of his grandchildren after their parents' death. He eventually became so exasperated with his adolescent grandson's behaviour that he asked the boy to leave his house. Blundell (1669–1737) did hit his daughters while they were young and did exert control over them as young adults, although not without a consideration for their wishes. For example, when Blundell went to fetch his daughters home from the convent school they attended in France, his elder daughter, then aged 19, refused to go home because she wished to stay and become a nun. Her father was annoyed and insisted she return to England; but conceded that if, after a period at home, she still wished to become a nun, she could do so. Morris (1659–1727) also inflicted some slight physical punishment, but did not regard it as very effective: 'Mr Nooth [son's tutor] telling my Son [aged 12] his Fault three or 4 times in Holding his Pen, & he committing the same again I struck him a slap on the Hinder Part of his Head with the Palm of my Hand; But that did not make him mend it' (91). Richards' (1660?–1721) method of disciplining his son resulted in a quarrel with his wife, as she believed that Richards was too severe: 'This evening, I beat Jack for his bad [behaviour] in play, apon that A. [wife] showed herself so insolent that I put her out of the room' (100). One month later, he wrote: 'At table I had words with A. about my son John, [Jack] which became at last very high, and the next day after dinner she began to renew the quarrel violently' (106).

The other diarists recorded alternative methods of discipline. *C. Mather (1663–1728) was the first to articulate any abstract concept of discipline:

The *first Chastisement*, which I inflict for an ordinary Fault, is, to lett the Child see and hear me in an Astonishment, and hardly able to beleeve that the Child could do so *base* a Thing, but beleeving that they will never do it again.

I would never come, to give a child a *Blow*; except in Case of *Obstinacy* or some gross Enormity.

To be chased for a while out of *my Presence*, I would make to be look'd upon, as the sorest Punishment in the Family. (vol. 7, pp. 535–6)

*Mather, in theory, wished to have total control over his offspring:

I first begett in them a high Opinion of their Father's Love to them, and of his being best able to judge, what shall be good for them.

Then I make them sensible, tis a Folly for them to pretend unto any Witt and Will of their own; they must resign all to me, who will be sure to do what is best; my word must be their Law. (vol. 7, p. 535)

In practice, *Mather did not possess such authority, for example against his father's wishes, Samuel underwent inoculation and *Mather had a lot of trouble from his elder sons. He did tell one son to leave home; but later asked him to return. *Mather would intervene on a child's behalf if he thought a punishment too harsh:

My little Son waits upon his Grandfather every Day, for his Instruction, as well as upon other Tutors and Teachers. This day, I sent him on an Errand, where the Person imposing on his flexible Temper, detained him so long, that his Grandfather was displeased at him, for coming so late; and his Punishment was, that his Grandfather, did refuse to instruct him, as he use to do. The Child unable to bear so heavy a Punishment, as that his Grandfather should not look favourably upon him, repairs to me, full of weeping Affliction. Hereupon, I applied myself with a Note, unto *my Father*, as an Advocate for the Child. I pleaded all that could be said by way of Apology for the Infirmity of the Child. I asked, that I might bear the Displeasure due for it, because of what had passed relating to it. (vol. 7, p. 583)

Peter Briggins (1672?–1717), while dying, wrote a letter of advice to his daughters, as earlier diarists had done for their offspring. He wished them to obey their mother, keep the faith, not to be extravagant and to help one another. E. Erskine (1680–1754) must have been against extreme forms of punishment, resolving as he did 'to be kind' to his children (290). Housman (1680?–1735) scolded her daughter of 7 years of age for forgetting 'to return Thanks to God for her Food' (80) and Morris (1659–1727) was annoyed with his 13-year-old daughter for refusing to do as he asked:

My dear Daughter Bettey refus'd to speak French with Mrs Keen; & I taking it unkindly from her, She fell into Tears, & continued grieving in that way even after she came home, so long that I was doubtful of her hurting her Constitution: & upon her being sorry for Refusing what was desir'd from her & promising it should be otherwise another time, I forgave her & she was extremely pleas'd with the reconciliation. (60)

153

Pledger (1665– ?) and Rule (1695?– ?) gave some indication of their modes of discipline for this period. Pledger's daughter at the age of 4 was very ill and was going to be sent away for her health. Pledger asked God 'to prevent her learning any ill words or actions' while away from home (MS, fo. 7) and Rule was upset by the behaviour of his children, particularly their 'insufferable Sloth' with respect to their education (MS, fo. 37v).

The child diaries provide additional information. Justinian Isham's (1687–1735) diary gives another example of the type of control that fathers would like to exert in theory; but did not achieve in practice. While abroad, at the age of 17 Isham wrote to his father telling him he had had his hair cut. His father replied: 'I am satisfy'd with the reasons you give me for cutting off your hair, but you might have writ to me about it before you had done it, and ask'it my leave' (187). Ryder (1691–1756) believed in theory 'that children ought from gratitude to behave so as to make their parents as easy as possible' (215). In practice, he often quarrelled with his father, although Ryder did regard the latter as 'a very fond father to me' (49).

Turning to the sample of the autobiographies, Fretwell and Pledger both recalled receiving physical punishment – the latter, harsh treatment. Fretwell (1699–1772) noted that he was sent to school but 'I suppose I did but continue here a few days, for growing weary of my book, and my dame not correcting me as my mother desired, she took me under her own pedagogy until I could read in my Bible' (183). Pledger (1665– ?), in his unpublished manuscript, wrote: 'I suffered very great severities from 2 mothers in law [stepmothers]' and complained that he was wrongfully accused of faults (MS, fo. 2). The other texts described alternative forms of parental control. Clegg (1679–1755) recalled his parents intervening when they did not approve of his behaviour. He was away at a private school, but neglected his studies for a love affair. When his parents were informed by one of the teachers, they removed him from the school and sent him to college earlier than he would have gone. William Stout's father, like many of the parents in these texts, wished to leave his children advice. Stout (1665–1752) recalled that, when his father was dying 'he called us all, his children, before him, & gave us exhortations to live in the fear of God & in duty & obedience to our mother, & brotherly kindness to each other' (73). Stout and his sister reared two of their brother's children and Stout remarked: 'my sister was as careful to nurse and correct them as if they had been her own children' (142).

Discussion. For the period 1650–99 there is an increase in the proportion of diarists who reported inflicting physical punishment, ranging from a slap to a 'whipping'. However, the latter appears to have been inflicted on rare occasions when all else had failed, and, as Richards' diary shows, both parents may not necessarily agree with the use of physical punishment as a disciplinary technique. Stone, among others, has suggested that Puritan parents were particularly severe disciplinarians. In the texts studied here, of those who recorded administering a whipping, Newcome and *Sewall were Puritans, Blundell a Catholic, Morris belonged to the Church of England and *Byrd and Richards followed a religion but did not specify which in their diary. Moreover, another Puritan, *C. Mather, did not believe in physical punishment. It is at least equally likely that it was the personality of the parent which determined the method of discipline, rather than religious beliefs, or perhaps an interaction between the two. Neither do the texts vindicate the arguments that upper-class parents were more severe than middle-class. Of the relevant 17th-century texts, 32 per cent were written by a member of the upper class (Blundell, Brodie, *Byrd, Freke, Isham, Newdigate, Rich, Richards and Slingsby). Blundell, *Byrd and Richards did inflict whippings but these were not unduly harsh – *Byrd was notably against harsh discipline even when he thought a child's conduct warranted it. Other fathers such as Slingsby had a very affectionate relationship with their offspring.

The texts do provide some support for Greven's (*The Protestant Temperament*, 1977) views. He argues that 'evangelical' parents such as *C. Mather regarded whipping as a failure of discipline and preferred to achieve their aims by the use of shame to shape the conscience and so ensure obedience. 'Moderate' parents such as *Sewall were unwilling to use force to discipline their children. But, as *Sewall's diary reveals, when confronted by a wayward child, parents are forced to make a decision according to the domestic situation and may not always act in accordance with their beliefs. What is intriguing about Greven's hypothesis is that it is the 'genteel' parents (e.g. *Byrd), those who greatly indulge their children, who are most likely to use whipping as a mode of discipline. *Byrd did believe in the efficacy of physical punishment, but it is of note that he whipped only his niece and nephew, not his son and daughter. It seems that parental views on discipline are not so much shaped by class and religion, but by daily involvement with and intimate knowledge of the parent's *own* children and this is a factor which many researchers into the history of childhood have ignored.

As with the previous 50-year period, there was a wide gap between theory and practice. A few parents in theory may have wished to have totally submissive offspring – although there is no evidence in the texts to suggest they wished to 'break the will' of their children – but, in practice, they did not achieve that aim. Some parents also sympathised with a child's distress (see Heywood and *C. Mather) and therefore it seems highly unlikely they would 'batter' their children. It is of note that several 16th- and 17th-century texts provide concrete evidence that extreme forms of punishment were condemned by society and parents. Newcome, for instance, removed his grand-daughter from her home because he could not tolerate his son's abuse of the child. (See also the texts of *Byrd, Heywood, Machyn, *C. Mather, Morris and Richards.) Wrightson (*English Society*, 1982), from his study of 17th-century society, argues that moderate discipline was both the ideal of 17th-century parents and the method put into practice. Thus it seems improbable that children would be subjected to cruelty on a large scale.

Overall, there has been surprisingly little change from 1500 to 1699. The same range of disciplinary techniques is found in each period – apart from 1500–49 where the sample size (2) was so small. There is one development, though – the emergence of an abstract concept of discipline (*C. Mather). This corresponds with the results obtained in chapter 4 which showed that abstract concepts of childhood and of the nature of the parental role appeared first in some 17th-century Puritans. This could either be due to the impact of the non-conformist religions, forcing man to re-evaluate his existence and/or the influence of the Puritan conduct books. It is equally likely, of course, that the latter merely reflect normal practice. The most popular of these works – Gouge (*Of Domesticall Duties*, 1622) – warned that though parents should 'correct' their offspring when necessary, they should also be sure that such a punishment was deserved. He also suggested that parents should reprimand before resorting to whipping and they should consider the child – 'if he be young and tender, the lighter correction should be used' (536).

1700–49. As would be expected from the results contained in chapter 4, some of the 18th-century diarists expressed how they thought a child should be disciplined (Powys, J. Taylor and M. Woods). All wished to find a happy mean between excess severity and excess indulgence. For example, J. Taylor (1743–1819) stated:

I have thought a deal on 'Train up a child in the way he should go'. I have considered the New Testament precepts on the same subject; and I have endeavoured to practise them . . . I recollected my being a child myself; how I behaved to my father and how he behaved to me. . . . I took notice also of other families in the neighbourhood, and attempted to derive some improvement from them. I laboured to preserve the love, esteem and affection of my children . . . I endeavoured not to overburden them with work . . . I was especially determined to keep them from following any course of sin, and from sinful companions . . . I made a practice of talking with my children, to instruct them to impress their minds . . . I then understood how unreasonable and cruel it was in parents to scold and beat their children for acting in such and such a manner; when they had taken no pains to instruct them that such actions were wrong. (118–20)

M. Woods (1748–1821) described how she believed children should be disciplined:

Some parents throw the reins on the necks of their children at a very early period, and hold them with a very slack hand; while others seem scarcely willing to loosen them a little, so long as they are able to keep hold of them. Either extreme, I believe is prejudicial. Too tight a curb sometimes makes young people fret under it, and produces an impatience to be entirely free, when more gentle discipline might have produced submission.

Little benefit can arise from mere compulsion, either in doing or forbearing, further than as it may gain time for the understanding and judgement to ripen . . . To keep children in the proper state of obedience, without having them stand in too much awe, is sometimes difficult. I have always wished that they should be afraid of doing wrong, but not afraid of me. . . . I am, from judgement, no great disciplinarian; if I err, I had rather it should be on the lenient side. Fear and force will, no doubt, govern children while little, but having a strong hold on their affections will have most influence over them in their progress through life. (205, 427)

Powys (1739–1817) was also against repressing children.

Boscawen, Boswell, Stedman and Thrale did inflict corporal punishment when they thought it necessary.[5] Boscawen's husband 'whipped' one of his sons as a young child; but the diary does not give the reason. Boscawen (1719–1805) herself would resort to, or at least threaten, physical punishment if she felt she was losing control.

Billy [4 years] is now perfectly recovered [from inoculation], I thank God. Purging discipline all over, but *my* discipline to begin, for it has been slackened so long it is unknown, how perverse and saucy we are, and how much we deal in the words won't, can't, shan't, ect. Today he would not eat milk for breakfast, but the rod and I went to breakfast with him, and though we did not come into action, nor anything like it, yet the bottom of the porringer was very fairly revealed. (1940, p. 179)

Boscawen did not insist on total obedience. For example, an older son disliked dancing the hornpipe before strangers: 'I have seen him try when I have pressed it extremely, but he has come running back the first step,

"Mama, I'm ashamed don't ask me to dance'" (1940, p. 123), and Boscawen did not force the issue. Boswell (1740–95) recorded beating his eldest son for telling a lie; but Boswell did not regard himself as a strict father in general. When his son was an infant, Boswell noted: '[I] dreaded that he would be spoilt by indulgence, and had poor hopes of my own authority as a Father' (vol. 12, p. 106). Four years later, Boswell is still regretting his 'too little authority' over his children (vol. 15, p. 17).

Stedman (1744–97) noted that his 13-year-old son, Johnny, was 'terribly leathered for picking apples from the garden which now was Moore's' and four years later Johnny also got a severe lecture for overspending his allowance (314). Stedman, however, did not believe in excessive punishment.

This evening some words happened between Mama and Johnny, [12 years] about his learning, he being today one year at Tiverton School. She said, *'Well, what have you learnt in that time?'* which he being affronted at answered, *'so much in one year as you'd have done in two'*, when she struck him a black eye which made high words between she and I, and she was exceedingly ill all night. [The next day] Johnny now begged her pardon to no purpose; and he went crying to school. She and I again fell out about this, and neither of us took any dinner till in the evening the boy came home, and all was reconciled. (276)

Stedman also wrote an advice letter to his son, to be opened after Stedman's death. He wished Johnny to be honest and industrious, obey those above him, not be extravagant and to take proper diet, air, exercise and recreation.

Thrale (1741–1821) would strike her offspring if they disobeyed her; but she tended to caution first. For example, she threatened her two daughters of 6 and 4 with a whipping for going out of bounds. One of her daughters was a sickly, peevish child and Thrale disliked her. Fearing that she would therefore discipline her too roughly, Thrale decided not to teach Susanna at home, but sent her to boarding school when she was not quite 4. Thrale was not entirely happy with her method of discipline: in 1782, when she had been married for 19 years and had had numerous children, she wrote: 'I am beginning a new Year in a new Character, may it be worne decently, yet lightly! I wish not to be rigid & fright my Daughters by too much severity' (523). Thrale did allow her daughters autonomy of thought: '[They] were always allowed & even encouraged by me to reason *their own way*; & not suffer their Respect or Affection for me to mislead their Judgement' (661).[6] Another mother, *Bailey (1746–1815), disapproved of her husband's method of treating children. She wrote in her memoirs that her husband 'had ever been sovereign, severe and hard with his children, and they stood in the greatest fear of him' (33). *Bailey's husband also wished to form an incestuous relationship with one of his daughters and, on her refusal, hit her, either with a horse whip or stock – *Bailey described such punishments as 'barbarous corrections' (40).

*M. Cutler, Wale, Wesley and Young employed pleas and reproaches in an attempt to regulate their offspring's behaviour. *M. Cutler's (1742–1823) son complained to his father that his farm was too small, to which *Cutler replied: 'If it is not so large as you could wish, why complain, when it is your lot to be so circumstanced in life? You have all your Father is able to give you' (vol. 2, p. 125), and went on to advise his son how to make the best of things. Thomas Wale's (1701–96) wife and 17-year-old daughter, Polly, seemed to be in continual conflict for several years: 'Mrs. W. in a mild manner talked soundly and freely with her daughter Polly and proposed a reconsiliation upon her better behaviour, and a confession of her faults within 24 hours' (160). Three years later: 'Daughter Polly having this day behaved rudely and impudently to her Mamma (and that in my hearing) received my reproaches and chastisement' (168). Wale considered that both parties were to blame and that the problem was best solved by Polly going away to school: 'The mamma too severe and the daughter somewhat as obstinate and provoking. Have on all sides consented to part' (175). Wale also wrote a letter to his son advising the latter to ensure he always kept his word. Charles Wesley (1707–88) noted that his children 'readily received my warnings' without specifying what these warnings were (139). While away from home, he wrote to his children requesting that they should rise early and study regularly, that his son should improve his Latin and his daughter should stop wearing shoes with high, narrow heels if they were making her fall. He concluded his letter by saying he hoped his children would accept his advice. Young (1741–1820) felt that it was his daughter's duty to be obedient as he had her best interests at heart. (Bobbin, 14 years, was refusing to take some medicine.)

But, my dear Bobbin, you ought to bring some circumstances to your recollection; the expense I have been at is more than I can afford . . . It is surely incumbent upon you to consider, that when a father is doing everything on earth for your good, yet you ought from feelings of gratitude & generosity to do all you can for yourself. (271)

Other parents such as Anne Cooke, S. Day, *Hicks, Lettsom, Mascall, *May, Mill and J. Yeoman wished their offspring to be 'dutifull' and not spoilt. For example: *John May (1748–1812) wrote to his children while he

was away from home 'that they must behave extremely well' (121); Mill
(1712–1805) re-married after his wife's death because he was 'afraid my
Children would be spoiled thro' want of proper discipline' (29); S. Day
(1747–1826) was 'thankful for the present privilege we enjoy of dutifull
affectionate children' (156); and John Yeoman (1748–1824) wrote to his
daughter at school: 'I hope that You are Improved and You pay Attention
to what Your Mistress tells You' (7). One child diary also reveals the level
of obedience and respect expected by some parents. *Philip Fithian
(1747–76) believed that 'The Duty of a Child to a Parent, is Obedience,
Love & all kinds of Regard' and gives an example of his theory in practice.
At the age of 20, he wrote to his father, asking for permission to go to
college: 'Relying on the Affection of a Parent, I have in this manner, with
all due Submission, but at the same time with the strongest Desire of
obtaining my Purpose, attempted to intreat your Encouragement &
Assistance in getting me put to School' (1). The three other child diarists
of this period (*Eve, *John Holyoke and *Elizabeth Phelps) who described
their home life, did not mention discipline. From the information
contained in their diaries, they do not appear to be as submissive or hold
their parents in the same awe as did *Fithian. There was no mention of
corporal punishment in any child diary.

Three autobiographers recalled receiving physical punishment in their
childhood. Boswell (1740–95) wrote: 'I do not recollect having had any
other valuable principle impressed upon me by my Father except a strict
regard to truth, which he impressed upon my mind by a hearty beating at
an early age, when I lied, and then talking of the *dishonour* of lying' (vol.
14, p. 20), and *Joshua Evans (1731–98) noted: 'I was early inclined to folly
and full of pranks, for which my mother often corrected me' (5). From
Stedman's (1744–97) autobiography, it appears that he was harshly
treated as a child:

I was teached blindly to obey, without consulting either my feelings, or my senses
. . . All this may be intended for the best and term'd, good education, but I shall
ever insist, that nothing can be worse than never to consult a child's motives or
desires which not only makes them miserable, but ten to one must end in making
them bad men. (23)

He gave examples of the strict obedience required of him: to eat whatever
he was given and that he was once told to drown a live mouse but, as he
felt unable to kill it, he substituted a dead one and was then whipped for
telling a lie. He was also 'unmercifully whipt' for stealing (8). Stedman
believed he was so severely treated because his mother preferred his
younger brother, who was not subjected to such a strict discipline.

Fletcher (1739–1814) recalled receiving other forms of punishment. She wrote that, at the age of 8 years: 'I was oppressed beyond measure with the fear of sin . . . This was followed by temptations unspeakable afflicting . . . The consequent effect of these temptations on my temper, drew on me so much anger and reproach from my parents, as made me weary of life' (7). Fletcher later became a strict Methodist against her parents' religious inclinations. As she refused to promise that she would not attempt to convert her younger siblings, she was asked to leave home. Thomas Wright (1711– ?) recalled that he wished to study astronomy and with his mother's help bought a number of books. His father, however, did not approve and burnt all the books he could find – although when Wright went to London to continue studying his father did send him money. Other parents had less influence over their older offspring's lives. *Griffith (1713–76) did not think his parents had a great deal of authority over him: 'My godly parents were very careful to prevent my falling into evil company; notwithstanding which, I frequently, without their knowledge, found such, and joined them in those vanities which are incident to youth' (5). George Whitefield (1714–70) similarly recalled his 'debauched' youth.

Five autobiographers recalled receiving nothing but kindness as children: *Bailey (1746–1815) recollected: 'I can truly say, it was seldom that an angry word was ever spoken in my father's family – by parents, brothers, or sisters, against me . . . So that I passed the morning of my days in peace and contentment' (11). Robert Day (1745–1841) described the friendly relations which existed between his father and himself and also mentioned that his frequent demands for money while at university were met by his father. Lettsom (1744–1815) referred to the 'tenderness' of his parents (16) as did J. Taylor (1743–1819) who remembered 'the superlative kindness of my family and my mother' (6). (D. Taylor, older brother of John, observed, however, that their father was stern and kept his children at a distance.) Finally, Young (1741–1820) noted of his mother: 'her kindness and affection for me had never failed during the course of her whole life' (126).

Discussion. As with the earlier time periods, these texts reveal the large amount of individual variation: from parents such as Woods who did not think children should be compelled to obey, to parents such as Boscawen and Thrale who exerted considerably more control over their offspring – the former by physical punishment, if necessary, and the latter by her rigorous educative system. A few diaries contain evidence on more rebellious children (such as that of Wale) and so reveal that children were not totally in awe of their parents. It does seem as if British parents were stricter than the American – none of the latter noted inflicting physical punishment.

Again it is the autobiographies which contain evidence on more severe forms of discipline, particularly that of Stedman who was very bitter about his upbringing. However, it is only 17 per cent of the autobiographers for this period who recalled receiving physical punishment and, in the case of Boswell, it would appear to have been only one whipping. Thus, though some children were treated harshly, they were a minority and not, as many historians have argued, the majority. In addition, the child diarists (the youngest of whom was aged 14) did not refer to physical punishment – as punishment to a child is a salient event, if it occurred it is likely that it would be recorded in the diary. It is possible though that these child diarists were too old for physical punishment – it appears to be the younger children who were subjected to such discipline, whereas older offspring were more likely to be reasoned with. However, apart from *Fithian, these adolescents were not in awe of their parents.

It is interesting that the emergence of articulated policies of discipline (Powys, J. Taylor and Woods) would not appear to have any effect on the way children were treated. Although these three parents did all consciously wish not to spoil or be too severe with their offspring, it seems from the texts that this is precisely what parents, who (from their diaries) did not possess such policies, were also doing (e.g. Boswell and Young).

1750–99. *M. Bayard, M. Fox, Fry, Mary Hamilton, *Huntington, Sandford, *Shippen and Trench described how they thought children should be reared – generally in an affectionate atmosphere with some restraints. *M. Bayard (1769– ?) considered herself to be an exception from the usual type of parent with regard to this. When visiting a friend *Bayard remarked: 'She has two sweet Children and manages them after my system, which I was so much blamed for at home; but these are a proof that gentleness is by far the best, with reasonable tempers' (96). However, with reference to the other diarists, she may not have been so exceptional. *Huntington (1791–1823), for example, wrote:

I do not like the punishment of whipping, unless when the child exhibits strong passion, or great obstinacy. It ought to be the last resort. Neither do I like those punishments which are chiefly directed to the selfish principles of our nature, as depriving a child of cake, sweetmeats, & c. I should rather aim to cherish feelings of conscious rectitude, and the pleasure of being beloved. I would have a child consider his parents' declaration that he is not good, his worst punishment. (109)

*Huntington listed those punishments which she considered to be suitable if a child 'has done very wrong': 'I would tell him he must not stay with mamma, or must not take a walk, or see the company, or that he must eat his dinner alone; and all, because he is not good enough to be indulged in these usual privileges. But there are some cases in which the use of the rod is indispensable' (109). Fry (1780–1845), in a list of 'Questions for Myself', asked herself: 'Hast thou . . . been . . . a tender, yet steady mother with thy children, making thyself quickly and strictly obeyed, but careful in what thou requirest of them?' (115) She did try to subdue the will of her children: 'My little——[either aged 6 or 4] has been very naughty; his will I find very strong: oh, that my hands may be strengthened rightly to subdue it' (137), but felt that she was not strict enough, compared with other mothers: 'I am sensible I do not apparently manage them [her children] so well, as many others do their children . . . I sometimes indulge them too much when young, I mean when very little, and perhaps their nurses do so too' (151, 169). Trench (1768–1837) believed that 'Chastisement, whether in the form of whipping, caning, slapping, ear-pulling, hair-dragging or any other uncouth and barbarous shape, never can produce good in private education; and many of the wise are doubtful of its having a favourable effect, even in public schools' (1837, p. 69). Trench thought that suitable punishments were: a slight fine, a temporary privation and a word or look of displeasure. She also regarded the use of 'shame' as a disciplinary technique as a 'hazardous experiment' (1837, p. 69) contrary to *C. Mather in the 17th century. She believed that a child should see that no punishment is intended to be vindictive, but is an act designed to prevent him hurting himself and/or others.

*Alcott, Macready, Rathbone, Thomas Rumney, Steuart, John Strutt and William Wilberforce all referred to the use of physical punishment. *Alcott (1799–1888) took over the disciplining of his two daughters of 2 and 3 years because he did not think their mother was firm enough.

Today I have been more than usually observant of their conduct at home while under the supervision of their mother. Some habits, I regret to say, have been permitted to attain a strength and fixity that will require no small degree of skill, delicacy, and yet force of discipline to remove – more than the mother will be able to put forth in the fondness and timidity of her heart. (46–7)

His resolve to assume responsibility for the control of his children's behaviour led *Alcott to inflict a certain amount of physical chastisement, particularly in dealing with his volatile younger daughter Louisa. However, as the children became older, *Alcott advised and scolded them rather than use physical punishment as a means of discipline.

Macready (1793–1873) was quite strict with his children; for example he wrote (the 'offence' was not described):

Before I came down my tenderness was put to a severe trial by my dear child [4 years] repeating the offence for which I had punished her yesterday. I felt there was no alternative, and I punished her with increased severity. It *cut my heart* to look upon the darling little creature's *agony*, as she promised to be good. I ordered her to be put to bed, and came downstairs in low spirits. God bless the dear child – my heart dotes on her, and I could weep with her, while I make her suffer; but I love her too well to bring her up with false indulgence. (vol. 1, p. 115)

Later he recorded: 'I was obliged to punish my dear Willie [2 years] for obstinacy and ill-temper. I love these children so fondly that I must be cautious lest my affection lead me into extreme indulgence which can only terminate in their unhappiness and my own bitter self-reproach' (vol. 1, p. 171). At times his own state of mind affected how he treated his offspring. 'I came into the drawing-room, wishing to vent my confused and tumultuous thoughts for mere relief. I sent the children, rather abruptly and pettishly to bed, which I should not have done, but I was suffering very much, and had lost command of myself' (vol. 2, p. 47). Rathbone (1761–1839) noted that her 15-month-old son was 'whipped in the night for violent crying' (53). Strutt's (1765– ?) 6-year-old daughter was 'naughty' while the family was camping.

I took her by the hand into a tent pitched by the side of the house and there I reasoned, and inflicted with my open hand, alternately, till I observed her mind received the warm, kind, pathetic, parental observations I addressed to her. And then after this very painful exercise of my duty I sent her in to her mother, and all in the house esteemed me a cruel man. But I rejoiced in the parental exertions I had made. (95)

Strutt was not so strict with his older offspring; for example when his 13-year-old son was leaving for boarding school, Strutt 'desired John when he was packing his trunk not to take anything he did not want, and unfortunately he rejected those books I wish he had always with him' (69).[7]

Steuart's (1770?–1808) manuscript is mainly concerned with the disciplinary problems she experienced with her young children and contains much useful information on one 18th-century mother's method of discipline. Her favourite punishment appears to have been to deprive the children of after-dinner fruit.

John [7 years] was getting up from table before his time (which is when the cloth is removed). I desired him to sit down again – but he would not do it for a moment till he had got to his Papa to put him in mind of a Pear he brought from——. He was not allowed to have any of the gooseberries Mag brought down from —— nor any plumbs or pears. Seemed more sorry to miss the fruit than that he had done something wrong. (MS, fo. 92)

Charles aged 4 was punished in the same way for crying often during the night, 'his other punishment was not being allowed to come into my bed this morning as he used to do'. A few days later John was again to have no 'plumbs'.

John told a fib to Charles in the morning about a play thing wch he said was below stairs, tho' it was under his arm . . . [he] seemed to feel the punisht a little – it was very mild however – but that was because he has heard such little fibs said by older people & was not so much to blame as for other ones – but if he falls into the same fault now that he has heard so much about it he must be severely punished. (MS, fo. 92)

Steuart would also send, or at least threaten to send, a child to bed for being 'impudent' or behave coolly towards that child, and at times resort to coaxing, although she did not approve of this method. 'John behaved very ill at going to bed – he wanted to sit up later. – I almost coaxed him to go quietly because he was very sleepy but I was wrong. I think I must give him a Punishment if this happens again' (MS, fo. 93v). John was whipped on one occasion and generally Steuart found it difficult to devise an effective punishment for him: 'It is very difficult to find a punishment for him as he receives it with a sort of indifference & good humour that makes it quite thrown away upon him' (MS, fo. 94). At times Steuart ignored her offspring's behaviour, for example when John and Charles were fighting; when Margaret dissolved into tears 'because John was to get all his lessons first' and when John cried loudly when his demand for bread to be put under his pillow was refused.

Some diarists used alternative methods of discipline. Burney (1752–1840) prayed nightly with her young son. In general this was 'a recapitulation of the errors and naughtiness, or the forbearance and happiness, of the day: and this I find has more success in impressing him with delight in goodness, and shame in its reverse, than all the little or great books upon the subject' (vol. 6, p. 224). Frances Calvert (1767–1859) tried lecturing her 12-year-old daughter who she thought talked too much: 'It went to my heart to be obliged to lecture her. She means nothing wrong, but the love of talking is so strong in her that I think it necessary to check it whenever I can' (56). Steadman (1764–1837) resorted to a persuasion when he discovered his sons had spent their pocket money on playing cards, of which he disapproved. He first expressed his disapproval of such amusements, persuaded his sons to sell their cards to him at prime cost and then threw the cards in the fire.

*Adams, *Alcott, Jones and Sandford advised their older offspring. For example, *Adams (1767–1848) was sent as a diplomat to Russia and wrote a letter of advice to his two sons who were left behind in America and Jones (1755–1821) intended to write a letter of advice for his childen to be opened after his death. When his son was starting university, Sandford (1766–1830) wrote to him asking him never to forget the purpose for which he was at Oxford, to proceed steadily and resolutely without deviating and to be cautious and slow in forming friendships. Reynolds and Watkin noted that they disapproved of their children's behaviour; but mentioned no methods of discipline used. For example, Deborah Reynolds (1770?–1803) wrote: 'John not always so good as he should be, but not to find fault with on the whole' (165) and Watkin (1787–1861) that 'the boys trouble me by their violence, rather, however, from thoughtlessness than bad intentions' (189).

Hardy and Skinner wanted a great deal of respect from their older children. Louisa Hardy (1789–1877) recorded: 'Later this Evening a most painful scene took place between Louisa and me on the score of Mr MaGregor [sister's suitor], as she was still too positive in her own opinion, and quite forgot that it was to her Mother that she was speaking' (164). Skinner (1772–1839) frequently clashed with his eldest son, regarding him as 'undutiful and ungrateful' and finally wrote Owen a letter:

After the insults which you have this day coolly and premeditatedly offered to your Father – a Father who has overlooked and forgiven similar insults several times, it is incumbent on that Father to tell his son that his own peace of mind requires that his feelings should not again be put to the trial of fresh insults. He is therefore come to the determination of again quitting his own house; but as he cannot do so for any long period without great loss – there being no one who will superintend the tything and farming concerns in his absence – he has to request *nay more, to command his son to leave him.* This Father, however outraged, will still consider the interests of his son as far as the purchase of a commission will go; he moreover will request his Grandmother to receive him for a time till steps can be taken to accomplish this end, and however repugnant it may be to his Father's better judgment. (165)

Skinner continually reproved and admonished both of his sons for their idleness, their inability to choose a suitable career and their lack of respect for him. He was one of life's misfits – Skinner annoyed everyone with whom he came into contact – and finally committed suicide, firm in the belief that he was the one wronged against rather than the instigator of the disturbances.

None of the child diarists made reference to physical punishment; but instead recorded various other methods of parental control. *Julia Cowles (1785–1803) at 14, was being sent to school in town but: 'Mama is something unwilling I should go, for fear that the pleasures of the world and its fashionable enjoyments will gain an ascendancy over me and raise ambitious views and lead me to the circle of an unthinking crowd' (26). *Shippen (1763–1841) at 15, often quarrelled with her mother. After one quarrel her father wrote to her: 'Have you persuaded yourself that your dear Mamma knows better than you & that it is your duty to obey her cheerfully always, altho it may sometimes seem hard. She loves you & wishes to make you one of the finest women in Philadelphia this should excite your love & gratitude & I flatter myself does' (72).

The British child diaries contain similar information. Elizabeth Wynne (1778–1857) observed that her 4-year-old sister 'went to bed without any supper because she gave the cook such a smack that for two hours she could not open her eye' (vol. 1, p. 18), and the diary also gives some indication of the kind of control her parents exerted over their offspring. When staying in another household, her younger sister Eugenia (1780– ?) noted:

It is impossible to do anything that demands attention when the children are so rowdy and it is of no use to bid them to be quiet for it is as if one spoke to the wind, they take no notice. One comes in with a chair as his carriage, pulling it after him with a great noise, another escapes with cries from the blows of his brother . . . If it was my children or my sisters I would certainly have shown them the door for it is unsupportable. (vol. 1, p. 119)

In addition, Elizabeth wrote: 'My little sisters were found a keeping a very impudent conversation with the Boys they are no more to play with them' (vol. 1, p. 186). However, Elizabeth was obviously not in awe of her parents. At the age of 17, she went out for a long ride with the groom and was very late back. 'Papa was rather angry for it and had made a great noise because Mamma had let me ride with Charles alone . . . At length Papa's passion passed a little and we amused ourselves very well this evening' (vol. 1, p. 180). Elizabeth would also quarrel with her mother if the latter was unable to take her to a ball or party. However, it appears that her father anyway would overrule Elizabeth at times: 'I had a little discussion with Papa for the music. I am to play Thursday and he will have my harpsichord sent there, which vexes me exceedingly, as it is a pity to spoil that good instrument. But as it makes him very angry I am afraid it must be so' (vol. 2, p. 54).

It would seem as if parents did possess greater authority over their older offspring than they would today. H. Backhouse (1787–1850), aged 21, wrote: 'In the evening, owing to my father's obliging us to come in sooner than I liked, I fell into a sulky mood in my own mind, growling over the misery of parental restraint. I sometimes feel my want of freedom rather galling' (12). The next year Backhouse complained about her mother forbidding her to go to a party. Nevertheless Backhouse was allowed some autonomy, for example she wished to be an artist; but her parents, as Quakers, were opposed to paintings. Despite their opposition, they fitted a workroom for her 'where I am to unfold my talents (if I have any) without interruption' (6). Sophia Fitzgerald (1765?–1826) had her own household; but was still expected to obey her mother. For example, one evening she did not visit her mother before going to a ball and the next day her mother 'told me how very much displeased she was with my behaviour to her. I certainly was very much in the wrong, and shou'd have refused going with the Duchess as it prevented me going to my Mother' (31). Fitzgerald was extremely upset at this incident, noting that she cried all night at the thought of being disrespectful to her mother. John Allen (1757–1808) regarded his father as 'unreasonable' and, at 20, complained of 'not being able to do hardly anything without incurring his Displeasure' (54) and Strutt (1796–1873) also referred to the almost continual friction which existed between him and his father. In contrast, the diaries of many children (e.g. John Barclay, Hamilton, Mary Jesup and *Sally Wister) reveal the deep affection with which they regarded their parents.

Three diarists, all American, give specific instances which reveal that they were not repressed by their parents or held them in awesome respect. *Condict (1754–79) enlisted her mother's help to get rid of a suitor who was pressing her to go to town with him. *Condict pretended her mother had forbidden her to go: 'So I winkt to her to say No for She was Present so She told him it would Not Doe' (49). *Sally Fairfax (1760?–85?), at age 11, wrote to her father telling him she thought he should have her younger brother inoculated and sent to school and that he was to send her his decision. *Winslow (1759–79), when aged 12, reprimanded her parents for their delay in sending a requested hat. 'The black Hatt I gratefully receive as your present, but if Captain Jarvise had arriv'd here with it about the time he sail'd from this place for Cumberland it would

have been of more service to me, for I have been oblig'd to borrow'
(7).

Three writers of autobiographies recalled receiving physical punishment as a child – Grant's (1797–?) autobiography contains information on a particularly cruel rearing. As young children she and her siblings either had their ears boxed or were rapped with a thimble. As they grew older, they were shut up in dark cupboards for any misdemeanour or whipped. Grant did not like milk; but the children were forced to eat whatever they were given, even though the milk made her sick. Her father supervised the breakfast, whip in hand, and Grant recalled being whipped as many times as was necessary for her to finish the food. If any child still refused to eat, the same food appeared at every meal until hunger forced the child to eat it – Grant remembered often being 'faint with hunger'. Grant did not have a high opinion of her upbringing. With reference to the care given to children, she wrote (her mother did not visit the nursery): 'In those days it was the fashion to take none; all children alike were plunged into cold water, sent abroad in the worst weather, fed on same food, clothed in the same light manner' (56). She then described the horror induced by cold water bathing in winter:

a large long tub, stood in the kitchen court, the ice on the top of which had often to be broken before our horrid plunge into it; we were brought down from the very top of the house, four pairs of stairs, with only a cotton cloak over our night-gowns, just to chill us completely before the dreadful shock. How I screamed, begged, prayed, entreated to be saved . . . all no use. (56)

Despite the repressive discipline, Grant did recall more happy times, for example playing with her father after dinner: 'Whatever the play was it was always charming, and redeemed all troubles . . . no longer the severe master, he [father] was the best of play fellows' (61). H. Backhouse and Robinson, though subjected to physical punishment, recalled a much less severe discipline. Backhouse (1787–1850) wrote: 'I was born of parents possessing so many virtues especially that of so loving their children, that while giving them every indulgence proper for them, they did not withold salutary punishments' (2). Henry Robinson (1775–1867) similarly noted:

I had a happy childhood. The only suffering I recollect was the restraint imposed upon me on Sundays, especially being forced to go twice to Meeting; an injurious practice I am satisfied. To be forced to sit still for two hours, not understanding a word, was a grievance too hard to be borne, I was not allowed to look into a picture-book, but was condemned to sit with my hands before me, or stand, according to the service. The consequence was that I was often sent to bed without my supper for bad behaviour at Meeting . . . Once I recollect being whipped by my mother for being naughty at Meeting. (vol. 1, p. 8)

Robinson did not consider that his parents had much control over him: 'I was an unruly boy, and my mother had not strength to keep me in order. My father never attempted it' (vol. 1, p. 5).

Three autobiographers, though giving no specific examples, recollect a repressive upbringing. *Samuel Bacon (1781–1820) noted that his father was severe and that he was afraid of him and Jane Knox (1790?– ?) also wrote that she and her siblings were very strictly reared. Trench (1768–1837) was orphaned at the age of 4 and was reared by her grandfather for a few years. He was confined to a chair, and so the care of Trench was given over to servants. 'I shall not dwell on the cruelties I suffered, possibly from the best intentions; but they have impressed me with a deep horror of unkindness to the young, and of all that is fierce and despotic in every shape' (1862, pp. 4–5). Trench's grandfather was kind to her and in adulthood she could not understand why she did not complain to him of her ill-treatment. However, after her grandfather's death, she was adopted by a friend from whom 'I never heard the tone or saw the look, of reproach; I cannot remember even that of mildest reproof' (1862, p. 7).

Other autobiographers described alternative forms of discipline and control. Mary Capper (1755–1827) and her brother became Quakers while away at school and were not allowed to return home until they had changed their religion. Notwithstanding this ultimatum, they refused and, after their father's death, their mother accepted their religious beliefs. *Fenimore-Cooper's (1789–1851) diary includes a memoir of one of his daughters, Susan. She recalled that her father usually brought back presents for his children when he had been away. On one occasion, Susan was given four dresses and then asked to give each one away. She described feeling extremely upset at the request; but, on doing as she was asked, was greatly hugged and kissed. (This kind of training in renunciation reappears, in a much more severe form, in Hare's autobiography in the next century.) *Hull (1765–1834) recalled that his mother reproved him for 'levity' and that he 'replied to her in rather unhandsome terms' which upset her (242). Amelia Opie (1769–1853) wrote of her mother that 'her word was law' (12). Townsend (1757–1826) described his upbringing:

I owe much to the love and care of an affectionate mother, not only for her regard to my personal safety, but also for her instructions and admonitions . . . As a proof of her regard to my religious interests, I recollect that on one occasion, when I had committed a great fault, and then told a falsehood to conceal it, (having the strongest possible conviction of my guilt) she kept me fasting in my chamber till I confessed my sin. (3)

From the evidence contained in the diaries, it appears that parents, particularly fathers, regarded it as their duty to advise their offspring. Two autobiographers noted receiving advice from their father and all seemed to appreciate the advice, even if they did not accept it at the time. On the death of his father, Thomas Belsham (1750–1829) wrote that he had lost 'an earthly friend, guide, instructor and counsellor' (68). *John Warren (1778–1856) also remarked on the death of his father that 'the loss of his advice and aid was very much felt' (130). J. Scott (1792–1862) regretted rejecting his father's advice. He received a letter from his father while at university: 'concerning his most earnest dissuasions from vice, especially those vices which he believed me to be most prone to. So just and tender were his observations that I regret I have thrown them to the flames. Would that his advice had been more fully followed and acted upon' (49).

Most writers remembered the kindness with which they were treated by their parents.[8] For example, *Benjamin Cutler (1798–1863) wrote of his mother: 'thirty-eight years of unchanged and fervent affection have I experienced from that mother' (163). *L. Dow (1777–1834) recalled that 'My parents . . . were very tender toward their children' (1). *Tucker (1775–1806) was reared by her grandmother and recollected nothing but 'her tenderness at an age when I most wanted protection' (312). Several British autobiographers recalled similar treatment, for example Eliza Fox (1793–1861) wrote: 'I was seldom checked or chided at home' (6); Holland (1770–1845) that her parents left her 'from fondness and inactivity to follow my own bent' (vol. 1, p. 158) and Moore (1779–1852) recalled that his 'youth was in every respect a most happy one' (vol. 1, p. 15). Frances Shelley (1787–1873) was greatly indulged as a child and, in fact, thought her mother was not strict enough:

She was not judicious in the management of her 'lambkin' (as she used to call me), a name which I resented, as I felt that I had much more of the lion than the lamb in my disposition. I disliked her impetuous caressing, and early learnt to allow myself, as a favour to *her*, to be kissed; and not, as is usual with most children, to receive a caress as the reward of good conduct and maternal affection. Although my mother spoiled me, there was a strong sympathy between us, and I liked to sit on her knee and listen to the old Scottish Jacobite ballads, and the sweet poetry of Burns. (vol. 1, p. 1)

Shelley's upbringing was markedly different from that of Grant, despite living with a decade of one another. (See also the autobiographies of

Discipline and control

*Joanna Bethune, M. Fox, Lettsom, Owenson, Turner (1875) and Watkin.)

Discussion. There is more preoccupation revealed in the 18th-century texts (both American and British) with the nature and function of discipline than in the earlier texts. Those writers who considered discipline in the abstract were advocating a middle way between severity and indulgence. As with the earlier periods, the majority of parents would seem to be following similar guidelines even though they did not consciously articulate such a concept.

A greater percentage of British (12 per cent) than American (4 per cent) diarists used physical punishment and a larger proportion of British than American autobiographers recalled a repressive upbringing. It does seem as if British parents wished to exert more control over their offspring than American. The phenomenon that has already been noted – that increased evidence on physical punishment and strict discipline is found in the autobiographies – occurs again. In addition, as with the earlier time periods, the child diarists did not mention severe punishment at all. Therefore only a few children endured a strict discipline and an even smaller minority endured a cruel regime – Grant's autobiography is the first text to describe actual cruelty. Her parents would appear to have been influenced by such theorists as Locke (1694) who proposed cold water bathing as a means of hardening children, although her parents did carry such a theory to its extreme by insisting that the children were plunged into cold water outside.

Trumbach in *The Rise of the Egalitarian Family* (1978) claims that, although the 18th-century British aristocrats were affectionate parents, their method of discipline was designed to break the will of the child. He further argues that whipping was the preferred punishment prior to 1750 and declined in popularity thereafter. The texts studied do not support his claim. They reveal no drastic differences in middle- and upper-class methods of discipline and no evidence that most upper-class parents wished to break their child's spirit – the texts of Burney, Douglas, Holland, Moore, Owenson and F. Shelley explicitly contradict this view.

The great variation in disciplinary practices is again striking – from the harshness of Grant's rearing to the complete freedom and indulgence of that of Holland and Shelley. Parents employed a wide range of disciplinary techniques, whipping was only one of the methods which they had at their disposal. A number of parents were prepared to use such a method, but not as a general disciplinary technique. It was used to

172

punish certain behaviours which a parent felt warranted this punishment such as lying, or kept as a last-resort method if a parent felt he or she was losing control, as in the case of Boscawen. Greven (1977) argues that 'moderate' parents from the 17th and 18th centuries were concerned with shaping their offspring's behaviour, regarding it as an essential parental duty: so did the parents examined here. The ability to regulate a child's short- and long-term behaviour is something which modern parents as well feel to be a crucial component of their role (Newson & Newson, 1976). Parents in earlier centuries were very much aware of their child's temperament (see Burney and Steuart, for instance) and organised their methods of discipline in order to achieve the best results with that child. It also appears from the texts that many parents were aware of contemporary advice urging them to maintain complete authority over their children, but found it impossible to be so uncompromising with their own offspring (see Boswell and Fry). Thus parents were forced to take each child's character into account and this hindered the imposition of an inflexibly harsh rearing regime.

1800–49. *Judson, *Longfellow and *Todd described their views on discipline without recording any actual punishment. For example, *Judson (1817–54), when extremely ill, wrote that if she died her children 'will be in trouble and I cannot help them; they will sin, and I cannot teach and discipline them' (300). *Longfellow (1807–82), with reference to the quotation 'Suffer the little children to come unto me' wrote: 'After that benediction how can any one dare to deal harshly with a child?' (383) *Todd (1800–73) believed that a boy needed 'a firm, decided government over him to which his will shall bow without any reserve, and with cheerfulness' (285).

*Louisa Alcott, Cobden-Sanderson, E. Gaskell, *Hayes, *Lovell, Lucas and *M. Walker reported inflicting physical chastisement. For example, *Alcott (1832–88) recorded:

New Year's Day is made remarkable by my solemnly spanking my child [5 years]. Miss C. and others assure me it is the only way to cure her wilfulness. I doubt it; but knowing that mothers are usually too tender and blind, I correct my dear in the old-fashioned way . . . Her bewilderment was pathetic, and the effect, as I expected, a failure. Love is better; but also endless patience. (354)

*Lovell (1809?– ?) gives a very detailed account of the methods she used to train her daughter, Caroline. The diary will be quoted from at some length because it reveals the insistence on obedience by *Lovell and also her realisation of her own child's temperament. The diary in its detail and techniques of discipline is very similar to that of E. Gaskell.

When Caroline was about a year old it became necessary for me to teach her her first lesson in obedience. The shovel and tongs seemed to fascinate her and she would take them and carry them around the house. I forbade her to touch them. She seemed perfectly to understand me, but continued to get them. I tried various ways to dissuade her from her purpose and finally concluded the best method was to divert her attention to some other object . . . But she had yet to learn obedience. When she was nearly two years old she one day took a cushion out of a chair and was bringing it across the room. I told her to carry it back and put it in the chair. She did not obey, and after repeating the requisition several times, to no purpose, I felt obliged to use corporal punishment. She had never before heard of such a thing and of course knew nothing about it. So that it was some time before I could make her understand that there was any connection between the correction and the fault. But she finally yielded. (52)

After this, *Lovell merely referred to the smack and Caroline obeyed. *Lovell thought that her daughter at the age of 5:

was generally obedient and easily governed, but there seemed to be a nervous impetuosity in her nature that sometimes led her into disobedience. For example, if she was jumping over a cricket and I said, 'Caroline, don't jump over it again', she would in an instant be over. The impulse seemed to have been given and her quick and active temperament nerved for the effort, and the prohibition was unheeded. But she was always sorry, and I made allowance for her peculiar temperament, which to a stranger might appear like indulgence . . . We wished to train her to a habit of implicit obedience with our directions, and on this account we frequently had occasion to correct her in such a way as we thought would best promote this object. (84)

For example, when *Lovell saw Caroline drawing the ashes in the fireplace, she told Caroline to come to her; but Caroline ignored her mother.

I felt afraid that I had been too lenient with her in former instances of disobedience, and thought I must now do something that would make an abiding impression upon her mind. I took her into another room and expressed to her my regret on account of her disobedience, and told her that I would have to whip her now as she had disobeyed in the same way several times and I feared she would again . . . She seemed very penitent . . . she entreated me not to inflict it [whipping], saying she would try to remember and obey *immediately* in the future. I considered her request and told her I would excuse her if she thought she should remember. As she never liked to have any one see her when she had been crying, I told her she might stay in that room until she had dried her tears so that she could look pleasant and then she might come out. (85)

A few months later Caroline refused absolutely to say 'Good Morning' to a visitor. She was sent to her room and, as she still refused, was smacked. Then, as she continued to say, 'No, I shan't,' her father eventually threatened to hit her with a stick and at that Caroline gave in. Her parents regarded the saying of 'shan't' with great distress: 'It seemed as if the enemy had her completely in his power, and was trying to effect her ruin . . . This was to us one of the most painful events of her life. It showed us the depraved state of the unrenewed heart, even of a gentle, lovely, and generally obedient child' (88).

*M. Walker (1814–97) would seem to have 'whipped' her children on a regular basis. She noted that, as soon as her 10-month-old son 'is put on the bed he begins to frolic and I often have to whip him to make him be still' (136). *Walker, though, did not insist on total obedience. For example, when Cyrus at 20 months asked for something and refused, at his father's request, to say 'please', his parents did not press the point although they were annoyed at Cyrus going to sleep with a 'smile'. Later, when her son was aged 4 and her daughter 2½ years, *Walker remarked: 'I had occasion about sunset to give my children a little whipping upon which, Miss Abigail ran off towards the lodges, bawling and calling "father, father, come home, mother whipped me"' (176).

A number of British diarists also revealed a concern for obedience. Cobden-Sanderson (1840–1922) wished to rid his 18-month-old son of 'bad habits' and make his 'will supple' (vol. 1, p. 246). Therefore Richard was whipped for crying when put to bed and occasionally during temper tantrums. Cobden-Sanderson did change his method of discipline after he realised he had punished Richard for crying when the latter was actually ill. Richard had been placed on a small table to stop crying. Once he had done so, he was taken out to the garden where 'he was very fretful, and falling to crying again. I upbraided him. Alas, blind and brutal, I did not know that he was not well' (vol. 1, p. 249). Richard was ill with fever for a few days and once he had recovered, his father wrote: 'He has gusts and wells of passion, but we bear with him and let him alone, and presently he emerges from the storm cloud radiant amid tears and with lips out-stretching for a kiss' (vol. 1, p. 250).

E. Gaskell (1810–65) wished to teach her young daughter self-control at an early age. For example, at 14 months: 'When she does become angry now . . . we look grave (*not angry*) and sometimes put our hands before our faces, which always attracts her attention and by so doing stops her little passion' (17). Gaskell was puzzled how to discipline Marianne at 2 years of age. 'The usual one [punishment], putting the little offender into a corner, had no effect with her, as she made it into a game . . . so the last we have tried is putting her into a high chair, from which she cannot get out, and leaving her there (always in the same room with one of us) till some little sign of sorrow is shown' (25). At 3 years Marianne was punished by being left in a room by herself for five minutes or so and was also slapped for the first time. Gaskell had been trying to make Marianne repeat some letters of the alphabet but Marianne refused. Eventually her mother slapped her hand every time she refused until Marianne said the letter. Gaskell was, however, worried about this mode of punishment: 'Still, I am sure we were so unhappy that we cried, when she was gone to bed. And I don't know if it was right. If not, pray, dear Marianne, forgive us' (32). Gaskell thought Marianne was still 'obstinate' at the age of 4 so that, after trying several means, 'we have been obliged occasionally to give a slight whipping. It has been done sorrowfully and gently, and has never failed in making her more obedient, without producing the *least* resentful feeling' (35–6).

Only one autobiographer referred to the disciplining of his own children. Lucas (1804–61) did not approve of corporal punishment; but found that the behaviour of one of his sons caused him to inflict it. Lucas described his eldest son at the age of 7 as 'a trying, though, in some respects, a gratifying child . . . He is also impertinent and very apt to answer again and recriminate when he is reprimanded. Occasional corporal punishment appears the most effective procedure, but it is very unpleasant resorting to it' (165). Hare (1834–1903) included in his autobiography some extracts from his mother's journal, revealing her insistence on obedience. When Hare was 2½ years she wrote:

After dinner today, on being told to thank God for his good dinner, he would not do it, I would not let him get out of his chair, which enraged him, and he burst into a violent passion. Twice, when this abated, I went to him and tried partly by encouragement, partly by positively insisting on it, to bring him to obedience. (16)

Hare remained in the dining room until he had said what was required of him. On Hare at the age of 5 his mother wrote: 'Augustus would, I believe, always do a thing if *reasoned* with about it, but the necessity of obedience without reasoning is specially necessary in such a disposition as his. The will is the thing that needs being brought into subjection' (27). The editor of Johnston's (1808–52) diary included some extracts from her mother's journal. These reveal that Johnston's parents also disapproved of any signs of rebellion, although they were nowhere near as harsh as Hare's mother. Her mother wrote that at the age of 3: '[Priscilla] attempted to rebel against her father's will, and I remember my distress on seeing him strike her rather sharply when in his arms, and her screams in consequence; but it had the best effect upon her will, and I do not think she ever disobeyed him afterwards' (iv). Louisa Knightley (1842–1913), at the age of 14, had been asked to an outdoor party; but as it rained she had been refused permission to go. She went anyway and an hour or so later was handed a note from her mother: 'Louisa, you will come away directly you receive this. You ought not to have gone, and if you are at tea, you will come away all the same' (5). Knightley described her father as the 'kindest of men' in spite of 'occasional displays of severity' (6).

Allen, Bain and *Prentiss all insisted on implicit obedience from their young offspring, although they did not record using physical punishment to achieve their aim. Allen (1813–80) noted how difficult it was to rear one's own children:

It is one thing to look upon their errors and failings as a disinterested party but quite another to do for the best as each occasion arises for the varying dispositions of childhood and their different temperaments; . . . As little as possible correct them before others; speak to them privately on any matter. Loud reproof may sometimes provoke to wrath instead of leading to repentance, though of course there are occasions when instant rebuke *is* needful. (110–11)

Allen further believed that a parent should not 'wound the spirit of a child . . . or alarm a child in manner or speech' (167). She also provided an example of her discipline. When her 5-year-old son hit his brother, Allen was 'touched by the penitent look on his face' and prayed with him for forgiveness. Later she noted: 'I felt this time I had been helped to decide it best to *persuade* rather than to use severer measures' (93). These diarists, however, relaxed their control over their older offspring. Louise Bain (1803–83), for example, did not approve of the theatre: but although she objected to her children going to see plays, did not stop them.

In contrast, *Duncan, Guest and Hanover (1964) wished to retain a great deal of authority over their older offspring. *Duncan (1808–76) for instance wished to suppress the independent thinking of her daughter: 'my eldest [14 years] my pride & hope gave me some trouble. She did not feel well & then there were several circumstances which made me feel badly that she was not willing to attend school because she disliked the Teachers. I trembled for her independent feeling' (77). *Duncan gave her daughter the choice of returning to school or to be a 'Millenor' – she chose the former. Guest's (1812– ?) 22-year-old daughter visited friends without telling her mother. 'I think these things wrong. While she remains under my roof I must be responsible and keep her with me, and prevent independent action . . . I reproved her and she was insubordinate; and so we did not speak for the whole time of our Canford sojourn, after which I condoned the offence' (1952, p. 207). Hanover (1819–1901) continued to exert control over her eldest daughter even when the latter married and moved to Prussia. She wished to know every detail of her daughter's life and constantly advised her how to behave (1964 text).

Other parents possessed considerably less authority over their offspring. Alford, Alison Cunningham, Palgrave, Lady de Rothschild, K. & J. Russell, Tregelles and *William Walker tried such methods of discipline as scolding and lecturing. For example, *W. Walker (1800–74) noted: 'Lectured my children on morals and good breeding, warning them against various immoralities' (172). Alford, Palgrave, de Rothschild and Tregelles all regret speaking harshly to their children. To his daughter while he was away from home, Alford (1810–71) wrote: 'I know I sometimes speak harsh words to you, dearest, but I should not do so; we must try to bear one another's burdens and make allowances for one another' (214). Another father, Tregelles (1806–84), felt 'I am too hasty with my dear children' (75). John Russell (1842–76) did not regard outbursts of temper in children as being very serious; but he did find that his 7-year-old son sorely taxed his patience:

Frank has been troublesome this morning & depressed me a good deal. Having his clean white suit on, the first thing he did was to cover his trousers with mud (out with the children). It seems Eliza wanted him to go to some place, or come home, & that he refused and went down in the dirt when she pulled him. I should think it was partly her fault, but as he was so dirty I told him to go & write his copybook till I came to fetch him out, & to stay in my room. When I came back soon after I found he had not staid there, but gone out to the hall to amuse himself. I therefore told him to do a little more writing, which he refused. However I insisted he should do it before he had his dinner. He was exceedingly obstinate, threw his copybook into the fireplace, & c. I left him a little, & when I came back found him ensconced comfortably under a table. I told him if he would not come out I must take away some grasses he had gathered, & as he would not I at last did so very reluctantly. Then he began to be so unhappy that I was afraid he wd make himself ill, so I offered to take him out, wh at once put him in a good humour, & he promised me to write when he came home . . . I hope he will not often be like this. (vol. 2, p. 502)

Unfortunately for Russell, though, Frank seemed determined to be as annoying as possible. He kicked a ball about the dining room although told not to, until he broke a window; refused to obey any orders or requests of others while insisting his own demands were met; threw a stone at their hostess and, finally, when told by Russell not to call him a 'beast', Frank did so, non-stop for half an hour. In the last case Russell believed 'a good boxing of the ears wd be far the best treatment though he does not actually inflict it (vol. 2, p. 518). Both parents appeared to be at a loss how to control their son; Russell wrote to his wife:

Obedience is not the most important, but surely they [children] must be prevented from doing things wh. injure themselves or others & be taught that some little deference is due to others' wishes instead of requiring every body to defer to theirs. Public schools are of immense value in this way & for some I think almost indispensable. As to managing a boy like Frank by love I do not believe in it, as he loves you more than anyone & yet you know how angry he is when you oppose him. (vol. 2, p. 511)

Russell did believe that 'untruthfulness ought to be treated as a very grave offence' (vol. 2, p. 511).

Collins, *Hayes and *Francis Lieber tried advising their offspring. John Collins (1848–1908), for example, on going to America for a lecturing tour, wrote a letter for his children to be opened after his death, exhorting them 'earnestly to love and cherish and to obey' their mother (132). Caroline Owen and F. Russell encouraged their children to show independence of thought. F. Russell (1815–98) wrote to her daughter of 15: 'Every day will now bring you more independence of mind, more capacity to under-stand, not merely to adopt the thoughts of others, to reason and to form opinions of your own' (216).

Occasionally a parent would not punish some particular behaviour even if it annoyed him or her, for example *M. Walker's husband would not punish his son for telling a lie, although *Walker (1814–97) would have preferred to do so. Frances Wood (1812–60) was exceedingly exasperated by one of her children's behaviour: 'I cannot really conceive of anything more vexatious than G's mingled stupidity and obstinacy over the lesson which I give him daily in Geography, – it is a glorious trial of Patience' (78).

There was again no record of physical punishment in the child diaries, although other forms of discipline were recorded. *Alcott (1832–88) mentioned running away and being tied to the settee the next day to repent and, at the age of 12, being reproved by her father for selfishness. Hanover (1819–1901) was left alone in a room as a punishment (1912 text). Caroline and Anna *Richards (1842–1913) were reared by their parental grandparents who, from the diary entries, appear to have been indulgent. The two sisters did not always concur with their grandparents' wishes: 'just as I had finished it [letter to her father], Grandmother told me something to write which I did not wish to and I spoke quite disrespectfully, but I am real sorry and I won't do so any more' (23).

Discipline and control

Another time they participated in a night sleigh-ride after their grandparents had forbidden them to go. The next day their grandparents found out and *Richards wrote: 'they acted so sober, and, after a while, Grandmother talked with us about it' (55). After Caroline and Anna promised not to go again, the incident was forgiven and forgotten. Their misdeeds were not always discovered, however:

Anna wanted to walk down a little ways with the girls after school so she crouched down between Helen Coy and Pattie Paddock and walked past the house. Grandmother always sits in the front window, so when Anna came in she asked her if she had to stay after school and Anna gave her an evasive answer . . . we just change the subject and divert the conversation into a more agreeable channel. (118)

In some respects their grandparents were strict: the sisters were meant to come straight home from school and had to ask permission to go to forms of entertainment – and permission was not always granted. Caroline and Anna did regard their grandmother as strict; but did not seem to mind too much: 'Grandmother knows that we think she is a perfect angel even if she does seem rather strict sometimes. Whether we are 7 or 17 we are children to her just the same' (124).

Fleming's (1803–11) diary is mainly concerned with her outbursts of temper and railings against authority. At the age of 7 she wrote:

I confess that I have been more like a little young Devil than a creature for when Isabella went up the stairs to teach me religion and multiplication and to be good and all my other lessons I stamped with my feet and threw my new hat which she made on the ground and was sulky an was dreadfully passionate but she never whiped me but gently said Marjory go into another room and think what a great crime you are committing letting your temper git the better of you but I went so sulkely that the Devil got the better of me but she never never whip[s] me so that I think I would be the better of it and the next time that I behave ill I think she should do it for she never does it but she is very indulgent to me. (40–2)

A few months later: 'I am going to tell you that in all my life I never behaved so ill for when Isa bid me to go out of the room I would not go & when Isa came to the room I threw my book at her in a dreadful passion & she did not lick me but said go into room & pray' (73–4). The only other punishment Fleming recorded was being fined 2d every time she bit her nails.

C. de Rothschild (1843–1931) thought her mother was not strict enough with her 13-year-old sister: 'It really makes me sorry to see the impertinent answer that Annie often gives to Mamma without the slightest provocation for them' (86). Both sisters were enraged by a

180

restraint which their mother wished to impose on them. Annie (1844–1926) refused to let her mother read a letter she was writing: 'I really could not . . . it pained me to see how angry Mamma looked but I would not show it' (89). Lady de Rothschild then said she would now read all their letters.

I was dumbstruck and could not say a word but tearfully left the room; I told it to Connie who continued arguing a long time, about it, saying she intended never writing, that she much preferred not writing at all to being subjected to such rule. That it was unjust, ridiculous; and we both rose to a pitch of furious indignation which I could hardly restrain. (89)

The threat was later withdrawn. K. Russell (1842–74) provided some indication of how she regarded parental discipline. At the age of 18, while alone in the house, she wrote: 'I do not like being here alone & yet I do not mind it so much. I am afraid it is selfish it is because no one finds fault with me. I should learn to bear reproof better – if I was more humble I should' (vol. 1, p. 97). *Long and *May noted receiving advice from their parents. *John Long's (1838–1915) father wrote in his journal:

John Davis [aged 11], wake up! Perform your duties better. Let not your time be wasted and lost. *Consider.* Can these bright days and these rich opportunities of your boyhood return to you? If you do not improve them in acquiring knowledge and in fitting yourself for a useful and happy life, will it not cause you bitter remorse as long as you live? (41)

While away at college *May (1840?– ?) wrote: 'What can be more cheering than a letter from my dear mother, and what excellent advice she gave me. I must always follow her counsels and admonition, for in them are found peace and happiness' (23).

Many diarists appear to have had an informal relationship with their parents. Gladstone (1847–1927) could criticise and disagree with her parents. Shore's (1819–39) own wishes were respected: for example, when asked to throw away some of her things in preparation for moving house, Shore threw out a model boat: 'However, papa and mamma, to console me for the loss of my steam-packet, which cost me thirteen pennies, very kindly indeed gave me sixpence apiece, and papa offered me a shilling for every stuffed bird I should throw away, but I would not for a guinea' (25). *Victoria Wortley (1837–1922) did exactly as she pleased, even if her activities caused her mother a great deal of anxiety, for example going up on deck during a squall and walking behind the Niagara Falls. Robert Fowler, Mary Gilpin, *Mary Harker, Johnston and Timms referred to the great affection they felt for their parents.

181

Discipline and control

Ten of the autobiographies contain information on physical punishment, and, of these, eight were British. The two American autobiographers did not describe severe punishment. *Mary van Lennep (1821–44) recalled that at the age of 6 she often lied and her father said he would punish her the next time she lied. When she did, she was sent to her room and the next morning hit on the hand by her 'distressed' father. *Martin Philips (1806–89) did not note receiving any physical punishment; but as he described his father as 'harsh', it is probable that he was the recipient of some.

In contrast, the British texts, particularly those of Cooper and Hare, described a considerably harsher disciplinary system. Cooper (1801–85) recalled only an exceedingly unhappy childhood: 'I and my sisters . . . were brought up with great severity, moral and physical, in respect both of mind and body, the opinion of our parents being that, to render a child obedient, it should be in a constant fear of its father and mother' (vol. 1, p. 51). Hare (1834–93) was adopted by an aunt who seemed to be dominated by two religious friends, both of whom advocated an extremely harsh system of discipline for Hare. From the age of 4, Hare was not allowed to play with toys or other children. He was shut up in his room on bread and water for two days as a punishment 'to break my spirit' and was often whipped with a riding whip by his uncle. 'In the most literal sense, and in every other, I was "brought up at the point of the rod". My dearest mother was so afraid of over-indulgence that she always went to the opposite extreme' (26). Other methods of repression were also employed – Hare was not allowed to express his own wishes or make a noise while playing. He always had roast mutton and rice pudding for dinner and, based on this, a new discipline was thought of for Hare when he was 5:

The most delicious puddings were talked of, – *dilated* on – until I became, not greedy, but exceedingly curious about them. At length *le grand moment* arrived. They were put on the table before me, and then just as I was going to eat some of them, they were snatched away, and I was told to get up and carry them off to some poor person in the village. (27)

Under the authority of his mother's friends, the regime became even worse. Hare was not allowed anything at all which gave him pleasure; if he liked anything or anybody, it was removed.

In comparison, other British writers of this period recalled less severe punishments. The editor of Bright's (1811–89) diary included a memoir of Bright's son. He wrote that his father was against harsh punishment but 'he never hesitated to administer corporal punishment to his children when he thought they deserved it. He was eminently just, and for this we all admired him and never questioned his decisions' (xii). John Epps (1806–69) wrote: 'I understand from those who knew me then, that I was peevish and fretful: so much so, that my father felt obliged to testify to the fact of my being his child, by using correction, remembering doubtless, what the wise man saith, "Spare the rod", ect.' (29) His father also wanted to create in Epps a feeling of self-reliance and courage. Therefore, from an early age, Epps slept in a room by himself, right at the top of the house. However, after Epps woke in a great fright one night, believing he saw the devil looking in the window, his room was changed. Lucas (1804–61) described his mother: 'she was strict in the management of her children, and sometimes did not spare the old-fashioned implement of birch, once considered so efficacious in the bringing up of youth. Though she never used it with passion and soon healed the wound with tenderness' (21). George Müller (1805–98), at the age of 17, travelled round the country without paying any bills and was finally imprisoned. His father came to collect him, paid the debts, and beat him 'severely' when they returned home.

Allen and Cavendish recalled the harsh treatment they received from a nurse and a governess respectively. Allen (1813–80), as a child, was looked after by a cruel nurse who frightened all the children with horror tales and hit them frequently. None of the children considered telling their parents of the cruelty. Lucy Cavendish (1841–1925) recalled the severe treatment meted out to her by her governess: whippings, being taken for walks with her hands tied behind her back and put between doors. However, parental discipline was much more lenient; of her mother, Cavendish wrote: 'there was no fear of our getting cowed and spiritbroken while we had that gentle and loving care always over us, though she interfered little directly between us and our governess' (11).

Acland, *Chace, *Jackson and Sewell recollected that their parents did expect obedience. For example, *Mitchell Jackson (1816–1900) wrote of his parents: 'to the day of their decease I should have considered a request or reasonable command as binding upon me as though I was still a boy and subject to their control' (128). Elizabeth Sewell (1815–1906) described her home as a 'paradise of freedom. My mother insisted indeed upon implicit and instantaneous obedience, but she never fretted us, and she entered into all our amusements' (4). Acland and Wilberforce both referred to parental advice on how to organise their studies.

Many autobiographers did specifically mention looking back on their childhood with pleasure. *Burroughs (1837–1921), for example, was deeply attached to his mother, although of his father he wrote: 'Father knew me not. All my aspirations in life were a sealed book to him' (106). *Van Lennep (1821–44), who did receive mild physical punishment, looked back on a 'sunny lovely childhood' (80). *Judson (1817–54) recalled 'being much petted and indulged during my first years' and also gave an example of overriding her parents' wishes (15). At the age of 16, *Judson wished to attend a dancing school, but her parents refused to let her go. She discussed the subject so often that her father finally forbade her to mention it. At that, *Judson informed her parents she was going to leave home and so her parents conceded to her wishes. *Todd (1800–73) believed he 'had one of the kindest and best of fathers' (29). *Colt, *Howe and *Lawrence similarly were very attached to their parents.

Many British texts tell the same story. Dawson (1811–78) noted that, despite his father's faults, the latter was always kind to him. Palgrave (1824–97) recalled the 'blithesome days of childhood' and wrote a long poem on his recollections of his happy childhood (6). John Pollen (1820–92) described his childhood as 'Ah! the former days! the sweet harmless former days' (5). Trant (1800–44) wrote of her father: 'He has indeed always loved me far, far better than I deserved' (5). (See also the texts of Anna Kingsford, F. Russell, Tregelles and Wood.)

Discussion. A greater proportion of parents, American and British, used physical punishment and also insisted on total obedience in this period than in the 16th and 17th centuries – it is the British autobiographies, though, which recall the harshest treatment. This agrees with part of Stone's (1977) argument that parents in the early 19th century were imposing a stricter discipline on their children than in the 18th. However, clearly the majority of children did not experience such a discipline, although for some this increased severity did amount to cruelty. Was this insistence on obedience and conformity part of a reaction to the rapid changes which were taking place in society – the change from a rural to an industrialised society? Perhaps certain people wished to restore some kind of order to their lives and began by ensuring that they would not rear rebellious children. It is possibly this severity in the early 19th century which has led researchers to believe that parental discipline prior to the 19th century was also severe.

An examination of the upper-class texts reveals that there is still no real evidence to suggest that the upper classes were any more strict than the middle, even in an age when many children were reared more strictly. Of the two writers who described enduring cruelty as children, Cooper was a member of the aristocracy whereas Hare grew up in a middle-class home. Some aristocratic parents such as Guest and Hanover undoubtedly wished their offspring to be under their total control but others such as de Rothschild discovered that their children would not tolerate this imposition and yet others, for example F. Russell, had no such wish and in fact encouraged independent thought in their sons and daughters. If anything it was the middle-class parents of this period who were preoccupied with ensuring that their children would be implicitly obedient.

Again, as with the 16th, 17th and 18th centuries, there is an enormous variation in the strictness of discipline imposed by parents of all classes, ranging from J. Russell who was unable to control his son's behaviour to Gaskell and *Lovell who were constantly trying to ensure that their young daughters would be implicitly obedient; and from Allen who did not wish to 'wound the spirit of a child' to Hare's mother whose mode of discipline was designed to break Hare's spirit. Hare's text is the only one in the large sample studied which describes a disciplinary policy specifically aimed at breaking a child's will.

1850–99. No American text for this period contains any relevant information. The British texts of the late 19th century reveal a reduction in the severity of discipline imposed on children when compared with the early 19th century. Seven diarists referred to discipline but only one to physical punishment. Waugh (1903–66) recorded striking his 14-year-old daughter after she broke his 'acme' chair for the second time (1976 text). Brabazon and Gurney did wish their children to be obedient. Gurney (1851–1932), for example, wrote of her offspring:

> The children were implicitly obedient. I don't remember any instance of obstinacy that we did not overcome without trouble, but once a command was given it had to be obeyed. The great point was never to make anything obligatory that could not be easily and well carried out . . . Let the little ones understand from the very first that the parents' 'No' means 'No' and the parents' 'Yes' means 'Yes'. (38, 112)

Four British diarists did not describe actual punishment, but their diaries provide an indication of the type of discipline they imposed on their offspring. Hochberg (1873–1950?) was annoyed at her son's shyness: 'I felt really at one moment when he spoke in a whisper with his hat in front of his mouth, that I would like to go up and give him one shake' (195). Hutchinson (1880– ?) had decided when his son was born that comics would never enter the house. Unfortunately his son's wishes

185

upset Hutchinson's plans: 'how insidiously the dashed things come'. Hutchinson was unsure how to solve another problem:

I agree entirely that indiscriminate giving of money, or of presents, to children may well be the sowing of seeds ruinous to their characters and disastrous to their futures. But of, instead, direct payment for work done I am not so sure. There is a danger that way, too, and as grave a one – the danger of implanting the idea that service of whatsoever sort must be paid for. (230)

Arthur Weymouth (1895– ?) wished to be able to advise his 14-year-old son: 'I must, somehow or other, utilize my own experience, to prevent him making the mistakes I, and so many others have made . . . I should like to be able to write to Anthony in such a way that he accepts my advice and acts on it, Anyhow I'm going to try' (112). Dorothy White (1877– ?) described her stepdaughter arguing with her father:

When we were sitting at table an argument began in which Molly, as usual, held her own against her father, cheerful, obstinate and positive. Her father, neither cheerful, obstinate or positive, but clinging to the last shred of faith in his better judgement, mildly querulous, attempted a defence. One by one, however, his defences were swept down: 'he did not know this; he did not know that'. At last he was driven against the wall. 'My dear Molly', he burst out, 'I don't know *nothing* about everything!' (47)

Three child diarists referred to home discipline. The Bowen children (1864–?) would appear to have been strictly reared. They were largely confined to the nursery and schoolroom and their parents were aloof – the children, in fact seemed to be afraid of their father. Nevertheless, despite these restrictions, from the evidence contained in the diary, the children did not appear to be repressed. They had frequent holidays and plenty of time to play and they did not mention any specific punishment. John Colt (1916– ?) at the age of 17, noted a scolding from his father for omitting to write his usual weekly letter and also wrote that his father would be 'foaming' if Colt failed an exam he was about to sit. Later, his half-term report was bad and his father was annoyed, but as the end of term report was better, Colt did not have to do any school work during the holidays. Stephen King-Hall (1893– ?) did not seem to regard his parents with awe, writing while he was at college: 'I shan't wear a knickerbocker suit so its not much good sending one' (338).

In marked contrast to the autobiographies of the early 19th century, the later autobiographies contain no evidence on physical punishment. Three autobiographers recalled other forms of punishment. James Agate (1877–1947) remembered 'being perched on a chest-of-drawers for punishment' (28); Elsie Mildmay (1850?– ?) was deprived of cakes or jam at teatime for any misbehaviour and Gurney (1851–1932) recorded:

My earliest impression was made upon me by my own mother. I can well remember her punishing me for my violent temper, as a very tiny child, and in a way which I never forgot. She took me into a large, unused bedroom, and told me to remain there till my passion was over, and then closed the door quietly. At first I remained furious, and then feeling absolutely foolish I thought the best plan would be to go downstairs, which I did, deeply ashamed of myself and I don't think I ever gave way to such temper again. (18)

It does seem as if children, at least in some families, were expected to be obedient. Hutchinson (1880– ?) wrote that 'Sons did what their fathers told them in those days' (74) and Mildmay (1850– ?) remembered that 'obedience to parents was *then* not only taught, but also practised' (9). However, in other families, the parents had less control. Cummings (1889–1919), for example, believed that 'Ours was a family – not uncommon I imagine, at any time – in which the parents were under the tolerant surveillance and patronage of the children' (1920, p. 76). Sidney Horler (1888– ?) wished to leave school at the age of 14: 'My father, quite evidently, was puzzled; he did not know what to do with me. But my determination was far stronger than his arguments: I had my own way' (1933, p. 29). Hochberg (1873–1950?) observed that 'no one could have had a happier, freer, more joyous youth' (9) than she had and Waugh (1903–66) wrote that he was never shouted at or threatened at home.

Discussion. The level of strictness in this time period returns to the same level of severity as in the 16th to 18th centuries. Thus the first half of the 19th century was atypical in the harshness of the regime to which children were subjected – the peculiarity of the period would repay further study.

The lack of information on discipline in the American texts is striking. It seems that American parents of this epoch were not concerned with regulating the behaviour of their sons and daughters to any great extent and certainly were less concerned than the British parents. I can offer no explanation for this; there does not appear to be any difference in the status and composition of the 18th-century American sample when compared with the 17th. Bremner (*Children and Youth in America*, 1970–3), suggests that the growing leniency of American parents was due to the effects of the American Civil War of 1861–5. The war finally ended British influence in America, so causing American parents to reject the British method of rearing children. Moreover, Bremner argues that American parents after the Civil War consciously wished to bring up more independent and less controlled children as they considered this to be fitting to the creation of a new nation. However, I am reluctant to accept this solution and must leave it as an unsolved problem.

Discipline in school[9]

There can be no doubt whatever that severe flogging was a normal and daily occurrence in the sixteenth- and seventeenth-century grammar school. (Stone, 1977, p. 164)

Much less information is available on discipline in school than on discipline in the home. No relevant information is available for the period 1500–49; no manuscript and very few American texts referred to school discipline. Table 8 shows the number of sources which made reference to school discipline.

1550–99. Only one diarist referred to school discipline. Samuel Ward (1571–1643) regretted 'my little pity of the boy who was whipt in the hall at college' (103). Forman (1552–1601) in his autobiography recalled that his school teacher 'beate him' for not learning some of his work (14) and Norwood (1590–1675) wrote that he was apprenticed to a master who treated him harshly.

1600–49. Woodforde (1638–1730) referred to school discipline in her diary and she believed that her son should accept whatever punishment was due to him.

This evening I had the cutting news that my second boy was in rebellion at the College of Winton, where he and all his companions resolved not to make any verses, and being called to be whipped for it several of them refused to be punished, mine amongst the rest . . . if [they] do not, they must be expelled. God I beseech thee subdue their stubborn hearts, and give them grace to repent and accept of their punishment due to their fault, and let them not run on to ruin. (15)

Her husband went to the school and their son was persuaded to take the punishment. Not all teachers could control their pupils. *Edward Taylor (1642–1729) at 16 years wrote of his teacher: 'Mr. Graves, not having his name for nought, lost the love of the undergraduates by his too much austerity, whereupon they used to strike a nail above the hall door-catch while we were reciting to him, and so nail him in the hall' (15).

Information on school discipline is also provided by three autobiographies. Evelyn (1620–1706) recalled that it was intended he should go to

188

Table 8. *Number of sources containing information on discipline in school*

Time period	Source											
	Diary			Child diary			Autobiography			All		
	A	B	% of sample	A	B	% of sample	A	B	% of sample	A	B	% of sample
1550–99	0	1	8	0	0	0	0	2	33	0	3	14
1600–49	0	1	4	1	0	9	0	3	75	1	4	12
1650–99	0	2	7	0	0	0	0	1	50	0	3	9
1700–49	0	1	2	1	0	11	0	3	17	1	4	5
1750–99	1	6	9	1	3	14	1	7	21	3	16	12
1800–49	2	0	3	3	3	13	3	8	34	8	11	12
1850–99	0	1	8	0	3	50	0	2	17	0	6	18

Discipline and control

Eton, but he 'was so terrified at the report of the severe discipline there' that he refused to go (vol. 1, p. 5). Josselin (1616–83) noted he was never whipped at school: 'I thank god for his goodness to me insomuch as for not saying my lessons I remember not that I was ever whipt' (2). Martindale (1623–86) received corporal punishment from one school teacher, but his father did not approve: 'This [punishment] I concealed: yet at last it came out, and mightly offended my father, but the Schoolemaster crying "peccavi" and promising to do so no more, all was well again' (14).

1650–99. The diaries of J. Erskine (1679–1754) and Morris (1659–1727) provide information on school discipline, and both fathers were against severe punishments. The tutor of Erskine's son complained about the boy's 'perverseness'. Erskine was angry:

As to the perverseness of the poor young child, it rarely is unconquerable in a boy so very young, if proper methods be taken. I know the boy had a wantonness, as such of his age use to have, and is more plyable by perswasion than by rough treatment. But Cumming's crabbed peevish temper made him use the last method, and often to beat him severely for trifles, and sometimes when the boy was more in the right than he, till I put a stop to it, and now he says himself the boy does well. Lord be thanked he learns well and would learn better if he had a more painfull and better temper'd master. (73–4)

Morris' son complained of the harsh treatment he received at school and his parents wrote a letter to the headmaster about it. However, as his son was still being punished severely, Morris went to the school.

He [teacher] profess'd to me, He had not given him above three Lashes at a time since I talk'd with him about it: He said also I should tell his Mother he would Whip him no more. I answered him, then all would be spoil'd that way: No. I did not desire that; But only moderate Correction, which to him a Good-Natured & Flexible, though Lazy, Boy I hoped would be effectual. I desired also he would keep him in the School at Playtime when the other Boys were at Liberty. He said that would [be] no manner of Punishment to him; For he would sit in his Chamber by himself many hours together. However, I answer'd it might be grievous to him when he was forc'd to do so. (104)

Finally, one autobiographer for this period mentioned the treatment he received at school. Fretwell (1699–1722) recollected that, at one school he attended, his teacher, though good, was 'too severe, tho' I was never whip't at school by any of my masters' (185).

Discussion. The picture given by the 16th- and 17th-century texts is much less dramatic than the one put forward by Stone. Corporal punishment was certainly inflicted in schools; but not every pupil was subjected to it. Moreover, most parents disagreed with severe punishment and were prepared to intervene on their child's behalf (J. Erskine and Morris for example). This finding contradicts Ariès (1960), who argued that pupils were severely beaten at school because their *parents* wished them to be so disciplined. Parents did not wish their offspring to be unrestrained, but desired moderate as opposed to brutal punishments.

1700–49. Two diarists, one a school teacher, the other a tutor, described the method of discipline they imposed. In Fletcher's case, minor faults were generally overlooked, but 'when actual sin was committed' it was written down and discussed at the weekly meeting. At these meetings, Fletcher (1739–1814) noted 'we always adapted our conversation to the little criminal' (61). If the children continued to disobey: 'we would then add unto our words correction; making them feel pain, that the impression might be strong and more lasting; and that they must never resent or resist these corrections, for it was more painful for us to give, than it could be for them to receive them' (56). John Harrower (1735?– ?) was responsible not only for the education of his two pupils but also for the care of them. He would use corporal punishment, with the boys' father's approval. For example, he wrote:

one night in the Nursery I wheep'd Billie [aged 5] for crying for nothing and she [Billie's mother] came in and carried him out from me. Some nights after he got into the same humour and his Papa The Col°. hearing him call'd me and Asked why I cou'd hear him do so and not correct him for it; Upon that I told him how Mrs Daingerfield had behaved when I did correct him. At that he was angry wt her. (96)

*Ebenezer Baldwin (1745–75), aged 17, recorded the punishments meted out at his college:

At night, Nichols, Halliok, and Brewster were publickly admonished for having a Dance at Milford, and for their general conduct. Bull, for going to Milford without liberty and for his general conduct, was ordered to depart from College and to live under the care of some minister at a distance till he should show signs of reformation and be fit to take a degree. (445).

Three autobiographers referred to the punishment they received at school. Boscawen (1719–1805) recalled 'I never was whipped at school' (1940, p. 89), whereas Boswell (1740–95) wrote: 'I cannot say that I found my Punishments when at School to be pleasant' (vol. 1, p. 60). Stedman (1744–97) recorded both the punishment he received at school and his father's reaction to it:

Discipline and control

[I] was again put to learn English with one, MacWilliams, a soldier, and regimental schoolmaster, who, for a very paltry offence, almost tore one of my ears from off my head, and which so prodigiously incensed my father, that he not only again took me home, but would have effectually kild the military pedant had he not begg'd for mercy on his knees. (9)

Discussion. There is little change from the earlier centuries – some pupils were whipped, some not. Again, at least some parents would not tolerate any cruelty to their child (see Stedman's diary). In addition, as *Baldwin's and Fletcher's diaries reveal, whipping was not the only punishment inflicted, milder methods generally being tried first.

1750–99. Seven diarists described school discipline. Calvert's daughter was at boarding school and was often taken out by her mother. While visiting Isabella (aged 11) one morning, Calvert (1767–1859) noted: 'I had the inexpressible mortification of hearing that she had been very pert to Mrs D. who requested that I would not take her. I actually shed tears I was so hurt, but I applauded Mrs Devis for informing me, and I trust this will be a useful lesson to Isabella, she cried the whole time I was in the room' (24).

Other diarists were less than happy about the discipline imposed on their children. Hardy (1789–1877) was very concerned when she discovered that the governess had been beating her youngest daughter 'most cruelly' (71). Moore (1779–1852) did not think that the teachers at his daughter's school understood her temperament. He visited

my dear Anastasia, whom I found in trouble. Great complaints against her from the schoolmistress for inattention to her lessons. Perceived the schoolmistress had mistaken her disposition, and supposes that it is obstinacy prevents the child from answering what she knows; when, in fact, it is the confusion arising from a strong feeling of reproof or disgrace that puts all her ideas to flight and makes her incapable of any thing while she is in that state. Lectured my dear little girl very gravely as I walked with her to meet her mama, who also was as serious as she could be about it, though feeling all the while, with me, that the schoolmistress had (as she herself used to do) mistaken the child's disposition. (vol. 4, p. 132)

Moore also recorded his son being punished at school. He received a 'Letter from Tom's schoolmaster, confessing that he had given our poor little fellow an over-severe beating one day, for a supposed offence of which he afterwards found the child to be innocent. The fellow's confessing it is something, though the marks all over the child's body sufficiently tell the tale. Little Tom [11 years] very manly and sensible about it' (vol. 6, p. 49). Holland (1770–1845) did not describe the discipline

192

her children received at school; but she was worried when her son was about to start Eton because 'the *world* of a public school he will find very different from that of the world seen from under the paternal roof' (vol. 2, p. 236).

Two teachers recorded their own methods of discipline. When *Sewall (1797–1846) took over his school he wrote: 'I found that I could not get along without a stricter discipline – consequently I laid down my rules, but some of the large scholars did not feel willing to come under the regulations, and have this day while out of school threatened to ignore me as I have just heard from a friend to the school' (33). Jones (1755–1821) wrote of his four pupils:

My happiness with regard to my little Boys is very great. The eldest is rather opinionative, yet I can easily manage him. The two middlemost are possess'd of amazing *Sensibility*. Whatever home reproof I may give either or all of them upon occasion, it never causes any Variance which lasts many moments. They never seem to bear the least resentment, nor can I: we always sit down to dinner together on the most loving Terms. (29)

Evidence on school discipline was provided by four child diarists. None described severe treatment. For example, at Litchfield school, the pupils, all girls, received credit marks for doing well and lectures for doing badly or any misbehaviour. As *Lucy Sheldon (1788–1889) noted: 'I heard Miss Pierce tell our faults, had the pleasure to hear her say she had seen no fault in me for the week past' (44). The diaries of Anna Bower (1768– ?) and *Powhattan Robertson (1769– ?) described the enjoyable time the children had at school or university.

Five autobiographers recalled the punishments they received at school. Three were subjected to physical chastisement. W. Scott (1771–1832) believed: 'I was indifferently well beaten at school; but I am now quite certain that twice as much discipline would have been well bestowed' (322). F. Shelley (1787–1873) went to school at the age of 8 and later wrote the following account of her school days:

Marks of approbation, and of disgrace, were pinned on our frocks. I seem to have been always in disgrace! I was wilful, headstrong, and determined to have my own way. The youngest sister of Miss Dutton, who kept the school, took me in charge, but in spite of violence and smacking, she could not subdue me. On one occasion she hit me over the shoulders with a wooden case full of pens. They flew out over the room in all directions, much to the merriment of my companions, who left their books to pick them up, and restored them to their owner with mocking curtseys. After this the elder sister, a delicate gentle creature, took me under her care, and I shall never cease to remember her kindness, her judicious management, and the strong affection which she inspired. (vol. 1, p. 5)

Discipline and control

Corporal punishment was employed at Townsend's school as well; he described the steward as a 'rigid and vigilant disciplinarian'. However, it was possible to gain a reprieve from this form of punishment. Townsend (1757–1826) recalled that he was due to receive a whipping for 'profaning' the name of God; but instead lost his privileges (5). Owenson (1780?–1859) wrote that at her school the disgrace of doing wrong was usually substituted for a punishment. *Silliman (1779–1864) described the school discipline he experienced: 'The discipline of our almost infant school was parental and not severe discipline. The rod was rarely or never used; but milder methods were employed' (vol. 1, p. 19). *Silliman gave an example of one of these 'milder methods'; although it is arguable that, at least from the child's point of view, this punishment was not in the least milder. *Silliman recalled that one boy and girl, for whispering and playing indoors, were made to walk home as yoke-fellows by means of a double yoke of willow branches fastened to their necks. 'The little girl, not at all abashed, addressed her shrinking companion by epithets of endearment: he was compelled to bear the sly titter of his school-fellows, – a punishment not soon forgotten' (vol. 1, p. 19).

Moore, O'Connell and Robinson described the general discipline at their school, although they were not punished. Moore (1779–1852) recalled that his first teacher drank heavily and then whipped the pupils for disturbing his slumber. Daniel O'Connell (1775–1814) wrote that he was not beaten at school, although he was the only one in his class who was not – due to the fact that he paid attention. Robinson (1775–1867) would have wanted to go to grammar school but he 'had heard that Mr. Lawrence was a flogging master' and was therefore glad not to go.

Discussion. As with the previous time periods, although parents did wish their offspring to be subjected to some discipline and control while at school (see Calvert's diary), they did not approve of severe punishment (Hardy, Holland and Moore). Individual school teachers did vary in the type of discipline they imposed, for example Harrower whipped his pupils whereas Jones did not. No dramatic transformation in the range of school discipline which children experienced has been found. Although some were physically punished at school, many others were not. However, it does appear that the likelihood of receiving corporal punishment was increased if a boy was sent to an English public school.

1800–49. Two diarists, both American teachers, described their methods of discipline. *Howe (1801–76) ran a school for the blind, in which corporal punishment was forbidden, although he did cane two pupils who set fire to the school building for the second time. *Ward (1841–1931) was quite different. After a few weeks' teaching he noted: 'I got a whip this morning, but I hope I shall have no occasion to use it' (27). His hope was not realised as he described whipping a few pupils and also slapping another, causing the boy's nose to bleed. 'Then John Bush told me that the parents did not wish me to punish their children in this manner' (90). However, *Ward carried on, writing that he whipped one pupil for running away from school and was going to whip another but the pupil ran away first. He also kept some pupils in detention. He did not use his whip all the time, for example on one occasion he wrote: 'I whipped with my palm too savagely' (91). This would seem to mean that he merely slapped a pupil.

Three child diarists, two of them at Eton, recorded receiving physical punishment at school. *Long (1838–1915) wrote: 'I was *ferruled* for chewing boxberry leaves at school' (16). J. Gaskell (1810– ?) and Thomas Selwyn (1812–34) referred to the 'floggings' inflicted at Eton. For example, James Gaskell wrote: 'He [teacher] first flogged one of the collegers, then called for me. I begged him to give me my first fault. He answered that I had committed an error very early. I scarcely refrain from tears but did' (3).

Three diarists noted other forms of punishment. *Caroline Chester (1801–70), attending Litchfield school, was scolded for staying out after 9 p.m. She regarded this scolding as 'a blast which never no never will be erased from my memory' (154). *C. Richards (1842–1913) mentioned that she was kept in after school on two occasions; once for laughing and once for whispering in class. Mary Brown (1807–33) attended school in France, and did not have a high opinion of the teacher's authority. She described the pupils jumping over stools, squirting ink, tossing books and dancing on the tables. The most common punishments issued were to make the offenders kneel or wear a black bonnet or write out poems. The other diarists who wrote diaries while at school did not refer to punishment at all, which does imply that, for them, the discipline was not severe.

Many of the autobiographers for this period, particularly those at the English public schools, recalled being subjected to very strict, if not cruel, discipline. This parallels the increase in severity in home discipline of the same period. *Howe and *Lawrence both referred to unpleasant school days. *Howe (1801–76) recalled that all pupils were beaten at his school because the principal enjoyed inflicting pain. *Lawrence (1814–86) complained to his father of the harsh, inconsistent discipline imposed at the boarding school he attended – the teacher pulled the boys' hair and ears. He finally ran away; but at his father's request went back to school. *Chace (1806– ?) recollected that, at the public school she and her sister attended, the pupils were expected to bow or curtsy to the teacher every time they stood before her in class. *Chace and her sister, however, were Quakers and such obeisance was against Quaker principles. On refusing to curtsy, the girls were threatened with a whipping; but by the intervention of their father the next day, they were eventually excused from curtsying.

The British writers described much harsher treatment. Acland (1809–98) attended a private school, presided over by a severe master: the pupils were whipped for arrears in work and for being the last one down in the morning. Acland spent five years there and felt he was being 'crushed'. Bright (1811–89) was sent to a highly recommended Quaker school; the teachers were exceedingly strict, inflicting 'harsh if not barbaric' punishments. He was forced to take a cold bath once a week; regarding it with the same horror as did Grant in the 18th century: 'I cannot describe the terror which seized and afflicted me on the mornings when I had to undergo the inevitable plunge' (6). His parents removed Bright from the school and also began an inquiry into the state of other schools. Cooper (1801–85) wrote of his school: 'The memory of that place makes me shudder; it is repulsive to me even now. I think there never was such a wicked school before or since. The place was bad, wicked, filthy; and the treatment was starvation and cruelty' (vol. 1, p. 39). Cooper was, however, sent to Harrow at the age of 12 and there he spent much happier school days. Epps (1806–69) described his protective measures for the punishment he received at school: 'In the holidays, in order to prepare my hands for the stripes they were to receive during the next year, I every day gave myself twenty stripes on the hands with a switch. Also having heard that our gardner had acquired a thick skin by the use of the spade, I took to digging hard in my father's garden' (46). Unfortunately, Epps' efforts were all in vain – the teacher merely hit harder when he saw that the punishment did not hurt and wound a 'cobbler's cord' round the cane to make it more painful. Epps thought that the canings at his school were too frequent and severe – they were often given for trifling faults. Hare (1834–1903) attended two schools. The first was private and presided over by a 'cruel' schoolmaster who caned so often that the pupils were in terror of him. After this, Hare went to Harrow where he recalled some masters who caned for the least fault, because they enjoyed inflicting pain. Lucas (1804–61) was also sent to two schools. In the first the schoolmaster's wife used to pull the pupils' hair and hit them on the back of their hands with a hair brush; the second Lucas regarded as an improvement, but recalled 'castigation was always going on'.

Sewell (1815–1906) recalled that physical punishment was not used at her school; but a repressive disciplinary system was still employed. No talking of any kind was allowed in school and, if three mistakes were made in a lesson – a hesitation counted as a mistake – the girl had to do another; marks of disgrace such as 'brown paper ass's ears' were put on the offender and she then had to stand in front of the class. Sewell herself was punished for telling a lie: she had to stand in front of the class wearing a special gown and a 'liar's tongue', feeling very ashamed and disgraced.

Pollen (1820–92), however, recollected that, despite the image of brutality which Eton had, he had nothing but 'delightful memories' of it.

Discussion. The quotation from Stone given at the front of this section could be more appropriately applied to the early 19th-century schools than to schools of the 16th and 17th centuries. It has been found that home discipline also increased in severity during this period, but the increased severity in school discipline was more marked and appears to have been more widespread. In this finding there is some class bias – only the wealthier families could afford to send their offspring to public school and it is these establishments which subjected their pupils to a regime of, at times, inhumane cruelty. In fact, the English public school teachers seemed to have believed that brutal discipline was necessary for the education of boys. However, if Guest (1812– ?) is typical, not all parents agreed. When her son was about to go to Eton she wrote:

When I thought of all the sorrow and temptation my poor boys would have to go through in that place I quite shuddered and prayed that assistance might be granted them from above. It seems a sad prospect, but everybody says it is the only way to bring up boys; and what is to be done! How can a poor woman, judge against all the world? (1950, p. 164)

There is notable sex discrimination in the discipline meted out to boys and girls – the former were much more likely to be caned and whipped. Of the six child diarists, it was the three boys who described receiving physical punishment at school.

1850–99. Some schools continued to impose a harsh discipline during this period but even so the results indicate that there was a reduction in severity.

197

Discipline and control

Patrick Traherne (1885–1917) taught at a public school and discussed the discipline there:

it is far easier to make a boy work through fear than it is through love of work: to rouse enthusiasm in the work itself is an exceedingly arduous business. The difficulty is that I hate the idea of caning a boy almost as much as some of the staff relish it. They satisfy a sort of bestial lust by lashing a small boy and hearing him yell. They would be horrified at the suggestion, but I am certain that this is true . . . On the other hand, I firmly believe that there is a type of boy who can understand no other form of treatment. I only wish such types would not come under my jurisdiction. (27)

Traherne's views brought him into conflict with the headmaster who regarded Traherne as being too lax in punishing. King-Hall and Newbolt referred to the canings at the educational establishments they attended. King-Hall (1893– ?) was at a naval college where 'floggings', if rare, were brutal: 'Yesterday a chap got a flogging for swearing, they tie you down to a horse (gym) . . . they then flog you in front of yr term some cadets faint for it draws blood sometimes so that Dr. is always there' (337–8). Francis Newbolt (1863–1941) remarked on the 'slogging' – the laying about with a cane to keep order – at his public school. Colt (1916– ?), on the contrary, wrote that canings were rarely inflicted at his school, lines being given instead.

Horler and Waugh referred to school punishment in their autobiographies. Horler (1888– ?) recalled the beating of one boy for stealing a sheet of notepaper which he had intended to replace: 'I watched, incredulously, W—— undo his trousers, pull them down, lift up his shirt, kneel against the form and have his head imprisoned between the sergeant's legs. The sergeant, I was glad to see, had tears in his eyes' (1933, p. 21). This 'birching' also drew blood and marked the start of Horler's hatred of 'practically all schoolmasters'. Waugh's (1903–66) experiences were less severe. He first went to a day school where the teachers 'were mild enough, but I had never before been shouted at or threatened' (1964, p. 82). There were very few beatings at this school; they were generally reserved for 'outrageous' behaviour. At his boarding school, discipline was also fairly mild; three strokes was the normal punishment and Waugh believed 'There was seldom any justice' (1964, p. 106).

Discussion. Very few texts referred to school discipline in this period. As with discipline in the home, in the late 19th century, the savagery of punishments lessened in the schools, although some whippings were still severe. Taking the evidence on school discipline as a whole, American children had a better chance of escaping cruel punishments, particularly in the late 19th century, than British children. This corresponds with the evidence on home discipline – that British parents were more concerned with discipline than American.

Conclusion

The information provided by the sources reveals that parents, through the centuries studied, have tried to control, or at least regulate, their children's behaviour. Various methods have been employed to achieve this objective: physical punishment, deprivation of privileges, advice, lectures, making the child feel ashamed, and remonstrations. The method used to discipline a child varied according to the parent and child rather than the time period, with the possible exception of the early 19th century – in every century strict and indulgent parents appeared. British parents would, however, seem to be stricter than American. It would also appear that physical punishment was used to discipline the younger offspring, while parents tried to advise and reason with adolescents. Parents did wish, in theory, to have a great deal of authority over their children, but in practice they did not achieve that aim. At least some parents believed in a reciprocal parent–child relationship: they would have the best interests of their children at heart and, in return, expected their children to be obedient – for example, *Jefferay in the 16th century, Josselin in the 17th, Young in the 18th and Weymouth in the 19th.

There was no link between attitudes and behaviour. For instance, in the 17th century, Heywood, Housman and *C. Mather all regarded children as being full of Original Sin; but none recorded administering physical punishment – *C. Mather, in fact, specifically spoke out against it. In the 19th century, Allen, *Lovell and *M. Walker viewed their offspring as depraved; the last two used physical punishment as a means of discipline whereas Allen did not. In the 18th century Boscawen and Elizabeth Wynne both intended to take great care of their offspring. This wish resulted in Boscawen resorting to whippings to ensure her children would be obedient, whereas Wynne was less concerned with obedience and did not mention inflicting any whippings.

The evidence does not agree with the arguments of such writers as Ariès, de Mause or Stone that children were harshly, even cruelly, disciplined, but reveals that brutality was the exception rather than the rule.[10] There was, however, a definite increase in severity in the early 19th century, particularly in Britain. During this period some children were subjected to intense brutality at home and even more so at school. The autobiographies of this period, especially the upper-class texts containing evidence on school discipline, in particular document the ill-treatment endured by children (those of Cooper, Grant and Hare described the harshest discipline). These autobiographies differ significantly from the earlier ones in their descriptions of the discipline that parents applied. For example, it is one thing to recall the general method of discipline as did G. Mildmay (whipped to 'inculcate virtuous principles') and Norwood (prayed to escape beatings during the week) in the 16th century, and another to give detailed, specific examples of cruelty as did Grant and Hare in the early 19th. It should be remembered though that only a minority of children in the early 19th century were cruelly treated.

The autobiographies consistently contain more evidence on physical punishment than any other source of evidence. This poses problems for such authors as de Mause and Stone who have relied mainly on autobiographies to reveal the strict discipline meted out to children in the past. Apart from the fact that other autobiographers of the same time period recalled nothing but happy childhoods, when the autobiographies are compared with other sources of evidence, especially the child diaries, it can be seen that severe discipline was not widespread. There is also the problem of how accurate autobiographies are – the writer's memories of his childhood are affected by hindsight, and memory is, in itself, extremely selective. Nevertheless many autobiographers did recall specific instances of harsh discipline and in these cases it does seem that the picture given by the autobiographer is accurate.

The use of the term 'whipping' is also of interest. It appears to have been the blanket term used to cover a wide range of physical punishment regardless of whether an implement was actually used. *Ward stated he whipped with his 'palm' and *Lovell threatened to whip her daughter with a stick when the term 'beat' would be more appropriate. In some cases an implement was mentioned – Boscawen, Grant and *Ward for example; but in many cases it appears that the parents were using only their hands. The terms 'spanking' or 'smacking' did not occur in the texts studied till the 19th century (the texts of *Alcott and F. Shelley). The word 'whipping' does conjure up images of severe punishment, of a defenceless child being brutalised by the stronger adult, when perhaps this was not the case. Thus there is a problem of the meaning of words in texts from previous centuries and this should be considered in any assessment of past child-rearing methods. The use of implements was not confined to previous centuries; Newson & Newson (*Seven Years Old in the Home Environment*, 1976) discovered that, by the age of 7, 75 per cent of modern British children had been hit with or at least threatened with an implement. These implements varied from a wooden spoon or slipper to a cane or belt. Thus, if the term 'whipping' did mean the use of a whip or stick, then it would still be impossible to argue that past parents were more cruel than 20th-century parents are.

It is vital to understand why most parents do not and did not subject their children to the level of unremitting severity and cruelty which has been claimed. As Allen clearly stated (see p. 176) the crux of the matter is that parents are attempting to discipline their *own* children. It is far easier to proffer guidance to others on the correct method of discipline than cope with all the plethora of decisions and problems involved in rearing one's own offspring. Evidence on the special way in which parents regarded their children can be found in many texts. For example, Newcome in the 17th century advised a friend how to treat his rebellious son, but the friend rejected his counsel. At that Newcome wrote: 'Nay I saw so much of the weakness of parents towards their children in this' (97). Two centuries further on J. Russell was the recipient of criticism from a friend who thought Russell was too severe in his dealings with his son Frank (see p. 178). Russell wrote: 'I suppose his children are easy to manage, & he most likely has no idea what a child of Frank's temperament is like' (vol. 2, p. 523). One century later Hutchinson related the tale of an acquaintance who replied to some advice on child-rearing with 'that's no use to me. If he was your son so would I jolly well know what to do with him. The trouble is he's mine!' (145) Parents have a deep involvement with and an intimate knowledge of their own child. Thus parents are prepared to tolerate most of what would be considered wayward behaviour by others from their children (see the texts of Clifford, Hope, H. Mildmay in the 16th century; *Byrd, Heywood, Josselin, *C. Mather in the 17th; Burney, Steuart in the 18th; K. and J. Russell, *Lovell in the 19th). Parents had to take their child's character into account in their assessment of any disciplinary situation and this could affect their reaction to it. Modern parents are aware of the same problem. Backett ('Images of the family', 1982) studied 20th-century parents and found that family life was regarded as a 'learning situation'. Even when parents had definite views on child-rearing these views were altered through interaction with their children. As one mother said, 'we had strong principles . . . about things that we *were* and we were *not* going to do when we had children. But the children came along and they're *people* and it just doesn't work you know' (354). The unique, emotional relationship between parent and child is a crucial determinant of disciplinary methods and yet has been ignored by most writers on the history of childhood.

Apart from the early 19th century, there was considerable continuity and homogeneity in methods of discipline. As opposed to one century standing out as being noticeably cruel or kind, instead there was a great deal of individual variation in methods of discipline. The severity of the early 19th century was most unusual. It was possibly a reaction to the rapid changes in society and the increased severity in school was perhaps due to the English school cult. The evolutionary theories on parental discipline are not supported – rather than kind methods of discipline evolving through the centuries, a wide range of variation in discipline existed at any one time. It was perhaps the existence of harsh discipline in the 19th century which led to such theories. Past parents did seem to be concerned with trying to form their child's character, but as Newson & Newson (1976) in their study of modern child-rearing methods reveal, parents of this century also attempted to control their children's behaviour in order to make the latter socially acceptable. Thus, regulating a child's behaviour is a fundamental aspect of the parental role and therefore parents will be concerned with discipline. However, it seems that the protective nature of parental care inhibits most parents from enforcing their authority with brutality.

6. From birth to twelve

having arrived, the child's infant progress was deemed of too little interest or importance to his family to merit record. . .
Infancy was but a biologically necessary prelude to the sociologically all important business of the adult world.

(Pinchbeck & Hewitt, 1969, pp. 4, 8)

Good mothering is an invention of modernization. In traditional society mothers viewed the development and happiness of infants younger than two with indifference.

(Shorter, 1976, p. 168)

childhood was a state to be endured rather than enjoyed.

(Tucker, 1976, p. 229)

As has already been pointed out in chapter 2, despite all the recent work on the history of childhood, we still know little about actual childhood. Many historians have claimed that parents up to the 18th century regarded their offspring with indifference and therefore largely ignored them – apart from when the latter needed punishment. This is a claim, however, based on assumption not evidence. Furthermore, most historians have concentrated on punishment to the exclusion of all other childhood experiences. Although discipline is only one facet of the parent–child relationship, its part in the life of past parents and children has been greatly exaggerated and over-emphasised. Thus, there are many areas which have yet to be considered and which would add a great deal to our knowledge on child life in previous centuries. Such questions as: were children wanted? did children pass through the same developmental stages as today? did they play? and how were they educated? have still to be adequately answered.

This chapter will be concerned with some of the actualities of child life in order to provide answers to the above questions, wherever possible, and also to discover just how much parents, particularly in the 16th and 17th centuries, were aware of their children. It is hoped to demonstrate that the parent–child relationship in the past was very much a dyadic one,

203

that parents and children both contributed to the form of this relationship and that the wishes of children were both respected and accommodated.

Birth
Were children wanted?

The 16th century. No 16th-century diarist stated that his children were unwanted; but Assheton, Dee, Penry and Powell merely recorded that a child had been born, without revealing any emotion. On the other hand, the diaries of Boyle, Clifford, Hope, *Jefferay and Wallington give some indication that children were wanted. *Jefferay (1591–1675), for example, referred to his children as 'my latest blessings' (36). On the christening of his seventh son, Boyle (1566–1643) remarked: 'The god of heaven make him happy, & bless him with a long lyffe & vertuous: & make him blessed in having many good & Relegeous children' (vol. 2, p. 207). Later he recorded of a grand-daughter: 'whome I beseech god to bless, with his choicest blessings, and that her parents and ffrends may reap happiness and muche comfort in her' (vol. 4, p. 166). Wallington (1598–1658) counted it one of the 'mercies of God' when his children were born, referred to 'my sweete sonne John' and regarded children as 'a man's treasure' (MS, fos. 404, 422). Hope's (1585?–1646) diary was begun after his family was complete; but he did note the births of his grandchildren, for example he wrote that his daughter gave birth to a child 'for quhilk I blesse the Lord, and God mak hir parentis and me thankfull' (111). Clifford (1590–1676) also started her diary after her child was born, but she remarked that she 'wept bitterly' when her husband threatened to take the child (aged about 18 months) from her. (Clifford's husband wished her to sign over to him her claim to a large amount of land, which she refused to do.) Later Clifford wrote: 'this was a very grievous and sorrowful day to me' when the child was taken from her, fortunately only temporarily (26).

The 17th century. Of the American texts, *Adams, *Cooper, *E. Holyoke and *C. Mather only noted the day their child was born, whereas *Byrd and *Sewall did express pleasure at the birth of a child. *Byrd (1674–1744), for example, on the birth of his son, stated: 'I returned God humble thanks for so great a blessing and recommended my young son to his divine protection' (1941, p. 79).

The British diaries present a similar picture: 13 parents[1] recorded only that a child had been born, whereas Calverley, Hervey, Housman, Josselin, Martindale and Newcome revealed that they did want the child. For example, after a stillbirth, Housman (1680?–1735) wrote: 'the last Time prevented our Enjoyment of a living Child; at once disappointed our Hopes, and cutt of our Expectations, which was a great Trial to our weak Graces' (35). Martindale (1623–86) was delighted at the birth of his first child: 'God was pleased to bestow upon us a gallant boy, which was sweet company to his poore mother in my absence and a refreshing to me at my return' (154). One mother, though, Rich (1624–78), did describe her anxiety at the thought of having too many children (see the quote from her autobiography on p. 102).

Discussion. There is a lack of any expression of emotion in these early texts; but there is more evidence to support the view that parents in the past did want their children rather than that the children were unwanted. (See also Wrightson, *English Society*, 1982, who found from his study of 17th-century diaries that children 'were clearly desired' (104). The omission of any statement of joy at the birth of a child cannot be taken to mean that parents therefore ignored infants. *C. Mather's diary is full of his preoccupation with, and attention to, his offspring, and yet he revealed no emotion at their birth. The British diarists who similarly noted only the birth of a child revealed a great awareness of their offspring in their diaries.

The 18th century. For this century 12[2] American diarists gave no more details than the dates of their offspring's births; but *Adams, *Alcott, *M. Dow, *Huntington, *Benjamin Lynde, *Shippen, *Silliman and *Mary White all revealed considerable happiness at the birth of a child. These diarists, with their greater aptitude for analysing and noting their feelings, referred to the joy they experienced when one of their children was born. For example, *Alcott (1799–1888) described the birth of his first child, a daughter, as 'a new and interesting event in the history of our lives. How delightful were the emotions produced by the first sounds of the infant's cry, making it seem that I was, indeed a father! Joy, gratitude, hope, and affection, were all mingled in our feeling' (27). *Silliman (1779–1864), on the birth of his first child, also a daughter, related that the birth 'Sent joy to many hearts and grateful thanks to Heaven. With this new theme of gratulation came a new motive for exertion and a novel source of happiness' (255).

Of the British writers, 18[3] observed only that a child had been born and

From birth to twelve

23[4] diarists referred to the pleasure such an event brought them. Calvert (1767–1859) described the birth of her first child, a son, as 'Oh joyful moment! Never, never to be forgotten' (7). Stedman (1744–97), on the birth of his second child, noted he was 'a beautiful strong healthy boy which crowns my happiness' (246). Trench (1768–1837) recorded her feelings as she held her first child: 'when I looked in my boy's face, when I heard him breathe, when I felt the pressure of his little fingers, I understood the full force of Voltaire's declaration:- "Le chef d'oeuvre d'amour est le coeur d'une mere" . . . My husband's delight in the birth of his son nearly equalled mine' (1862, p. 16).

Two diarists, although their diaries reveal that they had been delighted at the birth of their first few children, were not pleased at the prospect of having too many children. Thrale (1741–1821), for example, wrote: 'this is a horrible Business indeed: five little Girls too, & breeding again, & Fool enough to be proud of it! Oh Idiot! What should I want more Children for?' (389) After five children, Elizabeth Wynne (1778–1857) was similarly displeased to find herself pregnant again: 'I have not been at all well for this week past, being most wretchedly sick & sleepy – c'est un mauvais signe!' (vol. 3, p. 155)

The 19th century. The diarists *Burroughs, *Duncan, *Lawrence, *Lieber and *Phelps merely referred to the actual birth of their children, whereas *Colt, *Hayes, *Virginia Hoffman, *Howe, *Judson, *Longfellow, *Lovell, *Prentiss, *Todd, *M. Walker and *Ward described their happiness at the event. *Colt (1817– ?), for example, wrote that the birth of her first child, a daughter, 'blessed our home' and the birth of her son was 'fondly welcomed as a lovely morn' (248–9). *Howe (1801–76) noted that the birth of his daughter 'has made our cup to over-run with gladness' (155). *Longfellow (1807–82) stated: 'This morning was born in the Craigie House a girl, to the great joy of all' (85).

The evidence contained in the British texts is very similar. Alford, Allen, John Bailey, Cobden-Sanderson, Mary Collier, Fowler, E. Gaskell, Gladstone, Owen and Wood all simply noted the birth of a child. Sixteen[5] diarists, though, referred to the joy they felt. For example, to Ewing (1814–73), the day his son was born was one 'of great joy and thankfulness – a living son has been given to us' (32). J. Russell (1842–76) described his baby as 'a dear little fellow & it is a great happiness to look at his face & feel he is our own, mine & my darling wifie's' (vol. 1, p. 403). Finally, Traherne (1885–1917) noted the specialness of their own child to parents: 'I had always thought men rather fools who raved about their

206

children's looks: all babies used to look alike to me. Now I know that there never was such a baby as mine' (275).

The only two diarists who stated they were not delighted at the birth of a child belonged to the 19th century. *Sterne (1801–52), on the birth of his sixth child, remarked that the birth of children 'was an event which happens in the best of families'. The next day he added 'child no name yet, bothered what to call it' (vol. 31, 1927, p. 64). *Sterne, however, from the evidence contained in his diary did appear to be fond of his children. Similarly, Waugh (1903–66) did not regard the birth of children as a joyful event. On the birth of his second child he noted that his wife was 'happier than she is likely to be again' (1976, p. 450); but gave no indication of his feelings. When his third child died shortly after birth, he wrote: 'Poor little girl, she was not wanted' (1976, p. 489). His children did not appear to 'grow on him' either as he noted later that 'the presence of my children affects me with a deep weariness and depression' (1976, p. 607).

Two other diarists, though they wanted the child when he or she arrived, did not regard the prospect of another child with their (as revealed in their diaries) usual pleasure. Hanover (1819–1901) believed 'What made me so miserable was – to have the two first years of my married life utterly spoilt by this occupation [child-bearing]! I could enjoy nothing' (1964, p. 94). *M. Walker (1814–97) found the care of her three children enough to cope with: 'I find my children occupy much of the time; that if their maker should see fit to withhold from me any more till they require less of my time and attention, I think I should be reconciled to such allotment' (176).

There may also be exceptional circumstances in which the birth of a child was not looked on with delight. Cummings (1889–1919) was terminally ill when his first child was born. He described the baby as a 'monster' and a few days later wrote: 'The Baby touch is the most harrowing of all. If we were childless we should be merely unfortunate, but an infant . . .' (1923, p. 288). He did, though, become attached to his daughter, writing a few weeks later: 'Yet, on the whole, I find it a good and satisfying thing to see her, healthy, new, intact on the threshold' (1923, p. 305). This attachment grew so that by the time his daughter reached the age of 2, Cummings could write: 'What I have always feared is coming to pass – love for my little daughter. Only another communication string with life to be cut. I want to hear "the tune of little feet along the floor". I am filled with intolerable sadness at the thought of her' (1920, p. 30).

Discussion. The texts contain basically the same information for all centuries: many diarists did not reveal any emotion at the birth of a child; but the vast majority of those who did revealed only delight and pleasure. Many of the diarists who did not express any feelings at the birth of a child, continually referred to their offspring in their diary, as has been shown in the previous chapters and will be demonstrated in this. Hence, the lack of any expression of pleasure at the birth of a child cannot be taken as evidence of indifference to the child. Overall, there is more information to suggest that parents in previous centuries did want children than the contrary, but no evidence that 18th-century children were more valued than 17th-century children.

None the less, there were a few texts which reveal that a child was not always desired. Apart from Waugh who simply disliked children, the writers who made this point (Hanover, Rich, *Sterne, Thrale, *M. Walker and Elizabeth Wynne) did wish for children; but they did not want *too many* children. Unfortunately, without an efficient method of contraception, they had little choice in the matter. In the case of Cummings, he struggled unsuccessfully not to become fond of his daughter because he knew he was dying. Thus, though in certain circumstances all children may not be desired, most children were welcomed. The next section will turn to the question of why children were wanted.[6]

Why were children wanted?

Busfield in 'Ideologies and reproduction' (1974) suggests a number of reasons why 20th-century parents want children. Children are seen as a source of emotional satisfaction and as providing interest and variety in life. They are also viewed as offering a second chance for an individual to achieve for his children the things he did not manage to have and as providing security and pleasure in later life for their parents. Why parents in past times wanted children is more difficult to discover.

The 16th century. In the 16th century children were valued for the amusement they offered and their company (Clifford, Dee, *Jefferay, G. Mildmay, H. Mildmay and Wallington). In addition, it seems that parents did want their children to do well in life: Boyle wished his children would 'prosper', *Jefferay provided his daughters with furniture to set up home and Powell bought all his sons apprenticeships. However, the texts give no indication of whether or not parents believed that their offspring should support them in old age.

The 17th century. In the 17th century the sources contain information on all the points suggested by Busfield. *C. Mather (1663–1728) described the parental desire to gratify their children's demands:

Lord we know, we know, wee that are Parents feel it so, that if one of our Children should come to us and say unto us, *Father there is one thing that would make us perfectly and forever Happy and it is a thing that you can do for us, by Speaking of one Word*; will you please to do it? Wee could sooner dy, than deny that thing unto them. (vol. 7, p. 204)

Moreover, there were references to the joy parents experienced from their children. Byrom (1692–1763) wrote to his son (aged 14), while away on business: 'I wish I had thee with me; if I take such another journey as this, I shall be desirous of thy company, or Beppy's, or some of you, to keep me company, and to tell me what you think of things' (vol. 40, p. 201). E. Erskine (1680–1754) recorded his feelings for his young daughter: 'She and I being alone, I took her on my knee and dandled her, and she was very fond of me, took me round the neck and kissed me; which engaged my heart very much' (302).

A. Brodie, Josselin and Martindale believed that children should offer some support to their parents. Brodie (1617–80) was angry that, despite having 'nourished and broght up children' and that 'infirmitie and age is creiping on upon' him, his son refused to provide a home for him (305).

The 18th century. In this century, the diaries also provide evidence for the pleasure which parents took in their children. *Alcott (1799–1888) referred to his daughters of 4 and 3 as 'the charm of my domestic life' and revealed the understanding he had of his own children: 'They are very susceptible, and need the more interest to be taken in their hearts' wants and aspirings. They require a deep and apprehending love, or their natures cannot flourish as will many children of a more hardy make' (64). *Tucker (1775–1806) would prefer to stay at home than go shopping: 'My heart would incline me to stay at home with my little pensioner [adopted daughter] who has two romping companions to frolic with her. I should not interrupt them for I am extremely well calculated to sport with little children; they are at least harmless company and not at all times uninstructive' (319).

Similarly, Boswell (1740–95) greatly enjoyed talking with his 4-year-old daughter:

I had a most pleasing conversation with my dear Veronica, sitting with her on the floor of my dining room while the sun shone bright. I talked to her of the beauties and charms of Heaven, of gilded houses, trees with richest fruits, finest flowers, and most delightful Musick. I filled her imagination with gay ideas of futurity instead of gloomy ones . . . One cannot give rational or doctrinal notions of Christianity to a Child. (vol. 12, p. 180)

Watkin (1787–1861) took his 8-year-old son to visit a castle:

I was particularly pleased with the enthusiastic ardour of my little Edward. If this boy is not spoiled he will assuredly prove superior to the herd of mankind . . . He talked with animation of the castle, of the rock on which it stands, of the deep well which is in the castle yard, and put a great number of questions which it gave me great pleasure to hear and to answer. (120)

Burney's (1752–1840) diary reveals the pride and exasperation which children can arouse in their parents. Burney was asked by the royal family to bring her 3-year-old son to court. Alexander was very shy and so toys were brought in:

He seized upon dogs, horses, chaise, a cobbler, a watchman, and all he could grasp; but would not give his little person or his cheeks, to my great confusion, for any of them . . . I was a good deal embarrassed, as I saw the Queen meant to enter into conversation as usual; which I knew to be impossible, unless he had some entertainment to occupy him. (vol. 6, pp. 152–4)

Alexander soon became restless and tried to get into the Queen's workbox despite his mother's efforts to stop him, until he was finally given the box to play with. However, growing tired of that, he ran into the next room and Burney was forced to fetch him out, feeling 'excessively ashamed'. Eventually cakes were sent for in an attempt to quieten Alexander. 'He took one with great pleasure, and was content to stand down to eat it. I asked him if he had nothing to say for it; he nodded his little head, and composedly answered "Sanky, Queen". This could not help amusing her, nor me, either, for I had no expectation of so succint an answer' (vol. 6, p. 156).

Stanley and Young regarded their children as a means of support in old age. On his youngest daughter's death, Young (1741–1820) wrote; 'there fled the first hope of my life, the child on whom I wished to rest in the affliction of my age' (279). One mother, Trench (1768–1837), referred to parental ambition: 'One may cut down one's own ambition, but the shoots will spring up for one's children' (1862, p. 333).

The 19th century. In the 19th century there were references to the variety and zest which children injected into life. *Lawrence (1814–86) greatly enjoyed spending time with his offspring: 'Across the fields with the children (how beautiful they are!) to Sunday-school. With such company how can any father wish for any situation in life better than mine' (152). *M. Walker was amused by her 5-year-old son's inquiring mind: 'He is constantly making inquiries in regard to everything he can hear of; wishes every word defined that he hears spoken that he does not understand' (177). Cyrus ran in one day to ask why he heard a noise after shouting in the mountains. Before his mother had time to explain, he answered himself by deciding that, just as he, trees and things had shadows, his voice had a shadow too.

Johnston (1808–52) enjoyed looking at life through the eyes of her children: 'O what a new world is unlocked, as it were, by having a child ten years old! It seems gradually to engross and occupy so large a portion of one's mind. I cannot say how many more thoughts they take as they grow older' (169). Wood's (1812–60) comment on her 4-year-old daughter is very similar to that of *M. Walker above. On her first visit to the seaside, Fanny loved to paddle but (her mother wrote): 'I have had some difficulty in persuading her that the sea is not *alive*; and the first day that there was any surf, she begged to know "who had been washing in the sea, for it was all over soap-suds!"' (323)

There is one diarist who disliked his children's company, and strangely enough he belonged to this century – Waugh (1903–66). He believed that 'the truth is that a child is easily replaced while a book destroyed is utterly lost' and added: 'My children weary me' (1976, p. 555). Not surprisingly, his children did not like spending much time with their father, in marked contrast to the other children described in the texts. Waugh noted on one occasion he 'Returned home to find that the children had greatly enjoyed my absence' (1976, p. 695).

Alford and Cooper saw their children as a source of comfort in later years. After his son's death, Alford (1810–71) wrote: 'I have only my two sweet girls left me to stay my declining years and those of their mother. They are, thank God, well able and well willing to do it' (196).

Discussion. Parents throughout the centuries have obviously wished their children well, enjoyed the latter's companionship and for the most part delighted in their childishness. Some parents did expect to be recompensed for all their care and attention through being looked after by their children in later life, but others did not. Parents, as Wrightson (1982) also discovered, asked little from their children when young but just enjoyed having them around.

Infancy

There is a lack of infancy data in the sources. Although 158 diaries and manuscripts do provide details on children under the age of 5 (49 American, 109 British), unfortunately these may often be only mere snippets of evidence, particularly in the case of the 16th- and 17th-century diaries. This could be due to the fact that most of the diarists studied were male who may not have been involved in the daily care of young children. Female diarists are particularly scarce for the 16th and 17th centuries – of the diarists studied only one American and seven British were female and born before 1700. In addition, as revealed in the comparison study in chapter 3, some details on infancy, such as the method of feeding, may have been omitted from the published text. (Any relevant details discovered from the comparison study will be included in the following discussion.) As references to the illness, death or discipline of young children have already been discussed, this leaves 91 texts (29 American, 62 British) which contain material on other facets of infancy.

The lives of infants in the past will be discussed in relation to such early milestones as weaning, teething, walking and talking, as well as the method of feeding. Any problems the parents described, such as excessive crying, unwillingness to sleep and whether or not to have a child inoculated, will also be looked at. The evidence is nearly all from the published diaries; where other sources have been used, these are specified.

Feeding

The information contained in the diaries on the preferred method of feeding is not sufficient to allow any systematic analysis. As can be seen from Table 9, all that can be said is that children were both breast-fed and wet-nursed in each century. Even when a mother did intend to breast-feed the child, the infant could still be fed by another first, for example *Sewall (1652–1730) noted, shortly after his son's birth 'The first Woman the Child sucked was Bridget Davenport' (vol. 5, p. 40). This may be due, as Fildes (1980) argues, to the reluctance to give newborns colostrum.[7] *Sewall's son was not fed by his mother until five days later.

The results imply that there was a preference among the 18th- and 19th-century American diarists to breast-feed. However, this could be due to their situation – they were generally living in recently settled areas

Table 9. *Number of diaries reporting a particular feeding method*

Method of feeding	16th		17th		18th		19th	
	A	B	A	B	A	B	A	B
Breast-fed	0	1	1	4	6	13	7	1
Wet-nurse used*	0	1	3	8	0	9	1	8
Both methods tried†	0	1	1	2	2	5	0	2

* In addition, in the 19th century, three British diarists, Allen, Head and Traherne) and two American (*Hayes and *Longfellow) stated that their children had a nurse; but did not specify who was feeding the infant. They have not been included in the above table and so there may be more infants who had a wet-nurse in the 19th century than appears from the table.
† Those diarists who used both feeding methods were: *M. Dow, Hay, Hochberg, *Huntington, Moore, Newcome, Oliver, K. Russell, *Sewall, Thrale, *M. Walker, Wallington and Weeton.

where wet-nurses were unobtainable – rather than a preference for breast-feeding. Two American 19th-century diarists who did not have enough milk to feed their infants had to resort to soup in the case of *Phelps, and cows' milk in the case of *M. Walker, because wet-nurses were not always available.

Hunt in *Parents and Children in History* (1972) argues that, at least in the 17th century, because of the hostility experienced by adults towards children which inhibited the supply of milk, infants often found it difficult to get enough food. From the diaries it does look as if breast-feeding was not without its problems, although these were not confined to the 17th century and, as will be shown, parents were concerned if an infant was not being fed adequately. One month after the birth of his son, Wallington (1598–1658) noted that his wife 'began to have sore brests so that the childe did not sucke for three days to gether that wee ware faine to put it forth to norse into the country for wife was in such paine with her brests' (MS, fo. 412). The same problem occurred in the next century. *Sewall's wife was unable to nurse her son herself for five days after the birth and had trouble when she first started to feed him, requiring *Sewall's (1652–1730) help: 'Saturday, first laboured to cause the child suck his mother, which he scarce did at all. In the afternoon my Wife set up and he sucked the right Breast bravely' (vol. 5, p. 40). Josselin (1616–83) noted that 'my wives breasts were sore' after the birth of their first child; 'which was a grievance and sad cutt to her' (13).

213

From birth to twelve

In the 18th century only two published texts refer to any breast-feeding difficulties (the diaries of Moore and Thrale); but the unpublished manuscripts of Bishop, Oliver and Viney and also the original manuscript of A. Darby's diary provide more information on problems. The most common hardship was insufficient milk. Elizabeth Bishop (1751–1801) weaned one of her children early as she had 'but very little milk'; Darby (1716–94) noted that she had no milk after the birth of her second child; Oliver (1741–1823) reported that his wife was unable to provide enough milk for their first child and Richard Viney (1700?– ?) noted that his wife's milk temporarily dried up after the birth of their sixth child. After having had her first two children nursed out, Moore's (1779–1852) wife attempted to feed the third child herself; but lacked sufficient milk. Moore then looked for a wet-nurse for his son 'who seems as if he wanted a reinforcement of this nature, and I wish I had insisted upon his having it from the first' (vol. 2, p. 242). In addition, Bishop and the wife of Oliver suffered from sore nipples. Thrale (1741–1821) breast-fed her first child for a while, but stopped after she (Thrale) lost too much weight.

A few 19th-century diarists also found breast-feeding difficult. *Phelps (1810?– ?) noted after the birth of her first child: 'I had but little milk for my child. I had to feed him soup' (217). The situation did not improve with the birth of her second child. *M. Walker (1814–97) was very upset when she found breast-feeding too painful to be continued: 'I was very anxious about my babe & extremely reluctant to relinquish the idea of nursing him but I had experienced so much torture that I was at last glad when no alternative was left me' (257). *Ward (1841–1931) wrote that his wife was often ill while she was breast-feeding their son; but she was determined to carry on. One British mother was unable to nurse her children. Her husband J. Russell (1842–76) described the problem:

Tho' perfectly well K. had much trouble today from baby not sucking. He would not or could not do it. . . In the evg b.d. I sucked a little thinking it might do good, but I could not get much. Since I had to apply all my sucking power to get any milk it is no wonder the infant found it too hard for him. (vol. 1, p. 403)

K. Russell did manage to feed their second child for two months until she became ill and was then advised by her doctor to stop breast-feeding. She achieved more success with her third infant.

Not all mothers experienced difficulty with breast-feeding. In the 18th century Shelley noted, after the birth of his son, that his wife (Mary Shelley, 1797–1851) was 'very well also; drawing milk all day' (39). Similarly, Elizabeth Wynne (1778–1857) wrote: 'My little boy begins to suck very nicely and I am not at all troubled with my milk' (vol. 2, p. 203). It is possible that the diarists who breast-fed their infants without relating any problems, did not experience any.

Stone in *The Family, Sex and Marriage in England* (1977) claims that in the 18th century there was a transformation in the preferred method of feeding infants – mothers then wished to breast-feed rather than use a wet-nurse. If the British diarists in Table 9 are looked at, then 43 per cent of mothers in the 17th century breast-fed for at least a time, compared with 67 per cent in the 18th century. Thus, there is an increase but so few texts actually specify how infants were fed that it is impossible to make an adequate comparison. It is of interest though that R. Day (1745–1841) obviously thought maternal breast-feeding, although commendable, was rarely carried out. He described his daughter (born 1776) as having 'the rare merit of suckling her own children' (186). A later diarist, Alford (1810–71), whose daughter (born 1836) was unable to nurse her first child, wrote to her revealing an interesting view on the function of breast-feeding:

Not being able to nurse it, is a physical relief to you; but on one account I rather regret it, that you lose the discipline in patience and long-suffering which makes the bloom of the maternal character. A mother who has borne with her infant's thousand wearing and worrying ways, who has given up her employ by day and her rest by night for it for months together, will be likely to bear with its moral faults and exercise patience in disciplining it for Christ, better, perhaps, than one who has been spared all this. (380)

It is not clear from the diaries why infants had a wet-nurse except in the case of those diarists who were unable to feed the infant themselves (*M. Dow, K. Russell and Weeton), or if a particular infant was not thriving (*Huntington, *Sewall and Wallington). Also, when Andrew Hay's sister had twins, one was sent to a wet-nurse which suggests that she was incapable of feeding two babies herself. Some diarists may have been subscribing to the belief that breast-feeding females should not indulge in sex as this would curdle the milk, for example in Blundell's (1669–1737) diary, he noted that after his wife's month of lying-in was over, the child was sent to a wet-nurse and 'we lay together' (vol. 110, p. 69). This may also be the case of another 17th-century diarist who stated that his first daughter was nursed out. Newcome (1627–95) recorded 'though after we were sensible of the neglect of duty in not having her nursed at home, which made her mother resolved to endeavour to nurse, if the Lord gave her any more children' (13). The 'neglect of duty' probably refers to the Puritan principle that children should be breast-fed by the mother

(Gouge, 1622; Perkins, 1609). These writers argued that the mother's milk was the best kind for the child, that women had been provided with breasts in order to feed children and that infants would absorb undesirable character traits from their lower-class wet-nurse. Not all Puritans put these precepts into practice: *C. Mather, a devout Puritan, had a wet-nurse for all his children.

The custom of wet-nursing has been put forward as evidence for the neglect of infants in previous centuries. However, Schnucker in 'The English Puritans and pregnancy' (1974) has shown that the continuance of wet-nursing was more evidence for the inertia of social custom than evidence for the neglect of infants. Furthermore, it is clear from these texts that infants sent to a wet-nurse were not ignored by their parents; frequent visits were made, particularly if the child was ill. Dee (1527–1608) visited his infants at nurse and removed one daughter who was not thriving. Wallington (1598–1658) sent his son to nurse in the country and was kept informed of his progress. In the 17th century two American diarists (*Cooper and *Sewall) and eight British diarists (Blundell, William Bulkeley, Freke, Lowe, Morris, Newcome, Newton and Isabella Twysden) stated that their infants were nursed out rather than at home. Of these, seven gave details on visits to the infant. Blundell and Morris noted regular visits to their babies and revealed anxiety when the infant was ill. *Cooper visited his child, as also did Roger Lowe with reference to his master's child. W. Bulkeley's grand-daughter was left behind at nurse when her parents went to Liverpool; but Bulkeley visited her. Similarly, Freke's child was also left at nurse when his parents returned to Ireland and he was visited by his grandfather. Moreover, Freke returned from Ireland when she was told of his ill-treatment by the nurse. *Sewall's son was sent to his grandmother's home in the country as he was sickly and *Sewall was kept informed of his progress.

In the 18th century, of the diarists who had their child nursed out, Holland, *Huntington, Moore, Oliver, William Roe and Turner, all mention visiting the infants. When Moore (1779–1852) removed house, he was reluctant to disturb a child still at nurse; but his wife was unhappy at the separation: 'The only drawback on my dear Bessy's happiness is the being removed from her little child so far. She has hardly had time to get acquainted with it yet; but it would have been a great pity to take her away from a nurse that seemed to be doing her so much justice' (vol. 1, p. 361). Turner (1793–1873) was very concerned when his infant was ill: 'A month of anxiety and sorrow, in consequence of the illness of dear little Edmund, at Crosby. My mind during the month has been so unstrung, as to be incapable of attending to anything save works of necessity. Went to Crosby very often' (1875, p. 152). Goff (1739?– ?) had several of her children nursed out in cottages around her home town and did not always visit them herself. At least one infant was visited by her (infant's) maternal grandmother, the latter writing to Goff about the child's progress. *M. Dow (1780– ?) was forced to send her child to nurse when she became too ill to feed her daughter. She was also too ill to visit the child, but was distraught when she was informed that the infant had died.

In the 19th century infants would appear to have been nursed at home, none of the diarists stating that their babies were nursed out.

There are no data in the American diaries on the choosing of a nurse, but at least some of the British nurses were chosen with care. Dee in the 16th century, Blundell in the 17th, Boswell and Moore in the 18th and K. Russell in the 19th all noted that they were searching for a suitable nurse. Hunt argues that nurses in the 17th century absorbed a mother's hostility to her infant and were therefore psychologically inhibited from producing enough milk. Boswell was unlucky in his first nurse who did not have enough milk. This would be support for Hunt's argument if it were not for the fact that this occurred in the 18th century and that Boswell found his son's second nurse to be 'an excellent one' so that his son 'was visibly fuller in flesh and healthier in looks' (vol. 10, p. 257). It seems more likely that some nurses simply produced less milk than others, probably because there was a delay between the weaning of their own child and the taking of an infant to nurse.

Having a child nursed could be a hazardous business. In the 17th century, Evelyn, Hervey and *C. Mather noted that their child was overlaid by the nurse. Other British diarists reported a few cases of children who had been ill-treated by their nurses. Freke's (1641–1714) father wrote to her about 'my son being Cripled by the Carlessnes of his Nurse, & Aboutt 14 of December brok his Legg shortt In the Hackle Bone [hip], which she kept pryvatte for neer a quarter of A yeare Til a Jelley was Grown between Itt; She keeping him in his Cradle, & everybody believed he was Breeding of his Teeth' (25). Once this was discovered the child was removed to another nurse, his bone reset and he recovered completely.

Holland (1770–1845) again referred to the carelessness of nurses in the 18th century: 'I was brought to bed of a lovely boy in October, but owing to the neglect of the nurses he fell into convulsions and died' (vol. 1, p. 136). In his autobiography at the beginning of his diary, Stedman (1744–97) wrote:

Four different wet-nurses were alternately turn'd out of doors on my account, and to the care of whom I had been entrusted, my poor mother being too weak a condition to suckle me herself. The first of these bitches was turn'd off for having nearly suffocated me in bed; she having sleep'd upon me till I was smother'd, and with skill and difficulty restored to life. The second had let me fall from her arms on the stones till my head was almost fractured, & I lay several hours in convulsions. The third carried me under a moulder'd old brick wall, which fell in a heap of rubbish just the moment we had passed by it, while the fourth proved to be a thief, and deprived me even of my very baby clothes. (5)

After this, his parents gave up and had Stedman weaned, even though this was earlier than they had intended. Weeton (1776–1850) also noted that she weaned her child early at the age of 7 months due to the nurse's conduct, although she does not explain what was wrong. 'I am sorry to wean the child so soon, but the nurse's conduct has been so very reprehensible that I must part with her' (vol. 2, p. 141).

The same problem reappeared in the 19th century. K. Russell (1842–74) had five nurses for her son, which caused him much distress. Having found a highly recommended nurse, she decided to leave the baby at home while she went on a visit, hoping that way he would settle down. When she was away the nurse took only in different care of her son and was dismissed.

It makes my blood boil for my precious little darling, to think what he has had to bear. I am too furious. When he cried she used to shake him – when she washed him she used to stuff the sponge in his little mouth – push her finger (beast!) in his dear little throat – say she hated the child, wished he were dead – used to let him lie on the floor screaming while she sat quietly by & said screams did not annoy her it was good for his lungs . . . She sat in her room most of the day I find reading novels & never nursed the baby or spoke to it . . . She always put it on wet diapers though the nurse asked her to let her air them & so it often had a stomach ache, then she gave it an empty bottle in its cot to suck the tube & keep it quiet so making it suck in only wind – No wonder it cried & was so unhappy. (vol. 1, pp. 414–15)

It is of interest that Russell referred to her son as 'it'. Shorter, in *The Making of the Modern Family* (1976) argues that the referring to children as 'it' only occurred up to the 18th century and was an example of the indifference with which adults regarded children up to that date. Russell lived during the 19th century and was clearly not indifferent to her son. The calling of a child 'it' has no connection with the possessing of a concept of childhood (see also the quotation from Alford (1810–71) earlier in this chapter).

Weaning

LeVine ('Child rearing as a cultural adaptation', 1977) states that children in rural Africa are not weaned until well into the second year of life and sometimes later depending on the size of the child and whether the mother becomes pregnant again. (Draper, 1976, and Leighton & Kluckhohn, 1948, provide similar information.) Newson & Newson (*Patterns of Infant Care*, 1965) found that most British babies today are weaned between the ages of 6 and 12 months, although many infants are not completely weaned from the bottle until after their first birthday.

The texts studied here reveal that the age of weaning differed according to each infant. As Table 10 shows, there was considerable variation, even within a single family. Fildes ('The age of weaning', 1982) argues that the age of weaning decreased through the centuries, particularly during the 18th century. Although she found no significant reduction in the suckling period when the 16th century was compared with the 17th, nor when the 17th was compared with the 18th, she did find a significant reduction when the 16th and 17th centuries were compared with the 18th, $t = 2.08$, $p < 0.01$.[8] A similar analysis performed on my data revealed a significant decrease in the age at weaning in the 18th century when compared with the 17th, $t = 2.21$, $p < 0.025$. This reduction in the suckling period during the 18th century may be due, as Fildes argues, to the greater availability of better food substitutes and feeding vessels and the increased acceptability of artificial feeding.

The texts illustrate that, for the majority of infants, weaning was a gradual process. In the 16th century Dee (1527–1608) noted of three of his children that they began to be weaned, for example he noted: 'Michael was begone to be weaned' and later: 'Margaret Dee begonne to be weaned' (21, 55). The weaning of his son Arthur took three days. In exceptional circumstances a child could be weaned abruptly as in the case of Katharine Dee. She was sent home from her first nurse because the maid was ill. When her parents visited Katharine at her second nurse, they found that this time their daughter was ill and so they took her home to be weaned. In the 17th century, *Sewall (1652–1730) remarked that he and his wife 'Began to wean little Hull' (vol. 5, p. 70). His last child, a daughter, started her weaning on 7 March and by 22 March *Sewall wrote: 'Judith is very well weaned' (vol. 6, p. 75). Josselin's diary also gave details on the length of weaning. With his second child, Josselin (1616–83) noted that his wife 'began to weane her sonne Thomas' and 11

Table 10. *Age at weaning (in months)*

Century	Diarist	Age at weaning according to birth order of infants	Mean	Standard deviation
16th	Dee	13.5, 14.5, 16.5, 16, 13.5, 7.5	13.6	3.2
17th	Blundell	9.5	13.2	3.6
	*Green	9		
	Josselin	12, 13, 18, 19, 16, 12		
	*Sewall	9.5, 14.5		
18th	Bishop†	11.5, 0.25	9.5	4.5
	Boscawen	10		
	Cooke	10		
	*Hazard	7		
	*Huntington	14		
	Moore	7.5, 15		
	Rathbone	14.5		
	Stedman	10		
	Eliz. Wynne	4.5		
19th	*Duncan	1.5	14.8	10.1
	*Lovell	13, 14.5		
	*Prentiss	30		
	*Sterne	15		

† Bishop weaned her second child so soon because she was not producing sufficient milk.

days later, 'my wife weaned her sonne with much ease to her self and the child also quiett and content'. For his third child he wrote: 'this weeke my wife weaned her daughter Jane: shee tooke it very contentedly'. Two weeks after he and his wife decided to wean their seventh daughter, he remarked: 'An does well in her weaning.'[9] In the 18th century a few diarists also noted that they 'began' to wean their infants (Bishop, F. Gray, *Hazard (1756–1845) and Rathbone). In the 19th, K. Russell's (1842–74) son was weaned gradually, being given solid foods while still nursing whereas *Lovell's (1809– ?) daughter was weaned abruptly as was *Sterne's (1801–52) daughter – the last case owing to his wife's illness. *Lovell gave an account of the weaning of her daughter and was not happy with her method. The child, aged 13 months, was placed upstairs with her aunt while her mother remained downstairs.

Toward night I went up and took her. She asked to nurse but did not cry much and soon got down on the floor and began to play. She was easily weaned, seeming to understand that she could not nurse again, but from that time for more than a month she would always cry if I left her for a moment when she was awake. I could not even get up to go across the room, when she was playing on the floor, without her crying. I attributed this to my leaving her all day when I weaned her, and should never advise any mother to do so. (56)

In contrast to the findings of Newson & Newson (1965) that weaning presented little, if any, difficulty to mothers of this century, from the evidence contained in the texts it appears that to parents of previous centuries it was a time of anxiety stemming mainly from the non-availability of suitable food for infants and the poor standard of medical care in existence at that time. The parents who did note that weaning was an anxious time were aware of the distressing effect it could have on the child. These parents at least must have possessed some concept of childhood in order to appreciate how the child could experience the event. Josselin's and *Sewall's concern for their children at weaning has already been noted. In the 18th century four British diarists gave information on their concern with regard to weaning.

Bishop (1751–1801) in her unpublished manuscript wrote that her baby was 'brave & very quiet considering she has no Brest' (3 Apr. 1787).[10] Moore (1779–1852) wrote to his mother: 'I know you must be anxious about your little grand-daughter's . . . getting over her weaning, and I have great delight in telling you that she hardly seems to have missed the nurse at all, but has taken to the bread and milk as naturally as if she and it were old acquaintances' (vol. 1, p. 299). Rathbone (1761–1839), on weaning her son, anticipated his distress and 'gave him 6 drops of laudanum and do. antiminial wine, but had a very bad night' (53). Elizabeth Wynne (1778–1857) noted: 'I weaned Charles . . . I hope the poor child will not mind it much, he was tolerably good all day, but never eats without fretting' (vol. 3, p. 24).

One American diarist in the 19th century (*Prentiss, 1818–78), recorded: 'now comes the dreaded, dreaded experience of weaning baby' (155). A few months later, though, she was delighted 'To see dear baby so improved by the very change I dreaded' (156). Dawson (1811–78) also referred to weaning as an anxious time.

Two male diarists, both American, seemed to bear the responsibility for weaning their offspring. *Green (1675–1715) noted that he 'carried my mother and Nanny to Wenham, and Ben carryed my wife. I left my wife and Nanny and came home to wean John' (222). *Sterne (1801–52) wrote:

From birth to twelve

'[I] sat up nearly all night, nursing the infant Laura who has to be weaned in consequence of my wife's Sickness' (vol. 33, 1929, p. 77). (Josselin in the 17th century also noted that he and his wife 'decided to wean' a child, as if this were a joint activity.)

As Fildes (1982) also discovered, the reason for weaning an infant varied according to the individual circumstances. In some cases a baby was weaned because the mother was ill (Josselin, *Sterne) or because the mother lacked sufficient milk (Bishop). In others, the nurse was ill (Dee, *Sewall) or the parents were dissatisfied with the nurse (Dee, Stedman, Weeton). The parents did however consider both the health and wellbeing of the child, before and during the weaning process.

Teething

The information on teething given by the diaries is again very miscellaneous and does not give an adequate representation of the different nationalities and times. What evidence there is does reveal the enormous individual variation (see Table 11) rather than that children were retarded physically in previous centuries due to poor care, as has been suggested by de Mause (1976).

The texts do contain some evidence that teething was a disrupting time. In the 16th century Clifford (1590–1676) noted when her daughter was ill while cutting her eye teeth: 'I spent most of my time in working and in going up and down to see the Child' (51). In the next century *Byrd (1674–1744) wrote: 'My son began to breed teeth which disordered him' (1941, p. 125). Similarly, Josselin (1616–83) noted that Jane was ill while cutting teeth. No 18th-century American diarists referred to teething, but those British diarists who did also remarked on it as an anxious period. Boswell (1740–95) stated when his son was ill with teething: 'His Mother and I were in great uneasiness about him' (vol. 14, p. 74) and M. Shelley (1797–1851) also noted when her son was teething: 'Babe unwell. We are unhappy and discontented' (134). The same concern is shown in the 19th century. For example, *Lovell, K. Russell and Elizabeth Wynne all called the doctor while their children were cutting teeth.

Crying

Ariès in *L'Enfant et la Vie Familiale* (1960) argues that in the past infants were ignored by their parents, but it is hard to see how infants could have been ignored to the extent he suggests. Apart from the fact that infants

222

Table 11. *Age at teething (in months (m))*

Century	Diarist	Age at 1st tooth†	Age at 2 teeth	Additional information
16th	Clifford	–	–	18 teeth at 32m
17th	Blundell	11	–	–
	*Byrd	4	–	–
	Freke	–	4.5	–
	Josselin	6, 6, 4, –, –	–, –, –, 6, 7	1st child teething again at 15m
	*Sewall	–	6	Another child 8 teeth at 14.5m
18th	Bishop	10	–	–
	Boscawen	–	–	Cutting 2nd teeth at 60m
	Boswell	4½	–	Teething again at 15.5m
	Calvert	–	–	4 teeth at 1.0m
	Moore	–	7, 9	Cutting eye teeth at 13m Another child teething at 14.5m
	M. Shelley	–	–	Teething at 14m
	Stedman	6, –	–, 9	–
	Eliz. Wynne	5, 4.25	–	1st child teething again at 11m
19th	*Alcott	–	–	Teething at 17m
	Allen	4	–	–
	*Duncan	–	–	Teething at 18m
	E. Gaskell	–	5	8 teeth at 12m, 12 at 16m & eye teeth at 22m. 2nd child 4 teeth at 8m
	*Hayes	–	16	2nd child teething at 18m
	*Lovell	6, –	–, 5	1st child has eye teeth at 27m, 2nd child has additional 2 teeth nearly through
	*Prentiss	–	–	6 teeth at 14.5m
	K. Russell	7	–	3 teeth at 9.5m
	Traherne	6	–	–
	*M. Walker	10	–	–

† Note the looseness of this criterion: it may refer to having 1 tooth or to teething.

have to be fed and changed, they cry – and in such a way that tends to bring a response from a parent (Newson & Newson, 1965). There is, however, relatively little reference to crying in the texts studied and none at all in the 16th-century texts. In the 17th century *Byrd (1674–1744) noted being wakened in the night by his daughter's crying and *Sewall (1652–1730) wrote of his last child that she 'gave us very little Exercise after 3 or 4 nights' as if it were a relief not to have a crying child (vol. 6, p. 75). The British texts provide similar information. Hay (1610–89) also recorded that his infant's cries wakened him in the night. Josselin's (1616–83) diary contains a number of entries on crying: for example he found his little ones 'a great griefe' in their 'sudden cryings out in the forepart of the night' (see Macfarlane, 1970, p. 89).

In the 18th century one American diarist and seven British diarists mentioned crying children. *Shippen (1763–1841) noted her daughter cried at night and also mentioned responding to her cries during the day. In Bower's diary, her little brother was referred to as rarely crying; another diarist, Rathbone (1761–1839), described one son crying during weaning and a later child as always crying: 'my crying baby, tho' seemingly in good health, leaves me little time either night or day' (90). Stedman (1744–97) noted giving his infant son a sedative to quieten his crying: 'I buy a bottle of *Godfrey's Cordial*, for making children sleep, since Geordy keeps all the house awake, also almost kills his poor mother' (269). Trench (1768–1837) believed that: 'The real wants of an infant should be satisfied, the moment they are known. To supply them before they are announced by tears and cries, will often wholly prevent those whimpering and noisy habits, so injurious to children and so distressing to their parents' (1837, p. 15). Trench also made reference to the feelings of incompetence a crying child can arouse in the mother. She broke off writing a letter to her husband (who was engaged in the war with France) because 'my poor baby is crying. I hope Buonoparte may have a sick child, as I think the cry of an infant, whose pain we cannot know or assuage, would make him feel his want of power, though nothing else has done it' (1862, p. 238). Steuart, D. Taylor and Elizabeth Wynne also remarked on the crying of their infants.

In the 19th century six American diarists referred to crying children: *Duncan, *Lovell, *Prentiss, *Todd, *M. Walker and *Ward. For example, *Duncan (1808–76) 'felt badly owing to my being disturbed in the Night with the crying of children' (55). *Prentiss' (1818–78) diary contains a graphic description of the parental fatigue induced by a continuously crying child: 'when racked with pain, dizzy, faint and exhausted with suffering, starvation and sleeplessness, it is terrible to have to walk the room with a crying child!' (115) *Todd (1800–73) would have sympathised with *Prentiss; his 4-month-old daughter also cried a great deal (see chapter 4).

Three British diaries contain information on crying. Cobden-Sanderson (1840–1922) frequently recorded his son's crying: at night; when put in his crib; if something was removed from Richard which he wanted and sometimes for no reason at all. The crying did exasperate Cobden-Sanderson, although he thought:

Why should I not get rid of the irritation that ever recurring crying at this moment produces on me? Surely that would be one gain?
And I thought of the innumerable babies all the world over crying at the same moment, of the babies who up to now had cried, and of the hosts of generations yet destined to do so. And I thought it was indeed absurd to be irritated. (vol. 1, pp. 250–1)

E. Gaskell (1810–65) did not wish to give in to her daughter's cries for attention: 'Once or twice we have had grand cryings, which have been very distressing to me; but when I have convinced myself she is not in pain, is perfectly well and that she is only wanting to be taken up, I have been quite firm; though I have sometimes cried almost as much as she has' (7). K. Russell's (1824–74) son often cried and, while cutting his first tooth, he cried so violently that she asked the doctor to recommend 'a good and safe narcotic'. He told her to put 20 drops of chloroform on a handkerchief and let the child inhale for five to ten minutes at the most!

A number of diarists did refer to their infant as 'unwell' while teething and this may mean the child was crying.

Walking

The age at walking has been used by de Mause ('The evolution of childhood', 1976) as a source of evidence for his argument that children were retarded in their development in the past. As he states: 'the combination of tight swaddling, neglect, and general abuse of children in the past seemed often to have produced what we would now regard as retarded children' (50). De Mause compiled a table of ages at first walking which would show that children did walk later in previous centuries; if it were accurate. For example, he refers to Clifford's child as walking for the first time at 34 months of age when this was actually the date at which the leading strings were removed from the child's clothes. He further notes that Marianne Gaskell did not walk until 22 months of age. Although this is true, de Mause ignores both the fact that Marianne was a very frail child who was often ill and that her mother considered Marianne backward in walking. De Mause also omits to mention that Marianne's sister was walking well at the age of 18 months.

Cross-cultural studies reveal the mean age at walking alone to be about 14 months. Marvin *et al.* ('Infant caregiver attachment', 1977) found that many Hausa infants can walk at 12 months and all can crawl at this age. Leighton & Kluckhohn (*Children of the People*, 1948) discovered that the infants of the Navaho Indians can walk when led between 10 and 11 months of age and walk alone between the ages of 13 and 16 months. Table 12 contains the evidence given in the diaries on the walking ability of children.

Walking was a stage of great interest to those parents who referred to it in their diaries. Clifford (1590–1676) observed: 'Upon the 1st I cut the Child's strings off from her coats and made her use togs alone, so as she had two or three falls at first but had no hurt with them' (66). Blundell (1669–1737) in the next century was pleased that his daughter aged 30 months was 'a very healthfull Lively child, very nimble of her Feet' (vol. 110, p. 147).

For the 18th and 19th centuries the diary entries become more detailed. Weeton (1776–1850), after taking her daughter aged 11 months for her first walk, wrote:

I have been much diverted with Mary today. I took her by the hand, and she walked all the way from hence as far as our late house in Chapel-lane. She had so many things to look at, that I thought we should scarcely ever arrive. She stopped at every door, to look into the houses. There were many groups of little children in the street, and she would walk up to them, and shout at them; she set her foot upon the step of a door where there happened to be a cake-shop, so I bought her a cake; and then she wanted to stand still in the street whilst she ate it. (vol. 2, pp. 143–4)

Moore (1779–1852) described the achievement of his 10-month-old daughter:

Our little Barbara is growing very amusing. She (what they call) *started* yesterday in walking; that is, got up off the ground by herself, and walked alone to a great distance without any one near her. Bessy's [mother] heart was almost flying out of her mouth all the while with fright, but I held her away, and would not let her assist the young adventurer. (vol. 1, p. 329)

*Lovell (1809– ?), a 19th-century mother, was similarly 'diverted' with her younger daughter learning to walk.

Table 12. *Age at walking (in months (m))*

Century	Diarist	Age at crawling	Age at walking	Additional information
16th	Clifford	–	–	Leading reins removed at 34m
17th	Blundell	–	–	Running at 30m
	Freke	–	–	Standing almost alone at 4.5m
18th	Boswell	–	–	Walking well at 24m
	Cooke	–	14	–
	Moore	–	10	–
	Stedman	–	15.5	Reins bought at 8.5m, removed at 28m
	*Warder	–	9	–
	Weeton	–	11	–
	Eliz. Wynne	–	14.5	–
19th	*Alcott	–	13.5	–
	Cobden-Sanderson	8	16	–
	E. Gaskell	–, 10	22, 18	1st daughter walking with chairs at 16.5m
	*Hayes	–	15	–
	Head	19	22	Walking with chairs at 20m
	Johnston	–	11	–
	*Judson	–	22, 9	–
	*Longfellow	–	12	–
	*Lovell	–	18	–
	*Parker	–		Walking, holding on to fingers, at 8m
	*Prentiss	–	14.5	Walking well
	K. Russell	–	11	Running at 30m
	Wood	6.5	11	–

Note. For some strange reason it appears that 19th-century infants took longer to learn to walk (mean age of 15.4m) than 18th-century infants (mean age of 11.7m). The difference between the two groups, however, is not statistically significant, $t_{(17)} = 1.54$, $p < 0.05$.

This was a time of interest to us all. Caroline [elder sibling] took great delight in enticing her to come to her. She was very fearful to take a step at first, and for several days would fall two or three times in going from one side of the room to the other, but soon became accustomed to it, and would laugh heartily whenever she fell, and jump up and continue her tottering walk. By degrees her limbs gained strength and she ventured to get out at the door and walk on the ground. She would frequently get her little sun bonnet, and putting it on with the front behind, and cape before, would be out and walking off towards the barn before we missed her from her play in the house. (58)

One 19th-century British mother was also interested in the walking ability of her child. Caroline Head (1852–1904) noted: 'Baby gets on every day he will soon walk, he stands so firmly, almost without any support, and gets along by chairs' (102). Two months later: 'He walks all round the room from one thing to another, sometimes only just touching the wall or door' (102).

Talking

As with other infantile developments, only a few details on the acquisition and mastery of speech are contained in the texts. These are listed in Table 13.

The 18th- and 19th-century diarists related the interest they felt in their child learning to talk. That is not to say that the earlier diarists were uninterested; but they tended to note developments more matter of factly. For example, in the 16th century, Clifford (1590–1676) liked to have her daughter of not quite 2 years brought to speak to her and Wallington (1598–1658) was amused by his young daughter 'pratteling' to him. In the 17th century *Sewall (1652–1730) was told of his son speaking for the first time as soon as he came home, which indicates that the event aroused interest and excitement. He noted it as 'Little Hull speaks *Apple* plainly . . . this the first word' (vol. 5, p. 122). *Sewall's description of the event is remarkably like that of a later father's remark on his son learning to talk. Addison (1869– ?) wrote: 'Came home by tea-time and found that young "Timothy" had a few minutes before risen to the heights of "Da-Da" for the first time' (vol. 1, p. 64). Moreover, the fact that Blundell (1669–1737) described his young daughter as backward in talking and that William Bagshawe (1628–1702) recorded of his young grandson: 'We are well pleased with the lispings and imperfect speeches of little John as well as the longer discourses of the elder children' (30) also demonstrate that parents in earlier centuries were aware of and concerned about children's development.

A few of the later texts do provide more details. *White (1780–1811) took great pleasure in her daughter's attempts at 'speech': 'I endeavour to make her say, "Papa, Papa", but she seems to prefer "bubble, bubble",

Table 13. *Age at learning to talk (in months ('m'))*

Century	Diarist	Single words	Phrases	Sentences	Additional information
16th	Clifford	–	–	–	Child 'brought to speak to me' at 22m
	Wallington	–	–	35	Child 'prattling prettily'
17th	Blundell	–	30	–	Child considered backward
	*Sewall	18.5	–	–',	Child said 'apple'
18th	Boscawen	–, –	–	–, 36	Child of 30m noticeably increasing her vocabulary
	Boswell	24, –	–		2nd child had large vocabulary: but imperfect pronunciation
	Burney	20	24	–	Child considered backward
	Moore	–	23	–	–
	Thrale	–	–	–	Children say 'I goed' and not 'I went'
	*White	–	–	–	Child being encouraged to speak at 7m
	Eliz. Wynne	16.25, –	–, 25	–	Another child considered backward as not talking at all by 16.5m
19th	Addison	10	–	–	Child said 'Da-da'
	E. Gaskell	11	–	29	Child understood simple sentences
	Head	10	–	–	Child said 'Bow-Bow'
	*Howe	17.5	–, 24	–	Child said 'Papa'
	*Lovell	18, –	20	–	1st child understood speech
	K. Russell	–		30	–
	Traherne	–	–	–	Child 'doing her level best to talk' at 6m
	Wood	–	–	22	Child a 'chatterbox'

From birth to twelve

. . . Her first perfect word can hardly afford me more pleasure than her first feeble effort at articulation. Cote laughed at me the other evening for saying she articulated very well, – it was true, nevertheless' (338). Burney (1752–1840) wrote that, at 2 years, her son 'has made no further advance [in speech] but that of calling out, as he saw our two watches hung on two opposite hooks over the chamber chimney-piece, "Watch papa, – watch, mamma"' (vol. 6, p. 79). However, three months later: 'he has repeated readily whatever we have desired; and yesterday while he was eating his dry toast, perceiving the cat, he threw her a bit, calling out, "Eat it, Buff!"' (vol. 6, p. 91). Moore (1779–1852) was only too pleased to gratify his young daughter's demands: 'Barbara has this moment interrupted me with her often-repeated demand for "pretty mookis", which means "pretty music", and I have accordingly set her up on a chair at the pianoforte, where she is inflicting all sorts of tones on my ears' (vol. 2, p. 9). The 19th-century diaries depict a similar interest. *Howe (1801–76) referred to 'the ecstasy I felt yesterday when my little Julia, toddling up to my knee, raised her sweet face and said for the first time distinctly, "Papa! Papa". Such sounds sweep over strings of the heart of whose existence we were not aware, and make sweet music within us' (195). Kitto (1804–54), who was deaf, lamented the fact he could not hear his children talk:

Is there anything on earth so engaging to a parent as to catch the first lispings of his infant's tongue? or so interesting as to listen to its dear prattle, and trace its gradual mastery of speech? If there be any one thing arising out of my condition which more than another fills my heart with grief, it is THIS: it is to *see* their blessed lips in motion and to *hear* them not, and to witness others moved to smiles and kisses by the sweet peculiarities of infantile speech, which are incommunicable to me, and which pass by me like the idle wind. (629–30)

Sleeping

Only the 18th- and 19th-century texts refer to sleeping problems; but Clifford (1590–1676) was concerned that her daughter would be able to sleep in a bed by herself without being upset. Up till the age of 5, Margaret slept with a maid, apart from spending an occasional night in her parents' bed. Just after her daughter's fifth birthday, Clifford wrote: 'This night was the 1st that Lady Margaret lay alone, Mary having a bed hard by' (104).

Seven diarists recorded problems in getting their infants to sleep. K. Russell and Stedman both resorted to sedatives and Rathbone found it difficult to persuade her son to sleep once he was weaned. *Lovell's

(1809– ?) youngest daughter was reluctant to go to sleep; but by the time Laura was 18 months, her mother had solved the problem: 'I got Laura so that she would go to sleep in her little crib. Sometimes I had some difficulty with her, but generally when she saw that I was decided, she would go quietly to sleep' (57). Her elder daughter was over the age of 3 before she was willing to 'be left in the dark to go to sleep'. *Prentiss and *Todd had one child who just would not sleep, in each case a child who cried continually. *Prentiss (1818–78) described her difficulty: 'We swung him in blankets, wheeled him in little carts, walked the room with him by the hour, ect., ect., but it was wonderful how little sleep he obtained after all. He always looked wide awake as if he did not *need* sleep' (116). Cobden-Sanderson (1840–1922) wrote a long description of how he persuaded his 18-month-old son to go to sleep:

The other night he cried after being put to bed, not of course from pain, but mere contrariness. I tried to induce him to be quiet and failed. I then took him out of bed and whipped him, and as he cried out even more, pressed him close to me and held his head and bade him to be quiet. In a moment, after a convulsive sob or two, he became quite quiet. I put him back into his cot, told him to be quiet and go to sleep, and left him. Not a sound more did he make, and he went to sleep. The next day at noon he cried again when put to bed. I went to him, told him he must not cry, that he must lie down – he stands up in bed on such occasions and usually is found arranging his blanket over the rails of his cot – be quiet and go to sleep. I placed him properly in bed, spread the clothes over him, and left him. He became and remained perfectly quiet, and went to sleep. He now goes to bed noon and night and to sleep without a cry. (vol. 1, p. 246)

This diarist became more lenient with regard to his son's sleeping after the latter suffered from a fever and was later prepared to get up in the night to 'soothe' Richard back to sleep rather than insisting he went back to sleep immediately.

Inoculation

Inoculation for smallpox was introduced to England in 1718. The custom met with great opposition, particularly from the church which was still denouncing it as wicked and unnatural in 1760. Inoculation involved lancing one or both arms and introducing infected smallpox matter. If successful, the person would then suffer from a less virulent form of smallpox and afterwards be immune from further infection. Unfortunately, the procedure was not without its risks; it proved to be fatal in a number of cases and also spread the disease. The vaccine for smallpox – a much safer procedure – was discovered in 1796 and made public in 1798. Table 14 lists

Table 14. *Age at inoculation*

Diarist	Approx. date of inoculation†	Age of child (years; months; weeks)
Boscawen	1755	3;9
Boswell	1776	0;11
Burney	1797	2;3
Calvert	1790s	As babies
Cooke	1770‡	6;4 5;3 3;11
Darby	1758	9;11 8;0 6;1 3;0
*Drinker	1797	0;5
*Hiltzheimer	1769	6;0 4;0 0;9
Holland	1794	0;11
*Holyoke	1789	12;0
Kilham	1790	0;6
*C. Mather	1721	15;0
Oliver	1752	11;0
	1789	0;4§
Powys	1799	4;6
Rathbone	1787	0;3
Roe	1779	2;4;2 1;1
Stedman	1786	12;1 2;0
*Stiles	1772	13;0
Thrale	1765–75	As children
Woods	1782	As children
Eliz. Wynne	1792	6;0
	1799	0;2
	1801	0;10
Fry	1801	3;6
Hochberg	1905	2;6
*Lovell	1839	2;4 0;3
Mantell	1820	1;9 0;11
*Sterne	1844	3;3 5;0
Watkin	1817	0;0;2

† Those after 1800 are vaccinations rather than inoculations.
‡ Quite often all of a family was inoculated at the same time.
§ This child died from the inoculation.

those diarists who decided to have their children protected from smallpox and entered thus in their diary.

The table reveals that young infants were rarely inoculated until the end of the 18th century – it was perhaps considered too hazardous a procedure to subject a baby to. It was mainly the 18th-century diarists who provided information on inoculation and their remarks reveal the anxiety they felt about this novel action.

The American diarists did record their child's progress with the infection and were pleased when the child recovered; but their diaries do not disclose the great anxiety evinced by the British diarists. Boscawen (1719–1805) related the elaborate preparation required for the inoculation of her son of almost 3 years. He had to have rhubarb the night before:

I have not been able to get it all down – he reached so. However, as 'tis prescribed, I shall attempt the remainder to-morrow morning, but now the sweet soul was so sleepy and tired, and tried so honestly to do his best to oblige "May", the little stomach heaving all the while, that I must have had a heart of flint to torment him any more. (1940, p. 168)

The next day:

I held the child myself and so effectually employed his eyes and attentions (by a bit of gold lace which I was putting into forms to lace his waistcoat) that he never was sensible of the first arm. For the second, he pretended to wince a little, but I had a sugar plum ready, which stopped the whimper before it was well formed. (1940, p. 170)

After Burney's (1752–1840) son was inoculated at 27 months, she wrote: 'Relieved at length from a terror that almost from the birth of my darling has hung upon my mind' and then described the proceedings. The doctor had wanted her to leave the child to him and a maid but: 'I could not endure to lose a moment from the beloved little object for and with whom I was running such a risk.' During the actual event, her son was given a barley sugar; the maid attracted his attention with a toy and his mother 'began a little history to him of the misfortunes of the toy we chose, which was a drummer'. Alexander screamed when the incision was made but this was 'momentary, and ended in a look of astonishment at such an unprovoked infliction, that exceeds all description, all painting – and in turning an appealing eye to me, as if demanding at once explanation and protection' (vol. 6, pp. 88–90). Fry (1780–1845) consulted her doctor over vaccination and, on his advice, agreed to have it done, although she was worried about her undertaking:

I think highly of his [Doctor's] judgement, and I believe it to be our duty to avoid evil, both bodily and mentally. So trifling a complaint as the cow-pox, being likely to prevent so dreadful a disease as the small pox, at least it appears justifiable to try it; although the idea is pleasant, it almost looks like taking too much on ourselves to give a child a disease. (95)

However, as the operation was easily performed and her daughter recovered, Fry decided: 'What a wonderful discovery it is, if it really prevents the small pox' (95). Woods' (1748–1821) entry in her diary regarding inoculation embodies the feelings of all the British diarists in Table 14.

If ever I undertook anything in the fear of the Lord, I think I may say I have this day had my four children inoculated in that most holy fear . . . Though it has been done with a firm persuasion of its propriety, I feel deeply anxious for the event, beyond what I think I should feel for the apprehension of any ill in which I could have no hand. (124)

Some parents did not approve of inoculation because it was in opposition to their religious beliefs. *C. Mather (1663–1728) described the dilemma which occurred when his duty as a minister clashed with his duty as a parent. At the onset of a smallpox outbreak in 1721, his 15-year-old son wished to be protected. However, *Mather, as a minister, believed that his congregation would turn against him, arguing that he was interfering with the acts of God, if he allowed it. On the other hand, if Samuel died from smallpox, *Mather felt his position as a parent would be 'unsupportable'. The dilemma was finally solved by the boy's grand-father suggesting he was inoculated in secret. This was done and *Mather could then plead ignorance in the face of any opposition. One autobiographer, Jane Pearson, also refused to have her children inoculated in the 1760s due to her religious beliefs.

Inoculation was by no means universal even for those parents who, from their diaries, did not appear to have religious or any other objection to it. A number of children suffered from smallpox because they were not inoculated, even when the option was available. For example, in 1794, F. Gray (1751–1826) wrote: 'Through the kind hand of our gracious God, all the five children got well thro' the small pox, not one of them likely to be at all marked' (80). *Prentiss' (1818–78) entry on smallpox in the mid-19th century is even more surprising because she regarded the disease with absolute horror, and yet took no preventative measures to safeguard her offspring: 'does it not seem almost incredible that this child, watched from her birth like *the apple of our eyes*, should yet fall into the jaws of this loathsome disease?' (140)

Discussion. As has been stated in the introduction to this chapter, there is not a great deal of information on infancy in any century. Nevertheless, the information the texts do contain suggests the following reconstruction. Most infants were desired: they were regarded as something to be valued, as pleasures and 'comforts' when young, and as supporters of their parents when older. They may have been sent to a wet-nurse or breast-fed by the mother. If the former was the case, the majority of infants were visited by their parents, or failing that, a relative. The parents were distressed if the infant was ill or was being ill-treated by the nurse. The infants may have had difficulty in obtaining enough food. In this situation parents were clearly concerned and took steps to solve the problem either by sending the child to a wet-nurse, changing the nurse or finding an alternative means of nourishment. For the majority of infants, weaning was a gradual process and here too the parents were anxious that the child should not be too upset and would survive the transition. The infants would appear to pass through such developmental stages as teething at approximately the same age as infants of today, although there was a great deal of individual variation. The wide range of individual variation revealed in these texts makes it difficult to understand how many historians have been able to select one or two families as representative of a particular time period. Parents were aware of, and showed interest in, these stages. From the 18th century onwards a number of children were inoculated and parents were very concerned that they had made a correct decision. In general, life for infants in the past, at least from the 16th century, was relatively pleasant. This finding is in direct opposition to the argument of most historians that, prior to the 18th century, infants were unwelcome, ignored and neglected by their parents. The texts reveal no significant change in the quality of parental care given to or the amount of parental affection felt for infants for the period 1500–1900.

One further factor which emerges from the sources studied is that nearly all these infants were attached to their parents (possible exceptions were Freke's son and Thrale's daughters). Bowlby in *Attachment and Loss* (1970) has argued that attachment between mother and child developed because it was necessary for protection from predators and was thus essential for the infant's survival. Bowlby at first claimed that an infant needed a continuous relationship with one mothering figure for normal social development. However, reassessments of Bowlby's theory (see Rutter, 1972) and various anthropological studies as Leiderman, Tulkin & Rosenfeld (1977), LeVine (1977) and Marvin *et al.* (1977) reveal that this relationship need not be continuous nor confined to one mother figure. That is, it was quite possible for infants sent away to wet-nurse to form emotional bonds with their visiting parents. The concern shown by parents in the welfare and development of their children from infancy to long after the offspring had set up their own independent households, coupled with the deep affection with which the children regarded their fathers and mothers and the amount of contact maintained between parents and children when the latter had left home, bears witness to the lasting attachment formed between past parents and their offspring. There were only a few exceptions to this.

The early years of past infants having been traced, the next section will deal with their childhood.

Childhood

Once children are beyond infancy they regularly appear in the diaries in conjunction with illness, death, discipline (all of which have been discussed), play and education. Outwith these themes, the vast majority of all diarists with older children mentioned taking them on visits, for drives and walks, to the seaside or to watch any unusual events. This section will be concerned firstly with children's play and secondly with their education.

Play

Children's play does not appear very often in the texts, although entries referring to it have been made in each century studied, and by both American and British diarists. Play was most often recorded in the more detailed 18th- and 19th-century diaries. Some parents disapproved of play, or at least, of too much play. *C. Mather (1663–1728) did talk of providing children with paints; but also wrote: 'I am not fond of proposing *Play* to them [children], as a Reward of any diligent Application to learn what is good; lest they should think *Diversion* to be a better and a nobler Thing than Diligence' (vol. 7, p. 536). When one of his sons reached the age of 11 *Mather wished to 'raise his Mind above the Sillier Diversions of Childhood' by teaching him geography, history and astronomy (vol. 8, p. 473). Thus it seems that, to *Mather, play was a component of childhood; but it was not something to be encouraged. One 17th-century British diarist was more outspoken in his opposition to play, because he believed it interfered with a child's education. Before Slingsby's son was 4 years old, he could give the Latin names for his clothes and parts of the body. However, this aptitude for learning did not increase, as Slingsby (1601–58) described (writing shortly after his son's fourth birthday):

I find him duller to learn this year yn ye last, wch would discourage one, but yt I think ye cause to be his too much minding Play, wch takes off his mind from his book; therefore they do ill yt do foment & cherish yt humour in a child, & by inventing new sports increase his desire to play, wch causeth a great aversion to their book; & their mind being at first season'd with vanity, will not easily loose ye relish of it. (53–4)

One 18th-century diarist also disliked play. While away from home, Harrower (1735?– ?) wrote to his wife advising her how to rear their daughter of approximately 8 years of age: 'keep her tight to her seam and stockin and any other Housold affairs that her years are capable of and do not bring her up to Idleness or play' (91).

Other diarists were not so disapproving and even appeared to be amused at their children's play.

The 16th century. *Jefferay (1591–1675) described his children's rambles in the woods near their home and his enjoyment in accompanying them. He also condemned the Quaker religion because it did not approve of 'sport and pastime' for children (65). Two British diarists also referred to play. Dee (1527–1608) described some fantasy play: 'Arthur Dee and Mary Herbert, they being but 3 yere old the eldest, did make as it wer a shew of childish marriage, of calling ech other husband and wife' (14). Furthermore, he referred to another son, aged 8, as 'going childyshly with a sharp stick' (25). Wallington (1598–1658) remarked that his young son was 'very merry . . . and fully of play' and also noted that his 3-year-old daughter went out to play with another child (MS, fos. 404, 435).

The 17th century. In the next century three American and five British texts contain information on play. *Byrd (1674–1744) noted that his 11-year-old son was hurt while throwing snowballs. *Green (1675–1715) remarked that his young sons went fishing and *Sewall (1652–1730) described children playing 'trap-ball' and also observed that his grandson 'played wicket on the common' (vol. 7, p. 372). Blundell (1669–1737) was amused at the mock funeral staged by his daughters, aged 8 and 6. '[They buried one of their dolls] with a great deal of Formallity, they had a Garland of Flowers carried before it, and at least twenty of their Playfellows & others that they invited were at the Buriall' (vol. 112, p. 29). Two years later Blundell 'made a shuttle-cock for my children but they could not play with it' (vol. 112, p. 115). Heywood (1630–1702) described one of his sons, about the age of 7, playing a game while coming home from school.

From birth to twelve

Eliezer had been tied to other children by his coat sleeves, but unfortunately he fell into a ditch and was almost smothered. Richards (1660?–1721) simply mentioned that his son had been playing. Newcome (1627–95) recalled playing 'trap-ball' in the rain as a child and noted that one of his sons almost fell into the river while playing on a bridge. Pringle (1625–67) also remembered being 'greatly given to playing' as a child (4).

The 18th century. The 18th-century texts provide more detailed information.[11] *Huntington (1791–1823) considered that play could perform a useful function.

I like a baby house for little girls, all that some sensible people have said to the contrary notwithstanding. They may have a closet, or part of one entirely to themselves, and the arrangement and order of it be entrusted to their care . . . And I think it desirable to accustom them, as soon as may be, to assist in doing what they can, that they may learn the pleasure of being useful. (340–1)

*Shippen (1763–1841) noted her daughter's preference for her doll: 'that ingroces all her time and all her care, next to the Harpsichord of which she is Extreamly fond' (164). *Drinker (1734–1807) did not altogether approve of her son's pastime: 'Billy came home about dinner-time, his Face much bruised. He had been Boxing with one of the Latin-School Boys – an exercise that by no means suits him' (140).

The British texts contain similar information. Braithwaite (1788–1859) described her young son as 'paddling in all the puddles he can find' (54) and, in addition, wrote: 'I am now sitting surrounded by my little flock, excepting Robert, who is gone to bed. They are amusing themselves with pencils and paper, and look very smiling and happy' (68). Another mother, Reynolds (1770?–1803), took her children to the seaside and described their pastimes: 'The children are delighted with standing on a little rock and seeing the water surround them . . . [they] have got a great collection of shells – no great variety, and only common ones but they please them very much' (158, 159). Macready (1793–1873) recorded running 'into the garden to enjoy a romping play with my dear children' (143). Calvert (1767–1859), as did *Drinker, noted her son had been fighting. '[Nicolson's] little tongue ran incessantly; he is delighted with school. He has, he says "licked" some boys, and has been "licked" himself, but he don't mind it' (101).

The 19th century. In the 19th century[12] *Hayes (1822–93) observed that his sons were playing at soldiers with a trumpet and drum and described them as generally noisy. *Longfellow (1807–82) noted that all his children

238

were 'wild with play among the haycocks; the seat in the old apple-tree turned into a fort; great scrambling for sugar-plums, and the like' (223). *Phelps (1810?– ?) described how her son of 4 years piled gunpowder on the floor and lit it. As the pile did not ignite, he called his 3-year-old sister to come over and blow it. Emily obligingly did so, resulting in a 'child so black I hardly knew her'; but Emily did recover (225). *M. Walker's (1814–97) son of 2 also had a bad day: 'Before noon he chased the pigs into the horse pen and then fell into a dirty puddle, and came crying back in a sad plight' (147).

The British children engaged in more conventional forms of play. Allen (1813–80) described the following scene:

Archie [aged 6] is lying on the hearth-rug kicking up his heels while he harnesses his donkey; baby Alfie [aged 2½] has found an old doll's head minus the trunk, and is loving and kissing it most amusingly. The parlour looks like Bedlam at the present moment, strewn with bricks, dominoes and picture books. Edie [aged 7] has just come in from the garden with glowing cheeks to show me a treasure of fifteen violets in a sunny corner. (130)

Bailey's (1864–1931) 3-year-old daughter insisted her father played with her: 'Jenny [insists on] banishing *The Times* with a roaring "No" and calling her half-reluctant Papa to take the floor and "build a house". She demands Johny Crow's Garden every morning, and when we come to the end cheerfully remarks: Now yead it again, Daddy' (91). Head's (1852–1904) son of 2½ years revealed a great deal of fantasy play: 'He constantly plays at being a gardner, or lamplighter, or engine driver, or coal-man, or man with organ and monkey. He is most imaginative, and such a chatterbox' (105).

Discussion. Children have obviously played through the centuries, although the texts do not provide a great deal of information on the specific games they enjoyed. It does appear as if childhood and play are two inseparable entities, even if some parents did not entirely approve of such behaviour. For young children it seems as if imaginative play was common, references being made to this in each century. This corresponds to Newson & Newson's (1968) finding in respect of fantasy play seen in modern British 4-year-old children.

Education

The texts contain more information on education than any other theme in this chapter. Table 15 illustrates the percentage of texts which refer to

Table 15. *Percentage of texts providing information on education*

Century	All texts	American	British
16th	33	0	35
n =	24	2	22
17th	46	40	48
n =	80	15	65
18th	46	44	47
n =	245	98	147
19th	51	45	55
n =	188	65	123

education. In this section academic and religious education will be discussed separately.

The 16th century. The 16th-century diarists who mention education were concerned that their children should receive at least some education. For example, Winthrop (1587– ?) wrote: 'I will have a speciall care of the good education of my children'; wishing them to be '"well and Christianly educated"' (73, 152). The children appeared to receive elementary education at home, as well as going to school. Dee (1527–1608) sent three sons and a daughter to school in 1590, remarked in 1594 that 'John Stokden cam to study with our children' and again noted in 1596: 'Mary Goodwyn cam to my servyce to govern and teach Madinia and Margaret, my young daughters' (49, 56). Rogers (1550?–1618) wondered if he should disrupt his family by taking a teacher into it and Edward Tudor (1537–53), as heir to the throne, was totally educated at home. There was no set age for going to school; Powell (1581–1656), for example, mentioned sending his sons aged 19, 15 and 12 to school for the first time and the next year they were joined by their 10- and 8-year-old brothers. Daughters did not seem to be sent to school but were educated at home – apart from the case of Boyle (1566–1643) who recorded sending his daughter to a Mrs Cleyton – who may have been a teacher. The sons of Boyle, H. Mildmay and Winthrop all went on to further education, whereas those of Powell began apprenticeships after a few years' schooling. Boyle and H. Mildmay sent their sons to boarding school and noted in their diary the sending of regular letters and gifts.

An early autobiographer, Forman (1552–1601) gave some details on his education. He was sent to school in 1560 at the age of 8.

And when he came to lerne 'In the name of the Father,' &c., because his capacity could not understand the mistery of spellinge, he prayed his master he mighte goe to scolle noe more, because he should never learn yt; but his said master beate him for yt, which made him the more diligent to his bocke, and after som four dais, when he had pondered thereon well and had the reason thereof, he learned yt. And after that his master never beat him for his bocke again. (4)

Forman went to another school a year later, then another between the ages of 11 and 13, and finally bound himself apprentice at 14.

The 17th century. The 17th-century texts, with the sample size increasing from 7 to 33, give more information on education. *Byrd (1674–1744) taught his niece and nephew himself (their mother was dead and they lived with *Byrd). From his diary entries he appears to have been a strict disciplinarian in this respect. His eldest daughter was sent to boarding school at 10 and was regularly visited by her father. *Byrd took a great deal of interest in his children's education: for example, there are frequent entries of the sort 'heard the children read' and 'examined my children's reading' (1942, pp. 125, 130). Another diarist (*Green, 1675–1715) was concerned about the lack of a school in his village and so wanted to have a school house built and also to have 'a good school master to teach their children to read and write and cypher and everything that is good' (78). He got his wish and noted that his sons went to school, although this does not appear to have been on a regular basis as he also wrote: 'Boys cyphering at home.' His eldest son was sent away to school at the age of 12 because *Green wished him to be well educated so that his son could be a minister: 'I went to Salem Lecture carrying son Joseph to School, intending (if God please) to make him a schollar and minister. He boards at Cos. Hides. I am to give 12£ per year certain and 13£ uncertain' (101). There is no mention of the education of his daughters; as this is one of the diaries which has had many of the family details removed, this information may be in the manuscript – the editor did state that much of the diary relates to the 'education of his children'.

*C. Mather (1667–1728) was exceedingly concerned with the education of his offspring, both academic and religious, and was prepared to give up a great deal of his time in order to attend to this. He wished his children to regard education as a privilege and reward. For example, when they had behaved well: 'I would have them come to propound and expect, at this rate, *I have done well, and now I will go to my Father; He will teach me some Curious Thing for it*. I must have them count it a *Privilege*, to be taught; and I sometimes manage the Matter so, that my Refusing to teach them Something, is their *Punishment*' (vol. 7, p. 536). Both his sons and daughters were sent to school and *Mather was continually devising ways to improve their education. On one occasion he wrote:

About this Time, sending my little Son [6 years] to School, where the child was learning to read, I did use every Morning for diverse Months, to write in a plain Hand for the Child, and send thither by him, a *Lesson* in *Verse*, to be not only *Read* but also gott by Heart. My Proposal was, to have the Child improve in *Goodness* at the same time, that he improv'd in Reading. (vol. 7, p. 555)

However, he did find his concern for his children's education very time consuming (he had 15 children): 'The *Education* of my *Children* to learn them *Things*, and sett them *Talks*, which none else can, spends me no little *Time*' (vol. 7, p. 547). *Sewall (1652–1730) also sent both his sons and daughters to school – one son, Joseph, was sent to school with his 'horn book' when he was not quite 3. *Hammond (1640–99) and *Holyoke (1689–1769) merely noted that their children went to school.

The British texts depict a similar concern for their children's education. Of these diarists, 42 per cent merely stated that their children went to school or had a tutor; but the rest provided more details. Blundell (1669–1737) taught his daughters to read and write: W. Bulkeley (1691–1760) reared his eldest grand-daughter, endeavouring to give her as good an education as possible and Heywood (1630–1702) was prepared to move house to improve his son's education: 'I determined to have removed into Lanc. that I might be quietly at home, and for the benefit of a good school-master for my sons' (vol. 1, p. 282). Morris' (1659–1727) diary gives a good description of the education of his son and daughter. His daughter went to day-school at the age of 7 at the cost of 6d a week. At 9 years she began to have violin and singing lessons at 3 guineas per annum. At 11 years she was sent to a boarding school costing £12 a year and, in addition, Morris paid quarterly: 10s for French, dancing and violin masters, 5s for a writing master, 5s for a teacher to dress Betty 'to encourage her care', 2s 6d to each of three maids. Betty was also to be given fruit each week to the cost of 6d and was liberally supplied with clothes and pocket money. Apart from music lessons, her education ended at 13. The education of Morris' son was rather different. At the age of 4, William was sent to a dame's school where he (and the maid) were taught for 6s 6d a quarter. However, William did not appear to learn much there, for at 7 he was sent to a tutor for six months to learn how to read, at a cost of 1 guinea. At 8, he went to grammar school as a day scholar, costing at first 2, later 4, guineas per annum plus 1 guinea entrance fee. William also had violin lessons. At 13 William went to a boarding grammar school to learn Greek and Latin. This cost his father £20 a year, which did not include the cost of pens, books or shoe cleaning. Moreover, Morris paid, per quarter, 7s 6d to a master to teach writing, arithmetic and drawing, 1s to a barber, 9d for the mending of clothes and 5s pocket money. Finally William went to university at the age of 18.

Slingsby's (1601–58) diary also reveals the differences in male and female education. His daughter was taught by her mother so that by the age of 5: 'she is able already to say all her prayers, answer to her catechisme, read & wright a little' (3). The education of Slingsby's son was much more formal and Slingsby had definite ideas on how Thomas should be educated:

I also committ'd my Son Thomas [aged 4] into ye charge & Tuition of Mr Cheny whom I intend shall be his schoolmaster, & now he doth begin to teach him his primer; I intend he shall begin to spell, & Read Latin together with his english, & to learn to speak it, more by practise of speaking yn by rule; he could ye last year, before he was 4 years old, tell ye Latin words for the parts of his body & of his cloaths . . . I will make Tryall of this way Teaching my Son Latin, yt is wth out Rule or grammer; & herein I do follow ye Pattern of Michael de Montaigne a frenchman who as he himself saith was so taught Lating, yt he could at 6 years old speak more Latin yn French. But I want yt means wth he had, having those about him yt could speak nothing but Latin; him I do take to be my Pattern herein of educating my son. (53–4)

In contrast to the other diarists, apart from perhaps Slingsby, Evelyn (1620–1706) appears to have reared a selection of infant prodigies, for example his 5-year-old son was 'a prodigy for witt and understanding':

he had learn'd all his catechisme . . . at 2 years and a halfe olde he could perfectly reade any of ye English, Latine, French, or Gothic letters, pronouncing the three first languages exactly. He had . . . not onley skill to reade most written hands, but to decline all the nouns, conjugate the verbs regular, and most of ye irregular; learn'd out 'Puerilis', got by heart almost ye entire vocabularie of Latine and French primitives and words, could make congruous syntax, turne English into Latin, and vice versa . . . The number of verses he could recite was prodigious . . . he had a wonderful disposition to mathematics, having by heart divers propositions of Euclid that were read to him in play, and he would make lines and demonstrate them. (vol. 2, pp. 96–7)

Evelyn clearly regarded his son as atypical, writing that the latter's knowledge was 'far exceeding his age and experience' and 'such a child I never saw' (97). His daughters were also well educated, speaking French and Italian fluently and had read the best Latin and Greek authors.

It does not seem as if many girls were taught either Latin or Greek in the 16th and 17th centuries. It was not that parents regarded the education of their daughters as unimportant – Blundell, Briggins, Evelyn, Josselin, Morris, Newcome and Slingsby were just as proud of their daughters' accomplishments as they were of their sons' – but more because there were virtually no career opportunities for women, the acquisition of Greek and Latin was considered unnecessary for girls. Eleven[13] of the diarists sent their children to boarding school, both sons and daughters. Like the 16th-century diarists, they gave no indication as to why they did so. It was quite likely that there were simply no schools near them and therefore, if the diarists wished to have their children educated, they had to send them away. It was certainly not that these parents were uninterested in their children as every diarist wrote letters and sent gifts to a child away at school.

Discussion. These parents did wish their children to receive some education even if, as in the case of Powell's offspring, it was only for a limited period and even though, as Morris' diary reveals, the tuition of children could be an expensive business. The children would seem to learn to read first and then to write. This is in agreement with Spufford's (1979) research into early education in the 17th century. The 16th- and 17th-century parents appreciated that it was to their offspring's advantage to be educated and therefore endeavoured to ensure that some tuition was available – some parents taught their children themselves. These results do not support the argument of Hunt (1972) and others who claim that parents in the 17th century were uninterested in the education of their offspring and attached little importance to it.

The 18th century. In the next century, 28 per cent of the diarists merely noted that their children went to school or had a tutor at home and give very little additional information. Eighteen[14] texts refer to the importance which the diarist attached to education. For example, *Adams (1767–1848) wrote: 'For your children, however, there is another duty not less sacred than that of giving them bread – the duty of education – of training them up in the way they should go; of preparing them for the conflicts which *they* may have in their turn to sustain with the world' (16). *Mitchell (1783–1857) wished his daughters to be educated as quickly as possible: 'With regard to things at home, push the girls along in their learning – which I acknowledge you [wife] are ready to do. But becoming convinced, as I do, as I travel the country, of the importance of ed., I can not help feeling a degree of impatience to have that of my daughters effected as rapidly as possible' (21).

Most of the British diarists were also concerned about the education of their children, if not quite so anxious as *Mitchell. M. Fox (1793–1844) remarked: 'The time spent with the dear children has brought us to the

244

conclusion, that some change must be made, ere long, in our plan for the education of the two younger ones, in order to secure for them greater advantages and more steady application. This has caused us much thoughtfulness, and earnest have been our desires for right direction in so important a matter' (385). Another mother, Trench (1768–1837), recorded: 'A superior education for our children, the power of enjoying all the innocent pleasures of life without injuring *their* future prospects by expense, and my own health, all conspire to detain us here [in Ireland]' (1862, p. 302). Boswell (1740–95), however, was not so anxious to accelerate his offspring's learning. He sent his 5-year-old son to 'reading School . . . but he did not like it, and as I think six an early age enough, I did not force him' (vol. 14, p. 154).

Many diarists at least partly educated their children themselves.[15] This was not considered an easy task by either American or British parents. *Alcott (1799–1888) wrote: 'They [daughters] are unwilling to pass their time within doors, or fix their thoughts on formal lessons. I spend an hour or more in the morning daily with them, but to small profit' (133). *Huntington (1791–1823) remarked: 'There is scarcely any subject concerning which I feel more anxiety, than the proper education of my children' (88). Boscawen (1719–1805) noted:

The instant breakfast is over, we [she and son] retire into another room to say our lesson . . . by which means he has made a considerable progress since we came into the country, and, if he had but half as much application as he has genius and capacity, he would read soon. But this same application is an ingredient seldom found in the composition of such a sprightly cub (1940, p. 92)

and Macready (1793–1873) recorded:

Coming down I heard dear Nina her lesson, in which, though with many attempts to control myself, I grew impatient and spoke with temper. This is without qualification *wrong*; it is the business of parents to endure the levity and inattention of these dear creatures, and be contented to assure themselves that a patient repetition of the often forgotten or unheeded precept insures for it a permanent place in the memory at last. Children should be lured to knowledge, until its acquisition, like that of meaner gain, creates a passion for its increase. (vol. 1, p. 166)

Macready, despite his determination to lure his children to knowledge, continued to criticise himself for being too impatient to advance them in learning. Steuart (1770?–1808) also remarked on her children's inattentiveness and her own impatience:

The children sometimes put me out of humour when they are inattentive at their lessons . . . I believe the great difficulty in the education of children is allowed to

245

be that of making them acquire habits of industrious attention & the power of studying – without giving them a disgust to learning by painful restraint . . . Mag [aged 10] likes to apply for a short time . . . but John [aged 8] not at all. (MS, fos. 133, 140)

Four diarists, all British, gave their reason for sending their children to boarding school: because it was to the children's advantage (Calvert, Fry, Sandford and F. Shelley). To his sons at school Sandford (1766–1830) wrote: 'My constant employment would have prevented me from attending to you, and without daily attention, at this crucial period, you could make no progress in Greek' (vol. 1, p. 259). F. Shelley (1787–1873) believed her son would be improved by going to public school: 'Frederick is a shy, amiable, industrious boy, not wanting in abilities, but a little cowed . . . by the superiority of his elder brother, which I think a year at Eton will remove; and the independence he will acquire there will be of use to him before he goes to sea' (vol. 2, p. 102).

Douglas, Gisborne, Mantell, Moore, Roe and Elizabeth Wynne described the distress they experienced when their child started school. Douglas (1743–1823) wrote of his son aged 10:

Fred went off with considerable emotion [to school], but he kept it under very well, and Barnes and I left him well satisfied with his behaviour, though if he had perceived my agitation I doubt if he would have done so quite as well. His poor mother . . . saw him leave Bruton Street like a heroine . . . this is a new epoch, and though the relation of mother and son will I am sure remain ever equally tender and affectionate between them, its mode and form will be different and till the new habit is formed must seem somehow less endearing. (vol. 1, p. 189)

Gisborne (1770–1851) was similarly distressed: 'My dear Frederic [aged about 9] is now on his road to school, and for the first time in his life. When I reflect on the many hours which we have pleasantly spent to-gether, I cannot refrain from tears at the loss of his company, and his empty chair in my study touches me more sensibly than perhaps it ought to do' (107).

*Huntington, *Shippen and Turner (1793–1873) disliked school for girls but the rest of the diarists were just as likely to send their daughters to school as their sons. Nevertheless, there were still the same differences in education already seen in the previous centuries: most girls were not taught Latin or Greek and did not go on to university. This difference is clearly seen in the child diaries – the boys studied Latin, Greek, arithmetic and social accomplishments such as dancing; the girls were taught French, a great deal of history, and some arithmetic, in addition to dancing, painting, sewing and the playing of a musical instrument.

Thrale (1741–1821) devoted her life to her children. She is a good example of the type of parent depicted by de Mause (1976) (for the 18th century) as 'intrusive'. She was constantly with her children, urging them on to ever higher intellectual attainments. For example, her eldest daughter Queeney, at the age of 2½, knew the solar system, the signs of the Zodiac, the nations, seas and European capital cities, among other things. Two years later she could read quite well and knew her Latin grammar to the fifth declension. (Her education was an exception to the general education for females.) At just over 6 years, Queeney excelled in Latin. However, as Queeney became older, she grew to dislike her mother and eventually Thrale, with her continual tuition, alienated the affections of all her daughters. Thrale finally decided that her eldest daughter was not improved by all her education. (Thrale's all-absorbing interest in the education of her offspring is very similar to that of *C. Mather in the 17th century.)

The 19th century. For the 19th century, 26 per cent of those diarists who remarked on education gave little information beyond the fact that their children either attended school or had a tutor. Of the rest, similar themes to those already documented reappear. Six diarists stressed the importance of education: *Erastus Beadle, E. Gaskell, Gurney, *Guthrie, Kitto and T. Powys. *Abelard Guthrie (1814–73), for example, wished his daughters to have a sound education.

I was anxious that their [daughters'] studies should be confined to the common branches of a good English education. But the ladies wished to give them lessons in music and drawing . . . I again forbade it but the ladies were very importunate . . . And when Mrs Guthrie visited the children they obtained her consent and thus the useful branches of their education were much neglected and they returned home very little improved in intellectual culture. (124)

Another father, T. Powys (1882– ?), regarded the education of his son as a 'really serious question' (114).

As with the earlier centuries, a number of diarists educated their children themselves for at least the elementary stages (Edward Benson, Cobden-Sanderson, Gurney, *Hayes and K. Russell, as well as the diarists discussed below). The American diarists appeared to find no difficulty in the task; *M. Walker (1814–97) noted that her children progressed well and *Lovell (1809– ?) remarked: 'It was very interesting to teach her [daughter], because she received ideas so readily, and although we did not attempt to give her regular school learning, and never sent her to school except during one summer to Sabbath school, yet she was always learning' (80). Conversely, Acland (1809–98) and Kingsford (1846–87) found themselves incapable of educating their children. E. Gaskell (1810–65) also noted some of the problems she encountered, for example she found it difficult to make Marianne repeat her letters. Mothers such as Lady de Rothschild (1821–1910) and Wood (1812–60) discovered that they lacked patience while teaching their offspring. The other British diarists, although aware of the responsibility of the task, did not mention any problems. Margaret Jeune (1819–91) and her husband decided to educate their children themselves. The latter was particularly able to draw out a child's 'powers of mind better than any governess' so that Jeune concluded: 'I shall hope for a similar result from the others when they are old enough to profit by his peculiar aptitude for teaching' (14). Johnston (1808–52) thoroughly enjoyed teaching her children: 'One of the leading interests and objects of the year has been the very tiny commencement of my boy's education. O what a delicate and what a most important work to begin' (137). When her son reached the age of 3 years and 4 months, Johnston described his lessons: 'Our lessons are very pleasant; we have to-day finished the second page of three-letter words, and I think shall begin them again. We spell, look at pictures in infantine knowledge, read over the alphabet, and, for a treat, find and mark all the O's or any other letter in a page' (142).

Only two diarists gave their reason for sending a child to school: Hutchinson (1880– ?) because his son needed companionship, and E. Gaskell (1810–65) wrote: 'our reasons for wishing her to go to school are . . . not to advance her rapidly in any branch of learning . . . but to perfect her habits of obedience, to give her an idea of conquering difficulties by perseverance, and to make her apply steadily for a short time' (34). Allen, *Burroughs, Hutchinson and Jeune recorded their distress at their children going to school. For instance, *Burroughs (1837–1921) observed: 'Never a morning does Julian start off for School but I long to go with him, to be his mate and equal; to share his enthusiasms, his anticipations, his games, his fun. Oh! to see life through his eyes again!' (188) Allen (1813–80) noted when her sons were sent to boarding school that 'it has cost me a good deal to part with my boys' (107). In addition, Bonar and Palgrave remarked that they missed their children when the latter were at school and looked forward to the holidays.

As the 19th century neared its end, there was a broadening of the school curriculum for girls to include the more academic subjects. None the less, in some families, girls and boys were still educated differently.

For example, Gurney's (1851–1932) daughters were taught at home, whereas her sons were sent to public school.

Discussion. The 18th- and 19th-century diarists were just as concerned with education as the 16th- and 17th-century diarists. Many, particularly mothers, taught the basic skills of reading, writing and arithmetic to their offspring and some appeared to be overwhelmed by the enormity of the task. As with the earlier centuries, it seems that parents wished their children to go to school, or at least be literate and numerate, because they believed it was important for the child to learn.

The texts studied reveal that at least some parents, from the 16th century onwards, were concerned about the education of their offspring. This suggests that these parents were therefore not indifferent to their offspring, but wished to ensure that the latter were given every opportunity to advance in life. Although, as all the diarists and autobiographers were literate, they were perhaps more interested in education than the population as a whole.[16]

Not only academic but also religious education featured prominently in the lives of many past children.

The 16th century. In the 16th century there is no reference to the religious education of children in the texts apart from those of G. Mildmay (1552–1620) who thought some religious instruction for children was necessary and Winthrop (1587– ?) who wished his children to be Christianly educated. From the 17th to the 19th century a number of parents were concerned that their children should possess some religious knowledge. This change was probably a result of the Protestant Reformation in the 16th century, followed by the rise of the non-conformist religions which caused people to think about and examine their faith.

The 17th century. A. & James Brodie, Byrom, E. Erskine, Heywood, Housman, Josselin, *C. Mather, Newcome and *Sewall were concerned with the religious education of their children – six of these were Puritans and another three non-conformist. A. & J. Brodie, E. Erskine and Newcome prayed with their children and discussed such religious works as the latter could understand. Josselin's description of his children's dreams indicates that the children had absorbed their father's religious beliefs and Byrom wished to ensure that his offspring would always please God in 'everything they do or see or hear' (vol. 40, p. 240).

Four diarists, all Puritans, provided more information. *C. Mather (1663–1728) was as preoccupied with the religious education of his children as he was with their academic.

I begin betimes to entertain them with delightful Stories, especially *scriptural* ones. And still conclude with some *Lesson* of Piety; bidding them to learn that *Lesson* from the *Story* . . .

When the Children at any time accidentally come in my way, it is my custome to lett fall some *Sentence* or other, that may be monitory and profitable to them . . .

I essay betimes, to engage the Children, in Exercises of Piety; and especially *secret Prayer*, for which I give them very plain and brief *Directions*, and suggest unto them the *Petitions*, which I would have them to make before the Lord, and which I therefore explain to their Apprehension and Capacity. And I often call upon them; *Child, Don't you forgett every Day, to go alone, and pray as I have directed you!* . . . When the Children are capable of it, [in practice between the ages of 9 and 11] I take them *alone*, one by one; and after my Charges unto them, to fear God, and serve Christ, and shun Sin, *I pray with them* in my Study and make them Witness of the Agonies, with which I address the Throne of Grace on their behalf. (vol. 7, pp. 534–6)

*Mather was prepared to go to extremes to ensure that this point was made. For example, he took his 9-year-old daughter into his study: 'and there I told my Child, that I am to *dy* shortly, and she must, when I am Dead, Remember every Thing, that I said unto her. I sett before her, the sinful and woful Condition of her *Nature*' (vol. 7, p. 239). *Sewall (1652–1730) also attempted to impress a child with the importance and suddenness of death – although, in this case, it was the child's death rather than *Sewall's:

Richard Dumer, a flourishing youth of 9 years old, dies of the Small Pocks. I tell Sam. [aged 11] of it and what need he had to prepare for Death, and therefore to endeavour really to pray when he said over the Lord's Prayer: He seem'd not much to mind, eating an Aple; but when he came to say, Our father, he burst out into a bitter Cry and when I askt what was the matter and he could speak, he burst out into a bitter Cry and said he was afraid he should die. I pray'd with him, and read Scriptures comforting against death, as, O death where is thy sting, & c. (vol. 5, pp. 308–9)

*Sewall did not mock his children's fears but instead attempted to assuage their distress; when his daughter told him that she was afraid she would go to Hell, *Sewall 'answer'd her Tears as well as I could and pray'd with many Tears on either part' (vol. 5, p. 432).

The British diarists revealed a similar concern with their child's salvation. Heywood (1630–1702) required his sons to learn psalms and passages from the Bible by heart and was pleased when this affected his sons. For example, he noted that his son John was 'weeping bitterly' because 'he had sinned agt god, and had offended him, blessed be god for this beginning of god's work upon his heart' (vol. 1, p. 233). Housman (1680?–1735) gives another instance of the conflict between religious duty and parental concern:

I have had this Evening, my dear Child [8 years] with me in my Closet, conversing with her, endeavouring to awaken her, and convince her of her Sin and Misery, by Nature and Practice. The Child was seemingly affected and melted into Tears, and in Distress; so much that I was fain to turn my Discourse, and tell her that God was good, and willing to pardon and receive Sinners, especially those Children that were willing to be good betimes, and in their younger Days set themselves to love and serve God. I told her she must pray to God to pardon her, and give her Grace to serve him. The child seemed willing to pray, but wanted words to express herself; I asked her if I should help her, and teach her to pray. (81)

Discussion. The religious education of the 17th-century Puritans does seem harsh, although it is clear that these parents sympathised with a child's distress and tried to calm the latter's fears – and not all Puritans were as concerned as *C. Mather or Housman with a child's religious training. It was fundamental to the Puritan doctrine that all people were innately sinful and it was essential that a child should be aware of this fact in order that the way be paved for that child's salvation. (See Beales, 1975; Gouge, 1622; Morgan, 1944; and Stannard, 1974 for a discussion of the Puritan religion and its relation to child-rearing.) If a parent believed in the Puritan faith he could not ignore a child's religious training – to do so would not only mean he failed as a Puritan but he also failed as a parent in that he had not done everything in his power to ensure that his child would be one of the elect.

This preoccupation by some Puritans with their child's religious education was also probably due to the fact that dissenters were often persecuted and imprisoned for their beliefs. Hence, they wished to ensure that their children would so thoroughly absorb the principles of their religion that they would continue to adhere to their faith as adults, no matter what.

The 18th century. Apart from those diaries which simply state that the children attended church or went to 'meetings', 16 of the 18th-century texts give some evidence on religious education. *Pemberton (1727–95) referred to religious meetings held with the children at home and

*Silliman (1779–1864) did wish his children to be religious but he did not force any conversion on them. For example, he wrote: 'the best news is, that my younger daughters, H—— and J——, have become deeply interested in religion, and I wrote to them to bid them God Speed on their way to the celestial city' (vol. 1, p. 393). *Huntington (1791–1823) wished to bring her children up 'in the paths of truth and holiness' and described how she effected this:

I begin to have my children in the room at prayers, within the month after their birth; and they always continue to be present, unless they are sick, or are excluded the *privilege* as a punishment for having been very naughty. It is difficult, when they are quite young, to keep them perfectly still . . . After they get to be two years, or more, old, and are able to understand the meaning of your conduct, if they play, or in any other way make a disturbance, they may be taken out [of the room]. (147)

As the 18th century progressed, there was a growing leniency on the part of some parents regarding the religious instruction of their children. For example, though Mascall (1702–94), like Housman, urged an awareness of their sins on her children:

I have been sometimes endeavouring to my utmost to convince my children of their natural sinful state, & ye nessecity of a Saviour, & to teach ym wt to believe & practice yt they may be saved, . . . while others are mourning over ye Sins & follys of their Children, I have the pleasure to hear mine mourn in Secret over their own Sins, & this they acknowledge to me has been occasioned by my talking seriously & affectionately to them. (13)

Woods (1748–1821), on the other hand, did not wish to force too much religious education on her offspring:

The fear of making religion a burden has prevented me from much conversation on the subject: till we love religion, we have very little relish for such conversation, and unless the youthful mind feels some touches of divine love, and desires to do that which is right in the sight of God, I believe all that we can do will avail but little. (169)

Fry and Gisborne, although concerned for their children's spiritual welfare, allowed the latter to make up their own minds about religion. Fry (1780–1845) for instance observed: 'My beloved children, who are come almost to an age of understanding, I long to see more under the Cross of Christ, and less disposed to give way to their own wills' (169).

Boswell (1740–95), however, was an exception to this. His conversation with his 4-year-old daughter describing the delights of Heaven has already been quoted (p. 210) and he also talked to Veronica of death when she was aged 3: 'how pretty angels would come and carry her from *the kirk hole* [grave] to heaven, where she would be with God and see fine things. I thought it best to please her imagination. But she seemed to dread death' (vol. 12, p. 10). All Boswell's religious training was in vain – it did not have the effect he expected:

At night, after we were in bed, Veronica spoke out from her little bed and said, 'I do not believe there is a God'. 'Preserve me', said I, 'my dear, what do you mean?' She answered, 'I have *thinket* it many a time, but did not like to speak of it'. I was confounded and uneasy, and tried her with the simple Argument that without God there would not be all the things we see. It is He who makes the sun shine. Said She, 'It shines only on good days'. Said I: 'God made you'. Said she: 'My Mother bore me'. It was a strange and alarming thing to her Mother and me to hear our little Angel talk thus. (vol. 14, pp. 5–6)

The next day Boswell discovered that Veronica was afraid of death and had decided if there was no God then there was no death. (At this stage Boswell tried reading an advice book on the religious education of children. Unfortunately the book was written from the standpoint that all children accepted the existence of God and was thus totally unhelpful.) Two months later Boswell was still discussing death with Veronica: 'I talked with earnest, anxious, tender apprehension of her death' (vol. 14, p. 37).

Burney, M. Fox, D. Taylor and Wilberforce discussed the scriptures with their children. J. Taylor (1743–1819) 'was especially determined to keep' his children 'from following any course of sin' and therefore 'made a constant and daily practice of praying; with my children' (120). He described his method of teaching:

I never had such a notion of as some have of teaching my children to *say their prayers*; either the Lord's prayer, or any other form. I am well persuaded that the Lord Jesus did not intend to teach his disciples to use those precise words. But suppose it were true, that his disciples and so all christians were taught to use that form, it is really a wonder if any sober man can believe, that those words are fit for children. (120)

Trench (1768–1837) believed that: 'The first object of education is to train up an immortal soul. The second (but second at an immeasurable distance) is to do this in a manner most conducive to human happiness' (1837, p. 7).

Two autobiographies also contain information on religious education. Carvosso (1750–1834) wished to see his youngest child accept religion and therefore resolved to take the first available opportunity to discuss this with his son. F. Gray (1751–1826) recalled her own religious training: 'Being taught to read at a very early age, I was required to repeat the catechism, collects, and portions of Scripture, and these occasionally led to serious examinations whether I loved God with all my heart, what would become of me if I died in my present state' (21).

Discussion. Parents in this century were still concerned with the spiritual welfare of their children; but there was a growing reluctance in some parents to force too much religious awareness on a child too soon. Children of the 18th century – unless one had the misfortune to be Veronica Boswell – were more likely than those of the 17th century to acquire religious knowledge at their own pace. Although parents would prefer their children to be religious and, although there were still a few parents, such as Mascall, who were excessively concerned with their child's sinful state, many parents were more prepared to let their children make up their own minds regarding God. This does coincide with the dampening of religious fervour for which the 18th century was known (Owen, 1974).

The 19th century. In this century Allen, Bonar, *Louisa Hopkins, Johnston, *Lovell, Tregelles and *M. Walker provided information on religious education in addition to statements that the children attended church or were confirmed. *M. Walker cited the following conversation between herself and her son, aged 5. Cyrus had asked: 'Why my heart is always bad and you tell me if I have a bad heart I will go to the bad place. He said he had asked God a great many times to make his heart good and he had not done it yet' (185). This attitude is very similar to the earlier parents who also wished their children to be aware of their sins. It is seen again in the diary of Allen (1813–80). Her 7-year-old son was concerned that he was so naughty that he would go to Hell. His mother informed him he should be thankful he felt so sinful, that he should seek a saviour and then prayed with him. Similarly, *Hopkins was anxious that her son should be a Christian. These parents are in marked contrast to Bonar and Tregelles. Bonar (1810–92), for example, wrote: 'I am sorely vexed too about my children. I do very little about their Souls, and they are not concerned about their salvation' (211). Tregelles' (1806–84) wife thought she had been too hasty in urging religious precocity: 'she spoke to me of the dear children, saying she feared she had been too earnest to make them understand every part of the Holy Scriptures, and feared it might lead to scepticism if they were taught to expect to understand before they believe' (122). Johnston and *Lovell both give a good résumé of their method of religious instruction. *Lovell (1809– ?) wrote:

It was soon after this [severe fever] that I first took particular pains to teach her [aged 3] of the existence and nature of God and of our relation and duty to Him. I took her to the window in the morning when the rising sun was tingeing the clouds with all the colors of the rainbow and told her that our Father in Heaven made all so beautiful . . . I said very little to her of death, wishing to wait until she could understand something of it . . . Young children, unless very judiciously taught among this subject, are apt to be terrified at the thought of death, especially when told that sometime they too must die. (53–4)

Johnston (1808–52) tried to make her son's religious instruction enjoyable: 'Then Scripture illustrations; we look at a picture and talk about it – one picture lasts us several days. Sunday is made very much of a treat: the cake, clean clothes, a large picture Bible, walks with papa and mamma in the garden' (142).

Discussion. There are two different attitudes to religious training in this century: parents such as Allen and *M. Walker wished their children to be aware of their sins whereas parents such as Johnston, *Lovell and Tregelles were reluctant to force too much religious education on their children and also wished to make it as pleasant as possible. Religious education was still regarded by many parents as essential and continued to arouse concern, but to a far less extent than in the 17th century.

The child diarists

The best way to reconstruct past childhood is to read diaries kept by children. Unfortunately, the only available diary kept by a child under the age of 13 prior to the 18th century is that of Edward Tudor. He had acceded to the throne when he started to keep a diary and so it is concerned with affairs of state, hardly a typical interest of children.

In the 18th century there were three American child diarists: *Julia Cowles (1785–1803), *Sally Fairfax (1760?–85?) and *Anna Winslow (1759–79) – all three diarists started their diary between the ages of 11 and 12. The three girls helped in the home with the washing, sweeping and cooking. They all could sew; Anna being particularly accomplished in this respect. She could do fine network, knit lace, spin linen thread and woollen yarn and embroider pocket-books. Julia and Anna went to school, the former to boarding school and the latter away from her home town, but living with her aunt and going to day-school. They do not appear to have been repressed or unhappy children. Julia, for example, described sleighing in winter, going to dances, getting new gowns, visiting friends, playing with her siblings and attempting to improve her schoolwork. She was greatly attached to her father; after he had been thrown from his horse she noted that she 'Found him in a distressing situation, looking worse than I expected; it quite overcame me, I had no command over myself' (70).

Sally too mentioned new clothes and going to dances. She also recorded her father measuring her height, visits to and from neighbours, spending her own money and was extremely displeased with a person who killed a cat, referring to him as a 'son of a gun'. She was attached to her father, writing to him while he was away: 'I wish I could write free and unreserved, for I have many things I would say to my dear & ever beloved father that I don't like the curious should see' (214).

Anna's diary is the most detailed of the three. She wrote it while away from home so that her parents would know what she was doing. Again she was very interested in her clothes, the more so because fashions were different in Boston from her home town and she wanted to look the same as the inhabitants of Boston. Her parents sent money so that she could buy what she needed: 'And I would tell you, that *for the first time, they all lik'd my dress very much*. My cloak & bonnett are really very handsome, & so they had need be. For they cost an amasing sight of money . . . I have got *one* covering, by the cost, that is genteel, & I like it much myself' (14). She went to parties, visited neighbours where 'there was much notice taken of me' and frequently exploded into an 'egregious fit of laughter' (7). She was often ill and so was kept at home during cold or snowy weather. She was more in awe of her father:

My Papa inform'd me in his last letter that he had done me the honor to read my journals and that he approv'd of some part of them, I suppose he means that he likes some parts better than other, indeed it would be wonderful, as aunt says, if a gentleman of papa's understanding & judgement cou'd be highly entertain'd with *every little* saying or observation that came from a girl of my years & that I ought to esteem it a great favor that he notices any of my simple matter with his approbation. (56–7)

There are also three British child diarists available for the 18th century – the Wynne sisters – Elizabeth (1778–1857), Eugenia (1780– ?) and Harriet (1786– ?). The first two commenced their diaries in 1789 and also kept more detailed diaries than Harriet, describing the very gay life the sisters led. They regularly went to balls and masquerades, returning home after midnight – although, after a late night, they rose late and went to bed very early the next night. In 1789, Elizabeth noted she learnt to make silk buttons and Eugenia that she was taught to darn stockings. They recorded playing games such as hide and seek and blind man's buff as well as playing tricks on the servants. Eugenia referred to the quarrel between Elizabeth and their tutor: 'First one gets angry and then the other for the first one and then the other wants to read. I let them quarrel as they like and say nothing but go on working the while' (vol. 1, p. 29). They were taken to see exhibitions and to the opera and theatre. Both seemed attached to their parents and Elizabeth at least was not above manipulating them. After receiving money from both of them in 1791, she wrote: 'It was my wit that gained me this money for I wrote verses to them both' (vol. 1, p. 53).

The three American child diarists of the 19th century depict a quieter lifestyle, living in villages rather than towns. These three diarists were *Louisa Alcott (1832–88), *John Long (1838–1915) and *Caroline Richards (1842–1913). All of them began to write a diary at the age of 10. Louisa did not go to parties or to the theatre; but she still had an entertaining time. She recorded climbing trees, leaping fences and running races. Her father also wrote a diary and it is interesting that he described his daughters as being uninterested in lessons: 'Their thoughts are on the distant hill, the wending river, the orchard, meadow or grove; and so I let them have the benefit of these' (132). Louisa played with dolls and she and her sisters acted plays as well as helping with the housework. She described her day as rising at 5 a.m. and having a bath, 'I love cold water' (35). This was followed by a singing lesson, then breakfast, after which she washed dishes and then ran on the hill until 9 o'clock. She had lessons till lunch time: spelling, arithmetic, story-reading and discussion. After dinner, she either read, walked or played. Louisa's diary is full of her attempts to regulate her quick temper. She regretted calling her sister 'mean', felt sad because 'I have been cross to-day, and did not mind Mother' and is upset when reproved by her father for selfishness (36). She was devoted to both her parents, particularly her mother.

*Long provided a good description of his life. He was at school, studying arithmetic and geography. He read a chapter of the Bible every day and three on Sunday. This would seem to be due more to bribery than any religious motive because, when he had read the whole Bible: 'Mother is to give me a knife, a wallet, and a sack coat for next summer. Father is to give me a dollar' (7). He milked the cows before breakfast and helped his father chop wood, although he still has time to play, mentioning sleighing, visits and reading *Ivanhoe*. In May 1849 he was sent to boarding school, but because he was extremely homesick, he returned home in July and went to school in his home town. He was paid for helping his parents: 'Father gives me .50 a week if I will write in my journal every day, and milk one cow and be a good boy, and mind him and mother to do all they require of me' (41).

*Caroline Richards kept a detailed diary of her childhood from the age of 10. As her mother had died, she and her sister were reared by their grandparents; but were in close contact with their father. He spoilt them. On one of his visits he took them to a shop and asked what they wanted: 'So we asked for several kinds of candy, stick candy and lemon drops and bull's eyes, and then they got us two rubber balls and two jumping ropes with handles and two hoops and sticks to roll them with and two red cornelian rings and two bracelets' (5). Caroline was more assiduous in Bible reading than *John Long; she read three chapters every day and five on Sunday. Although the sisters did not get paid for this, they did get money for learning moral poems.

The diary entries describe games, moonlight sleigh rides, their grandmother tucking them in bed each night, new clothes and is full of the quips of the younger sister, Anna, aged 7: for example, when asked to write an essay on 'A Contented Mind': 'Anna said she never had one and didn't know what it meant, so she didn't try to write any at all' (16). Both sisters clearly enjoyed life – a typical entry for a school-day was that they 'did not get along very well, because we played too much' (13).

More British child diarists were available for the 19th century – 11. The diaries of Mary (1808–25) and John (1810–27) Bingham are religious diaries, recording their trials and tribulations. Marie Ramés (1839–1908) and Louisa Knightley (1842–1913) kept similar types of diary; listing regular lessons, parties, exhibitions and drives with their parents. Rachael Hamilton-Gordon (1873?– ?) – diary unpublished – wrote her diary while sailing to America, describing the pleasures of the journey.

Marjory Fleming (1803–11) was the youngest of the child diarists, beginning her diary at the age of 7 – and incidentally the only Scottish one. She spent most of her sixth to eighth years at her aunt's, being taught by her cousin Isobella. Her diary gives the impression of a very lively child. She recorded such activities as washing her doll's clothes, playing and bathing in the sunshine, her wish to see a play and have 'Regency b[o]nnets' which 'are become very fashionable of late & everybody gets them save poor me but if I had one it would not become me' (3) and also her liking to sleep with Isobella – despite the fact that, because Marjory kicked while sleeping, she was relegated to the bottom of the bed where 'Oft I embrace her feet of lillys But she has goton all the pillies' (23). Marjory noted all her outbursts of temper: stamping her feet and throwing her new hat on the ground; calling a servant 'a Impudent Bitch'; refusing to go upstairs to bed, 'roaring like a bull' and, finally, throwing a book at Isobella (41, 51, 73).

Emily Shore (1819–39) lived in the country and did not lead as hectic a social life as other child diarists. She was more interested in natural history – she and her siblings played in and investigated the fields and shrubberies around their home and all kept a collection of small animals and insects. Emily was taken to see any interesting exhibitions in London, such as a demonstration of the making of glass ornaments.

The Bowens: Sarah, born 1864, Anne, born 1867, Mary, born 1867 and Charles, born 1868, wrote a diary, beginning in 1876, between them. Most of the entries were, however, by Sarah. They occupied the nursery and school room at the top of the house, did not appear to have much contact with their parents and were particularly in awe of their father. He did not totally ignore them; Sarah noted: 'We cut out a great many nice pictures that Papa gave us' (251) but there seemed to be little parent–child interaction. Despite this, the children all appear to have been perfectly happy. They recorded a day's holiday whenever it was someone's birthday and birthday presents, holidays in the country twice a year where they played for hours in the gardens, and a seaside holiday every second summer where they were allowed 'to run nearly wild'. At home they had their own garden, pony and pocket money and, moreover, they did have fun. One of Sarah's entries reads: 'the four of us took a long walk and crossed the river near the mill, where we had great fun placing stepping stones' (242). Furthermore, they were always present when visitors called rather than ignored.

Henry Alford (1810–71), described his life at the age of 10:

I sleep in a room by myself, and have done for half a year nearly, and have got a drawer for my playthings, a drawer for my clothes, a washing-stand, a large bed, a chest of drawers, a little red box to keep seeds in with two bottoms, half a dozen pill-boxes, a large box to keep my books in, and pens and slate, some silk-worms' eggs, an Ovid's Epistles of Heroes in Latin which I am learning, Cornelius, Nepos Clarke and a large Bible which my father gave me. (9)

He was at boarding school which he liked and was greatly interested in gardening. Frederic Post (1819–35) was a much quieter child than either Alford or Fleming. As he was delicate, he was educated at home. His father spent a lot of time with him, taking him to the zoo, to see the Colosseum and the new Thames tunnel which was being built under water. He kept pets – a tortoise and a pony; but mainly noted in his diary his religious meditations and attendance at meetings. John Salter

(1841–1932) was another lively schoolboy and, like Alford, also attended boarding school. He was invited to parties, at one of which in 1853, he noted: 'I was very much put out because Uncle William danced with Alice when she was engaged to me, and I would not speak to him for ever so long' (4). He visited the British Museum and the Drury Lane theatre, saw a fireworks display, spent money at bazaars, played cricket, went on picnics and to the regatta, cut his name on a church pew and had fun at Greenwich Park where he 'Scampered up and down the hills for a long time, and had a pony ride; the others had donkeys at Blackheath' (5).

Discussion. It is a great pity that the whereabouts is unknown of any diaries written by children in the 16th and 17th centuries – if any have survived, or indeed were written. They are the most reliable source for discovering how children regarded their lifestyle and what they actually did.

All the child diarists covered in this chapter, despite their various lifestyles, were clearly content and happy with their lives. The Bowen children's diary is particularly interesting in that they led a typical Victorian upper- and middle-class childhood, spending most of their time in a nursery separate from their parents. It has been argued by many authors (e.g. Pinchbeck & Hewitt, 1969; Robertson, 1976) that such children led restricted, repressive lives, strictly regimented. The diary of Sarah Bowen and her siblings does not support this argument – they had plenty of free time and amusement. Even though the children did not have a great deal of contact with their parents, the latter were not indifferent to their offspring but ensured that the children had facilities and time for play and were not totally isolated in the nursery.

Conclusion

Primary sources used as evidence present a much more vivid picture of parental care and child life in the past than secondary sources. They reveal the amount of concern and interest felt by parents – and also the large amount of individual variation. They bring actual children to life, as opposed to the ideal child depicted in child-rearing advice literature, in a way that no secondary source of information ever can.

The sources reveal that past parents were very much aware of their children and concerned with the latter's welfare and education. Some of the childhood experiences may have changed – for example, the amount of religious education – but much more remained the same. Children played, were taken to see whatever was interesting in their area, did their lessons, and from their diaries appear to have been happy, free from worry and certainly not oppressed or regimented. They were not, as Ariès has argued, ignored, nor, as Hunt has claimed, unwanted, but instead it seems that children formed an integral part of the family unit, from at least the 16th century on. Parents were unmistakably aware of the individuality of their offspring, of their varying needs and dispositions and endeavoured to suit their mode of child care to each particular child.

Of particular interest is the amount of paternal concern for children in earlier centuries, even infants. Though mothers shouldered the responsibility of the day-to-day care of young children, many fathers were prepared to nurse a sick child, rise in the night to quieten a crying baby, assist an infant through the trauma of weaning, concern themselves with the education of older children and generally take a pride in their children's achievements and development.

7. Summary and conclusions

To recapitulate the main theories on the history of childhood, it has been claimed by many authors that:

(a) There was no concept of childhood before the 17th century; children were regarded as being at the very bottom of the social scale and therefore unworthy of consideration (e.g. Ariès, 1960; Demos, 1970; Hoyles, 1979; Hunt, 1972; Shorter, 1976; Stone, 1977; Tucker, 1976).

(b) There was a formal parent–child relationship; parents were distant unapproachable beings and children were something inferior, whose demands and needs were not sufficiently valuable to be met (e.g. de Mause, 1976; Pinchbeck & Hewitt, 1969; Plumb, 1975; Stone, 1977; Thompson, 1974).

(c) Up to the 18th century, and again in the early 19th century, children were often brutally exploited and 'subjected to indignities now hard to believe' (Sears, 1975). (See also Ariès, 1960; Hoyles, 1979; Hunt, 1972; Lyman, 1976; de Mause, 1976; Pinchbeck & Hewitt, 1969; Plumb, 1975; Shorter, 1976; Stone, 1977; Tucker, 1976.)

The above authors then go on to argue that a concept of childhood appeared from the 17th century on, due to a 'renewal of interest in education' (Ariès; see also Pinchbeck & Hewitt; developments within the family (Ariès, Shorter, Stone); the rise of capitalism (Hoyles, Shorter, Stone); the emergence of some indefinable spirit of benevolence (Sears, Shorter, Stone) and the increasing maturity of parents (de Mause). This concept of childhood became more elaborated during the 18th and 19th centuries until the child was accorded a central role in family life and his rights were protected by the state. Thus, if these arguments are to be believed, we have indeed come a long way in our treatment of children and, if de Mause's theory is accepted, far from projecting our unacceptable feelings into our children and hence beating them into submission, we now defer to their every wish, so producing 'gentle, sincere' beings.

Notwithstanding the fact that these theories form the received view on the history of childhood, they are not universally accepted. Hanawalt (1977) and Kroll (1977) have demonstrated that there was a concept of childhood in the middle ages, as have Beales (1975), Cohen (n.d.) and Stannard (1974) with reference to the early Puritan colonies. Morgan (1944) and Macfarlane (1970) would disagree with the view that children were ill-treated on a large scale. Many historians have subscribed to the mistaken belief that, if a past society did not possess the contemporary Western concept of childhood, then that society had no such concept. This is a totally indefensible viewpoint – why should past societies have regarded children in the same way as Western society today? Moreover, even if children were regarded differently in the past, this does not mean they were therefore not regarded as children.

As has been shown in chapter 2, the sources used to support the received view are suspect and are certainly not a secure enough base to warrant the dramatic generalisations derived from them. The area in fact bears the hallmark of sloppiness: not only are the problems inherent in the sources used rarely considered, but some of the data used and conclusions arrived at are factually inaccurate. A number of points can be made to demonstrate this. Ariès states that children were beaten at school because their *parents* wished them to be, whereas from the evidence contained in the sources used in this study, parents clearly wished no such thing and were prepared to intervene if they considered their child was being punished too severely (see for example the autobiography of Martindale and the diaries of J. Erskine and Morris, all from the 17th century). De Mause includes a table on the age at walking which has at least two inaccurate entries. Pinchbeck & Hewitt claim that child abuse was ignored by the press until the late 19th century whereas the information contained in chapter 3 reveals that this was not the case. Pinchbeck & Hewitt have argued that the lack of any reported cases of child abuse is evidence of the indifference shown towards children. However, not only did the newspapers report cases of child abuse from the late 18th century on, but they did so in a way that reveals the general horror with which such cruelty was regarded. Stone suggests that 17th-century Puritans wished to break the will of a child, and did so by using severe physical punishment. On the other hand, Demos and Morgan provide evidence against this claim – and it is their arguments which are supported by the texts used here. Finally, there are also inaccuracies in the way in which the evidence is discussed. Stone organises his arguments around three family types, all of which he claims have very different ways of rearing children. Yet, Josselin appears as a

263

representative example in all three family types, and *C. Mather is put forward as an example of both the restricted patriarchal nuclear family and of the closed domesticated nuclear family![1]

Because most of the authors on the history of childhood were concerned with the severe discipline meted out to children in the past, their accounts of child life have largely been confined to this area. Thus the children of the past are indecipherable figures; little is known about their actual lifestyle. This study has endeavoured to bring actual parents and children to life, to reveal the parent–child interaction, how parents thought of their children, how they attempted to rear them and also how children regarded their parents. The information has been taken from three primary sources of evidence (adult diaries, child diaries and autobiographies) and it is of interest to see how much similarity there is in the depictions of childhood provided by the three sources.

It is always possible that the adult diarists were presenting an image – it would be very difficult to write an introspective diary without some element of egoism being present – and therefore perhaps did not relate treating their offspring as the latter actually were treated. A comparison of the child and the adult sample would reveal any such discrepancies. The child diarists, from the evidence contained in their diaries, were not repressed, severely disciplined beings. In fact, they noted less punishment than the adult diarists, which suggests that they were not subjected to a harsh discipline. They seemed to be happy and content with their lives and were clearly attached to their parents. Some of the adolescent diaries describe discord between parents and children, but this rarely continued for long and nearly all of the children kept in close contact with their parents after they had left home.

In addition, there have been cases where a parent and child both wrote a diary and also diaries which, in their published form, have had the recollections of the diarist's children included. The parents and children who both wrote diaries were: *Alcott and his daughter Louisa, Brodie and his son James, *Holyoke and his son John, *Lynde and his son Benjamin, *Parkman and his daughter Anna, *Sewall and his son Samuel, Yeoman and his daughter Mary. The published diaries which included evidence from the diarist's children are those by Acland, *Fenimore-Cooper, *Howe, Newcome, Pollen, *Silliman, Steadman and Wilberforce.

The accounts by the parents and offspring are similar. For example, *Alcott (1799–1888) noted that he used physical punishment to discipline his children while they were young, but after they reached about the age of 7, he tried reasoning and alternative methods. His daughter started her diary at the age of 10 and, although she did record scoldings received from her father, she did not note any physical punishment. Furthermore, *Alcott wrote that he found it difficult to teach his daughters because they preferred to be outside playing. Louisa's (1832–88) diary is full of references to running up hills and through fields with her sisters. Brodie (1617–80) described 'admonishing' his son for his behaviour and warning him 'how unfaithfullie and unprofitabli he walked' (179), which advice his son ignored. James (1637–1708), in his diary, wrote that he regretted not following his father's advice and, after the latter's death, James felt 'the want of a dear father and instructor' (426). *Parkman's (1703–82) diary contains no evidence on discipline and neither did that of his 12-year-old daughter – *Anna Parkman (1755– ?).

The accounts of their childhood and parents given by a diarist's children in the published text also match the image of parental care presented in the diary. Acland (1809–98) wished his children to enjoy the pleasures of nature, allowing them free run of the garden, stream and shrubbery. His daughter recollected her childhood:

What happy hours we spent lying in the grass by that pond basking in the sun, and watching the floats, of which the fish seldom took any notice . . . It is impossible to describe all that that shrubbery contained for us. There were the nut trees, whose boughs we wove into little dwellings . . . the plum-trees whose gum we thought such a priceless treasure, and the little stream that ran through it . . . How muddy we made ourselves in that stream, and what hours we spent in making ponds and water-falls, and watching the frogs and newts and beetles. (149–50)

Newcome (1627–95) was clearly devoted to his offspring, from the information in his diary, helping them throughout their lives. His sons wrote of him as a 'loving and faithful father to his children' (288) and also as a 'revered and dear father . . . whose authority we revered, and whose indulgent care over us was one of our greatest supports' (299). *Silliman (1779–1864) greatly enjoyed the company of his children, referring to them as 'delights'. His three daughters added their recollections of their father to his diary. All remembered a kind, loving father. To quote from one daughter: 'My earliest recollections are of a loving, sympathizing and reasonable parent. I cannot recall any instance of impatient or unjust treatment at his hands. When very young children we were allowed to be with him in his busiest hours' (vol. 2, p. 360).

The offspring of one diarist recalled disciplinary procedures not noted in the diary. Wilberforce (1759–1832) did record studying the tempers and dispositions of his children in order to rear them adequately but there was no mention of actual punishment in the text. His son, on the other hand, wrote of his father: 'tenderness was the distinctive feature of his domestic character. Though he never weakly withheld any necessary punishment, he did not attempt to dissemble the pain which its infliction cost him' (314). In general, though, parents and children were in remarkable agreement over the kind of life the latter led. Thus there is no reason to reject the material contained in the adult texts on the grounds that it is distorted by adult perception to a significant degree.

Most of the autobiographies contain similar information to the diaries; but it is the autobiographies as a genre which describe stricter discipline (see chapter 5) and also greater parental authority (see Pollock, 1981, chapter 8). It is unlikely that cruel parents would keep a diary recording the severe punishment they meted out to their offspring and therefore autobiographies are an important source of information on the harsh mode of rearing to which some children were subjected. It should be noted, however, that it was only a small minority of the autobiographies which contain evidence on strict discipline and, out of the 121 autobiographies which were studied, only four (Cooper, Forman, Grant and Hare) describe actual cruelty. This suggests that child abuse was not as prevalent as many historians have claimed. It is also the autobiographies which reveal the greater amount of parental authority and control wielded in such areas as marriage and career. Though none of these writers was forced to marry someone they disliked or stay in work they hated, many recalled that their parents did arrange such matters for them and would have preferred their offspring to have agreed with their choices (see for example Rich on marriage and Fretwell and Norwood on career). That autobiographers on the whole recalled a stricter rearing than diarists is a surprising result and highlights the need to use all available sources on the history of childhood since concentration on only one source will give a slightly distorted view. Such a distorted viewpoint occurs in the works of de Mause and Stone who have used autobiographies to illustrate the cruel treatment inflicted on children in the past. Thus they ignore the fact that, if autobiographies are examined in bulk, then only a minority of writers will describe such treatment – others (see for example *Bailey, E. Fox and Knightley) recall receiving nothing but kindness as children – and also that other primary sources, such as adult and child diaries, do not provide evidence to support their findings.

Not only should all available sources be studied together and in bulk, but also the whole of every text should be examined. People are inconsistent and the texts studied here demonstrate this, as well as how easy it is to use quotations which are unrepresentative of the text to support a theory. For example, Martindale (1623–86), on the death of his only son, worked out how much he had lost by his son's death; not only had the latter's education been expensive; but he also owed his father money and Martindale now had to provide for his son's wife and child. This has been used by Stone to illustrate the 'cold-blooded attitude' to children (113). However, that entry was not representative of Martindale's affection for his son. He referred to the child as 'a gallant boy' and 'sweet company' soon after the boy's birth (154). At the age of 2 the boy was 'a beautiful child' who could beat back a calf which used to run at children, much to his father's pride: 'I doe not think one child of 100 of his age durst doe so much' (154). Despite his low income, Martindale did manage to send John to university and later helped him to set up his own household. From the evidence in the diary, Martindale was obviously proud of, and attached to, his son. A similar attitude reappears over 100 years later, again in a father who was devoted to his offspring. J. Taylor (1743–1819) was upset when one of his daughters was ill because 'with respect to our little worldly business, we depended on her entirely' (54). The texts abound with other examples, only a few can be given. Boscawen (1719–1805) referred to her 2-year-old daughter as a 'slut' on one occasion because the child would not drink when she was ill (80). *C. Mather (1663–1728) decided that, with regard to his children, 'my word must be their Law' (vol. 7, p. 535), yet his son Samuel was both inoculated and decided to go to England against his father's will and another son, Increase, continually rebelled against his father, *Mather eventually giving in to his children's wishes on each occasion. Moore (1779–1852) noted that his wife was 'in the way of producing another little incumbrance for us (a little prisoner perhaps)' (vol. 2, p. 139) although he greatly enjoyed having his children. Elizabeth Wynne (1778–1857) on a few occasions described her children as 'brats'. The above attitudes would be evidence for the conventional view that previous parents were indifferent to their children, regarding them only as unwanted nuisances, were it not for the fact that they are not representative of all the evidence which the texts contain.

The results of this study, given in chapters 4 to 6, demonstrate that the main arguments put forward by many historians are incorrect – they are at best only applicable to a minority of parents and children. Contrary to the belief of such authors as Ariès, there was a concept of childhood in the 16th century. This may have become more elaborated through the centuries but, none the less, the 16th-century writers studied did appreciate that children were different from adults and were also aware of the ways in which children were different – the latter passed through certain recognisable developmental stages; they played; they required discipline, education and protection.

The sources used reveal that there have been very few changes in parental care and child life from the 16th to the 19th century in the home, apart from social changes and technological improvements. Nearly all children were wanted, such developmental stages as weaning and teething aroused interest and concern and parents revealed anxiety and distress at the illness or death of a child. Parents, although they may have found their offspring troublesome at times, did seem to enjoy the company of their children. In every century studied the texts contain abundant evidence to support this finding: for example, Clifford (1590–1676) and Wallington (1598–1658) enjoyed talking with their young children and *Jefferay (1591–1675) described the long forest rambles he and his children took; Blundell (1669–1737) made toys for his daughters and helped them to make a garden; and *Byrd (1674–1744) liked taking his young daughter into company because she was so well-behaved; Boswell (1740–95) spent many hours talking with his eldest daughter, while Burney (1752–1840) and *Shippen (1763–1841) were greatly entertained by the behaviour of their young children; as also were Johnston (1808–52) and Wood (1812–60) in the 19th century.

It is also clear that the majority of children were not subjected to brutality. Physical punishment was used by a number of parents, usually infrequently and when all else had failed. It is, of course, possible that the diarists, representing as they do the literate section of society, were unlikely to beat their children, particularly in the earlier centuries when literacy was the mark of a higher education. Nevertheless, the large amount of sources studied here, added to the newspaper reports, suggest that cruelty to children was not as widespread as has been claimed. A large section of the population – probably most parents – were not 'battering' their children.

The texts also reveal that the parent–child relationship was not formal. They abound in instances of the closeness of the parent–child bond: parents who sat up all night nursing their sick offspring; who worried over the latter's education; who were prepared to come to their children's aid when necessary – and the children also felt free to approach their parents with any problems they might have – who referred to physical contact between themselves and their children and who were also aware of the latter's activities. As the children reached adolescence, there were clashes of opinion between parents and children. Thus, the offspring were on sufficiently familiar terms with their parents to quarrel and/or state their own opinions. Furthermore, parents accepted their children's right to have minds of their own; though the parents did not always approve of their children's behaviour, they continued to support them financially and there was rarely any loss of contact for long periods. The evidence in the texts does not support the view that parents were distant and/or indifferent to their offspring's welfare.

Although parental care would appear to have altered little from the 16th century to date, there have been some changes. Even allowing for the fact that the 16th-century diaries are brief and factual on all topics, there was still an increased emphasis on the *abstract* nature of childhood and parental care from the 17th century onwards. For example, the diarists described their methods of discipline as opposed to the punishment of a specific action and also recorded their views on the duties of parents to children. This abstract thinking appeared first in the 17th-century Puritans and increased during the 18th century. From the 18th century on, parents began to be more concerned with 'training' a child in order to ensure that he or she absorbed the correct values and beliefs and would grow into a model citizen. Both mothers and fathers approached parenthood with apprehension and trepidation, worrying whether or not their modes of child care were correct and whether they were sufficiently competent to rear their children. It is possible that these developments were related more to the growth and spread of literacy as well as increasing expertise with writing as a form of communication than to any significant transformations in the parent–child relationship. The changes reported are certainly very minor compared with the image of continuity provided by the sources.

During the early part of the 19th century, there was a distinct intensification of adult demands for obedience and conformity, notably in the schools. Though this severity occurred in only a minority of texts, for the children involved it could at times amount to definite cruelty. I have already suggested that the industrialisation of society may have contributed to the strictness of discipline. This hypothesis could be tested by comparing a large sample of families living in rural districts with those inhabiting the new industrial areas. In contrast, the later 19th-century texts, as shown in Pollock, chapter 8, reveal a lessening of parental control in areas like career or marriage, and also a reduction in parent–offspring conflict. As industry and technology expanded and as

269

the state began to regulate family life, parents seem to have relinquished some of their control over their offspring's lives – perhaps such parental authority as in the arranging of marriages was no longer appropriate to the new society in which they lived.

Nevertheless, parents did not stop attempting to direct at least some aspects of their children's lives: parents today are concerned with the socialisation of their children. The regulation of a child's behaviour appears to be fundamental to the parental role. Newson & Newson (1976), from their study of 20th-century child-rearing practices, point out that

the role of smacking remains a means to a more important end than the immediate conflict: it serves the need which parents feel to maintain their credibility as power figures who must undoubtedly win in any significant battle of wills. The inevitable occasional clash of interests between parent and children may become testing-times, when parents suspect that their long-term ability to influence their child's behaviour (a basic notion to the parental role) could be irretrievably diminished if they are seen to fail. (359)

Thus, the parental 'controlling' of behaviour is not confined to previous centuries. The claim put forward by many historians that children were totally regulated prior to the 18th century and unregulated thereafter is far too clear cut and rigid. Parents, it appears, would feel they were failing in their duty if they exerted no control over their offspring.

The received view on the history of childhood does not include all the facets of child life in the past. Most historians have believed that parents operate in a vacuum, automatically applying the current advice of their time on child-rearing, without distortion, to each and every child. Children, though, are far from passive creatures; they make demands on their parents and parents are forced to operate within the context of these demands. The parents in every century studied accommodated to the needs of their offspring, from Clifford in the 16th century, who although irritated by the continuing ill-temper of her 5-year-old daughter, tolerated it because she believed her to be ill, to *Lovell in the 19th who appreciated the spontaneous nature of her young daughter and therefore did not always insist on total obedience.

It is difficult to formulate any one theory on parental care in the past – there was a great deal of individual variation. Neither can the possession of a certain attitude, such as the concept of Original Sin, be put forward as evidence of a certain behaviour, such as the use of whipping as a means of discipline. The sources reveal that there is little, if any, connection between attitudes and behaviour – the changes in attitudes to children described in chapter 4 are not accompanied by parallel changes in parental behaviour. However, despite the individual differences in child-rearing techniques, there are limits on variation. These limits are the dependency of the child and the acceptance of the responsibility for the protection and socialisation of that child by the parents. From the material gathered here, it is clear that the vast majority of parents from earlier centuries were operating within these constraints. Even where wet-nurses and other servants were employed, most parents accepted that the main responsibility of rearing their children lay with them. Parents were also unwilling to cause extreme distress to a child by the imposition of a harsh disciplinary regime.

The sources used for this book do not provide all the answers to questions on the history of childhood but they do provide an insight into the lives of actual parents and children in a way that no secondary source of information ever can. The material analysed here does not support the evolutionary theories on the history of childhood. Although there may be changes in feeding practices (Fildes, 1980), and some slight changes in attitudes, there is no dramatic transformation in child-rearing practices in the 18th century. It is a myth brought about by over-hasty reading, a burning desire to find material to support the thesis and a wilful misinterpretation of evidence. Our method of child care is by no means an easy system – one only has to witness the constant anxiety experienced by parents – and yet it appears to be an enduring one. Instead of trying to explain the supposed changes in the parent–child relationship, historians would do well to ponder just why parental care is a variable so curiously resistant to change.

Appendix: List of sources studied

Author	Source[1] P	M	Text[2] A	C	O	Author's life span	Dates of text	Date of publication	Length of text[3]	Type of entry[4]	Occupation[5]	Author's Religion[6]	No. of children[7]	No. of dead children
16th century														
Nicholas Assheton	+	+				1590–1625	1617–1618	1848	⅔ v.	SW	Landowner	Puritan	5	4
Richard Boyle	+	+				1566–1643	1611–1643	1886	8 v.	SW	Statesman	Protestant	12	2
William Brownlow	+	+				1594–1675	1626	1909	5 pp.	SM	Lawyer	–	19	11
Anne Clifford	+		+			1590–1676	1603–1619	1923	½ v.	MW	Countess	Protestant	5	3
John Dee	+		+			1527–1608	1577–1601	1841	⅓ v.	SW	Astrologer	Religious	6	0
Simon Forman					+	1552–1601	1564–1600	1849	32 pp.	–	Astrologer	–	0	0
Robert Furse					+	1555?–1594?	1593	1894	17 pp.	–	Yeoman	Religious	11	1
Thomas Hope		+				1585?–1646	1633–1646	1843	1 v.	MW	Lord Advocate	Religious	7†	1
*William Jefferay[8]		+		+		1591–1675	1591–1669	1889	1 v.	LW	Landowner	Religious	4†	0
Henry Machyn		+				1498–1563	1550–1563	1848	1½ v.	SW	Tailor	Catholic	1	0
Grace Mildmay				+		1552–1620	1570–1617	1911	20 pp.	–	Gentlewoman	Religious	1	0
Humphrey Mildmay		+				1592–1667	1633–1652	1947	1 v.	SD	Sheriff	Protestant	6†	1
Richard Norwood		+		+		1590–1675	1590–1620	1945	½ v.	–	Surveyor	Religious	0	0
John Oglander		+				1585–1655	1595–1648	1888	1 v.	MW	Deputy-Lieutenant	–	4†	0
John Penry	+	+				1563–1593	1592–1593	1944	½ v.	MW	Preacher	Puritan	4	0
Walter Powell	+	+				1581–1656	1603–1654	1907	48 pp.	SW	Gentleman	–	14	7
Richard Rogers	+	+				1550?–1618	1586–1590	1933	¼ v.	MW	Minister	Puritan	6	1
Edward Tudor	+			+		1537–1553	1549–1552	1857	2½ v.	SD	King	C of E	0	0
Nehemiah Wallington	+	+		+		1598–1658	1630–1658	1869	3 v.	LW	Shop-owner	Puritan	12	4
Samuel Ward	+	+				1571–1643	1595–1630	1933	20 pp.	SW	Doctor	Puritan	1	0
John Winthrop	+	+				1587–?	1607–1630	1864	2 v.	MW	Government official	Puritan	7	0

Name	P	M	A	C	O	Dates	Year	Extent	Code	Occupation	Religion		
17th century													
*William Adams	+	+				1650–1685	1852	20 pp.	SW	Student	Religious	0	0
Elias Ashmole	+	+	+			1617–1692	1927	1⅓ v.	MW	Astrologer	–	1	1
William Bagshawe	+	+	+			1628–1702	1886	16 pp.	MW	Minister	Non-conformist	2†	0
Jacob Bee	+					1636–1711	1910, 1914	1½ v.	SY	Spinner and glover	–	5	3
Nicholas Blundell	+	+				1669–1737	1968–1972	4½ v.	SD	Estate owner	Catholic	2	0
Peter Briggins	+	+				1672?–1717	1894	39 pp.	MW	Grocer	Quaker	5	0
Alexander Brodie	+	+				1617–1680	1746	2 v.	MW	Lord of Sessions	Presbyterian	2	0
James Brodie	+	+				1637–1708	1746	½ v.	SW	Son of above	Presbyterian	9	0
Mark Browell	+	+				1660?–1729	1915	14 pp.	SY	Attorney	–	7	1
Robert Bulkeley	+	+				1630–1636	1937	⅔ v.	SD	Landowner	Religious	7	0
William Bulkeley	+	+				1691–1760, 1747–1760	1936	1 v.	MD	Country squire	Religious	2	0
*William Byrd	+	+				1674–1744	1941, 1942, 1958	8 v.	MD	Estate owner	Religious	8	2
John Byrom	+	+				1692–1763	1854	6½ v.	MD	Poet	Religious	6	3
Walter Calverley	+	+				1669–1722	1886	½ v.	SY	Baronet	Religious	2	0
James Clegg	+	+	+			1679–1755	1899	½ v.	MW	Doctor	Non-conformist	6	1
*William Cooper	+	+				1693–1743	1876	14 pp.	SW	Minister	Puritan	1	1
Mary Cowper	+	+				1685–1724	1864	⅞ v.	MD	Lady-in-waiting	C of E	4	0
Thomas Crosfield	+	+		+		1602–1663	1935	⅞ v.	SW	Student	–	0	0
William Cunningham	+	+				1650–1720?	1887	¾ v.	MY	Landowner	Presbyterian	6	0
*Samuel Danforth	+	+				1626–1674	1880	20 pp.	SW	Minister	Religious	12	3
Ebenezer Erskine	+	+				1680–1754	1831	2 v.	LY	Minister	Secession Church	10	4
James Erskine	+	+				1679–1754	1843	½ v.	LY	Lord Justice Clerk	Religious	6	1

	P	M	A	C	O								7	5
17th century														
John Evelyn	+	+		+	+	1620–1706	1640–1706	1906	5 v.	MW	Country gentleman	C of E	7	5
Elizabeth Freke	+	+		+	+	1641–1714	1671–1714	1913	⅔ v.	MY	Middle class	Religious	1	0
James Fretwell	+	+				1699–1772	1718–1760	1879	½ v.	–	Yeoman	Religious	0	0
*Joseph Green	+	+		+		1675–1715	1700–1715	1866	39 pp.	SW	Minister	Puritan	7	0
*Lawrence Hammond	+	+		+		1640?–1699	1677–1691	1891	30 pp.	MW	Captain	Religious	8	6
John Harington		+	+			?	1646–1653	–	¼ v.	SD	MP	Religious	3	0
Andrew Hay	+	+				1510–1689	1659–1666	1901	1¼ v.	LD	Gentleman	Religious	6	0
John Hervey	+	+				1565–1751	1688–1742	1894	½ v.	SW	Politician	Religious	3	1
Oliver Heywood	+	+		+		1530–1702	1666–1702	1882	7 v.	SW	Minister	Puritan	3	1
*Edward Holyoke	+	+				1589–1769	1709–1768	1911	30 pp.	SD	Minister	Religious	6	2
Mrs Housman	+	+				1680?–1735	1711–1732	1744	¾ v.	LY	Middle class	Puritan	2	1
David Hume	+	+		+		1643–1707	1697–1700	1843	½ v.	–	Judge	Religious	5	0
Henry Hyde	+	+		+		1638–1709	1687–1690	1828	1 v.	MD	Lord Lieutenant of Ireland	C of E	1	0
Justinian Isham	+			+		1687–1735	1704–1735	1907	25 pp.	LY	Baronet	Religious	0	0
James Jackson	+	+				1620?– ?	1650–1683	1921	34 pp.	SW	Farmer	Religious	7	0
Archibald Johnston	+	+				1610–1663	1632–1660	1896	2 v.	SW	Statesman	Religious	12	2
Ralph Josselin	+	+		+		1616–1683	1616–1681	1908	1 v.	SW	Vicar	Puritan	8	3
*Sarah Knight	+	+				1666–1727	1704–1705	1825	⅓ v.	LW	Teacher	–	1	0
Roger Lowe	+	+	+			1648?–1679?	1663–1674	1938	½ v.	SW	Apprentice	Puritan	0	0
*Benjamin Lynde	+	+				1666–1745	1690–1742	1880	⅔ v.	SY	Judge	Puritan	2	0
Adam Martindale	+	+	+			1623–1686	1645–1686	1845	1⅙ v.	LW	Minister	Puritan	6	3
*Cotton Mather	+	+				1663–1728	1681–1724	1911, 1912	7 v.	LW	Minister	Puritan	15	9
*Increase Mather	+	+				1639–1723	1675–1676	1899	¼ v.	MW	Minister	Puritan	2	0
Giles Moore	+	+				1635–1679	1655–1679	1848	¼ v.	SY	Minister	Religious	1	0
Claver Morris	+	+				1659–1727	1709–1710, 1718–1726	1934	½ v.	MW	Doctor	C of E	5	3
Henry Newcome	+	+			+	1627–1695	1661–1663	1852	2 v.	MW	Minister	Puritan	5	0

Name	P	M	A	C	O								15	4
Richard Newdigate	+				+	1644–?1710	1680–1706	1901	¼ v.	SW	Country gentleman	Puritan	15	4
Samuel Newton	+	+				1622–1717	1644–1717	1890	⅔ v.	SW	Alderman	Religious	3	1
Thomas Osborne		+	+			1631–1712	1666–1712	–	1 v.	SY	Statesman	–	7	3
*John Pike	+		+			1653–1710	1678–1709	1875	31 pp.	SW	Minister	Puritan	5	3
Elias Pledger	+		+			1665–?	1665–1725	–	1 v.	MY	Minister?	Presbyterian	2	1
Walter Pringle	+			+		1625–1667	1662–1665	1751	½ v.	–	Covenanter	Religious	6†	0
Mary Rich	+			+		1624–1678	1660–1672	1848	38 pp.	–	Countess	Religious	2	1
John Richards	+			+		1660?–1721	1698–1701	1853	19 pp.	SY	Squire	Religious	4	0
Andrew Rule		+		+		1695–?	1715–1750	–	1 v.	LY	Teacher	Religious	5	2
Dudley Ryder	+				+	1691–1756	1715–1716	1939	1¾ v.	LD	Student	Non-conformist	0	0
*Samuel Sewall	+	+				1652–1730	1673–1729	1878	4 v.	MW	Judge	Puritan	14	7
*Richard Skinner	+	+				1662?–1727	1724–1725	1900	3 pp.	SW	Deacon	Religious	12	0
Henry Slingsby	+		+			1601–1658	1638–1648	1836	1 v.	LW	MP	Religious	3	0
Thomas Smith	+		+			1673–1723	1721–1722	1907	41 pp.	SD	Squire	C of E	4	0
Owen Stockton			+	+		1630–1680	1665–1680	–	1 v.	LW	Minister?	Religious	6	5
Mrs Stockton			+	+		?	1665?	–	25 pp.	LD	Wife of above	Religious	6	5
William Stout	+	+				1665–1752	1679–1752	1967	¾ v.	–	Grocer	Puritan	0	0
*Edward Taylor	+		+			1642–1729	1668–1672	1880	19 pp.	SW	Student	Religious	0	0
John Thomlinson	+		+			1692–1761	1715–1722	1910	½ v.	MD	Minister	Religious	0	0
Isabella Twysden	+			+		1605–1657	1645–1651	1939	24 pp.	SY	Lady	C of E	6	0
Thomas Tyldesley	+			+		1657–1715	1712–1714	1873	¾ v.	SD	Gentleman	Religious	6	0
Anthony Wood	+			+		1632–1695	1657–1695	1891	7 v.	MW	Antiquary	Religious	0	0
Mary Woodforde	+				+	1638–1730	1684–1690	1932	13 pp.	MY	Minister[H]	Protestant	8	0
18th century														
*John Adams	+	+				1767–1848	1787–1848	1874	32 v.	MW	President	Religious	3	0
*Amos Alcott	+	+				1799–1888	1826–1882	1938	2⅔ v.	LW	Author and teacher	Religious	5	1
John Allen	+				+	1757–1808	1777	1905	⅜ v.	SD	Brewer	Quaker	0	0

Name	P	M	A	C	O									
18th century														
Hannah Backhouse	+	+	+	+		1787–1850	1804–1849	1858	1½ v.	MW	Minister[H]	Quaker	6	3
James Backhouse	+	+				1721–1798	1747–1752	1918	6 pp.	SY	Lower middle class	Quaker	2	0
*Mary-Ann Bacon	+		+			1787–?	1802	1903	7 pp.	MD	Middle class	Puritan	0	0
*Samuel Bacon	+	+		+		1781–1820	1818–1820	1822	⅔ v.	–	Minister	Baptist	0	0
*Abigail Bailey	+	+		+		1746–1815	1767–1792	1815	1 v.	–	Major[H]	Religious	17	1
John Baker	+		+			1717–1779	1771–1777	1909	46 pp.	SW	Solicitor	–	3†	0
*Ebenezer Baldwin	+			+		1745–1775	1762	1879	3 pp.	MW	Student	Religious	0	0
John Barclay	+	+		+		1797–1838	1814–1832	1842	½ v.	MW	Banker[F]	Quaker	0	0
*Edward Bates	+	+		+		1793?–1869	1859?–1866	1933	3½ v.	MW	Statesman	Religious	17	9
*James Bayard	+	+		+		1767–1815	1813–1814	1913	32 pp.	MW	Senator	–	0	0
*Martha Bayard	+	+		+		1769–?	1794–1797	1894	¾ v.	MW	Lawyer[H]	Presbyterian	2	1
Katherine Bayly	+	+			+	1721–1774	1721–1756	1898	14 pp.	MD	Clerk of Exchequer[H]	Catholic?	6	0
Thomas Belsham	+	+		+		1750–1829	1779–1826	1833	3/8 v.	MW	Minister	Dissenter	0	0
*William Bentley	+	+				1759–1819	1785–1819	1905	6 v.	MW	Teacher	Religious	0	0
*Joanna Bethune	+	+			+	1770–1860	1824–1847	1864	⅔ v.	–	Teacher	Religious	3†	0
Elizabeth Bishop			+		+	1751–1801	1779+ / 1785–1801	–	4½ v.	SW	Baker[H]	Quaker	7	3
*Joseph Bissell	+		+			1747–1784	1766	1868	4 pp.	SW	Student	Quaker	0	0
*William Bolling	+		+			1777–?	1827–1828	1935–1939	½ v.	SD	Farmer	Religious	4	0
Frances Boscawen	+	+		+		1719–1805	1742–1805	1940, 1942	1¼ v.	LW	Admiral[H]	Religious	5	1
James Boswell	+	+		+	+	1740–1795	1754–1794	1928–1934	26 v.	LD	Biographer and lawyer	Religious	6	1
Anna Bower	+		+			1768–?	1780–1799	1903	⅞ v.	SW	Upper middle class	–	0	0
Anna Braithwaite	+	+		+		1788–1859	1830–1859	1905	1 v.	LY	Manufacturer[H]	Quaker	9	2
Charlotte Brown	+	+		+		?	1754–1756	1935	32 pp.	MW	Matron	Religious	1	1
Nicholas Brown	+	+		+		1722?–1797	1767–1796	1910	½ v.	SW	Attorney	–	6	0
Frances Burney	+	+		+		1752–1840	1778–1839	1854	12½ v.	LW	Novelist	Religious	1	0

Name	P	M	A	C	O						Occupation	Religion		
*Aaron Burr	+	+				1756–1836	1808–1812	1903	3 v.	LW	Vice-President	–	1	0
Frances Calvert	+	+				1767–1859	1789–1822	1911	1⅞ v.	SY	Upper class	Religious	12	4
Mary Capper	+	+		+	+	1755–1827	1769–1826	1848	¾ v.	MD	Lower middle class	Quaker	0	0
*Landon Carter	+		+			1709– ?	1770–1776	1905–1910	⅔ v.	MW	Estate owner	–	6†	0
William Carvosso	+	+		+		1750–1834	1817–1833	1836	1½ v.	MY	Farmer	Methodist	3	0
*Jemima Condict	+			+		1754–1779	1772–1779	1930	⅜ v.	SY	Farmer^F	Presbyterian	0	0
*Silas Constant	+	+				1750–1825	1783–1801	1903	2¾ v.	SW	Minister	Religious	4	0
Anne Cooke	+	+				1726–1809	1761–1776	1915	¼ v.	SW	Upper middle class	Religious	3	0
*Julia Cowles	+		+			1785–1803	1797–1803	1931	½ v.	MW	Middle class	Puritan	0	0
*Benjamin Cutler	+	+				1798–1863	1818–1860	1865	1½ v.	SD	Rector	Episcopal	2	2
*Manasseh Cutler	+	+				1742–1823	1765–1819	1888	3 v.	MW	Minister	Religious	4†	0
*George Dallas	+	+				1792–1864	1837–1839 / 1856–1861	1892	2¼ v.	MW	Diplomat	Religious	4†	0
Abiah Darby	+	+				1716–1794	1745–1769	1913	15 pp.	MY	Lower middle class	Quaker	9	4
Hannah Darby	+	+				? –1762	1761–1762	1905	7 pp.	SD	Middle class	Quaker	2	0
Robert Day	+	+		+		1745–1841	1770–1830	1938	¾ v.	SW	Judge	Protestant	1	0
Susanna Day	+	+				1747–1826	1797–1805	1909	6 pp.	SW	Wholesaler^H	Quaker	5	0
*Samuel Dexter	+	+				1700–1755	1720–1752	1859	22 p.	MW	Minister	Puritan	11	4
Sylvester Douglas	+	+				1743–1823	1793–1819	1928	4 v.	LW	MP	Religious	1	0
*Lorenzo Dow	+	+		+		1777–1834	1794–1816	1848	1¾ v.	MW	Preacher	Methodist	1	1
*Margaret Dow	+	+				1780– ?	1804–1816	1848	½ v.	LW	Preacher^H	Methodist	1	1
*Elizabeth Drinker	+	+				1734–1807	1759–1807	1889	2 v.	SW	Merchant^H	Quaker	5	0
John Dungett	+			+	+	1780–1830	1815–1823	1833	½ v.	–	Surgeon	Methodist	0	0
Grace Elliot	+			+	+	1764–1814	1789–1801	1859	1 v.	–	Lady	Religious	1	0
*Joshua Evans	+			+	+	1731–1798	1745–1798	1837	1 v.	–	Minister	Methodist	2†	0
*Sarah Eve	+			+	+	1749–1774	1772–1773	1881	33 pp.	MW	Sea-captain^F	Quaker	0	0
*Sally Fairfax	+			+	+	1760?–1785?	1771–1772	1904	3 pp.	SW	Middle class	–	0	0

	P	M	A	C	O										
18th century															
*James Fenimore-Cooper	+	+	+	+		1789–1851	1848	1922	36 pp.	SD	Novelist	Religious	7	2	
*Philip Fithian	+			+		1747–1776	1767–1774	1900	1½ v.	LD	Middle class	–	0	0	
Edward Fitzgerald	+	+		+		1763–1798	1794–1796	1904	1¼ v.	MW	Lord	–	3	0	
Sophia Fitzgerald	+			+		1765?–1826	1785	1904	31 pp.	LY	Lady	–	0	0	
Mary Fletcher	+	+		+		1739–1814	1772–1814	1818	2¾ v.	MW	Teacher	Methodist	1	0	
Eliza Fox	+			+		1793–1869	1793–1812	1809	½ v.	–	MP[H]	Presbyterian	3	0	
Maria Fox	+	+		+		1793–1844	1824–1843	1846	2 v.	MW	Middle class	Quaker	3	0	
*Charles Frankland	+	+				1716–1768	1755–1767	1865	47 pp.	SW	Baronet	–	1	0	
Elizabeth Fry	+	+				1780–1845	1797–1845	1853	3 v.	MY	Philanthropist	Quaker	11	1	
*Timothy Fuller	+		+			1778–1835	1798–1801	1916	21 pp.	SW	Student	Religious	0	1	
*James Gallatin	+	+	+			1797–1876	1813–1827	1914	1½ v.	MW	Statesman	–	1	0	
*Samuel Gardner	+		+			1740–1762	1759	1913	23 pp.	SW	Student	Religious	0	0	
John Gisborne	+	+				1770–1851	1800–1851	1852	¾ v.	MD	Middle class	Protestant	9†	1	
Elizabeth Goff	+	+				1759–1799	1759–1799	1918	27 pp.	MW	Middle class	Quaker	22	9	
*James Gordon	+	+				1713–1768	1758–1763	1903–1904	48 pp.	MW	Colonel	Puritan	9	1	
Elizabeth Grant	+	+		+		1797–?	1797–1830	1911	2 v.	–	Upper class	–	1	0	
Faith Gray	+	+		+		1751–1826	1764–1826	1927	1 v.	SY	Business partner[H]	C of E	7	2	
Jonathan Gray	+	+		+		1779–1837	1806–1815	1927	60 pp.	MW	Lawyer	C of E	2	0	
*William Greene	+	+				1754–?	1778	1920	3¼ v.	MW	Soldier	–	0	0	
*John Griffith	+	+	+			1713–1776	1713–1776	1779	2⅛ v.	LW	Preacher	Quaker	4	1	
Mary Hagger	+	+	+			1758–1840	1814–1839	1843	30 pp.	MY	Preacher	Quaker	4†	2	
Mary Hamilton	+	+		+		1756–1816	1774–1816	1925	1½ v.	MD	Lady-in-waiting	Religious	1	0	
Louisa Hardy	+	+				1789–1877	1807–1877	1935	1¼ v.	MW	Lady	–	3	0	
John Harrower	+	+				1735?–?	1773–1776	1901	43 pp.	MD	Teacher	Religious	3	0	
*Thomas Hazard	+	+				1720–1798	1750–1790	1893	1¾ v.	SW	Farmer	Puritan	5	2	
*Thomas Hazard	+	+				1756–1845	1778–1840	1930	4 v.	SD	Farmer	Puritan	5	2	
*Elias Hicks	+	+	+			1748–1830	1813–1820	1832	2⅙ v.	MW	Carpenter	Religious	11	6	
*Jacob Hiltzheimer	+	+				1729–1798	1765–1798	1893	2⅜ v.	SW	Farmer	Religious	7	2	

Name	P	M	A	C	O									
Elizabeth Holland	+	+				1770–1845	1791–1811	1908	2¾ v.	MW	Baroness	C of E	5	2
*John Holyoke	+		+			1734–1753	1748	1911	3 pp.	SD	Middle class	–	0	0
*Mary Holyoke	+	+				1737–1802	1760–1799	1911	½ v.	SD	Middle class	Religious	12	9
*Susanna Holyoke	+	+				?	1793–1856	1911	30 pp.	SD	Middle class	Religious	4	2
*Henry Hull	+			+		1765–1834	1786–1813	1840	½ v.	SW	Shopkeeper	Quaker	3†	0
*Susan Huntington	+	+				1791–1823	1812–1822	1828	1¼ v.	LW	Minister[H]	Puritan	4	2
Mary Jesup	+		+			1799–1837	1811–?	1940?	⅜ v.	SW	Middle class	Religious	0	0
William Jones	+	+				1755–1821	1777–1821	1929	1½ v.	MY	Minister	Methodist	12	2
*Jackson Kemper	+		+			1789–1870	1834	1898	¼ v.	LD	Bishop	Episcopal	3	0
Hannah Kilham	+		+	+		1774–1832	1796–1832	1837	2½ v.	MW	Philanthropist	Quaker	2	1
Jane Knox	+			+	+	1790–?	1813–1819	1909	¼ v.	SW	Sea-captain[H]	Religious	4	0
John Lettsom	+			+	+	1744–1815	1813–1814	1933	2¼ v.	SD	Doctor	Quaker	8	3
*Jean Lowry	+			+	+	1720?–?	1756	1760	31 pp.	LW	Lower middle class	Quaker	4	1
*Benjamin Lynde	+					1700–1781	1721–1780	1880	⅜ v.	SY	Judge	Puritan	3	0
William Macready		+				1793–1873	1833–1851	1912	5 v.	MD	Actor	Religious	9	2
Gideon Mantell	+					1790–1852	1819–1852	1940	1½ v.	SW	Surgeon	Religious	4	1
Elizabeth Mascall	+					1702–1794	1731–1794	1902	¼ v.	MY	Pewterer[H]	Methodist	6	0
*John May	+					1748–1812	1788–1789	1873	¾ v.	MD	Colonel	Religious	12	2
John Mill	+					1712–1805	1740–1803	1889	1⅛ v.	LY	Minister	Protestant	2	10
*William Mills	+					1718–?	1743–1778	1912	3 pp.	SW	Farmer?	Religious	14	4
*Elisha Mitchell	+					1783–1857	1827–1828	1905	⅜ v.	MD	Geologist	Religious	5	0
Thomas Moore	+			+		1779–1852	1818–1847	1853	14 v.	LW	Poet	Catholic	5	3
*Robert Morton	+			+		1760–1785?	1777	1877	39 pp.	MW	Merchant[F]	–	0	0
Carolina Nairne		+				1766–1845	1789–1845	–	4 v.	LY	Baroness	Religious	1	0
Benjamin Newton	+			+		1762–1830	1816–1818	1933	1⅜ v.	MD	Minister	Protestant	4	0
Daniel O'Connell	+					1775–1814	1795–1802	1906	1 v.	–	Gentleman	Catholic	0	0
Peter Oliver		+		+		1741–1823	1741–1821	–	⅔ v.	SY	Doctor	–	5	2
Amelia Opie	+			+		1769–1853	1827–1853	1854	1 v.	–	Novelist	Quaker	0	0
*Lucinda Orr	+					1764–?	1782	1871	¼ v.	MW	Upper middle class	–	0	0

Name	P	M	A	C	O									
18th century														
Sydney Owenson	+		+		+	1780?–1859	1825–1829	1863	5½ v.	MW	Writer	C of E	0	0
*James Parker	+		+			1744–1830	1770–1829	1915	½ v.	MW	Soldier	Puritan	8	0
*Anna Parkman	+			+		1755– ?	1777–1778	1899	3 pp.	SW	Minister[F]	–	0	0
*Ebenezer Parkman	+		+			1703–1782	1737–1782	1899	1½ v.	MD	Minister	Religious	16	2
*Moses Parsons	+		+			1716–1783	1748–1783	1904	¼ v.	MW	Parson	Religious	2	0
Jane Pearson	+		+		+	1735?–1816	1793–1814	1818	½ v.	LY	Manufacturer[H]	Quaker	7	3
Edward Pease	+		+		+	1767–1858	1824+ 1838–1857	1907	1⅙ v.	MY	Wool merchant	Quaker	8↑	4
*John Pemberton	+		+			1727–1795	1769–1795	1842	½ v.	MD	Preacher	Quaker	0	0
*Elizabeth Phelps	+		+	+		1747–1817	1763–1812	1891	½ v.	SW	Lawyer[H]	Puritan	3	0
Caroline Powys	+		+			1739–1817	1756–1808	1899	1¾ v.	LY	Upper class	–	4	1
*John Preston	+		+			1717–1771	1743–1760	1871, 1902	8 pp.	SW	Lieutenant	–	10	5
*Jonathan Proctor	+		+			1739–1821	1759–1760	1934	27 pp.	SW	Captain	–	8	0
Elizabeth Raper	+		+			1736?–1778	1756–1770	1924	37 pp.	MD	Doctor[H]	–	2	0
Hannah Rathbone	+		+			1761–1839	1784–1809	1905	1⅙ v.	SW	Businessman[H]	Quaker	8	3
Deborah Reynolds	+		+			1770?–1803	1800	1905	17 pp.	MW	Middle class	Quaker	6	0
George Ridpath	+		+			1717?–1772	1755–1761	1922	2 v.	MD	Minister	C of S	3	0
*Powhattan Robertson	+			+		1796?– ?	1816–1818	1931	8 pp.	SW	Student	–	0	0
Henry Robinson	+				+	1775–1867	1811–1867	1872	4 v.	–	Barrister	Calvinist	0	0
William Roe	+		+			1748– ?	1775–1809	1928	½ v.	SY	Civil servant	Religious	5	2
Elizabeth Rowntree		+	+			1765?– ?	1808–1835	–	2 v.	MY	Shop-owner[H]	Quaker	7↑	1
Thomas Rumney	+		+			1764–1835	1805–1806	1936	½ v.	SD	Yeoman	–	0	0
Daniel Sandford	+		+			1766–1830	1824–1829	1830	¾ v.	MD	Bishop	Episcopal	7	1
Thomas Scattergood	+		+			1748–1814	1784–1800	1844	1⅛ v.	SW	Turner	Quaker	4↑	0
John Scott	+				+	1792–1862	1812–1828	1930	2⅙ v.	–	Army officer	Religious	0	0
Walter Scott	+		+		+	1771–1832	1825–1829	1890	4 v.	LD	Novelist	C of S	4	0
Joseph Sedgwick	+		+		+	1797–1853	1829–1853	1853	⅔ v.	LY	Pastor	Baptist	7	0
*David Sewall	+			+		1735–1825	1754	1878	7 pp.	MW	Student	–	0	0
*William Sewall	+		+			1797–1846	1817–1846	1930	1½ v.	SW	Farmer/teacher	Calvinist	6	0
*Charlotte Sheldon	+			+		1780–1840	1796	1903	8 pp.	MD	Doctor[F]	Puritan	0	0

Name	P	M	A	C	O									
*Lucy Sheldon	+			+		1788–1889	1801–1803	1903	9 pp.	SD	Doctor^F	Puritan	0	0
Frances Shelley	+	+		+		1787–1873	1814–1869	1912	4 v.	LM	Lady	Protestant	4	0
Mary Shelley	+			+		1797–1851	1814–1840	1947	1 v.	MD	Novelist	–	4	3
*Nancy Shippen	+	+	+	+		1763–1841	1783–1791	1935	1¾ v.	LW	Upper class	–	1	0
*Benjamin Silliman	+	+				1779–1864	1795–1864	1866	1 v.	LW	Professor	Puritan	5	1
John Skinner	+			+		1772–1839	1822–1832	1930	1½ v.	LD	Rector	C of E	5	2
*John Smith	+			+		1722–1771	1743–1752	1904	⅜ v.	MW	Merchant	Puritan	4	0
*Richard Smith	+			+		1784–1824	1817–1824	1916	¼ v.	SW	Teacher	Quaker	0	0
Robert Southey	+			+		1774–1843	1815–1825	1903	2⅜ v.	LD	Poet	–	5	0
*John Stanford	+			+		1754–1834	1798–1834	1835	2¼ v.	MW	Chaplain	Religious	4	3
Catherine Stanley	+			+		1792–1862	1809–1862	1879	1 v.	LY	Bishop^H	C of E	5	0
William Steadman	+			+	+	1764–1837	1790–1813	1838	2½ v.	MW	Minister	Baptist	9	3
John Stedman	+			+	+	1744–1797	1744–1797	1962	2 v.	SW	Soldier and author	Protestant	5	0
Amelia Steuart		+		+		1770?–1808	1789–1808	–	1⅞ v.	LD	Upper middle class	Protestant	4†	1
*Henry Stevens	+			+		1791–1867	1838–1842	1931	14 pp.	SD	Farmer and mill owner	Religious	3	0
*Ezra Stiles	+			+		1727–1795	1769–1795	1901	4 v.	MW	President of Yale	Religious	8	7
John Strutt	+	+		+		1796–1873	1813–1837	1939	24 pp.	MW	Upper class	Religious	4	0
Dan Taylor	+	+		+		1738–1816	1764–1771	1820	37 pp.	MY	Minister	Baptist	13	5
John Taylor	+	+		+		1743–1819	1743–1809	1820	¾ v.	MY	Minister	Baptist	6	3
*Isaiah Thomas	+	+		+		1749–1831	1805–1828	1909	4 v.	SW	Printer and publisher	Religious	4†	0
Hester Thrale	+			+		1741–1821	1776–1809	1951	5½ v.	LW	Upper class	Religious	12	8
John Townsend	+	+		+		1757–1826	1818–1826	1828	⅜ v.	MY	Minister	Methodist	4†	0
Melesina Trench	+	+		+		1768–1837	1798–1827	1837, 1862	2½ v.	SW	Colonel^H	Religious	9	4
*Mary Tucker	+			+		1775–1806	1802	1941	33 pp.	MW	Clerk^H	–	2	0
Thomas Turner	+	+		+		1793–1873	1816–1873	1875	1¼ v.	SW	Surgeon	Religious	5	0
Thomas Turner	+			+		1729–1789	1754–1765	1925	½ v.	MY	Shopkeeper	Religious	2	0

	P	M	A	C	O									
18th century														
Richard Viney		+	+			1700?– ?	1744	–	1¼ v.	MD	Superintendent of Moravians	Moravian	6	0
Thomas Wale	+		+			1701–1796	1765–1794	1883	1⅜ v.	MW	Merchant	–	8	4
*Timothy Walker	+		+			1705–1782	1746–1780	1889	⅜ v.	SW	Minister and farmer	Religious	5	0
*Ann Warder	+		+			1758–1829	1786–1788	1893	33 pp.	LD	Merchant[H]	Quaker	3↑	1
*John Warren	+		+		+	1778–1856	1837–1856	1860	3¾ v.	MD	Surgeon	Episcopal	6	0
Absalom Watkin	+		+		+	1787–1861	1814–1856	1920	1½ v.	MY	Merchant	Religious	4	0
*Joshua Weeks	+		+			1738–1806	1778–1779	1916	¼ v.	MW	Minister	Puritan	8	0
Ellen Weeton	+		+		+	1776–1850	1807–1825	1936–1938	3¼ v.	LY	Governess	Dissenter	1	0
Charles Wesley	+		+			1707–1788	1736–1756	1849	3⅙ v.	MD	Minister	Methodist	8	1
Henry White	+		+			1733–1788	1780–1784	1898	42 pp.	SY	Parson	Religious	10	1
*Mary White	+		+			1780–1811	1803–1805	1903	2 v.	MW	Upper class	Religious	3	1
George Whitefield	+		+		+	1714–1770	1736–1741	1905	2½ v.	MD	Minister	Methodist	2↑	0
William Wilberforce	+		+			1759–1833	1783–1833	1868	2⅙ v.	MY	MP	Religious	6	0
*The Williams[9]	+			+		1765–80– ?	1793–1801	1858	10 pp.	MW	Farmer[F]	Quaker?	0	0
*Anna Winslow	+			+		1759–1779	1771–1773	1894	⅜ v.	LW	Commissary General[F]	Puritan	0	0
*Sally Wister	+			+		1761–1804	1777–1778	1902	1⅛ v.	MW	Merchant[F]	Quaker	0	0
*John Wiswall	+		+			1731–1821	1763–1797	1908	⅜ v.	MY	Minister	Episcopal	5	3
Nancy Woodforde	+		+			1757–1814	1792	1932	49 pp.	MD	Upper middle class	–	0	0
*John Woods	+		+			? –1829	1820–1821	1822	1½ v.	LW	Farmer	C of E	6	0
Margaret Woods	+		+			1748–1821	1772–1821	1829	2½ v.	LY	Middle class	Religious	4	0
*John Woolman	+		+		+	1720–1792	1755–1772	1922	1 v.	LW	Teacher and lawyer	Quaker	4	3
Thomas Wright	+		+		+	1711–?	1711–1762	1911	15 pp.	MY	Watchmaker	Religious	0	0
Elizabeth Wynne	+		+	+		1778–1857	1789–1820	1935–1940	3 v.	SD	Admiral[H]	Catholic	7	1
Eugenia Wynne	+		+	+		1780– ?	1789–1811	1935–1940	1 v.	SY	Upper class	Catholic	4	0
Harriet Wynne	+			+		1786– ?	1803–1806	1940	½ v.	SD	Upper class	Catholic	0	0
Elizabeth Yeardley		+	+			? –1821	1815–1821	–	⅔ v.	LY	Missionary[H]	Quaker	1	1

Name	P	M	A	C	O									
John Yeoman	+	+			+	1748–1824	1774–1777	1934	40 pp.	MD	Farmer	–	9	0
Mary Yeoman	+			+	+	1780–?	1800	1926	16 pp.	SD	Farmer[F]	–	0	0
Arthur Young	+	+			+	1741–1820	1797–1818	1898	2⅜ v.	LW	Author and agriculturist	Protestant	4	1

19th century

Name	P	M	A	C	O									
Thomas Acland	+	+			+	1809–1898	1829–1837	1902	2 v.	SW	M P	Religious	7	2
Christopher Addison	+	+				1869–?	1914–1918	1934	3 v.	LD	M P	–	4	0
James Agate	+					1877–1947	1932–1943	1935–1944	9 v.	–	Critic	Religious	0	0
*Louisa Alcott	+	+		+	+	1832–1888	1843–1886	1889	2 v.	SY	Novelist	Religious	1	0
Henry Alford	+	+			+	1810–1871	1826–1870	1873	2¼ v.	MW	Dean	Protestant	4	2
Hannah Allen	+				+	1813–1880	1835–1849	1884	⅜ v.	MW	Middle class	Quaker	10	2
*Anonymous	+					1820?–?	1837	1909	6 pp.	SW	Middle class	–	0	0
John Bailey	+					1864–1931	1886–1930	1935	1½ v.	MY	Critic	Religious	3	1
Louise Bain	+					1803–1883	1857–1883	1940	¼ v.	SY	Bookseller[H]	Religious	8	0
*Erastus Beadle	+					1821–1894	1857	1923	½ v.	MD	Businessman	Presbyterian	3	0
Edward Benson	+					1829–1896	1878–1896	1899	4 v.	LW	Archbishop	C of E	6	0
John Bingham		+		+		1810–1827	1822–1825	1832	⅜ v.	MY	Apprentice	Methodist	0	0
Mary Bingham		+		+		1808–1825	1822–1825	1832	1⅜ v.	MY	Middle class	Methodist	0	0
Andrew Bonar		+			+	1810–1892	1828–1892	1894	2 v.	SW	Minister	C of S	6	1
The Bowens[10]	+				+	1864–1868–?	1876	1942	12 pp.	SW	Upper class	Protestant	0	0
*Claude Bowers	+				+	1880–1958	1880–1950	1962	1¾ v.	–	Political writer	–	1	0
Mary Brabazon	+				+	1848–1918	1880–1918	1928	3 v.	MW	Countess	Religious	6	0
John Bright	+				+	1811–1889	1837–1887	1930	2¾ v.	SW	MP	Quaker	8	1
Ford Brown		+		+		1821–1893	1844–1856	1900	¾ v.	SW	Painter	Religious	3	0
Mary Brown					+	1807–1833	1821	1905	1 v.	MD	Upper middle class	–	0	0
*John Burroughs	+				+	1837–1921	1857–1921	1928	1¾ v.	MY	Author and naturalist	–	1	0
Elizabeth Butler	+					1850?–1918?	1862–1914	1922	1⅔ v.	–	Artist	Catholic	6	1
George Cambridge		+				1819–1904	1832–1903	1906	3 v.	SW	Duke	Religious	0	0
Lucy Cavendish	+				+	1841–1925	1854–1880	1927	3 v.	–	Lady	Religious	0	0
*Elizabeth Chace	+				+	1806–?	1806–1897	1937	49 pp.	–	Manufacturer[H]	Quaker	10	7

	P	M	A	C	O								
Isobel Gurney	+	+	+			1851–1932	1913	1935	1 v.	MW	Lady	C of E	9	1
*Abelard Guthrie	+	+	+			1814–1873	1858–1862	1899	37 pp.	MY	Politician	–	4	1†
*James Hadley	+	+	+			1821–1872	1843–1852	1951	1½ v.	MW	Professor	–	1	1†
Rachael Hamilton-Gordon			+	+		1873?– ?	1882	–	27 pp.	MD	Upper middle class	Religious	0	0
Victoria Hanover	+	+	+			1819–1901	1832–1882	1868, 1912	7 v.	LY	Queen	C of E	9	0
Augustus Hare	+			+		1834–1903	1834–1856	1952	½ v.	–	Writer	C of E	0	0
*Mary Harker	+			+		1836?– ?	1853	1935	21 pp.	SD	Upper middle class	Quaker	0	0
*Rutherford Hayes	+		+	+		1822–1893	1841–1893	1922–1926	8¾ v.	MW	President	Methodist	8	3
Caroline Head	+		+			1852–1904	1871–1893	1905	⅔ v.	SW	Middle class	Evangelical	3	2
Maurice Hewlett			+	+		1861–1923	1893–1923	–	¾ v.	SW	Novelist	Religious	2	0
*Harriet Hillard	+			+		1809–1872	1829–1834	1900	1⅔ v.	SW	Upper middle class	Unitarian	0	0
Mary Hochberg	+		+			1873–1950?	1892–1914	1950	1½ v.	MY	Princess	Religious	4	1
*Virginia Hoffman	+	+	+			1832–1855	1847–1855	1859	⅔ v.	MY	Missionary	Episcopal	1	1
*Louisa Hopkins	+		+			1812–1862	1835–1840	1882	19 pp.	SY	Teacher	Religious	1	0
Sidney Horler			+	+		1888– ?	1933	1933	1⅜ v.	–	Author	–	0	0
*Samuel Howe	+		+	+		1801–1876	1825–1829	1906	5 v.	LD	Doctor	Free-thinker	6	1
Arthur Hutchinson	+		+			1880– ?	1935	1935	1¾ v.	LD	Novelist	Religious	2	0
*Mitchell Jackson	+		+	+		1816–1900	1852–1863	1939	⅔ v.	SW	Farmer	Methodist	4	0
Margaret Jeune	+		+			1819–1891	1843–1865	1932	¾ v.	MW	Dean^H	Protestant	5	0
Priscilla Johnston	+			+		1808–1852	1820–1850	1862	½ v.	MY	Middle class	Quaker	4	0
*Emily Judson	+			+		1817–1854 1847–1850	1828–1833 1847–1850	1861	29 pp.	MW	Teacher	Baptist	7	1
Caleb Kemp		+		+		1836– ?	1853–1908	–	8 v.	LW	Businessman	Quaker	0	0
Stephen King-Hall	+					1893– ?	1909–1917	1936	⅞ v.	SW	Navy cadet	–	0	0
Anna Kingsford	+			+		1846–1887	1881–1887	1913	4⅜ v.	LY	Writer	Christian Scientist	1	0
John Kitto	+		+			1804–1854	1820–1833	1856	3½ v.	MW	Printer	C of E	9	3
Louisa Knightley	+			+		1842–1913	1856–1884	1915	1⅞ v.	MW	Lady	Religious	0	0

19th century	P	M	A	C	O									
*Amos Lawrence	+	+				1814–1886	1843–1883	1888	1⅛ v.	SY	Businessman	Episcopal	7	1
*John Lee	+	+				1812–187?	1844–1847+ 1859	1877	1⅞ v.	–	Preacher	Mormon	16†	3
*Mary van Lennep	+	+				1821–1844	1841–1844	1851	1¼ v.	–	Missionary	Religious	0	0
*Jane Lewis	+		+			1806?–?	1820	1903	4 pp.	MW	Middle class	Puritan	0	0
*Francis Lieber	+		+	+		1800–1872	1822–1857	1882	1¼ v.	MW	Professor	–	4	1
*John Long	+	+		+		1838–1915	1848–1915	1923	1¼ v.	SW	Governor	Religious	2	1
*Henry Longfellow	+	+				1807–1882	1829–1881	1886	2 v.	SW	Poet	Unitarian	6	1
*Lucy Lovell	+	+				1809–?	1840–1843	1937	¼ v.	LY	Minister[H]	Quaker	7	4
William Lucas	+					1804–1861	1829–1861	1934	3 v.		Brewer	Quaker	9	0
*Susan Magoffin	+	+				1827–1855	1846–1847	1926	1¼ v.	LD	Gentlewoman	Protestant	4	2
Katherine Mansfield	+		+			1888–?	1914–1922	1927	1¼ v.	–	Writer	–	0	0
*Anna May	+		+			1840?–?	1857	1941	½ v.	MD	Student	Religious	0	0
Elsie Mildmay	+		+			1850?–?	1860?–1880?	1900?	44 pp.	–	Upper class	Religious	0	0
*Abner Morse	+			+		1819–1881	1859–1861	1940	27 pp.	MW	Farmer	Religious	3†	0
*Jacob Motte	+	+				1811–1868	1831	1940	½ v.	MD	Student	Episcopal	0	0
George Müller	+			+		1805–1898	1830–1892	1905	3⅔ v.	MY	Minister	Baptist	2	1
Francis Newbolt	+	+				1863–1941	1879+ 1882–1883	1904 1927	½ v.	MD	At Eton	–	0	0
*Eliza Ogden	+	+				1802?–?	1816–1818	1903	17 pp.	MW	Middle class	Puritan	0	0
*James Otey	+	+		+		1800–1863	1833–1863	1898	4 pp.	SW	Bishop	Episcopal	9	3
Caroline Owen	+	+		+		1809?–1873	1834–1873	1894	4 v.	MW	Professor[H]	–	1	0
Francis Palgrave	+	+				1824–1897	1833–1890	1899	1 v.	MY	Anthologist	Tractarian	6	1
Ann Palmer	+	+				1806–1834	1827–1834	1839	¼ v.	MY	Tailor	C of E	0	0
*Ellen Parker	+	+		+		1833–1910	1852–1857	1915	33 pp.	SD	Teacher	Religious	0	0
*Caroline Phelps	+	+				1810?–?	1830–1840	1930	31 pp.	LY	Fur trader[H]	–	3	0
*Martin Philips	+	+		+		1806–1889	1840–1863	1909	⅞ v.	SW	Doctor	Religious	1	0
John Pollen	+		+			1820–1892	1834–1890	1912	1¾ v.	MW	Painter	Catholic	10	1
Frederick Post	+		+			1819–1835	1830–1835	1838	1¾ v.	MW	Middle class	Quaker	0	0
Llewellyn Powys	+		+			1884–?	1909–1912	1936	22 pp.	MW	Middle class	–	0	0
Theodore Powys	+	+		+		1882–?	1906–1909	1936	10 pp.	MW	Middle class	–	2	0
*Elizabeth Prentiss	+	+				1818–1878	1836–1856	1882	2⅝ v.	MW	Teacher	Presbyterian	6	2

| | P M A C O | | | | | | | | | |

19th century

Name	P	M	A	C	O	Dates	Diary period	Year	Length	Entry type	Occupation / Class	Religion		
*Catherine Webb	+		+			1801–1900	1815–1816	1903	2 pp.	MW	Middle class	Puritan	0	0
Arthur Weymouth	+	+	+			1895– ?	1939–1946	1948	1½ v.	MW	Doctor	Religious	3	0
Dorothy White	+	+	+			1877– ?	1907–1913	1924	2½ v.	MW	Middle class	–	1	0
Thomas Whitwell	+			+		1814–1828	1827–1828	1927	10 pp.	SW	Middle class	Quaker	0	0
Samuel Wilberforce	+		+		+	1805–1873	1830–1873	1880	7⅔ v.	MW	Bishop	Religious	6	1
*Mary Wilbor	+		+	+		1806– ?	1822	1903	8 pp.	MW	Middle class	–	0	0
James Wilson	+		+			1805–1860	1851–1859	1927	3⅓ v.	MW	Politician	Quaker	6	0
Frances Wood	+		+			1812–1860	1830–1842	1926	1⅔ v.	MW	Major[H]	Religious	4	0
*Victoria Wortley	+			+		1837–1922	1850–1851	1852	1¼ v.	MW	Upper middle class	–	0	0

1. Source: P = published text, M = manuscript.
2. Text: A = adult diary, C = child diary, O = autobiography.
3. The length of a text is given in volumes (a volume is taken to be about 200 pages long), but where a text is under 50 pages, the exact number of pages is given.
4. The typical type of diary entry is described:
    L = over one page in length
    M = a half to one page in length
    S = a few lines
    D = daily or almost daily entries
    W = a few entries weekly
    Y = a few entries monthly or yearly
    For example, LW signifies that the diary entries are generally over a page in length and occur a few times a week.
5. The specific occupation is given wherever possible. In some cases the father's, husband's or grandfather's employment is given and these are marked by [F], [H] or [G/F] respectively. When a writer's career is unknown, an estimate of his social class is provided.
6. Religion: – signifies that religion is not mentioned in the text.
7. The total number of children born to an author is given, followed by the number of children who died. In some texts it is unclear whether the writer is referring to his or her children, relatives, friends or servants. In these cases (marked by a †), an estimate of the number of offspring is provided.
8. An asterisk indicates an American author.
9. The *Williams: this text comprises extracts from the diaries kept by six sisters. Only a few extracts from each diary are provided by the editor.
10. The Bowens: this text comprises a few entries from the diary kept by four siblings.

Notes

1. Past children. A review of the literature on the history of childhood

1. The system of referencing is as follows: authors discussed in the text are referred to by title, name and date at the first mention in each chapter. After that the author–date system is employed. Merely illustrative references are referred to by author and date only. A complete bibliography is given at the end of the book. In the case of Stone, the work referred to is always his 1977 text. Quotations from Ariès and Badinter are first given in the original language, followed by the English translation.
2. Although Ariès' work was the first to attract a great deal of attention and interest to the history of childhood, there are in fact a number of earlier studies. See Bayne-Powell (1939), Findlay (1923) and Lynd (1942), all of whom claim that children were cruelly treated in previous centuries. For alternative views see Crump (1929), Godfrey (1907), Lochead (1956), Morgan (1944) and Roe (1959). A review of these works is contained in Pollock (1981).
3. Ariès was mainly concerned with attitudes to children and so does not discuss the actual lifestyle of children.
4. Ariès (1960) and Demos (1970) believe that there was no concept of adolescence until the 19th century. For a criticism of this view see Beales (1975), Davis (1971) and Smith (1973).
5. The method of inferring the actual experience of children from attitudes which is so much a feature of this literature will be discussed in chapter 2.
6. See Marvick (1974): 'The character of Louis XIII: the role of his physician in its formation'.
7. A notable exception to this is Greven (1977) who stresses 'continuities of child-rearing methods over long periods of time' (corresponding to particular types of religious temperaments) rather than constant evolution (16). His work is referred to in later chapters. Greven is, however, very much an exception. Even recent works such as Porter (1982) emphasise the great change in the status and treatment of children in the 18th century. (Porter follows the same lines as Stone (1977) and Trumbach (1978).)

2. The thesis re-examined: a criticism of the literature

1. De Mause (1976) has attempted to argue that, in the past, children were developmentally retarded because they were ill-treated; but the data he used

to reveal the supposed level of retardation (age at walking) are inaccurate (see p. 225).

2. Inclusive fitness: number of adult offspring left in the next generation (Wilson, 1975).

3. This is an example of the misconception that adaptive behaviour is for the benefit of the species rather than the individual.

4. Van Lawick-Goodall (1967) extensively studied chimpanzees in their natural setting over a long period of time. Her report reveals how subtle and complex the development of young chimpanzees is.

5. Even when the economy of a society dictates that children have to work at an early age, this does not mean they were therefore seen as adults. The children of the Navaho Indians had to help in order that the family could survive, but only so much was expected from a child at each age level and the children continued to engage in such childish activities as play while working (Leighton & Kluckhohn, 1948).

6. This behaviour of the Ik is not an inevitable response to famine; Turnbull's book has also been much disbelieved.

7. Ferguson (1966) notes that even though the children he studied had been treated with compassion and competence, yet after leaving the institution, their performance fell seriously short of that of the ordinary run of young people.

8. In addition, see Clarke & Clarke (1976) who discuss a number of child isolation cases and also children grossly neglected by their parents.

9. Stern (1977) studied the first relationship between mother and infant and found that the lack of reciprocal interaction which can lead to child abuse is evident very early on.

10. This section was prepared before the publication of Ferdinand Mount's book *The Subversive Family* (1982). In this he provides an excellent critique of the prevailing viewpoint on family life and goes on to suggest why historians have depicted family life in past times in the way they have.

11. There has been little systematic analysis of child-rearing advice literature – indeed of any source of evidence. What is needed is a comparison of the *prevalence* of varying types of advice literature through the centuries. This could then be compared with similar analyses of other sources of evidence such as diaries, as it is possible that parallels of change could be found.

12. Effective contraceptive measures became widespread and acceptable in the 19th century; the welfare state was not fully in existence until the mid-20th century.

13. Wrigley (1968) has demonstrated that infant and adult mortality rates were subject to fluctuation in the past. Hence, though Trumbach (1978) claims there was a fall in infant mortality after 1750, Wrigley's research reveals that the rate merely returned to its previous level.

14. For a more detailed discussion of the effects of and response to industrialisation, see Pollock (1981), chapter 3.

15. Parents of the same period would not be viewed as treating their children in the same way, but rather as providing at least adequate mental, emotional and

physical care. Thus, society's treatment of children is not necessarily paralleled by parental treatment.
16. See also Anderson (1980) on this point.

3. Issues concerning evidence

1. Diaries were the largest source type used and thus the methodological discussion is mainly concerned with them. Much, however, is also applicable to autobiographies. In 'The wrong way through the telescope' (1976), Laslett examines the problem of using literary sources as evidence for the past and puts forward the case for a more sophisticated literary sociology. See also the sections in *Household and Family in Past Time* (1972) and *Family Life and Illicit Love* (1977).
2. In this and every other case where parts of a manuscript are published at different times, the relevant publication date is given.
3. This quotation was written in a letter by Boswell and is cited in Spalding (1949), p. 1.
4. There was not total approval of physical punishment for children. Some theorists through the centuries have spoken out against the use of such discipline, particularly in schools. For example: Pluto 400 BC, Plutarch AD 1000, Asham and Ingeland in the 16th century and Locke and L'estrage in the 17th century were all opposed to physical punishment (Helfer & Kempe, 1968). (This does seem to be a continuing debate: corporal punishment in schools today is both regarded as necessary and condemned by sections of society.)
5. Mill noted that his daughter was 'too forward in drawing up with young men' (52).
6. The manuscript sample was small and so where a manuscript referred to a relevant topic, it was included either in the diary or autobiography section and the use of such a text specified by MS.
7. For convenience, the diary of Machyn (born 1498) was considered with the 16th-century sources and the diaries of Cole (born 1916) and Waugh (born 1903) were considered with the 19th-century data.
8. The year 1785 was the earliest date for which an index to the newspaper was available.

4. Attitudes to children

1. The type of child care provided by the parents is considered in the following two chapters. In order to avoid too much repetition of quotations, only those relating to attitudes will be given in this section.
2. As will be shown in chapter 6, some fathers did take quite an active part in the physical care of their young.
3. &c = et cetera.
4. There is as yet no adequate survey of the child advice literature – only the main theorists are reviewed, notably Locke, Rousseau and works of a Calvinistic denomination and there is little discussion of other theorists of the same

period. As the works of Locke and Rousseau were widely available and were re-published a number of times, it is likely that many people read them. It seems that some of the texts studied do reflect the ideas of these two theorists and so it was decided, because of the lack of alternative knowledge, to concentrate on them. (There is a great need for a systematic analysis of child advice literature.) Of course, it is equally likely that the parents studied here were not affected by these theorists' views.

5. See also the following texts: Addison, Bailey, Bright, C. Brown, Cobden-Sanderson, Collier, Collins, Dawson, Ewing, E. Gaskell, Guest, Head, Hewlett, Hochberg, Hutchinson, Jeune, Johnston, Kitto, Müller, Owen, Palgrave, F. Russell, J. Russell, K. Russell, Sopwith, Traherne, Tregelles, Wilberforce, Wood.

6. See also the following texts: Allen, Bonar, Cobden-Sanderson, Dawson, Ewing, E. Gaskell, Gurney, Hochberg, Palgrave, Lady de Rothschild, F. Russell, Trant, Tregelles, Wood.

7. Waugh was a notorious 'poser' and was writing in the knowledge that he would be read. Although it is debatable how much of what he wrote can be taken to represent his true feelings, with reference to his children, it does appear as if he put his theories into practice. Waugh had his own residence in London, rarely saw his children as infants and, as they all went to boarding school, did not see much of them as they grew up.

8. The Puritan conduct books advised Puritans on every aspect of their lives, particularly family relations. See Powell (1917) for a review of such conduct books. As Mechling (1975) has shown (see chapter 2), advice literature must be used with caution. However, it seems reasonable to assume that denominational literature will at least be read by those who subscribe to that religious belief.

9. See also: H. Backhouse, Boscawen, Boswell, Calvert, Fry, Harrower, Lettsom, Macready, Skinner, Thrale, Wesley.

10. See also: Bagshawe, Blundell, W. Bulkeley, Byrom, Clegg, E. Erskine, *Green, Hay, Heywood, Josselin, Martindale, Morris, *Sewall, T. Smith.

11. See also: *M. Bayard, Bishop, Braithwaite, Calvert, Cooke, A. Darby, H. Darby, *Dexter, Douglas, *Drinker, Gisborne, F. Gray, Hardy, *Hazard (1756–1845), *Hicks, Holland, *E. Holyoke, *M. Holyoke, *Huntington, Jones, Kilham, *Lynde, Macready, Mantell, *May, Moore, Newton, Pease, T. Powys, Rathbone, Reynolds, Roe, Rowntree, Sandford, *W. Sewall, M. Shelley, Skinner, Southey, Stedman, Steuart, D. Taylor, J. Taylor, Thrale, Turner, *White, Elizabeth Wynne, Young.

12. See also: Alford, Allen, Bailey, Benson, Bright, Cobden-Sanderson, Collins, *Colt, Cowell, Cunningham, Dawson, *Duncan, Ewing, Gladstone, Guest, Hanover, Head, *Jackson, Jeune, *Longfellow, *Otey, Palgrave, *Phelps, *Philips, *Sterne, Tregelles, *Walker, *Ward, Wood.

13. Two 16th-century diarists lost an older child, Hope and H. Mildmay. The latter did not grieve long for his adolescent son's death, having a party within two weeks of his loss.

14. The diaries of Clegg, *Danforth, Evelyn, *Hammond, Josselin, Martindale, *C. Mather, Newcome and Osborne contain information on parental reaction

to the death of an older child. Only *Danforth revealed no emotion. The autobiographies of Rich and Stout also reveal parental distress at the death of an older child.

15. Though Josselin referred to this child as 'it', it could hardly be argued that he was unaware of her presence.

16. See also: Bishop, Boswell, Calvert, *B. Cutler, A. Darby, *L. Dow, *M. Dow, Fry, F. Gray, *Griffith, Holland, Kilham, Lettsom, *Mills, Moore, Oliver, Rathbone, Roe, M. Shelley, D. Taylor, J. Taylor, Thrale, *Warder, *White, *Wiswall, Elizabeth Wynne.

   For those texts which describe the death of older children see: *Alcott, H. Backhouse, Boscawen, C. Brown, Burney, *Drinker, Goff, Hagger, *Hicks, *Hiltzheimer, Knox, Lettsom, Macready, Mascall, Moore, Pearson, Pease, Rowntree, Sandford, Skinner, *Stiles, Thrale, Townsend, Young.

   Goff, *Hicks and *Hiltzheimer recorded no emotion.

17. See also: Alford, Allen, Bonar, *Bowers, *Colt, *Duncan, Ewing, *Hoffman, *Judson, *Longfellow, Palgrave, *Prentiss, J. Russell, *Todd.

   Alford, Bailey, Benson, Bright, Cooper, Fowler, *Long, *Otey and Sopwith all lost an older child. All were distressed.

5. Discipline and control

1. The extent of parental control over a child's choice of career or marriage partner has been discussed in Pollock (1981), chapter 8.

2. There is no way of telling from the diary if this was accidental or a punishment.

3. This punishment Machyn noted was also given on another occasion for 'sedyssyous wordes & rumors & conseles agaynst the quen'[s] mageste' (102) which reveals the extent of the condemnation against the beating of the child with rods. (Treason to 16th-century England was a very serious crime.)

4. This quote was not contained in the published text. Again note the use of 'it' to refer to his daughter (see Josselin, p. 135).

5. Viney (1710?– ?) reported a case of child abuse: a woman was 'taken up for burning a child in ye oven to whom she was step mother' (MS, fo. 6).

6. Douglas, *Hiltzheimer and *Stiles also gave examples in their diaries of allowing children a degree of autonomy.

7. These extracts were written by John Strutt's father and have been included in the published version of Strutt's diary.

8. See also the autobiographies of Belsham, Burney, Fry, F. Gray, Hagger, *Huntington, Pease, *Silliman and Watkin.

9. This section includes the treatment of apprentices.

10. Stone (1977) also found that discipline was severe in the early 19th century. This aspect of his argument is confirmed here. However, my results do not support his assertion that strict discipline was the norm in the 16th and 17th centuries.

6. From birth to twelve

1. See the texts of Blundell, Browell, Byrom, E. Erskine, J. Erskine, Evelyn, Freke, Johnston, Osborne, Pledger, Rule, Stockton, Twysden.
2. See the texts of *M. Bayard, *Dexter, *Drinker, *Hazard, *Hiltzheimer, *M. Holyoke, *Parker, *E. Parkman, *Preston, *W. Sewall, *Stiles, *Wiswall.
3. See the texts of H. Backhouse, Bishop, Boscawen, Braithwaite, Cooke, A. Darby, H. Darby, F. Gray, Macready, Nairne, Powys, Raper, Rathbone, Roe, Steuart, D. Taylor, Viney, Watkin.
4. See the texts of H. Backhouse, Boswell, Burney, E. Fitzgerald, Fry, Hamilton, Holland, Jones, Kilham, Knox, Mantell, Moore, Oliver, M. Shelley, Steadman, Thrale, Turner (1793–1873), Weeton, Wilberforce, Elizabeth Wynne.
5. See the texts of Bonar, Cooper, Guest, Hanover, Head, Hewlett, Hochberg, Johnston, Palgrave, F. Russell, Timms, Tregelles, Wilberforce.
6. Napier's case notes depict the despair of many women who were barren or unable to have any more children (MacDonald, 1981, p. 83).
7. Fildes (1980) argues that there was a 'radical change in neonatal feeding practices' after 1750 (319). After this date, no text she examined considered colostrum to be bad for or harmful to an infant and many recommended that the first milk was good for the child. This, Fildes believes, was the crucial factor in reducing the endogenous mortality rate.
8. Fildes (1982) used the median test (a non-parametric test) to analyse her data because the results were not from a normal distribution. In fact even great deviations from the normal distribution do not affect the validity of the t test.
9. These entries are contained in the manuscript of Josselin's diary and cited in Macfarlane (1970), pp. 87–8.
10. The manuscript pages are not numbered and therefore the date of the entry is given.
11. See also the texts of H. Backhouse, Boscawen, Burney, Cooke, *Dallas, Douglas, Goff, J. Gray, Hamilton, *Hazard (1756–1845), Lettsom, Mantell, Moore, Rathbone, Steuart, Thrale, Weeton.
12. See also the texts of Addison, *Colt, Gregory, Guest, Hochberg, *Howe, Kitto, *Lawrence, *Lovell, Owen, Palgrave, *Prentiss, F. Russell, K. Russell, Tregelles, Waugh, Wood.
13. See also the texts of Blundell, Briggins, *Byrd, Freke, Jackson, Josselin, Morris, Richards, T. Smith, Twysden, Woodforde.
14. See also the texts of *Alcott, H. Backhouse, Braithwaite, Hamilton, Hardy, Harrower, *Huntington, Mill, M. Shelley, *Shippen, Skinner, *Stiles, Yeoman, Young.
15. See also the texts of H. Backhouse, Boscawen, Burney, Calvert, Douglas, M. Fox, Lettsom, Nairne, Rathbone, Skinner, J. Smith, Steadman, J. Taylor, Thrale, Trench, Wesley.
16. Spufford's (1979) article reveals the importance which the poorer members of society attached to education.

7. Summary and conclusions

1. See also Macfarlane (1979a) who points out the mix-up in Stone's (1977) time periods. For example, Stone states at the beginning of his book that the 'Closed Domesticated' phase in family life lasted from 1640 to 1800. However, on other occasions the phase starts at 1620 or even as late as towards the end of the 17th century (Macfarlane, p. 121).

Bibliography and citation index

Primary sources

In this section those texts which contain information on childhood are signified by C.

PUBLISHED TEXTS

Acland, Thomas (1902). *Memoir and Letters of The Right Honourable Sir Thomas Dyke Acland*; ed. Acland, Arthur; printed privately, London.   C.   *pp.* 131, 183, 196, 248, 265

Adams, John (1874). *Memoirs of John Quincy Adams*; ed. Adams, Charles; J. B. Lippincott, Philadelphia.   C.   *pp.* 116, 166, 205, 244

Adams, William (1852). Memoir of the Rev. William Adams. *Massachusetts Historical Society Collections*; 4th series, vol. 1, pp. 8–22.   C.   *pp.* 135, 204

Addison, Christopher (1934). *Four and a Half Years*; Hutchinson, London, 2 vols.   C.   *pp.* 132, 228

Agate, James (1935). *Ego. The Autobiography of James Agate*; Hamish Hamilton, London, 9 vols.   C.   *pp.* 186–7

Alcott, Amos (1938). *The Journals of Bronson Alcott*; ed. Shepard, Odell; Little, Brown, Boston.   C.   *pp.* 117, 129, 163–4, 166, 205, 209, 245, 264–5

Alcott, Louisa (1889). *Life, Letters and Journals*; ed. Cheney, Ednah; Roberts Brothers, Boston.   C.   *pp.* 173, 179, 200, 257, 264–5

Alford, Henry (1873). *Life, Journals and Letters of Henry Alford, D.D.*; ed. Alford, F.; Rivingtons, London.   C.   *pp.* 108, 140, 178, 206, 211, 215, 218, 259

Allen, Hannah (1884). *A Beloved Mother*; Samuel Harris, London.   C.   *pp.* 108, 110, 122, 177, 183, 185, 199, 201, 206, 239, 248, 254, 255

Allen, John (1905). *Leaves from the Past*; ed. Sturge, Clement; J. W. Arrowsmith, Bristol.   C.   *p.* 168

Anonymous (1909). Travels in Western America in 1837. *The Journal of American History*, vol. 3, pp. 511–16.   C.

Arbuthnot, Harriet (1950). *The Journal of Mrs. Arbuthnot*; eds. Bamford, Frances & Duke of Wellington; Macmillan, London.

Asbury, Francis (1852). *Journal of Rev. Francis Asbury*; Lane & Scott, New York.

Ashmole, Elias (1927). *The Diary and Will of Elias Ashmole*; ed. Gunther, R.; Butler & Tanner, Oxford.   C.   *p.* 150

Assheton, Nicholas (1848). *The Journal of Nicholas Assheton*; ed. Raines, E.; Chetham Society Publications, Manchester, vol. 14.   C.   *pp.* 134, 204

Backhouse, Hannah (1858). *Extracts from the Journal and Letters of Hannah Chapman Backhouse*; printed privately, London. C. *pp.* 119, 168, 169

Backhouse, James (1918). The diary of James Backhouse. *The Journal of the Friends' Historical Society*, vol. 15, pp. 21–7. C.

Bacon, Mary-Ann (1903). Diary in Vanderpoel, Emily: *Chronicles of a Pioneer School*; Cambridge University Press, Massachusetts, pp. 66–71. C.

Bacon, Samuel (1822). Diary in Ashmun, J.: *Memoir of the Life and Character of Rev. Samuel Bacon*; Jacob Gideon, Washington City, pp. 138–274. C. *p.* 170

Bagshawe, William (1886). *The Bagshawes of Ford*; Mitchell & Hughes, London. C. *p.* 228

Bailey, Abigail (1815). *Memoirs of Mrs Abigail Bailey*; Samuel Armstrong, Boston. C. *pp.* 106, 119, 137, 158–9, 161, 266

Bailey, John (1935). *Letters and Diaries*; ed. Bailey, Sarah; John Murray, London. C. *pp.* 206, 239

Bain, Louisa (1940). Diary in Bain, James: *A Bookseller Looks Back*; Macmillan, London, pp. 39–89. C. *p.* 177

Baker, John (1909). Extracts from diary. *Sussex Archaeological Collections*, vol. 52, pp. 38–83. C.

Baldwin, Ebenezer (1879). Diary in Kingsley, William, ed.: *Yale College*; Henry Holt, New York, vol. 1, pp. 444–6. C. *pp.* 191, 192

Barclay, John (1842). A selection from letters and papers. *The Friends' Library*, vol. 6, pp. 385–478. C. *p.* 168

Bates, Edward (1933). *The Diary of Edward Bates*; ed. Beale, Howard; Government Printing Office, Washington, DC. C.

Baxter, Henry (1927). Diary. *The Pennsylvania Magazine of History and Biography*, vol. 51, pp. 27–78, 143–71, 207–43.

Bayard, James (1913). Papers of James A. Bayard, ed. Donnan, E.; *Annual Report of the American Historical Association*, vol. 2, pp. 385–516. C.

Bayard, Martha (1894). *The Journal of Martha Pintard Bayard*; ed. Dod, S.; Dodd, Mead, New York. C. *pp.* 104, 107, 131, 138, 142, 162

Bayly, Katharine (1898). Notes from the diary of a Dublin lady in the reign of George II. *The Journal of the Royal Society of Antiquaries of Ireland*, 5th series, vol. 8, pp. 141–55. C.

Beadle, Erastus (1923). *To Nebraska in Fifty-seven*; New York Public Library. C. *p.* 247

Bee, Jacob (1910). Diary. *North Country Diaries*; Surtees Society, 2nd series, vol. 118, pp. 43–63; also (1914) 2nd series, vol. 124, pp. 54–175. C.

Belsham, Thomas (1833). *Memoirs of the Late Reverend Thomas Belsham*; ed. Williams, John; printed privately, London. C. *p.* 171

Benson, Arthur (1926). *Diary of A. C. Benson*; ed. Lubbock, Percy; Hutchinson, London.

Benson, Edward (1899). *The Life of Edward White Benson*; ed. Benson, Arthur; Macmillan, London. C. *p.* 247

Bentley, William (1905). *The Diary of William Bentley, D.D.*; The Essex Institute, Massachusetts. C.

Beresford, John, ed. (1927). *Memoirs of an Eighteenth-Century Footman*; George Routledge & Sons, London.

Bibliography and citation index

Bethune, Joanna (1864). Diary in Bethune, George: *Memoirs of Mrs. Joanna Bethune*; Harper & Bros., New York, pp. 125–250.   C.   *p. 172*

Bingham, John (1832). *A Memoir of Mr. John Bingham*; ed. Bustard, John; John Mason, London.   C.   *p. 258*

Bingham, Mary (1832). *A Memoir of Miss Mary Helen Bingham*; ed. Bustard, John; John Mason, London.   C.   *p. 258*

Bissell, Joseph (1868). Extracts from diary. *Yale College Courant*, 12 September, pp. 131–3.   C.

Blackader, John (1824). *The Life and Diary of Lieutenant Colonel J. Blackader*; ed. Crichton, Andrew; H. S. Baynes, Edinburgh.

Blundell, Nicholas (1968). The great diurnal of Nicholas Blundell. *The Record Society of Lancashire and Cheshire*, vol. 110; also (1970) vol. 112; (1972) vol. 114.   C.   *pp.* 72, 100, 124, 152, 155, 215, 216, 217, 226, 228, 237, 242, 243, 268

Bolling, William (1935). Diary. *The Virginia Magazine of History and Biography*, vol. 43, pp. 237–50, 330–42.

Also:

(1936) vol. 44, pp. 15–24, 120–8, 238–45, 323–34.

(1937) vol. 45, pp. 29–39.

(1938) vol. 46, pp. 44–51, 146–52, 234–9, 321–8.

(1939) vol. 47, pp. 27–31.   C.

Bonar, Andrew (1894). *Andrew A. Bonar. Diary and Letters*; ed. Bonar, Marjorie; Hodder & Stoughton, London.   C.   *pp.* 132, 133, 248, 254

Boscawen, Frances (1940). *Admiral's Wife*; ed. Aspinall-Oglander, Cecil; Longmans, Green, London.   C.   *pp.* 80, 118, 129, 133, 157–8, 173, 191, 199, 200, 233, 245, 267

Boscawen, Frances (1942). *Admiral's Widow*; ed. Aspinall-Oglander, Cecil; The Hogarth Press, London.   C.

Boswell, James (1928–34). *The Private Papers of James Boswell from Malahide Castle, in the Collection of Lt.-Colonel Ralph Heyward Isham*; eds. Scott, Geoffrey & Pottle, Frederick; printed privately, New York, 18 vols.   C.   *pp.* 75, 78, 79, 87, 105, 130, 139, 142, 158, 160, 162, 173, 191, 209–10, 217, 222, 245, 252–3, 254, 268

Bowen, Sarah (1942). Diary of four Bowen children in Bowen, Elizabeth: *Bowen's Court*; Longmans, Green, London, pp. 241–52.   C.   *pp.* 186, 259, 260

Bower, Anna (1903). *The Diaries and Correspondence of Anna Catherina Bower*; printed privately, London.   C.   *pp.* 193, 224

Bowers, Claude (1962). *My Life. The Memoirs of Claude Bowers*; Simon & Schuster, New York.   C.

Boyle, Richard (1886). Diaries of Sir Richard Boyle in Grosart, A.; ed.: *The Lismore Papers*, Chiswick Press, London, 1st series, vols. 1–5.   C.   *pp.* 97, 98, 204, 208, 240

Boynton, Lucien (1933). Selections from the journal of Lucien C. Boynton. *Proceedings of the American Antiquarian Society*, new series, vol. 43, pp. 329–80

Brabazon, Mary (1928). *The Diaries of Mary Countess of Meath*; ed. Brabazon, Reginald; Hutchinson, London.   C.   *pp.* 108, 185

Bradstreet, Simon (1854). Diary. *New England Historical and Genealogical Register*, vol. 8, pp. 325–33; also (1855) vol. 9, pp. 43–51, 78–9.

Braithwaite, Anna (1905). *Memoirs of Anna Braithwaite*; ed. Braithwaite, J. Bevan; Headley Brothers, London. C. *pp*. 137, 238

Briggins, Peter (1894). Peter Briggins' diary in Howard, Eliot, ed.: *The Eliot Papers*; John Bellows, Gloucester, no. 2, pp. 29–67. C. *pp*. 153, 243

Bright, John (1930). *Diaries*; ed. Walling, R.; Cassell, London. C. *pp*. 78, 182–3, 196

Brodie, Alexander (1746). *The Diary of Alexander Brodie*; ed. Laing, David; The Spalding Club, Aberdeen. C. *pp*. 100–1, 149, 151, 209, 249, 265

Brodie, James (1746). *The Diary of James Brodie*; ed. Laing, David; The Spalding Club, Aberdeen. C. *pp*. 249, 265

Browell, Mark (1915). Diary. *North Country Diaries*; Surtees Society, 2nd series, vol. 124, pp. 176–89. C. *p*. 135

Brown, Charlotte (1935). The journal of Charlotte Brown, Matron of the General Hospital with the English Forces in America in Calder, I. M.: *Colonial Captivities, Marches and Journeys*; Macmillan, New York, pp. 169–98. C.

Brown, Ford (1900). Madox Brown's diary in Rossetti, William: *Praeraphaelite Diaries and Letters*; Hurst & Blackett, London, pp. 61–202. C.

Brown, Mary (1905). *The Diary of a Girl in France*; ed. Shore, H. N.; John Murray, London. C. *p*. 195

Brown, Nicholas (1910). The diary of Nicholas Brown. *North Country Diaries*; Surtees Society, 2nd series, vol. 118, pp. 230–323. C.

Brown, William (1939). Diary in Loehr, Rodney: *Minnesota Farmers' Diaries*; The Minnesota Historical Society, Saint Paul, pp. 37–82.

Brown, William (1941). *My War Diary*; John McQueen & Son, Galashiels.

Browning, Orville (1925). Diary. *Collections of the Illinois State Historical Library*, vol. 20; also (1933) vol. 22.

Brownlow, William (1909). Diary in Cust, Elizabeth: *Records of the Cust Family*; Mitchell, Hughes & Clarke, London, pp. 120–4. C. *pp*. 134–5, 142

Buchanan, George (1932). *Passage through the Present*; Constable, London.

Budgett, Sarah (1840). *A Memoir of the Late Mrs. Sarah Budgett*; ed. Gaskin, John; Simpkin & Marshall, London. C.

Bulkeley, Robert (1937). The diary of Bulkeley of Dronwy. *Anglesey Antiquarian Society and Field Club Transactions*, pp. 26–168. C.

Bulkeley, William (1936). *Mr. Bulkeley and the Pirate*; ed. Roberts, B. D.; Oxford University Press, London. C. *pp*. 216, 242

Burney, Frances (1854). *Diary and Letters of Madame D'Arblay*; ed. Barrett, Charlotte; Hurst & Blackett, London, new edition, 6 vols. C. *pp*. 74, 165, 172, 173, 201, 210, 230, 233, 253, 268

Burr, Aaron (1903). *The Private Journal of Aaron Burr*; The Genesee Press, Rochester, New York. C.

Burritt, Elihu (1937). Diary in Curti, Merle: *The Learned Blacksmith*; Wilson-Erickson, New York, pp. 11–138.

Burroughs, John (1928). *The Heart of Burroughs's Journals*; ed. Barras, Clara; Houghton Mifflin, Boston & New York. C. *pp*. 108, 183–4, 206, 248

Bustard, John (1829?). *The Thoughtful Child. A Memoir of Mary Ann Bustard*; John Mason, London. C.

Bibliography and citation index

Butler, America (1940). Diary of Rogue River Valley. *Oregon Historical Quarterly*, vol. 41, pp. 337–66.

Butler, Elizabeth (1922). *An Autobiography*; Constable, London. C.

Byrd, William (1941). *The Secret Diary of William Byrd of Westover 1709–1712*; eds. Wright, Louis & Tinling, Marion; The Dietz Press, Virginia. C. *pp.* 78, 83, 99, 116, 125, 128, 133, 135, 151–2, 155, 156, 201, 204, 222, 224, 241, 268

Byrd, William (1942). *Another Secret Diary of William Byrd of Westover*; ed. Woodfin, M.; The Dietz Press, Virginia. C. *pp.* 100, 237, 241

Byrd, William (1958). *The London Diary*; eds. Wright, Louis & Tinling, Marion; Oxford University Press, New York. C. *p.* 79

Byrom, John (1854). *The Private Journal and Literary Remains of John Byrom*; ed. Parkinson, Richard; Chetham Society Publications, Manchester, vols. 32, 34, 40, 44. C. *pp.* 80, 100, 101, 115, 120, 136, 209, 249–50

Callender, Hannah (1888). Extracts from diary. *The Pennsylvania Magazine of History and Biography*, vol. 12, pp. 432–56.

Calverley, Walter (1886). Memorandum book of Sir Walter Calverley, Bart. *Yorkshire Diaries and Autobiographies; Surtees Society*, vol. 2. C. *pp.* 84, 205

Calvert, Frances (1911). *An Irish Beauty of the Regency*; ed. Blake, Mrs Warrenne; The Bodley Head, London. C. *pp.* 165, 192, 194, 206, 238, 246

Cambridge, George (1906). *George Duke of Cambridge. A Memoir of his Private Life*; ed. Sheppard, James; Longmans, Green, London. C.

Capper, Mary (1848). A memoir of Mary Capper. *The Friends' Library*, vol. 12, pp. 1–145. C. *p.* 170

Carlyle, Jane (1883). *Letters and Memorials of Jane Welsh Carlyle*; ed. Froude, James; Longmans, Green, London.

Carter, Landon (1905). Diary of Col. Landon Carter. *William & Mary College Quarterly Historical Magazine*, vol. 13, pp. 45–53, 157–64, 219–24.
Also:
(1906) vol. 14, pp. 38–44, 181–6, 246–53.
(1907) vol. 15, pp. 15–20, 63–9, 205–11.
(1908) vol. 16, pp. 149–56, 257–69.
(1909) vol. 17, pp. 9–18.
(1910) vol. 18, pp. 37–44. C. *pp.* 85–6, 104, 128

Cartwright, George (1911). *Captain Cartwright and his Labrador Journal*; ed. Townsend, Charles; Dana Estes, Boston.

Carvosso, William (1836). *A Memoir of Mr. William Carvosso*; ed. his son; John Mason, London. C. *pp.* 119, 253

Cavendish, Lucy (1927). *The Diary of Lady Frederick Cavendish*; ed. Bailey, John; John Murray, London. C. *p.* 183

Chace, Elizabeth (1937). Diary in Lovell, Malcolm, ed.: *Two Quaker Sisters from the Original Diaries of Elizabeth Buffum Chace and Lucy Buffum Lovell*; Liveright, New York, pp. 1–49, 110–83. C. *pp.* 133, 183, 196

Chamberlain, Benjamin (1935). Diary in Ellis, Isabel: *Records of Nineteenth-Century Leicester*; printed privately, pp. 183–92. C.

Chandler, Samuel (1901). Diary; ed. Mulliken, Sarah. *The Harvard Graduates' Magazine*, vol. 10, pp. 376–81, 529–35.

Chester, Caroline (1903). Diary in Vanderpoel, Emily: *Chronicles of a Pioneer School*; Cambridge University Press, Massachusetts, pp. 150–4. C. *p. 195*

Clegg, James (1899). *Extracts from the Diary of Rev. James Clegg*; ed. Kirke, Henry; Smith, Elder, London. C. *pp. 75, 154*

Clifford, Anne (1923). *The Diary of the Lady Anne Clifford*; ed. Sackville-West, Victoria; William Heinemann, London. C. *pp. 97, 99, 110–11, 124, 125, 128, 133, 137, 146–7, 148, 201, 204, 208, 222, 225–6, 228, 230, 268, 270*

Clubb, Stephen (1809). *Journal Containing an Account of the Wrongs, Sufferings and Neglect, Experienced by Americans in France*; no publisher, Boston.

Cobden-Sanderson, Thomas (1926). *The Journals of Thomas James Cobden-Sanderson*; Richard Cobden-Sanderson, London. C. *pp. 122, 123, 141, 175, 206, 225, 231, 247*

Coke, Mary (1889). *The Letters and Journals of Lady Mary Coke*; David Douglas, Edinburgh.

Cole, William (1931). *The Blecheley Diary of the Rev. William Cole*; ed. Stokes, Francis; Constable, London.

Collier, Mary (1944). *A Victorian Diarist*; ed. Collier, E. C. F.; John Murray, London. C. *p. 206*

Collins, John (1912). *Life and Memoirs of John Churton Collins*; ed. Collins, L. C.; The Bodley Head, London. C. *p. 179*

Colt, John (1936). *Young Colt's Diary*; ed. Terrott, C.; Grayson & Grayson, London. C. *pp. 186, 198*

Colt, Miriam (1862). *Went to Kansas*; L. Ingalls, Watertown. C. *pp. 107, 184, 206*

Compton, Thomas (1900). Diary. *The Essex Review*, vol. 9, pp. 33–7.

Condict, Jemima (1930). *Her Book, being the Diary of an Essex County Maid*; Catereret Book Club, Newark, New Jersey. C. *pp. 75, 168*

Constant, Silas (1903). *The Journal of the Reverend Silas Constant*; ed. Roebling, Emily; J. B. Lippincott, Philadelphia. C. *p. 128*

Cooke, Anne (1915). Diary. *Journal of the County Kildare Archaeological Society*, vol. 8, pp. 104–32, 205–19, 447–63. C. *p. 159*

Cooper, Anthony (1886). *The Life and Work of the 7th Earl of Shaftesbury*; ed. Hodder, Edwin; Cassell, London. C. *pp. 76, 87, 108, 182, 184, 196, 200, 211, 266*

Cooper, William (1876). Diary. *New England Historical and Genealogical Register*, vol. 30, pp. 435–41; also (1877) vol. 31, pp. 49–55. C. *pp. 135, 204, 216*

Cory, William (1897). *Extracts from the Letters & Journals of William Cory*; ed. Cornish, Francis; printed privately, Oxford.

Cowell, Emilie (1934). *The Cowells in America*; ed. Disher, M.; Oxford University Press, London. C. *pp. 139–40, 142*

Cowles, Julia (1931). *The Diaries of Julia Cowles*; ed. Moseley, Laura; Yale University Press, New Haven, Connecticut. C. *pp. 167, 255–6*

Cowper, Mary (1864). *Diary of Mary, Countess Cowper*; John Murray, London. C. *pp. 115, 124*

Crosfield, Thomas (1935). *The Diary of Thomas Crosfield*; ed. Boas, F. S.; Oxford University Press, London. C. *p. 150*

Cummings, Bruce (1920). *A Last Diary*; Chatto & Windus, London. C. *pp. 207, 208*

Bibliography and citation index

Cummings, Bruce (1923). *The Journal of a Disappointed Man*; Chatto & Windus, London. C. *pp.* 132, 207, 208

Cunningham, Alison (1926). *Cummy's Diary*; ed. Skinner, Robert; Chatto & Windus, London. C. *p.* 178

Cunningham, William (1887). The diary and general expenditure of William Cunningham; ed. Dodds, James; *Scottish History Society*, vol. 2. C.

Cutler, Benjamin (1865). Diary in Gray, Horatio: *Memoirs of the Rev. Benjamin C. Cutler, D.D.*; A. D. F. Randolph, New York, *passim*. C. *p.* 171

Cutler, Manasseh (1888). *The Life, Journals and Correspondence of Rev. Manasseh Cutler*; eds. Cutler, William & Julia; Robert Clarke, Cincinnati. C. *pp.* 104, 159

Dallas, George (1892). *Diary of George Mifflin Dallas*; ed. Dallas, Susan; J. B. Lippincott, Philadelphia. C.

Damer, Mary (1841). *Diary of a Tour in Greece*; Henry Colburn, London. C. *p.* 75

Danforth, Samuel (1880). Diary. *New England Historical and Genealogical Register*, vol. 34, pp. 85–9, 162–6, 297–301, 359–63. C. *pp.* 125, 128, 135

Darby, Abiah (1913). Extracts from the diary of Abiah Darby. *The Journal of the Friends' Historical Society*, vol. 10, pp. 79–92, 295. C. *pp.* 86, 131, 142

Darby, Hannah (1905). Diary in Greg, Emily, ed.: *Reynolds-Rathbone Diaries and Letters 1753–1839*; printed privately, London, pp. 13–19. C.

Dataller, Roger (1933). *A Pitman Looks at Oxford*; J. M. Dent & Sons, London.

Dawson, Henry (1891). *The Life of Henry Dawson*; ed. Dawson, Alfred; Seeley, London. C. *pp.* 123, 184, 221

Day, Robert (1938). *Mr. Justice Day of Kerry*; ed. Day, Ella; William Pollard, Exeter. C. *pp.* 161, 215

Day, Susanna (1909). Diary of Susanna Day. *The Essex Review*, vol. 18, pp. 151–6. C. *pp.* 84, 159

Dee, John (1841). The private diary of Dr. John Dee. *The Camden Society*, vol. 19. C. *pp.* 97, 98, 125, 128, 144, 148, 204, 208, 216, 217, 219, 222, 237, 240

Dexter, Samuel (1859). Diary. *New England Historical and Genealogical Register*, vol. 13, pp. 305–10; also (1860) vol. 14, pp. 35–40, 107, 112, 202–5. C. *p.* 86

Douglas, Sylvester (1928). *The Diaries of Sylvester Douglas*; ed. Bickley, Francis; Constable, London. C. *pp.* 82, 172, 246

Dow, Lorenzo (1848). *History of Cosmopolite*; Joshua Martin, Vancouver. C. *pp.* 142, 171

Dow, Margaret (1848). Journal in Dow, Lorenzo: *History of Cosmopolite*; Joshua Martin, Vancouver, pp. 607–709. C. *pp.* 142, 205, 215, 217

Drinker, Elizabeth (1889). *Extracts from the Journal of Elizabeth Drinker*; ed. Biddle, Henry; J. B. Lippincott, Philadelphia. C. *pp.* 75–6, 117, 238

Dudley, Dorothy (1876). Diary in G., A., ed.: *The Cambridge of 1776*; no publisher, Cambridge, pp. 18–88.

Duncan, Elizabeth (1928). Diary of Mrs. Joseph Duncan. *Journal of the Illinois State Historical Society*, vol. 21, pp. 1–91. C. *pp.* 121, 142, 177, 206, 224

Dungett, John (1833). *Memoir of Mr. John Dungett*; ed. Heaton, Joseph; John Mason, London. C.

Dymond, Mary (1857). *Memoir of Mary Dymond*; ed. Dymond, Henry; William & Frederick Cash, London. C.

Elliott, Grace (1859). *Journal of my Life during the French Revolution*; Richard Bentley, London. C.

Emerson, J. (1910–11). Diary. *Massachusetts Historical Society Proceedings*, vol. 44, pp. 262–82.

Epps, John (1875). *Diary of the Late John Epps*; ed. Epps, E.; Kent, London. C.   *pp.* 183, 196

Erskine, Ebenezer (1831). *The Life and Diary of Rev. Ebenezer Erskine*; ed. Fraser, Donald; William Oliphant, Edinburgh. C.   *pp.* 128, 136, 142, 153, 209, 249

Erskine, James (1843). *Extracts from the Diary of a Senator of the College of Justice*; ed. Maidment, J.; Thomas Stevenson, Edinburgh. C.   *pp.* 79–80, 100, 125, 136, 190, 191, 263

Esberger, Christian (1902). *Christian Frederick Esberger, his Relatives and his Journal*; ed. Goulding, R.; J. W. Goulding & Son, Louth.

Evans, Joshua (1837). Journal. *Friends' Miscellany*, vol. 10, pp. 43–212. C *p.* 160

Eve, Sarah (1881). Extracts from journal. *The Pennsylvania Magazine of History and Biography*, vol. 5, pp. 19–36, 191–205. C.   *pp.* 74, 160

Evelyn, John (1906). *Diary and Correspondence of John Evelyn*; ed. Wheatley, Henry; Bickers & Son, London, 2 vols. C.   *pp.* 100, 136, 137, 142, 150, 151, 188–90, 217, 243

Ewing, Alexander (1877). *Memoir of Alexander Ewing*; ed. Ross, Alexander; Daldy, Isbister, London. C.   *pp.* 81, 206

Eyre, Adam (1875). A dyurnall or catalogue of all my accions and expences. *Yorkshire Diaries and Autobiographies; Surtees Society*, vol. 65, pp. 1–118.

Fairfax, Sally (1904). Diary of a little colonial girl. *The Virginia Magazine of History and Biography*, vol. 11, pp. 212–14. C.   *pp.* 168, 255–6

Fenimore-Cooper, James (1922). Journal in Fenimore-Cooper, James, ed.: *Correspondence of James Fenimore-Cooper*; Yale University Press, New Haven, Connecticut, vol. 2, pp. 727–52. C.   *pp.* 117, 170, 264

Fithian, Philip (1900). *Journal and Letters*; ed. Williams, John; The University Library, Princeton, New Jersey. C.   *pp.* 160, 162

Fitzgerald, Edward (1904). Letters in Campbell, Gerald: *Edward and Pamela Fitzgerald*; Edward Arnold, London, *passim*. C.

Fitzgerald, Sophia (1904). The diary of Lady Sophia Fitzgerald in Campbell, Gerald: *Edward and Pamela Fitzgerald*; Edward Arnold, London, pp. 28–58. C.   *p.* 168

Fleming, Marjory (1934). *The Complete Marjory Fleming*; ed. Sidgwick, Frank; Sidgwick & Jackson, London. C.   *pp.* 75, 180, 258–9

Fletcher, Mary (1818). *The Life of Mrs. Mary Fletcher*; ed. Moore, Henry; Thomas Cordeux, London. C.   *pp.* 130, 161, 191, 192

Forman, Simon (1849). *The Autobiography and Personal Diary of Dr Simon Forman*; ed. Halliwell, J.; Richards, London. C.   *pp.* 87, 147, 149, 188, 240–1, 266

Fowler, Robert (1893). *Sir Robert N. Fowler. A Memoir*; ed. Flynn, John; Hodder & Stoughton, London. C.   *pp.* 181, 206

Bibliography and citation index

Fox, Eliza (1809). *Memoir of Mrs Eliza Fox*; ed. Fox, Franklin; N. Trubner, London. C. *pp.* 171, 266

Fox, Maria (1846). *Memoirs of Maria Fox*; ed. Fox, S.; Charles Gilpin, London. C. *pp.* 119, 130, 162, 172, 244–5, 253

Fox, Sarah (1874). Extracts from the diary of Sarah Fox. *The Friend*, new series, vol. 14, pp. 72–3. *p.* 86

Frankland, Charles (1865). *Sir Charles Henry Frankland*; ed. Nason, Elias; J. Munsell, New York, pp. 51–97. C.

Freke, Elizabeth (1913). *Her Diary*; ed. Carbery, Mary; Guy, Cork. C. *pp.* 87, 88, 115, 124, 126, 149, 151, 155, 216, 217, 235

Fretwell, James (1879). A family history. *Yorkshire Diaries and Autobiographies; Surtees Society*, vol. 65, pp. 163–245. C. *pp.* 127, 154, 190, 266

Frizzell, Lodisa (1915). *Across the Plains to California in 1852*; ed. Paltsits, Victor; New York Public Library. C.

Fry, Elizabeth (1853). *Life of Elizabeth Fry*; by Corder, Susanna; W. & F. G. Cash, London. C. *pp.* 74, 80, 105, 106, 119, 130, 131, 142, 163, 173, 233–4, 246, 252

Fuller, Timothy (1916). Extracts from diary. *The Publications of the Cambridge Historical Society*, vol. 11, pp. 33–53. C.

Furse, Robert (1894). Diary. *Reports and Transactions of the Devonshire Association for the Advancement of Science, Literature and Art*, vol. 26, pp. 168–84. C.

Gale, Walter (1857). Extracts from journal. *Sussex Archaeological Collections*, vol. 9, pp. 182–207.

Gallatin, James (1914). *A Great Peace Maker*; William Heinemann, London. C. *p.* 129

Gardiner, Thomas (1894). Extracts from a memorandum book in Daniell, J. J.: *The History of Chippenham*; Houlston & Sons, London, pp. 189–92.

Gardner, Samuel (1913). Diary for the year 1759. *Essex Institute Historical Collections*, vol. 49, pp. 1–22. C.

Gaskell, Elizabeth (1923). *My Diary*; printed privately, London. C. *pp.* 75, 122, 123, 132, 133, 175–6, 185, 206, 225, 226, 247, 248

Gaskell, James (1883). *Records of an Eton Schoolboy*; ed. Gaskell, Charles; printed privately, London. C. *p.* 195

Gilmor, Robert (1922). Diary. *Maryland Historical Magazine*, vol. 17, pp. 231–68, 319–47.

Gilpin, Mary (1841). *Memoir of Mary Ann Gilpin*; Edmund Fry, London. C. *p.* 181

Gisborne, John (1852). *A Brief Memoir of the Life of John Gisborne Esq.*; Whittaker, London. C. *pp.* 246, 252

Gladstone, Mary (1930). *Her Diaries and Letters*; ed. Masterman, Lucy; Methuen, London. C. *pp.* 82, 181, 206

Goddard, Lucy (1930). The diary of Mrs Lucy Goddard in Bell, Eva, ed.: *The Hamwood Papers*; Macmillan, London, *passim*.

Goff, Elizabeth (1918). The Goff letters. *The Journal of the Friends' Historical Society*, vol. 15, pp. 69–86, 129–37. C. *pp.* 128–9, 130, 141, 217

Gordon, James (1903). Journal of Col. James Gordon. *William & Mary College*

Quarterly Historical Magazine, vol. 11, pp. 98–112, 217–36; also (1904) vol. 12, pp. 1–12.   C.   *p.* 129

Grant, Elizabeth (1911). *Memoirs of a Highland Lady*; ed. Lady Strachey; John Murray, London.   C.   *pp.* 87, 130, 133, 169, 171, 172, 200, 266

Gray, Faith (1927). Faith Gray and her diaries in Gray, E.: *Papers and Diaries of a York Family*; The Sheldon Press, London, pp. 20–226.   C.   *pp.* 131, 142, 220, 234, 253–4

Gray, Jonathan (1927). Jonathan Gray in Gray, E.: *Papers and Diaries of a York Family*; The Sheldon Press, London, pp. 121–96.   C.

Green, Joseph (1866). Diary of Rev. Joseph Green of Salem Village. *Essex Institute Historical Collections*, vol. 8, pp. 215–24; also (1869) vol. 10, pp. 73–104; (1900) vol. 36, pp. 325–30.   C.   *pp.* 99, 100, 114, 221, 237, 241

Greene, William (1920–1). Diary. *Massachusetts Historical Society Proceedings*, vol. 54, pp. 84–138.

Gregory, Isabella (1946). *Lady Gregory's Journals 1916–1930*; ed. Robinson, Lennox; Putnam, London & Dublin.   C.

Griffith, John (1779). *A Journal of the Life, Travels, and Labours in the Work of the Ministry of John Griffith*; James Phillips, London.   C.   *pp.* 116, 161

Guest, Charlotte (later Schreiber) (1950). *Lady Charlotte Guest. Extracts from her Journal*; ed. Earl of Bessborough; John Murray, London.   C.   *pp.* 79, 197

Gurney, Isobel (1935). *Isobel, Mrs. Gurney*; ed. Gurney, S.; Jarrold & Sons, Norwich.   C.   *pp.* 80–1, 108, 122, 185, 187, 247, 249

Guthrie, Abelard (1899). Extracts from journal in Connelley, William, ed.: *The Provisional Government of Nebraska Territory*; The Nebraska State Historical Society, Lincoln, Nebraska, pp. 116–52.   C.   *p.* 247

Hadley, James (1951). *Diary of James Hadley*; ed. Moseley, Laura; Yale University Press, New Haven, Connecticut.   C.

Hagger, Mary (1843). Memoranda. *The Friends' Library*, vol. 7, pp. 432–61.   C.

Hamilton, Mary (1925). *At Court and at Home*; eds. Anson, E. & F.; John Murray, London.   C.   *pp.* 162, 168

Hammond, Lawrence (1891–2). Diary. *Massachusetts Historical Society Proceedings*, 2nd series, vol. 7, pp. 144–72.   C.   *p.* 242

Hanover, Victoria (1868). *Leaves from the Journal of our Life in the Highlands*; ed. Helps, Arthur; Smith, Elder, London.   C.

Hanover, Victoria (1884). *More Leaves from the Journal of a Life in the Highlands*; Smith, Elder, London.   C.

Hanover, Victoria (1912). *The Girlhood of Queen Victoria*; ed. Esher, Viscount; John Murray, London.   C.   *pp.* 132, 179

Hanover, Victoria (1964). *Queen Victoria: Dearest Child*; ed. Fulford, Roger; Evans Brothers, London.   C.   *pp.* 108–9, 122, 178, 185, 207, 208

Hardy, Louisa (1935). *Nelson's Hardy and his Wife*; ed. Gore, John; John Murray, London.   C.   *pp.* 166, 192, 194

Hare, Augustus (1952). *The Years with Mother*; ed. Barnes, Malcolm; George Allen & Unwin, London.   C.   *pp.* 87, 133, 176, 182, 185, 196, 200, 266

Harker, Mary (1935). Journal of a Quaker maid. *The Virginia Quarterly Review*, vol. 11, pp. 61–81.   C.   *p.* 181

Bibliography and citation index

Harrower, John (1901). Diary. *The American Historical Review*, vol. 6, pp. 65–101. C.   *pp.* 191, 194, 237

Hay, Andrew (1901). The diary of Andrew Hay; ed. Reid, Alexander; *Scottish History Society*, vol. 39. C.   *pp.* 215, 224

Hayes, Rutherford (1922–6). *Diary and Letters of Rutherford B. Hayes*; ed. Williams, Charles; Ohio State Archaeological and Historical Society. C.   *pp.* 107, 121, 123, 139, 173, 179, 206, 238, 247

Hazard, Thomas (1893). *College Tom*; ed. Hazard, Caroline; Cambridge University Press, Boston. C.

Hazard, Thomas (1930). *Nailer Tom's Diary*; The Merrymount Press, London. C.   *pp.* 137, 220

Head, Caroline (1905). Diary of Caroline Head in Hanbury, Charlotte (1911): *Life of Mrs. Albert Head*; Marshall Brothers, London, pp. 42–160. C.   *pp.* 228, 239

Hervey, John (1894). *The Diary of John Hervey*; Ernest Jackson, Wells. C.   *pp.* 135, 137, 205, 217

Heywood, Oliver (1882). *The Rev. Oliver Heywood. His Autobiography, Diaries, Anecdote and Event Book*; ed. Turner, J. Horsfall; T. Harrison, Bingley, 4 vols. C.   *pp.* 101, 115, 150, 151, 156, 199, 201, 237–8, 242, 249, 251

Hickey, William (1950). *Memoirs of William Hickey*; ed. Spencer, Alfred; Hurst & Blackett, London.

Hicks, Elias (1832). *Journal of the Life and Religious Labours of Elias Hicks*; Isaac Hopper, New York. C.   *pp.* 84, 106, 107, 159

Hillard, Harriet (1900). *My Mother's Journal*; ed. Hillard, Katharine; George H. Ellis, Boston. C.

Hiltzheimer, Jacob (1893). *Extracts from the Diary of Jacob Hiltzheimer*; ed. Parsons, Jacob; Wm. F. Fell, Philadelphia. C.   *p.* 128

Hoby, Margaret (1930). *The Diary of Lady Margaret Hoby*; ed. Meads, Dorothy; George Routledge & Sons, London.

Hochberg, Margaret (1950). *The Private Diaries of Daisy Princess of Pless*; ed. Chapman-Huston, D.; John Murray, London. C.   *pp.* 132, 185, 187

Hoffman, Virginia (1859). Diary in Cummins, George: *Life of Mrs. Virginia Hale Hoffman*; Lindsay & Blakiston, Philadelphia, pp. 31–161, *passim*. C.   *p.* 206

Holland, Elizabeth (1908). *The Journal of Elizabeth, Lady Holland*; ed. Earl of Ilchester; Longmans, Green, London, 2 vols. C.   *pp.* 79, 171, 172, 192–3, 194, 216, 217

Holyoke, Edward (1911). Diary in Dow, George, ed.: *The Holyoke Diaries*; The Essex Institute, Massachusetts, pp. 1–30. C.   *pp.* 204, 242, 264

Holyoke, John (1911). Diary in Dow, George, ed.: *The Holyoke Diaries*; The Essex Institute, Massachusetts, pp. 44–6. C.   *pp.* 160, 264

Holyoke, Mary (1911). Diary in Dow, George, ed.: *The Holyoke Diaries*; The Essex Institute, Massachusetts, pp. 47–138. C.   *p.* 137

Holyoke, Susanna (1911). Diary in Dow, George, ed.: *The Holyoke Diaries*; The Essex Institute, Massachusetts, pp. 175–204. C.   *p.* 137

Hooke, Robert (1935). *The Diary of Robert Hooke*; eds. Robinson, Henry & Adams, Walter; Taylor & Francis, London.

306

Hope, Thomas (1843). *A Diary of the Public Correspondence of Sir Thomas Hope 1635–45*; Bannatyne Club, Edinburgh. C.   *pp.* 97, 98, 125, 146, 148–9, 201, 204

Hopkins, Louisa (1882). Diary in Prentiss, George: *The Life and Letters of Elizabeth Prentiss*; Hodder & Stoughton, London, pp. 203–6, 541–55. C.   *p.* 254

Horler, Sydney (1933). *Excitement. An Impudent Autobiography*; Hutchinson, London. C.   *pp.* 187, 198

Horler, Sydney (1934). *Strictly Personal*; Hutchinson, London.

Housman, Mrs (1744). *The Power and Pleasure of the Divine Life*; ed. Pearsall, Richard; J. Oswald, London. C.   *pp.* 101–2, 115, 126, 128, 136, 153, 199, 205, 249, 251, 252

Howe, Samuel (1906). *Letters and Journals of Samuel Gridley Howe*; ed. Richards, Laura; Dana Estes, Boston. C.   *pp.* 121, 131, 184, 194–5, 206, 230, 264

Hull, Henry (1840). Life of Henry Hull. *The Friends' Library*, vol. 4, pp. 236–325. C.   *pp.* 117, 124, 170

Hume, David (1843). *Domestic Details*; Thomas G. Stevenson, Edinburgh. C.   *p.* 151

Huntington, Charles (1924). Diary. *Proceedings of the Massachusetts Historical Society*, pp. 244–69.

Huntington, Susan (1828). *Memoirs of the Late Mrs. S. Huntington*; ed. Wisner, B.; William Collins, Glasgow, 2nd edition. C.   *pp.* 104, 116–17, 120, 129, 131, 138, 141, 162–3, 205, 215, 216, 238, 245, 246, 252

Hutchinson, Arthur (1935). *A Year that the Locust—*; Ivor Nicholson & Watson, London. C.   *pp.* 76, 185–6, 187, 201, 248

Hutchinson, Thomas (1883). *Diary and Letters of His Excellency Thomas Hutchinson Esq.*; ed. Hutchinson, Peter; Sampson, Law, Marston, Searle & Rivington, London.

Hyde, Henry (1828). *The Correspondence of Henry Hyde, Earl of Clarendon and of his Brother Laurence Hyde, Earl of Rochester, with their Diaries*; ed. Singer, Samuel; Henry Colburn, London, vol. 11, pp. 141–332. C.

Isham, Justinian (1907). The diaries of Sir Justinian Isham. *Transactions of the Royal Historical Society*, 3rd series, vol. 1, pp. 181–205. C.   *pp.* 154, 155

Jackson, James (1921). Diary. *Transactions of the Cumberland and Westmorland Antiquarian and Archaeological Society*, new series, vol. 21, pp. 96–129. C.

Jackson, Mitchell (1939). Diary in Loehr, Rodney: *Minnesota Farmers' Diaries*, The Minnesota Historical Society, Saint Paul, pp. 83–220. C.   *p.* 183

Jefferay, William (1889). *Journal of William Jefferay, Gentleman. A Diary that might have been*; ed. Austin, John; R. L. Freeman & Sons, Providence. C. *pp.* 97, 98, 99, 124–5, 144–6, 148, 149, 199, 204, 208, 237, 268

Jesup, Maria (1940?). *Extracts from the Memoranda and Letters of Maria Jesup*; printed privately, York. C.   *p.* 168

Jeune, Margaret (1932). *Pages from the Diary of an Oxford Lady*; ed. Gifford, Margaret; The Shakespeare Head Press, Oxford. C.   *p.* 248

Johns, James (1936). Diary. *Proceedings of the Vermont Historical Society*, new series, vol. 4.

Johnston, Archibald (1896). Diary of Sir Archibald Johnston. *Publications of the Scottish History Society*, vol. 26, pp. 34–98; also (1911) vol. 61. C.

Bibliography and citation index

Johnston, Priscilla (1862). *Extracts from Priscilla Johnston's Journal*; ed. MacInnes, E.; Charles Thurnam & Sons, Carlisle. C. *pp.* 77, 109, 132, 176–7, 181, 211, 248, 255, 268

Jones, William (1929). *The Diary of the Revd. William Jones*; ed. Christie, O. F.; Brentano's, London. C. *pp.* 73, 76, 80, 104–5, 107, 118, 131, 138, 142, 166, 193, 194

Josselin, Ralph (1908). The diary of the Rev. Ralph Josselin. *Camden Society*, 3rd series, vol. 15. C. *pp.* 100, 101, 103, 111, 136–7, 142, 149–50, 151, 190, 199, 201, 205, 209, 213, 219–20, 221, 222, 224, 243, 249, 263

Judson, Emily (1861). Diary in Kendrick, A. C.: *The Life of Mrs. Emily C. Judson*; Thomas Nelson & Sons, London, pp. 16–30, 231–4, 299–307. C. *pp.* 121, 123, 133, 173, 184, 206

Kay, Richard (1968). *The Diary of Richard Kay*; Chetham Society publications, Manchester, 3rd series, vol. 16.

Kemper, Jackson (1898). Journal of an Episcopalian missionary's tour to Green Bay 1834. *Collections of the State Historical Society of Wisconsin*, vol. 14, pp. 394–449. C.

Kilham, Hannah (1837). *Memoir of the Late Hannah Kilham*; ed. Biller, Sarah; Darton Harvey, London. C. *pp.* 131, 142

King-Hall, Stephen (1936). *Sea-Saga*; ed. King-Hall, L.; Victor Gollancz, London. C. *pp.* 186, 198

Kingsford, Anna (1913). *Her Life, Letters, Diary and Work*; ed. Maitland, Edward; John M. Watkins, London. C. *pp.* 184, 248

Kitto, John (1856). *Memoirs of Dr. John Kitto*; ed. Ryland, J. E.; William Oliphant & Sons, Edinburgh. C. *pp.* 122, 133, 230, 247

Knight, Sarah (1825). *The Journal of Madam Knight*; Wilder & Campbell, New York. C. *pp.* 100, 107

Knightley, Louisa (1915). *The Journals of Lady Knightley of Fawsley*; ed. Cartwright, Julia; John Murray, London. C. *pp.* 177, 258, 266

Knox, Jane (1909). *Memoirs of a Vanished Generation*; ed. Blake, Mrs Warrene; The Bodley Head, London. C. *p.* 170

Lake, Edward (1847). Diary. *Camden Miscellany*; Camden Society, vol. 1, pp. 5–31.

Landreth, James (1921). *A Grampian Diary*; Alexander Gardner, Paisley.

Lawrence, Amos (1888). Diary in Lawrence, William: *Life of Amos Lawrence*; Houghton Mifflin, Boston & New York, pp. 50–273, *passim*. C. *pp.* 107–8, 121, 184, 195–6, 206, 210–11

Lee, John (1877). *Life and Confessions*; Bryan Brand, St Louis. C. *p.* 139

van Lennep, Mary (1851). Diary in Hawes, Louisa: *Memoir of Mrs. Mary E. van Lennep*; Wm. Jas. Hamersley, Hartford, pp. 84–323. C. *pp.* 182, 184

Lettsom, John (1933). *His Life, Times, Friends and Descendants*; ed. Abraham, James; William Heinemann, London. C. *pp.* 138, 159, 161, 172

Lewis, Jane (1903). Diary in Vanderpoel, Emily: *Chronicles of a Pioneer School*; Cambridge University Press, Massachusetts, pp. 230–4. C.

Lieber, Francis (1882). *The Life and Letters of Francis Lieber*; ed. Perry, Thomas; James R. Osgood, Boston. C. *pp.* 179, 206

Long, John (1923). *America of Yesterday*; ed. Mayo, Lawrence; The Atlantic Monthly Press, Boston. C. *pp.* 181, 195, 257–8

Longfellow, Henry (1886). *Life of Henry Wadsworth Longfellow*; ed. Longfellow, Samuel; Ticknor, Boston. C. *pp.* 107, 173, 206, 238–9

Lovell, Lucy (1937). Diary in Lovell, Malcolm, ed.: *Two Quaker Sisters from the Original Diaries of Elizabeth Buffum Chace and Lucy Buffum Lovell*; Liveright, New York, pp. 49–110. C. *pp.* 108, 110, 121, 139, 173–4, 185, 199, 200, 201, 206, 220–1, 222, 224, 226–8, 230–1, 247–8, 254–5, 270

Lowe, Roger (1938). *The Diary of Roger Lowe*; ed. Sachse, William; Longmans, Green, London. C. *p.* 216

Lowry, Jean (1760). *A Journal of the Captivity of Jean Lowry*; no publisher, Philadelphia. C. *p.* 104

Lucas, F. L. (1939). *Journal under the Terror*; Cassell, London.

Lucas, William (1934). *A Quaker Journal*; eds. Bryant, G. E. & Baker, G. P.; Hutchinson, London. C. *pp.* 109–10, 123, 176, 196–7

Luttig (1920). *Luttig's Journal of a Fur Trading Expedition on the Upper Missouri*; ed. Drum, Sheila; Missouri Historical Society, St Louis.

Luttrell, Narcissus (1857). *A Brief Historical Relation of State Affairs*; Oxford University Press, London.

Lyman, Simeon (1899). Journal. *Collections of the Connecticut Historical Society*, vol. 7, pp. 111–34.

Lynde, Benjamin (1880). *The Diaries of Benjamin Lynde and Benjamin Lynde Jr*; ed. Oliver, Fitch; printed privately, Boston. C. *pp.* 205, 264

Lyon, George (1824). *The Private Journal of Captain G. F. Lyon*; John Murray, London.

MacKenna, Stephen (1936). *Journal and Letters of Stephen MacKenna*; ed. Dodds, E.; Constable, London.

Machyn, Henry (1848). Diary. *The Camden Society*, London, vol. 42. C. *pp.* 144, 148, 156

Macready, William (1912). *The Diaries of William Charles Macready*; ed. Toynbee, William; Chapman & Hall, London, 2 vols. C. *pp.* 81, 105, 118, 131, 138, 142, 164, 238, 245

Magoffin, Susan (1926). *Down the Santa Fe Trail and into Mexico*; ed. Drumm, Stella; Yale University Press, New Haven, Connecticut. C.

Mansfield, Katherine (1927). *Journal of Katherine Mansfield*; ed. Murry, J. Middleton; Constable, London. C.

Mantell, Gideon (1940). *The Journal of Gideon Mantell*; ed. Curwen, E. Cecil; Oxford University Press, London. C. *pp.* 82, 118, 246

Martindale, Adam (1845). *The Life of Adam Martindale*; ed. Parkinson, Richard; Chetham Society Publications, Manchester, vol. 4. C. *pp.* 78, 101, 103, 150, 151, 190, 205, 209, 263, 267

Mascall, Elizabeth (1902). *Elizabeth Mascall. Remnants of a Life*; ed. Matthews, A. Weight; printed privately, London. C. *pp.* 105, 107, 118, 129, 130, 159, 252, 254

Mather, Cotton (1911). Diary. *Massachusetts Historical Society Collections*, 7th series, vol. 7; also (1912) 7th series, vol. 8. C. *pp.* 83, 99–100, 102, 103, 114, 116, 126, 128, 135–6, 137, 141, 142, 152–3, 155, 156, 163, 199, 201, 204, 205, 209, 217, 234, 236, 241–2, 247, 250, 251, 264, 267

Mather, Increase (1899). Diary. *Massachusetts Historical Society Proceedings*, 2nd series, vol. 13, pp. 340–74, 398–411.   C.   *pp.* 84, 125–6, 128

May, Anna (1941). *Journal of Anna May*; ed. Robinson, George; printed privately, Cambridge, Massachusetts.   C.   *pp.* 74, 132, 181

May, John (1873). Journal and letters of Col. John May of Boston; ed. Darlington, W.; *The Historical and Philosophical Society of Ohio*; new series, vol. 1.   C.   *pp.* 159–60

Mildmay, Elsie (1900?). *Elsie: a Naughty Little Girl*; printed privately, London (?).   C.   *p.* 187

Mildmay, Grace (1911). The journal of Lady Mildmay. *The Quarterly Review*, vol. 215, pp. 119–38.   C.   *pp.* 98, 99, 113, 124, 147–8, 149, 200, 208, 249

Mildmay, Humphrey (1947). *Sir Humphrey Mildmay: Royalist Gentleman*; ed. Ralph, Philip; Rutgers University Press, New Brunswick.   C.   *pp.* 97, 98, 125, 141, 146, 148, 201, 208, 240

Mill, John (1889). The diary of the Reverend John Mill. *Publications of the Scottish History Society*, vol. 5.   C.   *pp.* 76, 82, 160, 291 n. 5

Mills, William (1912). Notes from the account books of William Mills in Clarke, George: *History of Needham, Massachusetts*; Cambridge University Press, USA, pp. 49–51.   C.

Mitchell, Elisha (1905). *Diary of a Geological Tour*; ed. Battle, Kemp; University of North Carolina Press, Chapel Hill.   C.   *pp.* 117, 244

Mkeevor, Thomas (1819). A voyage to Hudson's Bay. *New Voyages and Travels*, vol. 11, pp. 1–76.

Moore, Giles (1848). Extracts from the journal and account book. *Sussex Archaeological Collections*, vol. 1, pp. 65–127.   C.

Moore, Thomas (1853). *Memoirs, Journal, and Correspondence of Thomas Moore*; ed. Russell, Lord John; Longman, Brown, Green & Longmans, London, 6 vols.   C.   *pp.* 118, 138, 171, 172, 192, 194, 214, 216, 217, 221, 226, 230, 246, 267

Morris, Claver (1934). *The Diary of a West Country Physician*; ed. Hobhouse, Edmund; Stanhope Press, Rochester.   C.   *pp.* 79, 101, 152, 153, 155, 156, 190, 191, 216, 242–3, 244, 263

Morris, Gouverneur (1939). *A Diary of the French Revolution*; ed. Davenport, Beatrice; George C. Harrap, London & Sydney.

Morris, Robert (1940). An American in London. *The Pennsylvania Magazine of History and Biography*, vol. 64, pp. 164–217, 356–406.

Morse, Abner (1940). Diary. *The Wisconsin Magazine of History*, vol. 23, pp. 62–88.   C.

Morton, Robert (1877). Diary. *The Pennsylvania Magazine of History and Biography*, vol. 1, pp. 1–39.   C.

Motte, Jacob (1940). *Charleston goes to Harvard*; ed. Cole, Arthur; Harvard University Press, Cambridge, Massachusetts.   C.

Müller, George (1905). *Autobiography of George Müller*; ed. Bergin, G. F.; J. Nisbet, London.   C.   *p.* 183

Neville, Sylas (1950). *The Diary of Sylas Neville*; ed. Cozens-Hardy, Basil; Oxford University Press, London.

Newbolt, Francis (1904). *The Diary of a Fag*; F. E. Robinson, London.   C.   *p.* 198

Newbolt, Francis (1927). *The Diary of a Praeposter*; Philip Allan, London. C. *p.* 198

Newcome, Henry (1852). *The Autobiography of Henry Newcome*; ed. Parkinson, Richard; Chetham Society Publications, Manchester, vol. 1. C. *pp.* 88, 100, 101, 107, 115, 124, 126, 131, 149, 155, 201, 205, 215, 216, 238, 243, 249, 265

Newdigate-Newdegate, Richard (1901). *Cavalier and Puritan*; ed. Lady Newdigate-Newdegate; Smith, Elder, London. C. *pp.* 101, 149, 151, 155

Newell, Timothy (1852). Diary. *Massachusetts Historical Society Collections*, 4th series, vol. 1, pp. 261–76. *p.* 83

Newton, Benjamin (1933). *The Diary of Benjamin Newton*; eds. Fendal, C. P. & Crutchley, E. A.; Cambridge University Press. C. *p.* 74

Newton, Samuel (1890). *The Diary of Samuel Newton*; ed. Foster, J. E.; Cambridge Antiquarian Society, Cambridge. C. *pp.* 135, 216

Norwood, Richard (1945). *The Journal of Richard Norwood*; eds. Craven, Wesley & Hayward, Walter; Scholars Facsimiles and Reprints, New York. C. *pp.* 148, 149, 188, 200, 266

O'Connell, Daniel (1906). *His Early Life, and Journal*; ed. Houston, Arthur; Sir Isaac Pitman & Sons, London. C. *p.* 194

Ogden, Eliza (1903). Diary in Vanderpoel, Emily: *Chronicles of a Pioneer School*; Cambridge University Press, Massachusetts, pp. 160–76. C.

Oglander, John (1888). Diary in Long, W. H.: *The Oglander Memoirs*; Reeves & Turner, London, *passim*. C. *pp.* 97, 98, 125

Opie, Amelia (1854). *Memorials of the Life of Amelia Opie*; ed. Brightwell, Cecilia; Fletcher & Alexander, Norwich. C. *p.* 170

Orr, Lucinda (1871). *Journal of a Young Lady of Virginia*; ed. Mason, Emily; John Murphy, Baltimore. C. *p.* 75

O'Sullivan, Humphrey (1936–7). Diary. *Irish Texts Society*, vols. 30, 31, 32, 33.

Otey, James (1898). Diary in Hotchkin, S. F.: *Memoir of Bishop Otey*; printed privately; Bustleton, Philadelphia, *passim*. C.

Owen, Caroline (1894). Diary in Owen, Richard: *The Life of Richard Owen*; John Murray, London, *passim*. C. *pp.* 179, 206

Owen, William (1906). Diary. *Indiana Historical Society Publications*, vol. 4, pp. 1–134.

Owenson, Sydney (1863). *Lady Morgan's Memoirs*; ed. Dixon, W. Hepworth; W. H. Allen, London. C. *pp.* 76, 172, 194

Palgrave, Francis (1899). *Francis Turner Palgrave. His Journals and Memories of His Life*; ed. Palgrave, Gwenllian; Longmans, Green, London. C. *pp.* 122, 178, 184, 248

Palmer, Ann (1839). *Extracts from the Diary of Ann Palmer*; ed. Richards, G. P.; Simmons, London. C. *p.* 132

Parker, Ellen (1915). Journal. *Collections of the New Hampshire Historical Society*, vol. 11, pp. 132–62. C.

Parker, James (1915). Diary of James Parker. *New England Historical and Genealogical Register*, vol. 69, pp. 8–17, 117–27, 211–24, 294–308; also (1916) vol. 70, pp. 9–24, 137–46, 210–20, 294–308. C. *p.* 128

Parkman, Anna (1899). Diary in Parkman, Ebenezer: *The Diary of Rev. Ebenezer*

Parkman; ed. Forbes, Harriette; The Westborough Historical Society, Massachusetts, pp. 60–2. C. *p. 265*

Parkman, Ebenezer (1899). *The Diary of Rev. Ebenezer Parkman*; ed. Forbes, Harriette; The Westborough Historical Society, Massachusetts. C. *pp. 104, 128, 265*

Parsons, Moses (1904). Diary in Ewell, John: *The Story of Byfield*; George E. Littlefield, Boston, pp. 101–58. C.

Pearson, Jane (1818). *Sketches of Piety in the Life and Religious Experiences of Jane Pearson*; Wm. Alexander, York. C. *p. 234*

Pease, Edward (1907). *The Diaries of Edward Pease*; ed. Pease, Alfred; Headley Brothers, London. C.

Pemberton, John (1842). Life of John Pemberton; eds. Evans, William & Evans, Thomas; *The Friends' Library*, vol. 6. C. *pp. 83, 251*

Penry, John (1944). The notebook of John Penry. *Camden Society*, 3rd series, vol. 67. C. *pp. 146, 151, 204*

Pepys, Samuel (1942). *The Diary of Samuel Pepys*; ed. Wheatley, Henry; Limited Editions Club, New York.

Peter, John (1934). Diary. *The Mississippi Valley Historical Review*, vol. 21, pp. 529–42.

Phelps, Caroline (1930). Diary. *Journal of the Illinois State Historical Society*, vol. 23, pp. 209–39. C. *pp. 75, 213, 214, 239*

Phelps, Elizabeth (1891). A diary of long ago in Huntington, Arria: *Under a Colonial Roof-tree*; Houghton Mifflin, Boston. C. *pp. 160, 206*

Philips, Martin (1909). Diary of a Mississippi planter. *Publications of the Mississippi Historical Society*, vol. 10, pp. 305–481. C. *p. 182*

Pike, John (1875–6). Diary. *Massachusetts Historical Society Proceedings*, 1st series, vol. 14, pp. 121–50. C. *pp. 125, 128, 135*

Polk, James (1910). *The Diary of James K. Polk*; ed. Quaife, Milo; A. C. McClurg, Chicago.

Pollen, John (1912). *John Hungerford Pollen*; ed. Pollen, Anne; John Murray, London. C. *pp. 184, 197, 264*

Post, Frederic (1838). *Extracts from the Diary of the Late Frederic James Post*; printed privately, London. C. *pp. 75, 77, 259*

Powell, Walter (1907). *The Diary of Walter Powell*; ed. Bradney, J.; John Wright, Bristol. C. *pp. 75, 97, 98, 125, 128, 134, 146, 148, 204, 208, 240, 244*

Powys, Caroline (1899). *Passages from the Diaries of Mrs. Philip Lybbe Powys*; ed. Climenson, Emily; Longmans, Green, London. C. *pp. 84, 157, 162*

Powys, Llewelyn (1936). Diary in Marlow, Louis: *Welsh Ambassadors*; Chapman & Hall, London, pp. 212–40. C. *p. 132*

Powys, Theodore (1936). Diary and letters in Marlow, Louis: *Welsh Ambassadors*; Chapman & Hall, London, pp. 160–210. C. *pp. 108, 109, 111, 122, 247*

Prentiss, Elizabeth (1882). Extracts from journal in Prentiss, George (1882): *The Life and Letters of Elizabeth Prentiss*; Hodder & Stoughton, London, *passim*. C. *pp. 80, 108, 121, 131, 177, 206, 221, 224–5, 231, 234*

Preston, John (1871). Extracts from the diary of Lieut. John Preston, of Salem Village. *Essex Institute Historical Collections*, vol. 11, pp. 256–62; also (1902)

Diary. *New England Historical and Genealogical Register*, vol. 56, pp. 80–3. C. *p. 137*

Pringle, Walter (1751). *Memoirs of Walter Pringle of Greenknow*; William Hamilton, Edinburgh. C. *pp.* 102, 115, 127, 150–1, 238

Procter, Jonathan (1934). Diary kept at Louisburg, 1759–60 by Jonathan Procter. *Essex Institute Historical Collections*, vol. 70, pp. 31–57. C.

R., I (1887). *A Lady's Ranche Life in Montana*; W. H. Allen, London.

Ramés, Marie (1911). Marie Louise Ramés' journal in Huntington, Henry: *Memories, Personages, Peoples, Places*; Constable, London, pp. 228–96. C. *p. 258*

Raper, Elizabeth (1924). *The Receipt Book of Elizabeth Raper*; The Nonesuch Press, London. C.

Rathbone, Hannah (1905). Diary in Greg, Emily, ed.: *Reynolds-Rathbone Diaries and Letters 1753–1839*; printed privately, London, pp. 19–150. C. *pp.* 82, 105, 131, 164, 220, 221, 224, 230

Reynolds, Deborah (1905). Diary and letters in Greg, Emily, ed.: *Reynolds-Rathbone Diaries and Letters 1753–1839*; printed privately, London, pp. 154–70. C. *pp.* 166, 238

Rich, Mary (1848). The autobiography of Mary, Countess of Warwick. *The Percy Society*, vol. 22. C. *pp.* 83, 102, 115, 124, 127, 133, 151, 155, 205, 208, 266

Richards, Caroline (1913). *Village Life in America*; Henry Holt, New York. C. *pp.* 132–3, 179–80, 195, 258

Richards, John (1853). Extracts from diary. *The Retrospective Review*, vol. 1, pp. 97–101, 201–5, 408–16. C. *pp.* 152, 155, 156, 238

Ridpath, George (1922). The diary of George Ridpath. *Publications of the Scottish History Society*, 3rd series, vol. 2. C.

Robertson, Powhattan (1931). Diary. *William & Mary College Quarterly Historical Magazine*, 2nd series, vol. 11, pp. 61–8. C. *p. 193*

Robinson, Henry (1872). *The Diary, Reminiscences, and Correspondence of Henry Crabb Robinson*; ed. Sadler, Thomas; Macmillan, London, 2 vols. C. *pp.* 169–70, 194

Robson, William (1922). Journal. *The Journal of the Friends' Historical Society*, vol. 19, pp. 105 7.

Roe, William (1928). *The Private Memorandums of William Roe*; ed. Thomas-Stanford, Charles; printed privately, Brighton. C. *pp.* 216, 246

Rogers, Richard (1933). Diary in Knappen, M., ed.: *Two Elizabethan Puritan Diaries*; The American Society of Church History, Chicago, pp. 53–102. C. *pp.* 84, 97, 240

de Rothschild, Annie (1935). Diary in de Rothschild, Lady: *Lady de Rothschild and her Daughters*; ed. Cohen, Lucy; John Murray, London, pp. 75–108. C. *p. 181*

de Rothschild, Constance (1935). Diary in de Rothschild, Lady: *Lady de Rothschild and her Daughters*; ed. Cohen, Lucy; John Murray, London, pp. 75–108. C. *p. 180*

de Rothschild, Lady (1935). *Lady de Rothschild and her Daughters*; ed. Cohen, Lucy; John Murray, London. C. *pp.* 178, 185, 248

313

Rumney, Thomas (1936). *Tom Rumney of Mellfell*; ed. Rumney, A. W.; Titus Wilson & Son, Kendal. C. *p.* 163

Russell, Frances (1910). *Lady John Russell*; eds. MacCarthy, Desmond & Russell, Agatha; Methuen, London. C. *pp.* 122, 179, 184, 185

Russell, John (Lord Amberley) (1966). *The Amberley Papers*; eds. Russell, Bertrand & Patricia; George Allen & Unwin, London, 2 vols. C. *pp.* 178–9, 185, 201, 206, 214

Russell, Kate (Lady Amberley) (1966). *The Amberley Papers*; eds. Russell, Bertrand & Patricia; George Allen & Unwin, London, 2 vols. C. *pp.* 88, 111, 178, 181, 201, 214, 215, 217, 218, 222, 225, 230, 247

Ryder, Dudley (1939). *The Diary of Dudley Ryder*; ed. Matthews, William; Methuen, London. C. *pp.* 79, 154

Salter, John (1933). *Dr. Salter*; ed. Thompson, J. O.; The Bodley Head, London. C. *pp.* 259–60

Sandford, Daniel (1830). *Remains of the Late Right Reverend Daniel Sandford*; Waugh & Innes, Edinburgh. C. *pp.* 81, 105, 131, 142, 162, 166, 246

Scattergood, Thomas (1844). Memoirs. *The Friends' Library*, vol. 8, pp. 2–225. C.

Schnell, Leonhard (1903). Extracts from diary. *The Virginia Magazine of History and Biography*, vol. 11, pp. 115–31, 370–93; also (1904) vol. 12, pp. 55–61.

Schreiber, Charlotte (formerly Guest) (1952). *Lady Charlotte Schreiber: Extracts from her Journal*; ed. Earl of Bessborough; John Murray, London. C. *pp.* 177–8, 185

Scott, John (1930). *An Englishman at Home and Abroad*; ed. Mann, Ethel; Heath Cranton, London. C. *pp.* 75, 171

Scott, Walter (1890). *The Journal of Sir Walter Scott*; David Douglas, Edinburgh. C. *pp.* 75, 105, 130, 193

Sedgwick, Joseph (1853). *A Memoir of Mr. Joseph Sedgwick*; ed. Milner, Samuel; Houlston & Stoneman, London. C.

Selwyn, Thomas (1903). *Eton in 1829–30*; ed. Warre, Edmond; John Murray, London. C. *p.* 195

Sewall, David (1878). Diary. *Massachusetts Historical Society Proceedings*, 1st series, vol. 16, pp. 5–11. C.

Sewall, Samuel (1878). Diary. *Massachusetts Historical Society Collections*, 5th series, vol. 5; also (1879) 5th series, vol. 6; (1882) 5th series, vol. 7. C. *pp.* 66, 78, 99, 100, 114, 135, 137, 151, 155, 204, 212, 213, 215, 216, 219, 221–2, 224, 228, 237, 242, 250, 264

Sewall, Samuel (1892). Diary. *Massachusetts Historical Society Proceedings*, 2nd series, vol. 8, pp. 221–5. *p.* 264

Sewall, William (1930). *Diary of William Sewall*; ed. Goodell, John; Hartman, Beardstown, Illinois. C. *pp.* 104, 117, 193

Sewell, Elizabeth (1907). *The Autobiography of Elizabeth Sewell*; ed. Sewell, Eleanor; Longmans, Green, London. C. *pp.* 183, 197

Sheldon, Charlotte (1903). Diary in Vanderpoel, Emily: *Chronicles of a Pioneer School*; Cambridge University Press, Massachusetts, pp. 10–19. C.

Sheldon, Lucy (1903). Diary in Vanderpoel, Emily: *Chronicle of a Pioneer School*; Cambridge University Press, Massachusetts, pp. 43–53. C. *p.* 193

Shelley, Frances (1912). *The Diary of Frances, Lady Shelley*; ed. Edgcumbe, Richard; John Murray, London, 2 vols. C.   *pp.* 171, 172, 193, 200, 246

Shelley, Mary (1947). *Mary Shelley's Journal*; ed. Jones, Frederick; University of Oklahoma Press, Norman. C.   *pp.* 214, 222

Shippen, Nancy (1935). *Nancy Shippen: her Journal Book*; ed. Armes, E.; J. B. Lippincott, Philadelphia. C.   *pp.* 117, 129, 133, 162, 167, 205, 224, 238, 246, 268

Shore, Emily (1898). *Journal of Emily Shore*; Kegan Paul, Trench, Trübner, London. C.   *pp.* 74, 82, 133, 181, 259

Silliman, Benjamin (1866). *Life of Benjamin Silliman, M.D., L.L.D.*; ed. Fisher, G.; Charles Scribner, New York. C.   *pp.* 104, 117, 138, 194, 205, 252, 265

Skinner, John (1930). *The Journal of a Somerset Rector*; eds. Coombs, Howard & Bax, Arthur; John Murray, London. C.   *pp.* 76, 86, 87, 105, 142, 166–7

Skinner, Richard (1900). Diary. *New England Historical and Genealogical Register*, vol. 54, pp. 413–15. C.

Slingsby, Henry (1836). *The Diary of Sir Henry Slingsby*; ed. Parsons, Daniel; Longman, London. C.   *pp.* 101, 124, 150, 151, 155, 236–7, 243

Smith, Frank (1875). Diary in Smith, Hannah: *Frank. The Record of a Happy Life*; Morgan & Scott, London, *passim*. C.   *p.* 132

Smith, Hannah (1896). *Educate our Mothers or Wise Motherhood*; James Nisbet, London. C.

Smith, John (1904). *Hannah Logan's Courtship*; ed. Myers, Albert; Ferris & Leach, Philadelphia, pp. 65–324, 326–45. C.

Smith, Richard (1916). Journal. *The Journal of the Friends' Historical Society*, vol. 13, pp. 49–58, 89–97, 129–39; also (1917) vol. 14, pp. 15–23, 56–69, 108–18. C.

Smith, Thomas (1907). Diary of Thomas Smith of Shaw House in Neale, John: *Charters and Records of Neales of Berkeley*; Mackie, Warrington, pp. 169–209. C.   *p.* 80

Sopwith, Thomas (1891). *Thomas Sopwith·* ed. Richardson, Benjamin; Longmans, Green, London. C.   *p.* 80

Southey, Robert (1903). *Journal of a Tour in the Netherlands*; ed. Nicoll, William; William Heinemann, London. C.

Stanford, John (1835). *Memoir of the Rev. John Stanford, D.D.*; ed. Sommers, Charles; Swords, Stanford, New York. C.

Stanley, Catherine (1879). *Memoirs of Edward and Catherine Stanley*; ed. Stanley, Arthur; John Murray, London. C.   *pp.* 105, 210

Steadman, William (1838). *Memoir of the Rev. William Steadman*; ed. Steadman, Thomas; Thomas Ward, London. C.   *pp.* 77, 138, 165–6, 264

Stedman, John (1962). *The Journal of John Gabriel Stedman*; ed. Thompson, Stanbury; The Mitre Press, London. C.   *pp.* 87–8, 105, 158, 160, 162, 191–2, 206, 217–18, 222, 224, 230

Steele, Millicent (1926). Diary of a voyage from London to Clipper Canada in 1833. *Papers and Records of Ontario Historical Society*, vol. 23, pp. 483–510. C.

Sterne, Adolphus (1926). Diary. *The Southwestern Historical Quarterly*, vol. 30, pp. 139–55, 219–32, 305–24.
Also:
(1927) vol. 31, pp. 63–83, 181–7, 285–91, 374–83.

(1928) vol. 32, pp. 87–94, 165–79, 252–7, 344–51.
(1929) vol. 33, pp. 75–9, 160–8, 231–41, 315–25.
(1930) vol. 34, pp. 69–76, 159–66, 257–65, 340–7
(1931) vol. 35, pp. 77–82, 151–68, 228–42, 317–24.
(1932) vol. 36, pp. 67–72, 163–6, 215–29, 312–16.
(1933) vol. 37, pp. 45–60, 136–48, 215–22, 320–3.
(1934) vol. 38, pp. 53–70, 149–52, 213–28. C.   *pp.* 73, 111, 207, 208, 220, 221

Stevens, Henry (1931). Diary. *Proceedings of the Vermont Historical Society*, vol. 2, pp. 115–28. C.

Stewart, Agnes (1928). Journey to Oregon. *The Oregon Historical Quarterly*, vol. 29, pp. 77–98. C.

Stiles, Ezra (1901). *The Literary Diary of Ezra Stiles*; ed. Dexter, F.; Charles Scribner & Sons, New York. C.   *pp.* 104, 128

Stout, William (1967). *The Autobiography of William Stout of Lancaster*; ed. Marshal, J.; Chetham Society Publications, Manchester, vol. 14. C.   *p.* 154

Strang, James (1830). Diary in Quaife, Milo: *The Kingdom of Saint James*; Yale University Press, New Haven, Connecticut, pp. 195–234. C.   *p.* 139

Strickland, Hugh (1858). *Memoirs of Hugh Edwin Strickland*; ed. Jardine, Sir William; John Van Voorst, London. C.

Strother (1912). *Strother's Journal*; ed. Caine, Caesar; A. Brown & Sons, London.

Strutt, John (1939). Diary in Strutt, Charles: *The Strutt Family of Terling*; printed privately, pp. 71–94. C.   *pp.* 164, 168

Stuart, Granville (1925). *Forty Years on the Frontier*; ed. Phillips, Paul; Arthur H. Clark, Cleveland. C.

Swift, Jonathan (1948). *Journal to Stella*; ed. Williams, Harold; Clarendon Press, Oxford.

Taylor, Dan (1820). *Memoirs of the Rev. Dan Taylor*; ed. Taylor, Adam; printed privately, London. C.   *pp.* 131, 142, 161, 224, 253

Taylor, Edward (1880). Diary. *Massachusetts Historical Society Proceedings*, 1st series, vol. 18, pp. 5–18. C.   *p.* 188

Taylor, John (1820). *Memoirs of the Rev. John Taylor*; ed. Taylor, Adam; printed privately, London. C.   *pp.* 80, 118, 156–7, 161, 162, 253, 267

Teedon, Samuel (1902). *The Diary of Samuel Teedon*; ed. Wright, Thomas; Sign at the Unicorn, London.

Thomas, Isaiah (1909). Diary. *Transactions and Collections of the American Antiquarian Society*, vols. 9 & 10. C.

Thomlinson, John (1910). The diary of John Thomlinson. *North Country Diaries*; Surtees Society, 2nd series, vol. 118, pp. 64–167. C.   *p.* 83

Thoreau, Henry (1962). *The Journal of Henry D. Thoreau*; eds. Torrey, Bradford & Allen, Francis; Dover, New York.

Thrale, Hester (1951). *Thraliana: the Diary of Mrs. Hester Lynch Thrale*; ed. Balderstone, Katharine; Clarendon Press, Oxford, 2nd edition, 2 vols. C.   *pp.* 73, 79, 87, 105, 138, 158, 161, 206, 208, 214, 235, 247

Timms, Mary (1835). *Memoirs of the Late Mrs. Mary Timms*; ed. Morgan, E.; T. Whitehorn, London. C.   *pp.* 140, 142, 181

Todd, John (1876). *The Story of his Life*; ed. Todd, John; Sampson Law, London. C.   *pp.* 108, 121, 131–2, 133, 142, 173, 184, 206, 225, 231

Tompkins, John (1930). The Tompkins diary. *Sussex Archaeological Collections*, vol. 11, pp. 11–56.

Townsend, John (1828). *Memoirs of the Rev. John Townsend*; J. B. & John Courthope, London.   C.   *pp.* 74, 119, 170–1, 194

Traherne, Patrick (1918). *A Schoolmaster's Diary*; ed. Mais, S.; Grant Richards, London.   C.   *pp.* 198, 206–7

Trant, Clarissa (1925). *The Journal of Clarissa Trant*; ed. Luard, C. G.; The Bodley Head, London.   C.   *pp.* 87, 184

Tregelles, Edwin (1892). *Edwin Octavius Tregelles*; ed. Fox, Sarah; Hodder & Stoughton, London.   C.   *pp.* 74, 122–3, 124, 178, 184, 254, 255

Trench, Melesina (1837). *Thoughts of a Parent on Education*; John W. Parker, London.   C.   *pp.* 118, 163, 253

Trench, Melesina (1862). *The Remains of the Late Mrs. Richard Trench*; ed. The Dean of Westminster; Parker, Son & Brown, London.   C.   *pp.* 138–9, 141, 170, 206, 210, 224, 245

Tucker, Mary (1941). Diary. *Essex Institute Historical Collections*, vol. 77, pp. 306–38.   C.   *pp.* 104, 116, 171, 209

Tudor, Edward (1857). *Literary Remains of King Edward the Sixth*; ed. Nichols, J.; J. B. Nichols & Sons, London.   C.   *pp.* 240, 255

Turner, Thomas (1875). *Memoir of Thomas Turner, Esq.*; Simpkin, Marshall, London.   C.   *pp.* 106, 172, 216–17, 246

Turner, Thomas (1925). *The Diary of Thomas Turner*; ed. Turner, Florence; The Bodley Head, London.   C.   *p.* 80

Twysden, Isabella (1939). Diary. *Archaeologia Cantiana*, vol. 51, pp. 113–36.   C.   *p.* 216

Tyldesley, Thomas (1873). *The Tyldesley Diary*; eds. Gillow, Joseph & Hewitson, Anthony; A. Hewitson, Preston.   C.

Van Curler, Arent (1895). Journal in *Annual Report of the American Historical Association*; Government Printing Office, Washington, DC, pp. 81–101.

Wale, Thomas (1883). *My Grandfather's Pocket Book*; ed. Wale, Henry; Chapman & Hall, London.   C.   *pp.* 159, 162

Walker, Mary (1940). Diary in Drury, Clifford: *Elkanah and Mary Walker*; The Caxton Printers, Caldwell, Idaho, *passim*.   C.   *pp.* 75, 108, 110, 121, 175, 179, 199, 206, 207, 208, 211, 213, 214, 224, 239, 247, 254, 255

Walker, Timothy (1889). *The Diaries of Rev. Timothy Walker*; ed. Walker, J.; Concord, New Hampshire.   C.

Walker, William (1899). Journals in Connelley, William, ed.: *The Provisional Government of Nebraska Territory*; The Nebraska State Historical Society, Lincoln, 2nd series, vol. 3, pp. 153–400.   C.   *p.* 178

Wallington, Nehemiah (1869). *Historical Notices of Events in the Reign of Charles I*; Richard Bentley, London.   C.   *pp.* 74, 84, 97, 98, 111, 131, 134–5, 137, 142, 148, 149, 204, 208, 228, 268

Ward, Lester (1935). *Young Ward's Diary*; ed. Stern, Bernhard; G. P. Putnam's Sons, New York.   C.   *pp.* 78, 107, 139, 195, 200, 206, 214, 224

Ward, Samuel (1933). Diary in Knappen, M., ed.: *Two Elizabethan Puritan Diaries*; The American Society of Church History, Chicago, pp. 103–32.   C.   *p.* 188

Warder, Ann (1893). Extracts from the diary of Mrs Ann Warder; ed. Cadbury, Sarah; *The Pennsylvania Magazine of History and Biography*, vol. 17, pp. 444–62. C. *p. 84*

Warren, John (1860). Diary in Warren, Edward: *The Life of John Collins Warren*; Ticknor & Fields, Boston, *passim*. C. *p. 171*

Washington, George (1925). *The Diaries of George Washington*; ed. Fitzpatrick, John; Houghton Mifflin, Boston & New York.

Watkin, Absalom (1920). *Extracts from his Journal*; ed. Watkin, A. E.; T. Fisher Unwin, London. C. *pp. 106, 166, 172, 210*

Waugh, Evelyn (1964). *A Little Learning*; Chapman & Hall, London. C. *pp. 187, 198*

Waugh, Evelyn (1976). *The Diaries of Evelyn Waugh*; ed. Davie, Michael; A. D. Peters and Weidenfeld & Nicolson, London. C. *pp. 109, 131, 139, 141, 185, 207, 208, 211, 292 n. 7*

Webb, Catherine (1903). Diary in Vanderpoel, Emily: *Chronicles of a Pioneer School*; Cambridge University Press, Massachusetts, pp. 148–9. C. *p. 133*

Weeks, Joshua (1916). Journal of Rev. Joshua Weeks. *Essex Institute Historical Collections*, vol. 52, pp. 1–16, 161–76, 197–208, 345–56. C.

Weeton, Ellen (1936). *Miss Weeton. Journal of a Governess 1807–11*; ed. Hall, Edward; Oxford University Press, London, 2 vols. C. *pp. 75, 80, 87, 215, 218, 222, 226*

Wesley, Charles (1849). *The Journal of the Rev. Charles Wesley*; ed. Jackson, Thomas; John Mason, London. C. *p. 159*

West, John (1827). *The Substance of a Journal*; L. B. Seeley & Son, London. C.

Weymouth, Arthur (1948). *Journal of the War Years and One Year Later*; Worcester Press, Worcester. C. *pp. 186, 199*

Whalley, Thomas (1863). *Journals and Correspondence of Thomas Sedgewick Whalley*; ed. Wickham, Hill; Richard Bentley, London.

White, Dorothy (1924). *The Groombridge Diary*; Oxford University Press. C. *p. 186*

White, Henry (1898). The Diary of Rev. Henry White in Clutterbuck, Robert: *Notes on the Parishes of Fyfield*; Bennet Brothers, Salisbury, pp. 10–51. C.

White, Mary (1903). *Memorials of Mary Wilder White*; ed. Tileston, M.; The Everett Press, Boston. C. *pp. 205, 228–30*

Whitefield, George (1905). *George Whitefield's Journal*; ed. Wale, William; Drane, London. C. *p. 161*

Whitwell, Thomas (1927). A Darlington schoolboy's diary. *The Journal of the Friends' Historical Society*, vol. 24, pp. 21–30. C.

Wilberforce, Samuel (1880). *The Life of the Right Reverend Samuel Wilberforce*; ed. Ashwell, A. R.; John Murray, London. C. *p. 183*

Wilberforce, William (1868). *Life of William Wilberforce*; ed. Wilberforce, S.; John Murray, London. C. *pp. 139, 163, 253, 265–6*

Wilbor, Mary (1903). Diary in Vanderpoel, Emily: *Chronicles of a Pioneer School*; Cambridge University Press, Massachusetts, pp. 234–41. C.

Williams (1858). The Williams' Journal in Sumner, William: *A History of East Boston*; J. E. Tilton, Boston, pp. 331–9. C.

Wilson, James (1927). Diary in Barrington, Emilie: *The Servant of All*; Longmans, Green, London, *passim*. C.

Winslow, Anna (1894). *Diary of a Boston School Girl*; ed. Earle, Alice; Houghton Mifflin, Boston. C.   *pp.* 129, 168–9, 255–6

Winthrop, John (1864). *Life and Letters of John Winthrop*; ed. Winthrop, R.; Cambridge University Press. C.   *pp.* 97, 98, 99, 125, 134, 146, 148–9, 240, 249

Wister, Sally (1902). *Sally Wister's Journal*; ed. Myers, Albert; Ferris & Leach, Philadelphia. C.   *p.* 168

Wiswall, John (1908). The life and times of the Rev. John Wiswall. *Collections of the Nova Scotia Historical Society*, vol. 13, pp. 1–73. C.

Wood, Anthony (1891). *The Life and Times of Anthony Wood*; ed. Clark, Andrew; Clarendon Press, Oxford. C.   *p.* 150

Wood, Frances (1926). *A Great-Niece's Journals*; ed. Rott, Margaret; Constable, London. C.   *pp.* 179, 184, 206, 211, 248, 268

Woodforde, Mary (1932). Diary in Woodforde, Dorothy, ed.: *Woodforde Papers and Diaries*; Peter Davies, London, pp. 3–35. C.   *pp.* 127, 188

Woodforde, Nancy (1932). Diary in Woodforde, Dorothy, ed.: *Woodforde Papers and Diaries*; Peter Davies, London, pp. 35–89. C.

Woods, John (1822). *Two Years' Residence in the Settlement on the English Prairie*; Longman, London. C.

Woods, Margaret (1829). *Extracts from the Journal of Margaret Woods*; John & Arthur Arch, London. C.   *pp.* 105, 106, 107, 118, 156–7, 161, 162, 234, 252

Woolman, John (1922). *The Journal and Essays of John Woolman*; ed. Gummere, Amelia; Macmillan, London. C.

Wortley, Victoria (1852). *A Young Traveller's Journal*; T. Bosworth, London. C.   *p.* 181

Wright, Thomas (1911). Journal. *County Louth Archaeological Society*, vol. 2, pp. 171–85. C.   *p.* 161

Wynne, Elizabeth (1935). *The Wynne Diaries*; ed. Fremantle, Anne; Oxford University Press, London, *passim*, 3 vols. C.   *pp.* 118–19, 120, 167–8, 199, 206, 208, 214–15, 221, 222, 224, 246, 256–7, 267

Wynne, Eugenia (1935). *The Wynne Diaries*; ed. Fremantle, Anne; Oxford University Press, London, *passim*, 3 vols. C.   *pp.* 167, 256–7

Wynne, Harriet (1940). *The Wynne Diaries*; ed. Fremantle, Anne; Oxford University Press, London, *passim*, 3 vols. C.   *p.* 256

Yeoman, John (1934). *The Diary of John Yeoman*; ed. Yearsley, Macleod; Watts, London. C.   *pp.* 160, 264

Yeoman, Mary (1926). *The Diary of Mary Yeoman*; ed. Reid, R. D.; Journal Office, Wells. C.   *p.* 264

Young, Arthur (1898). *The Autobiography of Arthur Young*; ed. Betham-Edwards, M.; Smith, Elder, London. C.   *pp.* 105, 159, 161, 162, 199, 210

MANUSCRIPTS

Anon. Diary; The National Library of Scotland, George IV Bridge, Edinburgh, no. 1658.

Bibliography and citation index

Bishop, Betty. Diary; The Friends' Society Library, Euston Road, London, no. S.83. C.   *pp.* 214, 220, 221, 222

Byrd, William. Diary; University of North Carolina, Chapel Hill, North Carolina. C.   *p.* 83

Calverley, Walter. Diary; The British Library, Great Russell Street, London, Additional MSS 27418.   *p.* 84

Carter, Landon. Diary; University of Virginia Library. C.   *pp.* 85–6

Darby, Abiah. Diary; The Friends' Society Library, Euston Road, London. C.   *pp.* 86, 214

Day, Susanna. Diary; The Friends' Society Library, Euston Road, London, Box D. C.   *p.* 84

Dexter, Samuel. Diary; Dedham Historical Society, Dedham, Massachusetts. C.   *p.* 86

Dunne, R. E. Diary; Dr Williams' Library, Gordon Square, London, no. 24.77.

Fox, Sarah. Diary; The Friends' Society Library, Euston Road, London, Box D.   *p.* 86

Hamilton-Gordon, Rachael. Diary; The British Library, Great Russell Street, London, Additional MSS 49271, fos. 207–28. C.   *p.* 258

Harington, John. Diary; The British Library, Great Russell Street, London, Additional MSS 10114. C.

Hewlett, Maurice. Diary; The British Library, Great Russell Street, London, Additional MSS 41075. C.   *pp.* 80, 122

Hicks, Elias. Diary; Friends' Historical Library, Swarthmore College, Philadelphia, Pennsylvania. C.   *p.* 84

Hyde, Henry. Diary; The British Library, Great Russell Street, London, Additional MSS 22578 and Stowe Collection 770. C.   *p.* 83

Jeffries, Joyce. Diary; The British Library, Great Russell Street, London, Egerton Collection 3054.

Keith, Margaret. Diary; The National Library of Scotland, George IV Bridge, Edinburgh, no. 984.

Kemp, Caleb. Diary; The Friends' Society Library, Euston Road, London, no. S3–8. C.

Mackenzie, Francis. Diary; The National Library of Scotland, George IV Bridge, Edinburgh, no. 2540.

Mather, Cotton. Diary; American Antiquary Society, Worcester, Massachusetts. C.   *p.* 83

Mather, Increase. Diary; American Antiquary Society, Worcester, Massachusetts. C.   *p.* 84

Nairne, Carolina. Diary; The National Library of Scotland, George IV Bridge, Edinburgh, no. 981. C.

Newell, Timothy. Diary; New York Public Library.   *p.* 83

Oliver, Peter. Diary; The British Library, Great Russell Street, London, Egerton Collection 2674. C.   *pp.* 111, 130, 131, 214, 216

Osborne, Thomas. Diary; The British Library, Great Russell Street, London, Additional MSS 28040–1. C.

Pemberton, John. Diary; Historical Society of Pennsylvania, Philadelphia, Pennsylvania. C.   *p.* 83

Petiver, James. Diary; The British Library, Great Russell Street, London, Sloane Collection 3220–6.

Pledger, Elias. Diary; Dr Williams' Library, Gordon Square, London, no. 28.4. C.   *pp.* 127, 128, 136, 154

Powys, Caroline. Diary; The British Library, Great Russell Street, London, Additional MSS 42160–73. C.   *pp.* 84–5

Rich, Mary. Autobiography; The British Library, Great Russell Street, London, Additional MSS 27357. C.   *p.* 83

Rogers, Richard. Diary; Dr Williams' Library, Gordon Square, London, no. 61.13. C.   *p.* 84

Rowntree, Elizabeth. Diary; The Friends' Society Library, Euston Road, London, Box T. C.   *p.* 131

Rule, Andrew. Diary; The National Library of Scotland, George IV Bridge, Edinburgh, no. 34.7.12. C.   *pp.* 101, 127, 136, 137, 154

Russell, Helen. Diary; The National Library of Scotland, George IV Bridge, Edinburgh, no. 3233. C.

Skinner, John. Diary; The British Library, Great Russell Street, London, Additional MSS 33633–730. C.   *p.* 86

Steuart, Amelia. Diary; The National Library of Scotland, George IV Bridge, Edinburgh, no. 983. C.   *pp.* 90, 106, 118, 141, 164–5, 173, 201, 224

Stewart, Mrs. Diary; The National Library of Scotland, George IV Bridge, Edinburgh, no. 982.

Stockton, Mrs. Diary; Dr Williams' Library, Gordon Square, London, no. 24.8. C.   *pp.* 127, 136

Stockton, Owen. Diary; Dr Williams' Library, Gordon Square, London, no. 24.7. C.   *pp.* 127, 136

Thomlinson, John. Diary; The British Library, Great Russell Street, London, Additional MSS 22560. C.   *p.* 83

Tonson, Jacob. Diary; The British Library, Great Russell Street, London, Additional MSS 28276.

Upcott, William. Diary; The British Library, Great Russell Street, London, Additional MSS 32558.

Viney, Richard. Diary; The British Library, Great Russell Street, London, Additional MSS 44935. C.   *pp.* 214, 293 n. 5

Wallington, Nehemiah. A record of the mercies of God; Guildhall Library, Aldermanbury, London, MS 204. C.   *pp.* 85, 147, 213, 215, 216, 237

Warder, Ann. Diary; Historical Society of Pennsylvania, Philadelphia, Pennsylvania. C.   *p.* 85

Winthrop, Adam. Diary; The British Library, Great Russell Street, London, Additional MSS 37419.

Yeardley, Elizabeth. Diary; The Friends' Society Library, Euston Road, London, Box R. C.

Secondary sources

Abbott, Grace (1938). *The Child and the State*; University of Chicago Press.

Ainsworth, M. D. S. (1967). *Infancy in Uganda: Infant Care and the Growth of Love*; Johns Hopkins University Press, Baltimore.   *pp.* 38, 51

Bibliography and citation index

Allport, Gordon (1935). Attitudes in Murchison, C., ed.: *Handbook of Social Psychology*; Clark University Press, Worcester, Massachusetts, pp. 798–884.   *p. 45*

Altick, Richard (1973). *Victorian People and Ideas*; J. M. Dent & Sons, London.   *p. 62*

Anderson, Michael (1971). *Family Structure in Nineteenth Century Lancashire*; Cambridge University Press.   *p. 70*

Anderson, Michael (1980). *Approaches to the History of the Western Family, 1500–1914*; Macmillan, London.   *p. 291 n. 16*

Anderson, Michael, ed. (1982). *Sociology of the Family*; Penguin Books, Middlesex.

Ariès, Philippe (1960). *L'Enfant et la Vie Familiale sous l'Ancien Régime*; Librairie Plon, Paris. All quotations are taken from the 1973 edition, identical to the first except for the addition of a new preface. English translation (1962) *Centuries of Childhood*; Baldick, R.; Jonathan Cape, London.   *pp. 1–3, 4, 5, 10, 13–14, 18, 22, 23–4, 25, 26, 27, 28, 29–30, 46, 49, 54–5, 56, 57, 59, 64, 96, 120, 143, 191, 199, 222, 261, 262, 263, 267*

Arling, G. L. & Harlow, H. F. (1967). Effects of social deprivation on the maternal behaviour of rhesus monkeys. *Journal of Comparative and Physiological Psychology*, vol. 64, pp. 371–7.

Ashton, T. S. & Sykes, Joseph (1964). *The Coal Industry of the Eighteenth Century*; Manchester University Press.   *p. 61*

Axtell, James (1974). *The School upon a Hill. Education and Society in Colonial New England*; Yale University Press, New Haven, Connecticut.

Backett, K. C. (1982). Images of parenthood in Anderson, Michael, ed.: *Sociology of the Family*; Penguin Books, Middlesex, pp. 350–69.   *pp. 141, 201–2*

Badinter, Elisabeth (1980). *L'Amour en Plus*; Flammarion, Paris. English translation (1981) *The Myth of Motherhood*; DeGaris, R.; Souvenir Press (E & A), London.   *pp. 7, 10, 16, 24, 25, 26, 50, 103*

Bakwin, H. (1949). Emotional deprivation in infants. *Journal of Pediatrics*, vol. 35, pp. 512–21.

Barash, David (1977). *Sociobiology and Behavior*; Elsevier, New York.   *pp. 34, 36*

Bates, John (1976). *British Manuscript Diaries of the Nineteenth Century: an Annotated Listing*; Centaur Press, London.

Bayne-Powell, Rosamond (1939). *The English Child in the Eighteenth Century*; John Murray, London.   *p. 289 n. 2*

Beales, Derek (1969). *From Castlereagh to Gladstone 1815–1885*; Thomas Nelson & Sons, London.

Beales, Ross (1975). In search of the historical child. Miniature adulthood and youth in colonial New England. *American Quarterly*, no. 27, pp. 379–98.   *pp. 53–4, 251, 263, 289 n. 4*

Beaver, M. W. (1973). Population, infant mortality and milk. *Population Studies*, vol. 27, pp. 243–54.

Berkner, Lutz (1973). Recent research on the history of the family in Western Europe. *Journal of Marriage and the Family*, vol. 35, pp. 395–405.

Berry, Boyd (1974). The first English pediatricians and Tudor attitudes toward childhood. *Journal of the History of Ideas*, vol. 35, pp. 561–77.

Birch, R. C. (1974). *The Shaping of the Welfare State*; Longman, London.   *p. 60*

Blager, F. & Martin, H. P. (1976). Speech and language of abused children in Martin, Harold: *The Abused Child*; Bollinger, Cambridge, Massachusetts, pp. 83–92.   *p. 41*

Blurton-Jones, N., ed. (1972). *Ethological Studies of Child Behaviour*; Cambridge University Press.

Booth, Charles (1889–1903). *Life and Labour of the People in London*; Macmillan, London.

Bowlby, John (1966). *Maternal Care and Mental Health and Deprivation of Maternal Care*; Shocken Books, New York.   *pp. 27, 41*

Bowlby, John (1970). *Attachment and Loss*; The Hogarth Press, London.   *p. 235*

Brazelton, T. B. (1972). Implications of human development among the Mayan Indians of Mexico. *Human Development*, vol. 15, pp. 90–111.   *pp. 39, 50*

Bremner, Robert, ed. (1970–3). *Children and Youth in America*; Harvard University Press, Cambridge, Massachusetts, 3 vols.   *pp. 4, 10–11, 17, 22, 45, 59, 113, 187–8*

Briggs, Asa (1959). *The Age of Improvement*; Longmans, Green, London.   *p. 60*

Briggs, Asa (1972). The history of changing approaches to social welfare in Martin, Ernest, ed.: *Comparative Development in Social Welfare*; George Allen & Unwin, London, pp. 9–24.   *p. 62*

Brobeck, Stephen (1976). Images of the family: portrait paintings as indices of American family culture, structure and behaviour, 1730–1860. *Journal of Psychohistory*, vol. 5, pp. 81–106.   *pp. 44, 46, 47, 49, 66*

Bronfenbrenner, Urie (1958). Socialisation and social class through time and space in Maccoby, E., Newcomb, T. & Hartley, E., eds.: *Readings in Social Psychology*; Methuen, London, pp. 400–25.   *p. 43*

Bruce, Maurice (1968). *The Coming of the Welfare State*; B. T. Batsford, London.   *p. 62*

Bruner, Jerome (1974). Nature and uses of immaturity in Bruner, J. & Connolly, K.: *The Growth of Competence*; Academic Press, London & New York, pp. 11–49.

Busfield, Joan (1974). Ideologies and reproduction in Richards, M. P. M.: *The Integration of a Child into the Social World*; Cambridge University Press, pp. 11–36.   *p. 208*

Campbell, D. T. (1975). On the conflicts between biological and social evolution and between psychology and moral tradition. *American Psychologist*, vol. 30, pp. 1103–26.   *p. 36*

Carpenter, Clarence (1965). The howlers of Barro Colorado Island in Devore, Irven, ed.: *Primate Behaviour*; Holt, Rinehart & Winston, New York & London, pp. 250–92.   *p. 38*

Carr, Edward (1961). *What is History?* Macmillan, London.   *p. 68*

Carter, Jan, ed. (1974). *The Maltreated Child*; Priory Press, London.   *p. 42*

Chance, Michael & Jolly, Clifford (1970). *Social Groups of Monkeys, Apes and Men*; Jonathan Cape, London.   *p. 38*

Chesser, Eustace (1951). *Cruelty to Children*; Victor Gollancz, London.

Children's Employment Commission (1816–17). Report of the minutes of evidence on the state of children employed in the manufactories. *British Parliamentary Papers*, no. 1, vol. 3.

Children's Employment Commission (1831–2). Report from the Select Committee on the labour of children in the mills and factories. *British Parliamentary Papers*, no. 2, vol. 15.   pp. 62–4

Children's Employment Commission (1833). First report. Employment of children in factories. *British Parliamentary Papers*, no. 3, vol. 20.

Children's Employment Commission (1842). First report of the Commissioners. Mines. *British Parliamentary Papers*, no. 6, vol. 15.

Clarke, Ann & Clarke, A. D. B. (1976). *Early Experience. Myth and Evidence*; Open Books, London.   pp. 28, 290 n. 8

Clarke-Stewart, K. A. (1978). Popular primers for parents. *American Psychologist*, vol. 33, no. 4, pp. 359–69.

Clegg, Alec & Megson, Barbara (1968). *Children in Distress*; Penguin Books, Middlesex.

Cleverley, J. & Philips, I. (1976). *From Locke to Spock*; Melbourne University Press.   pp. 4, 11–12, 15

Cohen, Charles (n.d.). Palatable children: White American attitudes towards childhood in paintings 1670–1860; unpublished paper, University of California, Berkeley & Los Angeles.   pp. 47–8, 263

Coveney, Peter (1957). *Poor Monkey. The Child in Literature*; Rockliff, London.

Crump, Lucy (1929). *Nursery Life Three Hundred Years Ago*; George Routledge & Sons, London.   pp. 7, 23, 289 n. 2

Daly, Martin & Wilson, Margo (1981). Abuse and neglect of children in evolutionary perspective in Alexander, R. D. & Tinkle, D. W., eds.: *Natural Selection and Social Behaviour. Recent Research and New Theory*; Blackwell Science, London, pp. 405–16.   p. 41

Davis, Glen (1976). *Childhood and History in America*; The Psychohistory Press, New York.

Davis, Natalie (1971). The reasons of misrule: youth groups and charivaris in sixteenth century France. *Past and Present*, no. 50, pp. 41–75.   p. 289 n. 4

Davoren, Elizabeth (1968). The role of the social worker in Helfer, Ray & Kempe, C. Henry: *The Battered Child*; Chicago University Press, pp. 135–50.   pp. 41, 42

Demos, John (1970). *Family Life in a Plymouth Colony*; Oxford University Press.   pp. 3, 4, 14, 15–16, 23, 24, 27, 49, 53, 96, 262, 263

Demos, John (1972). Demography and psychology in the historical study of family life in Laslett, Peter, ed.: *Household and Family in Past Time*; Cambridge University Press, ch. 21, pp. 561–71.

Demos, John (1973). Developmental perspectives on the history of childhood in Rabb, T. & Rotberg, R., eds.: *The Family in History*; Harper & Row, New York & London, pp. 127–40.   pp. 4, 15–16, 27

Devore, Irven (1965). *Primate Behaviour*; Holt, Rinehart & Winston, New York & London.

Dicey, A. V. (1905). *Law and Opinion in England*; Macmillan, London.

Dimond, Stuart (1970). *The Social Behaviour of Animals*; B. T. Batsford, London.

Doyle, G. A., Anderson, A. & Bearder, S. K. (1969). Maternal behaviour in the lesser bushbaby. *Folia Primat*, vol. 11, pp. 215–38.

Draper, Patricia (1976). Social and economic constraints on child life among the !Kung in Lee, Richard & Devore, Irven, eds.: *Kalahari Hunter-Gatherers*;

Harvard University Press, Cambridge, Massachusetts, pp. 199–217.   *pp.* 39, 51, 219

Durham, W. H. (1976). The adaptive significance of cultural behaviour. *Human Ecology*, vol. 4, pp. 89–121.   *p.* 36

Earle, Alice (1899). *Child Life in Colonial Days*; Macmillan, New York.

Erikson, Eric (1963). *Childhood and Society*; W. W. Norton, New York.   *p.* 27

Ferguson, Thomas (1966). *Children in Care and After*; Oxford University Press, London.   *pp.* 41, 290 n. 7

Fildes, Valerie (1980). Neonatal feeding practices and infant mortality during the eighteenth century. *Journal of Biosocial Science*, vol. 12, pp. 313–24.   *pp.* 134, 212, 271, 294 n. 7

Fildes, Valerie (1982). The age of weaning in Britain. *Journal of Biosocial Science*, vol. 14, pp. 223–40.   *pp.* 219, 222, 294 n. 8

Findlay, J. (1923). *The Children of England*; Methuen, London.   *p.* 289 n. 2

Firestone, Shillamith (1971). *The Dialectic of Sex*; Jonathan Cape, London.   *p.* 4

Fishbein, Martin & Ajzen, Icek (1975). *Belief, Attitude, Intention and Behaviour. An Introduction to Theory and Research*; Addison-Wesley, Amsterdam & London.   *p.* 89

Flandrin, Jean-Louis (1976). *Familles: Parenté, Maison, Sexualité dans l'Ancienne Société*; Librairie Hachette, Paris. English translation (1979) *Families in Former Times*; Southern, Richard; Cambridge University Press.   *p.* 50

Fleming, Sandford (1933). *Children and Puritanism: the Place of Children in the Life and Thought of the New England Churches, 1620–1847*; Yale University Press, New Haven, Connecticut.

Flint, Elizabeth (1967). *The Child and the Institution*; University of London Press.

Franklin, Alfred (1977). *The Challenge of Child Abuse*; Academic Press, London.   *pp.* 41, 42

Fraser, Derek (1973). *The Evolution of the British Welfare State*; Macmillan, London.

Friedman, Lawrence (1977). *Law and Society*; Prentice-Hall, Englewood Cliffs, New Jersey.

Friedmann, W. (1959). *Law in a Changing Society*; Stevens & Sons, London.

Fuller, Peter (1979). Uncovering childhood in Hoyles, Martin, ed.: *Changing Childhood*; Writers and Readers Publishing Cooperative, London, pp. 71–108.   *p.* 48

Gillis, John (1979). Affective individualism and the English poor. *Journal of Interdisciplinary History*, vol. 10, pp. 121–8.   *pp.* 19, 70

Godfrey, Elizabeth (1907). *English Children in the Olden Time*; Methuen, London.   *pp.* 22, 289 n. 2

Goldberg, S. (1972). Infant care and growth in urban Zambia. *Human Development*, vol. 15, pp. 77–89.   *pp.* 39, 51

Goody, John, ed. (1973). *The Character of Kinship*; Cambridge University Press.   *p.* 37

Goody, John, ed. (1976). *Family and Inheritance*; Cambridge University Press.

Gouge, William (1622). *Of Domesticall Duties*; John Haviland, London.   *pp.* 116, 156, 216, 251

Greven, Philip (1977). *The Protestant Temperament. Patterns of Child-rearing,*

Religious Experience, and the Self in Early America; Alfred A. Knopf, New York.   *pp.* 103, 110, 113, 116, 120, 141, 155, 173, 289 n. 7

Hall, K. R. & Devore, Irven (1965). Baboon social behaviour in Devore, Irven, ed.: *Primate Behaviour*; Holt, Rinehart & Winston, New York & London, pp. 53–111.   *p.* 38

Hamilton, W. D. (1966). The genetical evolution of social behaviour. *Journal of Theoretical Biology*, vol. 7, pp. 1–52.   *pp.* 34, 36

Hanawalt, Barbara (1977). Childrearing among the lower classes of late medieval England. *Journal of Interdisciplinary History*, vol. 8, no. 1, pp. 1–22.   *pp.* 49, 54, 55–6, 70, 263

Hansen, E. (1966). The development of maternal and infant behaviour in the rhesus monkey. *Behaviour*, vol. 27, pp. 107–49.

Hareven, Tamara (1973). The history of the family as an interdisciplinary field in Rabb, T. & Rotberg, R., eds.: *The Family in History*; Harper & Row, New York & London, pp. 211–26.

Harlow, H. & Harlow, M. (1962). Social deprivation in monkeys. *Scientific American*, vol. 207, pp. 136–46.

Harlow, H. & Harlow, M. (1963). A study of animal affection in Southwick, Charles: *Primate Social Behaviour*; D. Van Nostrand, New Jersey, pp. 174–85.   *p.* 40

Harris, R. W. (1963). *England in the Eighteenth Century*; Blandford Press, London.

Helfer, Ray & Kempe, C. Henry (1968). *The Battered Child*; University of Chicago Press.   *pp.* 61, 291 n. 4

Helmholtz, R. H. (1975). Infanticide in the province of Canterbury during the fifteenth century. *History of Childhood Quarterly*, vol. 2, pp. 379–90.   *p.* 49

Heywood, Jean (1978). *Children in Care*; Routledge & Kegan Paul, London.   *p.* 62

Hill, Christopher (1967). *Reformation to Industrial Revolution*; Weidenfeld & Nicolson, London.

Hinde, R. A. (1970). *Animal Behaviour*; McGraw-Hill, New York & London.   *p.* 38

Hinde, R., Spencer-Booth, Y. & Bruce, M. (1966). Effects of six-day maternal deprivation on rhesus monkey infants. *Nature*, no. 210, pp. 1021–3.

Hird, Frank (1898). *The Cry of the Children*; James Bowden, London.

Holt, John (1975). *The Needs and Rights of Children*; Penguin Books, Middlesex.

Houghton, Walter (1957). *The Victorian Frame of Mind*; Oxford University Press, London.

Housden, Leslie (1955). *The Prevention of Cruelty to Children*; Jonathan Cape, London.   *p.* 60

Hoyles, Martin (1979). Childhood in historical perspective in Hoyles, Martin, ed.: *Changing Childhood*; Writers and Readers Publishing Cooperative, London, pp. 16–29.   *pp.* 4, 14, 28, 31, 46, 262

Humphrey, N. K. (1976). The social function of intellect in Bateson, P. P. G. & Hinde, R. A., eds.: *Growing Points in Ethology*; Cambridge University Press, pp. 303–17.

Hunt, David (1972). *Parents and Children in History*; Harper & Row, New

York.   *pp.* 4, 6–7, 16, 23, 24–5, 26, 27, 46, 49, 55, 56–7, 103, 213, 217, 244, 261, 262

Illich, Ivan (1973). *Deschooling Society*; Penguin Books, Middlesex.   *p.* 4

Illick, Joseph (1976). Child-rearing in seventeenth-century England and America in de Mause, Lloyd, ed.: *The History of Childhood*; Souvenir Press, London, pp. 303–50.   *pp.* 7, 15, 116

Isaacs, Susan (1948). *Childhood and After*; Routledge & Kegan Paul, London.

Itani, Junichiro (1963). Paternal care in the wild Japanese monkey, Macaca luscata in Southwick, Charles: *Primate Social Behaviour*; D. Van Nostrand, New Jersey, pp. 91–8.

James, Thomas (1962). *Child Law*; Sweet & Maxwell, London.

Jay, Phyllis (1965). The common langur of North India in Devore, Irven, ed.: *Primate Behaviour*; Holt, Rinehart & Winston, New York & London, pp. 197–249.   *pp.* 37, 38

Jensen, G. (1968). Reaction of monkey mothers to long-term separation from their infants. *Psychonomic Science*, no. 11, pp. 171–2.

Jensen, G. & Tolman, C. (1962). Mother–infant relationship in the monkey, Macaca nemestrina; the effect of brief separation and mother–infant specificity. *Journal of Comparative and Physiological Psychology*, vol. 55, pp. 131–6.

Jolly, Alison (1966). *Lemur Behaviour*; University of Chicago Press.

Jolly, Alison (1972). *The Evolution of Primate Behaviour*; Macmillan, New York.   *p.* 40

Kagan, J. & Klein, R. E. (1976). Cross cultural perspectives on early development; paper presented at Bung Wartenstein Symposium, Vienna.   *p.* 39

Kaufman, I. C. & Rosenblum, L. A. (1967). Depression in infant monkeys separated from their mothers. *Science*, no. 155, pp. 1030–1.

Kelly, R. G. (1974). Literature and the historian. *American Quarterly*, no. 26, pp. 141–59.

Kelman, Herbert (1974). Attitudes are alive and well and gainfully employed in the sphere of action. *American Psychologist*, vol. 29, pp. 310–24.

Kempe, C. Henry & Helfer, Ray, eds. (1972). *Helping the Battered Child and his Family*; J. B. Lippincott, Philadelphia & Toronto.   *p.* 41

Kempe, Ruth & Kempe, C. Henry (1978). *Child Abuse. The Developing Child*; Fontana/Open Books, New York.   *p.* 41

Kessen, William (1974). *The Child*; John Wiley & Sons, London & New York.

King, Truby (1937). *Feeding and Care of Baby*; Oxford University Press, London.   *p.* 45

Kluckhohn, Clyde (1951). Values and value-orientations in the theory of action. An exploration in definition and classification in Parsons, T. & Shils, E., eds.: *Toward a General Theory of Action*; Harvard University Press, Cambridge, Massachusetts, pp. 388–433.   *p.* 45

Konnor, Melvin (1977). Infancy among the Kalahari Desert San in Leiderman, P. H., Tulkin, S. R. & Rosenfeld, A., eds.: *Culture and Infancy. Variations in the Human Experience*; Academic Press, New York & London, pp. 287–328.   *pp.* 49, 137

Bibliography and citation index

Kroll, Jerome (1977). The concept of childhood in the middle ages. *Journal of the History of Behavioural Sciences*, vol. 13, no. 4, pp. 384–93.   *pp.* 52–3, 263

Lack, David (1954). *The Natural Regulation of Animal Numbers*; Oxford University Press.   *p.* 34

Lack, David (1966). *Population Studies of Birds*; Oxford University Press.

Lack, David (1968). *Ecological Adaptations for Breeding in Birds*; Methuen, London.

de Laguna, Frederica (1965). Childhood among the Yakuta Tlingit in Spiro, Melford, ed.: *Context and Meaning in Cultural Anthropology*; The Free Press, New York.   *p.* 137

Laslett, Peter (1971). *The World we have Lost*; Souvenir Press, London.   *p.* 61

Laslett, Peter (1976). The wrong way through the telescope: a note on literary evidence in sociology and in historical sociology. *British Journal of Sociology*, vol. 27, pp. 319–42.   *p.* 291 n. 1

Laslett, Peter (1977). *Family Life and Illicit Love in Former Generations*; Cambridge University Press.   *pp.* 57–8, 65–6, 291 n. 1

Laslett, Peter & Wall, Richard, eds. (1972). *Household and Family in Past Time*; Cambridge University Press.   *pp.* 54, 291 n. 1

van Lawick-Goodall, Jane (1967). Mother–offspring relationships in free-ranging chimpanzees in Morris, Desmond: *Primate Ethology*; Weidenfeld & Nicolson, London, pp. 287–345.   *pp.* 38, 290 n. 4

Lee, Richard & Devore, Irven, eds. (1976). *Kalahari Hunter-Gatherers*; Harvard University Press, Cambridge, Massachusetts and London.

Leiderman, P., Tulkin, S. & Rosenfeld, A., eds. (1977). *Culture and Infancy. Variations in the Human Experience*; Academic Press, New York & London.   *p.* 235

Leighton, Dorothea & Kluckhohn, Clyde (1948). *Children of the People*; Harvard University Press, Cambridge, Massachusetts.   *pp.* 70, 137, 219, 226, 290 n. 5

Le Roy Ladurie, Emmanuel (1978). *Montaillou: Village Occitan de 1294 à 1324*; Editions Gallimard, Paris. English translation (1978) *Montaillou: Catholics and Cathars in a French Village*; The Scolar Press, London.   *pp.* 51–2, 54, 70

LeVine, Robert (1977). Child rearing as a cultural adaptation in Leiderman, P. H., Tulkin, S. R. & Rosenfeld, A., eds.: *Culture and Infancy. Variations in the Human Experience*; Academic Press, New York & London, pp. 15–27.   *pp.* 38–9, 43, 51, 137, 219, 235

Lewis, Hilda (1954). *Deprived Children*; Oxford University Press, London.

Lewis, M. & Ban, P. (1971). Stability of attachment behaviours: a transformational analysis; paper presented at the meeting of the Society for Research in Child Development, Minneapolis.   *p.* 38

Lochead, Marion (1956). *Their First Ten Years*; John Murray, London.   *pp.* 23, 289 n. 2

Locke, John (1694). *Some Thoughts Concerning Education*; A. & J. Churchill, London.   *pp.* 107, 120, 122, 124, 172

Lumsden, C. J. & Wilson, E. O. (1981). *Genes, Minds and Culture*; Harvard University Press, Cambridge, Massachusetts.   *p.* 36

Lyman, Richard (1976). Barbarism and religion: late Roman and early medieval childhood in de Mause, Lloyd, ed.: *The History of Childhood*; Souvenir Press, London, pp. 75–100.   *pp.* 4, 15, 22, 24, 143, 262

Lynd, S. (1942). *English Children*; William Collins, London.   *pp.* 12, 58, 289 n. 2

MacDonald, Michael (1981). *Mystical Bedlam. Madness, Anxiety, and Healing in Seventeenth-Century England*; Cambridge University Press.   *pp.* 51, 70, 103, 128, 131, 137

McKendrick, Neil (1974). Home demand and economic growth: a new view of the role of women and children in the Industrial Revolution in McKendrick, Neil, ed.: *Historical Perspectives. Studies of English Thought and Society*; Europa Publications, London, pp. 152–210.   *p.* 61

McLaughlin, Mary (1976). Survivors and surrogates: children and parents from the ninth to the thirteenth centuries in de Mause, Lloyd, ed.: *The History of Childhood*; Souvenir Press, London, pp. 101–82.   *pp.* 4–5, 12, 15, 22, 24, 45, 49, 143

Macfarlane, Alan (1970). *The Family Life of Ralph Josselin*; Cambridge University Press.   *pp.* 8, 16, 22, 23, 27, 49, 66, 69, 72, 73, 86–7, 263

Macfarlane, Alan (1979a). 'The family, sex and marriage in England 1500–1800' by Lawrence Stone. *History and Theory*, vol. 18, pp. 103–26.   *pp.* 19, 51, 52, 58–9, 103, 137, 295 n. 1

Macfarlane, Alan (1979b). *The Origins of English Individualism. The Family, Property and Social Transition*; Cambridge University Press.   *pp.* 54, 58, 59

Marshall, Dorothy (1962). *Eighteenth-Century England*; The Camelot Press, London.

Marshall, Dorothy (1973). *Industrial England 1778–1851*; Routledge & Kegan Paul, London.

Marshall, J. D. (1968). *The Old Poor Law 1795–1834*; Macmillan, London.

Martin, Harold (1972). The child and his development in Kempe, C. Henry & Helfer, Ray, eds.: *Helping the Battered Child and his Family*; J. B. Lippincott, Philadelphia & Toronto, pp. 93–114.   *p.* 42

Martin, Harold, ed. (1976). *The Abused Child*; Bullinger, Cambridge, Massachusetts.   *pp.* 41, 57

Martin, J. P., ed. (1978). *Violence and the Family*; John Wiley & Sons, New York.   *pp.* 41, 57

Marvick, Elizabeth (1974). The character of Louis XIII: the role of his physician in its formation. *Journal of Interdisciplinary History*, vol. 4, no. 3, pp. 347–74.   *pp.* 7, 56–7

Marvick, Elizabeth (1976). Nature versus nurture: patterns and trends in seventeenth-century French child-rearing in de Mause, Lloyd, ed.: *The History of Childhood*; Souvenir Press, London, pp. 259–302.   *pp.* 22, 46, 50

Marvin, R., Vandevender, T., Iwanaga, M., LeVine, S. & LeVine, R. (1977). Infant caregiver attachment among the Hausa of Nigeria in McGurk, Harry, ed.: *Ecological Factors in Human Development*; North-Holland, Amsterdam & Oxford, pp. 247–59.   *pp.* 39, 51, 226, 235

Mason, W. A. (1968). Early social deprivation in the nonhuman primates: implications for human behaviour in Glass, D. C.: *Environmental Influences*; Rockefeller University Press, New York, pp. 70–100.   *p.* 40

Bibliography and citation index

Matthews, William (1945). *American Diaries*; University of California Press, Berkeley & Los Angeles. *p. 69*

Matthews, William (1950). *British Diaries*; Cambridge University Press, London. *pp. 69, 72, 82*

Matthews, William (1974). *American Diaries in Manuscript*; University of Georgia Press, Athens. *p. 82*

de Mause, Lloyd (1976). The evolution of childhood in de Mause, Lloyd, ed.: *The History of Childhood*; Souvenir Press, London, pp. 1–74. *pp. 4, 5, 8–9, 15, 19–20, 21, 22, 24, 25, 27, 28, 31, 42, 49, 50, 57–8, 120, 143, 199, 200, 222, 225–6, 262, 263, 266*

May, Robert (1978). Human reproduction reconsidered. *Nature*, vol. 272, pp. 491–5.

Mead, Margaret & Wolfenstein, Martha, eds. (1955). *Childhood in Contemporary Cultures*; University of Chicago Press. *p. 38*

Mechling, Jay (1975). Advice to historians on advice to mothers. *Journal of Social History*, vol. 9, pp. 44–63. *pp. 43–4, 45*

Menzel, E. W., Davenport, R. K. & Rogers, C. M. (1963). Effects of environmental restrictions upon the chimpanzee's responsiveness in novel situations. *Journal of Comparative Physiology and Psychology*, vol. 56, pp. 329–34. *p. 40*

Middleton, Nigel (1971). *When Family Failed*; Victor Gollancz, London. *p. 61*

Miller, R. E., Caul, W. F. & Mirsky, I. A. (1967). Communication of affect between feral and socially isolated monkeys. *Journal of Personal Social Psychology*, vol. 7, pp. 231–9.

Minturn, Leigh & Lambert, William (1964). *Mothers of Six Cultures. Antecedents of Child Rearing*; John Wiley & Sons, New York.

Mitterauer, Michael & Sieder, Reinhard (1977). *Vom Patriarchat zur Partnerschaft: zum Strukturwardel der Familie*; C. H. Beck'sche Verlagsbuchhandlung, Munich. English translation (1982) *The European Family*; Oosterveen, K., Hörzinger, M.; Basil Blackwell, Oxford. *pp. 26, 28, 29, 31*

Morgan, Edmund (1944). *The Puritan Family*; Trustees of the Public Library, Boston. *pp. 14, 23, 27, 251, 263, 289 n. 2*

Mount, Ferdinand (1982). *The Subversive Family. An Alternative History of Love and Marriage*; Jonathan Cape, London. *p. 290 n. 10*

Murphey, Murray (1965). An approach to the historical study of national character in Spiro, Melford, ed.: *Context and Meaning in Cultural Anthropology*; The Free Press, New York, pp. 144–63. *pp. 44, 45, 46*

Napier, J. R. & Napier, P. H. (1967). *A Handbook of Living Primates*; Academic Press, London.

National Society for the Prevention of Cruelty to Children (1976). *At Risk*; Routledge & Kegan Paul, London. *p. 42*

Newson, John & Newson, Elizabeth (1965). *Patterns of Infant Care in an Urban Community*; Penguin Books, Middlesex. *pp. 44, 70, 88, 141, 219, 221, 224*

Newson, John & Newson, Elizabeth (1968). *Four Years Old in an Urban Community*; Penguin Books, Middlesex. *pp. 44, 70, 88, 141, 239*

Newson, John & Newson, Elizabeth (1974). Cultural aspects of child rearing in the English speaking world in Richards, M. P. M., ed.: *The Integration of a Child into a Social World*; Cambridge University Press, pp. 53–83.   *pp.* 4, 11, 21, 45–6

Newson, John & Newson, Elizabeth (1976). *Seven Years Old in the Home Environment*; George Allen & Unwin, London.   *pp.* 39–40, 70, 77, 88, 116, 141, 173, 201, 202, 270

Oastler, Richard (1830). Slavery in Yorkshire; letter in *Mercury* newspaper, Leeds.

Owen, John (1974). *The Eighteenth Century 1714–1815*; Thomas Nelson & Sons, London.   *p.* 254

Perkin, Harold (1969). *The Origins of Modern English Society, 1780–1880*; Routledge & Kegan Paul, London.   *pp.* 60, 61, 62

Perkins, William (1609). *Workes*; J. Legatt, London.   *p.* 216

Pinchbeck, I. & Hewitt, M. (1969). *Children in English Society*; Routledge and Kegan Paul, London, 2 vols.   *pp.* 4, 6, 10, 15, 20–1, 22, 26, 27, 28, 29, 46, 59, 62, 91–2, 99, 203, 260, 262, 263

Plumb, J. H. P. (1975). The new world of children in eighteenth-century England. *Past and Present*, no. 67, pp. 64–93.   *pp.* 8, 15, 18, 22, 23, 26, 65, 143, 262

Pollock, Linda (1981). The forgotten children; unpublished doctoral dissertation, University of St Andrews.   *pp.* 33, 99, 101, 266, 269, 289 n. 2, 290 n. 14, 293 n. 1

Porter, Roy (1982). *English Society in the Eighteenth Century*; The Pelican Social History of Britain, Penguin Books, Middlesex.   *pp.* 26, 289 n. 7

Powell, Chilton (1917). English Domestic Relations 1487–1653; Columbia University Press, New York.   *pp.* 102, 292 n. 8

Quinlan, Maurice (1941). *Victorian Prelude*; Columbia University Press, New York.

Rabb, Theodore & Rotberg, Robert, eds. (1973). *The Family in History*; Harper & Row, New York & London.

Rheingold, Harriet (1963). *Maternal Behaviour in Mammals*; John Wiley & Sons, New York & London.

Richerson, P. J. & Boyd, R. (1978). A dual inheritance model of the human evolutionary process. I: basic postulates and a simple model. *Journal of Social and Biological Structures*, vol. 1, pp. 127–54.   *p.* 36

Roberts, David (1969). *Victorian Origins of the British Welfare State*; Archon Books, London.

Roberts, Jacquie (1978). Social work and child abuse: the reasons for failure and the way to success in Martin, J. P., ed.: *Violence and the Family*; John Wiley & Sons, New York, pp. 255–91.   *p.* 42

Robertson, Priscilla (1976). Home as a nest: middle class childhood in nineteenth-century Europe in de Mause, Lloyd, ed.: *The History of Childhood*; Souvenir Press, London, pp. 407–31.   *pp.* 10, 21, 46, 60, 260

Rodgers, Brian (1968). *The Battle against Poverty*; Routledge & Kegan Paul, London.

Roe, F. Gordon (1959). *The Victorian Child*; Phoenix House, London.   *p.* 289 n. 2

Roe, F. Gordon (1961). *The Georgian Child*; Phoenix House, London.   *p.* 289 n. 2

Roebuck, Janet (1973). *The Making of Modern English Society from 1850*; Routledge & Kegan Paul, London.   *p.* 60

Rokeach, Milton (1968). *Beliefs, Attitudes and Values. A Theory of Organization and Change*; Jossey-Bass, San Francisco.   *p.* 45

Bibliography and citation index

Rosenberg, C., ed. (1975). *The Family in History*; University of Pennsylvania Press, Philadelphia.

Rosenblum, Leonard (1968). Mother–infant relations and early behavioral development in Rosenblum, Leonard & Cooper, Robert, eds.: *The Squirrel Monkey*; Academic Press, New York & London, pp. 209–33. *p. 38*

Rothman, David (1973). Documents in search of a historian: toward a history of childhood and youth in America in Rabb, T. & Rotberg, R., eds.: *The Family in History*; Harper & Row, New York & London. *pp. 59, 65*

Rousseau, Jean-Jacques (1763). *Emile or on Education*; J. Nourse & P. Vaillant, London. *pp. 107, 120*

Rowell, Thelma (1972). *The Social Behaviour of Monkeys*; Penguin Books, Middlesex. *p. 38*

Rowntree, Benjamin (1901). *Poverty: a Study of Town Life*; Macmillan, London.

Rutter, Michael (1972). *Maternal Deprivation Reassessed*; Penguin Books, Middlesex. *p. 235*

Ryder, Judith & Silver, Harold (1970). *Modern English Society*; Methuen, London. *pp. 60, 62*

Ryerson, Alice (1961). Medical advice on child rearing 1550–1900. *Harvard Educational Review*, vol. 31, pp. 302–23. *pp. 45, 50*

Saveth, Edward (1969). The problem of American family history. *American Quarterly*, no. 21, pp. 311–29. *pp. 59, 65*

Schnucker, R. V. (1974). The English Puritans and pregnancy, delivery and breast-feeding. *History of Childhood Quarterly*, vol. 1, pp. 637–58. *pp. 50, 216*

Schücking, Levin (1969). *The Puritan Family. A Social Study from Literary Sources*; Routledge & Kegan Paul, London. *p. 102*

Scott, John (1979). The history of the family as an affective unit. *Social History*, vol. 4, no. 3, pp. 509–16. *pp. 19, 70*

Sears, R. (1975). *Your Ancients Revisited. A History of Childhood Development*; University of Chicago Press. *pp. 4, 8, 17–18, 20, 21, 26, 29, 31–2, 144, 262*

Seay, B., Hansen, E. & Harlow, H. (1962). Mother–infant separation in monkeys. *Journal of Child Psychology and Psychiatry*, vol. 3, pp. 123–32.

Seay, B., Alexander, B. & Harlow, H. (1964). Maternal behaviour of socially deprived rhesus monkeys. *Journal of Abnormal and Social Psychology*, vol. 69, no. 4, pp. 345–54.

Shore, Miles (1979). The psychogenic theory of history. *Journal of Interdisciplinary History*, vol. 9, no. 3, pp. 517–23. *pp. 28, 58*

Shorter, Edward (1976). *The Making of the Modern Family*; William Collins, London. *pp. 3–4, 6, 9, 10, 18, 22, 23, 24, 25, 26, 28, 29, 30, 31, 46, 50, 65, 70, 99, 111, 134, 144, 203, 218, 262*

Skinner, Angela & Castle, Raymond (1969). *Seventy-eight Battered Children: a Retrospective Study*; National Society for the Prevention of Cruelty to Children, London. *p. 42*

Smelser, Neil (1959). *Social Change in the Industrial Revolution*; Routledge & Kegan Paul, London.

Smelser, Neil (1974). Sociological history. The Industrial Revolution and the British working-class family in Flinn, M. W. & Smout, T. C., eds.: *Essays in Social History*; Clarendon Press, Oxford, pp. 23–38.

Smith, Daniel (1977). Autonomy and affection: parents and children in eighteenth-century Chesapeake families. *The Psychohistorical Review*, vol. 6, pp. 32–51.   *pp.* 9, 17, 23, 113, 143

Smith, Peter (in press). Biological, psychological and historical aspects of reproduction and child-care in Davey, G., ed.: *Animal Models and Human Behaviour*; John Wiley & Sons, London.   *pp.* 36, 49–50

Smith, Stephen (1973). Communication. The London apprentices as seventeenth-century adolescents. *Past and Present*, no. 61, pp. 149–61.   *p.* 289 n. 4

Spalding, P. A. (1949). *Self-Harvest. A Study of Diaries and the Diarist*; Independent Press, London.   *pp.* 73–4

Spence, J. C., ed. (1897). *The Dawn of Civilization; or England in the Nineteenth Century*; Watts, London.

Spitz, René (1945). Hospitalism. *The Psychoanalytic Study of the Child*, vol. 1, pp. 53–74.   *pp.* 41, 62

Spufford, Margaret (1979). First steps in literacy: the reading and writing experiences of the humblest seventeenth-century spiritual autobiographers. *Social History*, vol. 4, no. 3, pp. 407–37.   *pp.* 244, 294 n. 16

Stannard, David (1974). Death and the Puritan child. *American Quarterly*, no. 26, pp. 456–76.   *pp.* 49, 53, 251, 263

Steel, Brandt & Pollock, Carl (1968). A psychiatric study of parents who abuse infants and small children in Helfer, Ray & Kempe, C. Henry: *The Battered Child*; Chicago University Press, pp. 89–133.   *p.* 41

Stein, Peter & Shand, J. (1974). *Legal Values in Western Society*; Edinburgh University Press.

Stern, Daniel (1977). *The First Relationship*; Open Books, London.

Stone, Lawrence (1975). The rise of the nuclear family in early modern England in Rosenberg, C., ed.: *The Family in History*; University of Pennsylvania Press, Philadelphia.

Stone, Lawrence (1977). *The Family, Sex and Marriage in England 1500–1800*; Weidenfeld & Nicolson, London.   *pp.* 6, 9, 10, 12, 14, 15, 18–19, 21, 22, 24, 26, 27, 28, 29, 30–1, 46, 49, 50, 58–9, 65, 66, 70, 89, 96, 103, 110, 126, 137, 143, 144, 155, 184, 188, 190, 197, 199, 200, 215, 262, 263–4, 266, 267, 293 n. 10

Thane, Pat, ed. (1978). *The Origins of British Social Policy*; Croom Helm, London.

Thompson, E. P. (1977). Review of Lawrence Stone. *New Society*, 8 Sept., pp. 499–501.   *p.* 58

Thompson, R. (1974). *Women in Stuart England and America*; Routledge & Kegan Paul, London.   *pp.* 22, 27, 46, 113, 262

Tizard, Jack & Tizard, Barbara (1974). The institution as an environment for development in Richards, Martin, ed.: *The Integration of a Child into a Social World*; Cambridge University Press, pp. 137–53.

Trivers, Robert (1974). Parent–offspring conflict. *American Zoologist*, vol. 14, pp. 249–64.   *pp.* 34, 36, 37

Trumbach, Randolph (1978). *The Rise of the Egalitarian Family*; Academic Press, New York & London.   *pp.* 4, 8, 20, 23, 26, 27, 28, 29, 32, 50, 172

Tucker, M. J. (1976). The child as beginning and end: fifteenth- and sixteenth-century English childhood in de Mause, Lloyd, ed.: *The History of*

Childhood; Souvenir Press, London, pp. 229–58.   *pp. 5–6, 12, 15, 22, 24, 46, 49, 99, 144, 203, 262*

Tuckwell, Gertrude (1894). *The State and its Children*; Methuen, London.

Turnbull, Colin (1973). *The Mountain People*; Jonathan Cape, London.   *p. 40*

Vandeberg, Brian (1978). Play and development from an ethological perspective. *American Psychologist*, vol. 33, no. 8, pp. 724–39.

Vigne, T., ed. (1975). Parents and children 1890–1918; distance and dependence. *The Journal of the Oral History Society*, Family History Issue, vol. 3, no. 2.

van de Walle, Etienne (1973). Recent approaches to past childhoods in Rabb, T. & Rotberg, R., eds.: *The Family in History*; Harper & Row, New York & London.   *p. 56*

Walzer, John (1976). A period of ambivalence: eighteenth-century American childhood in de Mause, Lloyd, ed.: *The History of Childhood*; Souvenir Press, London, pp. 351–82.   *pp. 9, 10, 16–17*

Watson, John (1928). *Psychological Care of Infant and Child*; George Allen & Unwin, London.   *p. 45*

Wells, Robert (1971). Family size and fertility control in eighteenth-century America. A study of Quaker families. *Population Studies*, vol. 25, pp. 73–83.

West, F. (1974). Infant mortality in the East Fen parishes of Leake and Wrangle. *Local Population Studies*, vol. 13, pp. 41–4.

Whiting, Beatrice, ed. (1963). *Six Cultures. Studies of Child Rearing*; John Wiley & Sons, New York.   *p. 39*

Wilson, Adrian (1980). The infancy of the history of childhood: an appraisal of Philippe Ariès. *History and Theory*, vol. 19, pp. 132–54.   *pp. 47, 55, 56*

Wilson, Edward O. (1975). *Sociobiology*; The Belknap Press, Cambridge, Massachusetts.   *pp. 34–5*

Winnicott, D. W. (1957). *The Child and the Family*; Tavistock, London.

Wishy, Bernard (1968). *The Child and the Republic. The Dawn of Modern American Child Nurture*; University of Pennsylvania Press, Philadelphia.   *pp. 4, 11, 12*

Wrightson, Keith (1975). Infanticide in early seventeenth-century England. *Local Population Studies*, vol. 15, pp. 10–21.   *p. 49*

Wrightson, Keith (1982). *English Society 1580–1680*; Hutchinson Social History of England, London.   *pp. 8, 50, 52, 58, 61, 103, 128, 131, 134, 156, 205, 211*

Wrigley, E. A. (1966). Family limitations in pre-industrial England. *The Economic History Review*, 2nd series, vol. 19, no. 1, pp. 82–109.

Wrigley, E. A. (1968). Mortality in pre-industrial England: the example of Colyton, Devon, over three centuries. *Daedalus*, vol. 97, pp. 546–80.   *p. 290 n. 13*

Wrigley, E. A. (1977). Reflections on the history of the family. *Daedalus*, vol. 106, pp. 71–85.

Zuckerman, Michael (1970). *Peaceable Kingdoms: New England Towns in the Eighteenth Century*; Random House, New York.   *pp. 3, 24, 49*